JENNIFER RUSSELL

Her Place Was With God

~ The Road to God's Promises ~

The opinions expressed in this manuscript are solely the opinions of the author and do not represent the opinions or thoughts of the publisher. The author has represented and warranted full ownership and/or legal right to publish all the materials in this book.

Her Place Was With God
All Rights Reserved.
Copyright © 2014 Jennifer Russell
v6.0

Cover Photo © 2014 Jennifer Russell. All rights reserved - used with permission.

This book may not be reproduced, transmitted, or stored in whole or in part by any means, including graphic, electronic, or mechanical without the express written consent of the publisher except in the case of brief quotations embodied in critical articles and reviews.

ISBN: 978-0-578-13353-9

PRINTED IN THE UNITED STATES OF AMERICA

I dedicate this book to my Jesus that loves me and all of you. To all my family, friends, others in this world I don't know and all of the women I was told I would help one day – To all of you and your children, your loves and family's that are enduring the chaos that these life-choices leave us with and the reality of such, that brings us to our knee's.

Authors Note

My life is connected by my heart to the people I love, some of whom possibly wouldn't have chosen to have their stories told at this time or in this way. I quickly found that I couldn't tell my story without telling part of theirs also. I changed names and identifying characteristics of some of the people in my book to protect their privacy but I can't promise anything. The conversations have been constructed by memory (… that comes in bits and pieces. To those who know me and our lives lol it could be backwards, inside out and upside down), and it might be different from others memories of the same conversations or happening. Also, the spell check is correct on my in-correct English, but I wrote my story the way I spoke it and heard it in myself throughout my life.

Thank you and God Bless. I'm grateful to my family and friends for allowing me to portray them in my version of my memories during the events in God's story. I hope and pray that those who love me now, will love me after they have read mine and Gods book.

Introduction

… I hit the wall to brace myself, threw my leather over Jas and started to pray. Every time he flung the machete to one side of us, Darby would scream and he would swing the machete towards her which is where Jas was …

My story 'Her Place Was With God', was written for you and for me. I wrote it for my kids, my grandkids, my mom, my dad's, my sisters and brothers and for all of my family and friends as a whole. I wrote it for you and your neighbor and for the family who had one of their loved ones come home from war and their heart is broke when they are so angry and torn up inside that slowly and loudly the abuse is everywhere. It's about you or someone you love or all of the others we don't know who are growing up in a world of drug use. It's a part of their everyday life and they know no different or for the young teenager alone and scared. He or she is offered to get high and a warm place to sleep and food to eat in exchange for the un-mentionable. It's for the family whose sole provider lost their job because of cut backs or gets hurt at work and is laid off. Money is hard and moods change, relationships grow weary and trust fades. Abuse, any and all types, physical, sexual, verbal, emotional and drug abuse can happen in these families and in anyone's home, in many different ways.

When someone is abused it will always be a part of you, but with God it doesn't have to define who you are as a person or what you can accomplish in your life.

When I started drinking alcohol and smoking weed I was 12 years old and I didn't know what the word addict meant. I knew what an alcoholic was and I knew what a stoner was because everyone drank and smoked. In those days' drugs, i.e. Meth (Crank, Speed, Ice), Cocaine (Crack), Heroin, Oxycontins, LSD, Ecstasy, Mushrooms (Silosybin Mushrooms) and Inhalants, were all kept under wraps and what was happening to the kids was not paid any attention to. Everyone was sweeping it under the table, no one knew what to do about it. It came in so quick and messed up so many people, it was like an atom bomb going off and killing out almost a whole generation.

A lot of people died and some have continued to live to today still using these drugs and destroying their lives. Children are taken from moms and dads who really do love their kids. We just got caught up and didn't see it happening, we became broken souls. Marriages fall apart daily, someone is hurt, someone is beaten, someone is yelled at and someone is scared. There are so many different roads you have to choose from and the incentives aren't always enough to guarantee we make the right choices.

When you get caught up in something it begins so innocently and before you know it, it's something you can't and won't live without. No, you don't have to listen to my words but hear your own heart, God already knows it and hears it.

We start doing drugs and then down the road, a short time could have passed or years could be flying by, and you get clean. What happens is, the way you know of surviving and living your life is that of a child or person of the age you were when the drugs took over … everything becomes so confusing. When I quit using drugs it had been 21 years of use, I didn't know how to do anything. I couldn't keep job or stay off of welfare and had done a lot of damage to my body and soul. I hadn't learned anything about life other than what was in front of me so I said a lot of prayers, went with it and ran.

The drugs will lead you to lose your sense of what you are living for and why you are put here on this earth. They will forget to tell you that you are a child of Christ and that he died on the Cross so that our sins could be forgiven and that he loves you so much!

Thank you for sharing your time and reading my story. I pray it helps to let you know that Jesus loves you and that you're not alone. If it helps any one of you in any way, you are one of my answered prayers.

God Bless you in your walk through life and with God.

Table of Contents

Younger Days and Beautiful Times 1
Growing Up a Teenager 7
Bachmann Hill - Juvenile Correctional School 18
Switzerland 28
Growing Up Into a Teenage Mommy 42
Starting Over in Mendocino and Unexplainable Loses 55
The Downward Spiral Was Sure To Come 71
Living Life as His Prisoner - The County Jail Was Better 84
On The Road Again 92
A Double 2nd Chance 120
Alaska Bound 134
February 14, 1993 - Our Valentine's Day Wedding 145
The Talkeetna Blue Grass Festival - Summer 1993 151
We Live in Houston … Houston, Alaska That Is! 157
Fear of the Night 162
Blue Grass #2 168
Our Love Story Destroyed 171
The Beginning of the End 176
Home Sweet Home? 187
2nd Time On the Road to California 196
Third Times a Charm? 209
The First Days of the Rest of Our Lives 220
Is That a Rainbow God? 235
Another Sad Good-Bye 239
Michelle and Jereme's Wedding - September 2002 253

Sometimes the Colors Fade ... Will They Get Brighter God? 270
Answered Prayers and Lessons Learned 274
Love and Loss, Lives and Family 317
My Place Was With God and He Knew the Whole Time 320
Resources for Help 327
Acknowledgments 328
My Writing and Publishing Process 332

Younger Days and Beautiful Times

Beautiful times of my life include the time I spent with my grandma and grandpa, everything was good when I was with them. Their fruit and vegetable stand was known throughout the county and then some for the best tasting produce. It was grown with the deepest love and hard work of this amazing God loving family. Grandma would stand outside on the back porch and ring the dinner bell as a signal for grandpa to come in from the fields. Memories of him working in the garden and of how loving he was will always remain in the front of my mind.

 They always went to church and when I was there to visit I was the one that everyone wanted to hug and say hello too. I was so lucky that my grandma was a Sunday school teacher, I always got to stay in her class even though I was younger than most of the kids. Before they went to bed in the evenings I would run down the hallway from my room and jump in bed with grandma while she read me stories out of her bible. I wish today that I could still remember them but I always fell asleep. She would wake me, kiss me on the forehead and send me back to my own bed for the night.

 Holidays were something we all looked forward to, the women would always be bustling around in the kitchen preparing the best meal in the world. Eventually a phone line would form in the hallways with everyone waiting to speak with the family member who couldn't make it. For us kids, playing on the feather bed in the back room or swinging in the tree swing out back was only part of the perfection of grandma and grandpa's house.

 Running around and working at the stands was the best and we were never too tired to consume one of grandma's frozen blackberry treats, the taste was amazing!

HER PLACE WAS WITH GOD

The other safe place in my world was at my granny's house, she was our dad's mama. Dody (Vernon), died in a car accident in 1966 when I was 4 years old and my sister Dru was 6. Visiting them on the holidays and summer vacations were our escapes from our reality. We were the love and memory of their baby they had lost and we belonged like it was our own home. They spoiled us and always gave us money for the little 'five and dime' store across the street and we got to go to the grocery store to pick out our cereal (mine is froot loops) and anything else we wanted. Then we'd go to the auto shop to visit our grandpa and uncle and get soda pop and candy. W & L Auto was the name and tow trucks and gas were their game, what a wonderful place and the most wonderful family I got to grow up with!

There was a bus and for some reason, it never ended up in the junk yard. It was parked up between the shop and the houses, to cool. It was painted blue with stars and planets all over it and was our hide-out of all hide-outs, we called it the 'hippie van'. It's something myself and my cousins will always remember with a smile. The canal out back was full of crawdads. Our granny would give us bologna or hotdogs and with our little wooden stick fishin poles and string we caught as many of them as we could and sold their tails for a penny a piece at the store. Go us!

Before our dad passed away he played a lot of baseball, our mom did to. When he was gone, mom still played ball at Hooker Oak Park. When I was about 5 and Dru was 7 we were both given the honor of being batgirl for her team the Peppers.

The park had everything you could ask for. A playground, plenty of picnic tables, basketball courts and a creek that we swam in every summer and more, there were even bathrooms! My favorite part of the park was the enormous oak tree, the Hooker Oak Tree that greeted you at the entrance. It was beautiful and seemed to know the secret to life. I often envisioned it sharing that secret with me but just knowing that it knew, was good enough for me.

The park had something else though, it also had a coach for mom's team, our soon to be step-dad, Geoffrey.

In the beginning I remember things were always pretty peaceful. Some times in the evenings their friends would come visit. Already in bed I would wander out since I could hear everyone and wanted to see who was there. They would all be sitting around in a circle singing and talking, smoking (weed) and drinking wine. Everyone got happy when they saw me and I would get tones of hellos with hugs and kisses then I was sent back to bed.

PICTURE OF MOM, DRU AND I

It didn't stay that way though, as I got older I seemed to always be in the way. As the years went by the fighting and the yelling became a regular thing, it was obvious he was mean to my mom and to my sister but I would take off. I'd climb out my bedroom window and for however long the fighting lasted, I'd stay at my best friend's house. Her and her dad and the rest of their family treated me as theirs. It was easy to change my reality when I was there. There never fought and yelled, at least not like my parents did and when things mellowed out my mom would know where I was and call me to tell me I could come home.

After school one day myself and a couple of my friends walked in the house and Geoffrey was sitting there in his underwear in his chair with girly magazines open to nude pictures and they were laying all around him. I pushed my friends back as quick as I could telling them we had to go somewhere else, I was so embarrassed … my friends didn't come over much after that.

Soon I pretty much did what I wanted, when I wanted and with whomever I wanted to do it with. My mom was stuck in his world and I'm sure it was all she could do to keep herself above water having to deal with life. Eating breakfast or dinner at the table with him also became something that could easily have been done without. We weren't allowed to talk, sing, or laugh, so no conversations and I wasn't good at listening to rules so I always got hollered at for one thing or another.

One weekend Geoffrey took me and a friend of ours with us to Heavenly Valley to go skiing, she was about my sisters' age. It was night time and we had all gone to bed when I woke to noises coming from the other room. I got up to go see what was going on and saw our friend and my step-dad having what I know now as sex, but at that moment I thought he was hurting her or something. I felt so stupid! I ran back into my room and got into bed and covered my head. The next thing I knew she was getting me a cup of water and he was asking if I was alright and if I needed anything. I don't think I had ever been as confused.

After that I knew I didn't like him and I knew I wouldn't spend much time at home. It wasn't like I could tell my mom what happened, I didn't know if she would be angry with me or even believe me or if he would get mad at me for telling her. I had no idea what to do, I was so scared all the time.

I started leaving school at lunch and going home since everyone was gone then, it seemed like the perfect time to drink. My friends and I would set up on the kitchen counters and drink the booze we could find that my mom and Geoffrey had 'put up', it sure made some of the icky stuff go away for a little bit. I felt bad, our mom is a good mom, she loves me and my sister and we were always loved on and kissed and hugged on. She never yelled at me and we never fought. If I thought my situation was bad, I knew it was worse for my sister. She and our step-dad got along even worse than he and I did. She had a type of contempt for him that was another level than mine. My sister was more beautiful than I was and did better in school and since she was also the out-spoken one, she received the majority of the crap from him.

Acting out (and being noticed) wasn't something I did very often. I like to stay quiet but sometimes situations got out of hand. One night I was staying the night with my friend Laura. We snuck out and went to a frat party thinking that for sure we would be back before anyone would notice. We met a couple of boys and instead of going home we left and went to their place with them. Their apartment was (for the lack of even knowing what the word meant), alluring, and romantic, at least from what I had imagined 'romantic' would be. The lights were down low and candles were lit in separate areas of the room. The guy I was with took me to his bed and my friend went with the other guy. For a couple of hours all my worries drifted to a world I didn't know existed, it was like I was in a movie. It ended soon though and it was time to leave. As we tried to sneak back into her house we dreadfully discovered that we were locked out, oh my God! Laura called her mom and she came to the door, she unlocked it and told me that I had to leave, that I couldn't stay the night. I knew she was mad but I had no idea what I was going to do, my mom was going to kill me!

I found my way to the closest payphone to call her. By the time I got there I had worked myself into a frenzy, enough of one that my mom would believe me as I cried to her on the phone telling her that I had been raped. As the words were coming out of my mouth my brain was telling me to shut up but my mouth kept talking. Soon my mom and sister picked me up and took me to the police department and we filed a report. It just kept getting worse. All I wanted to do was to go home and go to sleep and make the most beautiful moment of my life be just a dream as I woke up in my happy warm bed. But it didn't happen that way. The police made me get in the car with them, tell them a story about where he took me and what happened then finally they took me home. I hated myself as I wrote out my description of this guy because he was nothing but amazing to me and I was just trying to cover up getting caught and being in trouble.

Finally the night was over and the whole situation was swept under the table. I couldn't get this boy off of my mind, I hoped every day that nothing ever happened to him, I knew it wasn't rape and I'm sure the police figured that out to. To say the least I'm sure my friends parents thought I was a pretty bad influence … I suppose they were right.

I loved getting to visit my cousin Carol in Yuba City. My aunt and uncle loved me like their own, I even got to ride the bus and go to school with her for a week or so at a time, it seemed easier for everyone if I were somewhere else.

My sister Dru and I weren't very good friends growing up which made matters so much worse for both of us I'm sure. Being friends would have helped more than we could have known. I do know that we both longed for the life we would have lived if our real father were still alive.

My regular routine consisted of spending time at my friend's house and hanging out at the mall or at Shakey's pizza parlor, i.e. wherever and whenever I wanted. But the most important thing on my mind was that going home wasn't a happy event very often and it didn't seem like I was very welcome or wanted. I figured then that leaving, running away, was the way to go and taking my sister clothes and weed with me gave me something to be happy about, at least I'd be stoned and look great.

Adventure, excitement, people who didn't know me or anything about me. I could be anyone I wanted and that was so much easier than being me.

Growing Up a Teenager

My friend Kat's checking account was closed but the checkbook still had checks in it. Since she still had it in her possession we figure it was fair game, more so, if cashing the checks worked then we would be happy campers. We were of course very responsible … lol. K-mart was our store of choice since it was close to my house and of course we only picked up the necessities which included a blow dryer, a curling iron, make-up and a few outfits for each of us. Everything we would need on a runaway journey to San Francisco. We walked up to the cashier as if we knew what we were doing, placed our items on the counter and paid for them by check, of course.

Who would have thought that 'no' money could purchase all these items we needed! As we headed for the bus depot I imagined we were explorers going on a new adventure, rock stars about to board our tour bus. All of the trips to my granny's house on the holidays and during school break made me a bus connoisseur. The greyhound smell was something you could always count on, it had been that way for as long as I could remember. I wished we were headed there this time but we weren't. The many bus rides there brought the actress out in me. Pretending to be whomever I wanted, Id change my heritage, life style and my age. No one had any idea of who I was, so I became whoever I desired to be. Now I was with Kat giving yet another performance. In my mind I wasn't running away from home, I was running to me. Escaping to be whom I would have been if my mom and Geoffrey had never met because my dad was still alive. Of course none of that mattered at the moment, because at the moment none of it was real. For now, I was a rock star going on tour.

Kat and I struggled with our bags as we climbed the stairs onto the bus. No one had to worry about us taking the 'good' seats as we headed for the back of the bus. Continuously I stretched my neck peering toward the rear to be sure no one sat in our VIP section. Whenever someone ahead of us sat down we sighed in relief. Finally we were there, first class section – aka – the last three seats, awesome!

"I'm so tired." Kat Said. She sat down on the first of the three seats and I climbed over her to the window. Tucking our bags around us we were finally able to take a deep breath and get some rest.

"Now we can get a little sleep maybe." I said, moving my things to make a pillow.

"I hope no one pays any attention to us." She replied.

"Everything's going to fine Kat, I promise." Thinking about what I had just said I realized that all this pretending must be going to my head, how could I promise her anything? I was just a kid to.

The continuous driving motion put us both into a deep sleep until the sounds of other busses inside a terminal woke us up. As if in a musical everyone on the bus stood up and grabbed their things. Of course our section had to get off the bus last, it gave us more time to get our things together so that was a good thing. We did the best we could while we drug our bags down the aisle trying not to hit the people remaining on the bus in their heads. Stumbling down the three small steps I smiled back at Kat.

"Cool, we made it. Let's get something to eat from inside, I'm starving!" I'm so glad she was still smiling to.

"Me to Jenn, we'll figure something out. Let's rest for a second and go smoke a cigarette."

"Good idea, I forgot we hadn't smoked in all that time, no smoking on the bus." I said laughing.

Knowing quite well that the 'no smoking on the bus' rule didn't apply to us. We learned how to smoke out the little window in the bathroom without getting caught. The feeling of getting away with it was better than actually smoking whether it was a cigarette or a joint.

We headed directly the VIP section at the bus station, you know, the area with the connected little black chairs that have televisions on them. There was a woman sitting on the floor having a conversation with a seagull that had happily landed to retrieve a popcorn kernel, obviously left behind for him. There was a janitor sweeping, he appeared to have been working his job far too long. He seemed very un-enthused, poor guy, he did manage to smile our way as he swept past us.

It was still daylight so we had plenty of time to decide what we would do next so we made pillows out of our back packs and decided to lie our heads down for a few minutes. When we woke up we were bummed to see it was dark and really cold. Being cold was actually an understatement, we were freezing and we were unsuccessful at all attempts of transforming our jackets into blankets.

"Come on Jenn, I want to go." Kat whispered.

It only took one glance around the place and it was apparent that this was where homeless people came to sleep. Not looking the part of the 'regulars' made us stand out and within moments of waking, all creepy eyes were on us. The feeling I had of someone watching us while we slept was justified.

"You know girls, it can be dangerous here, are you alright?" said the eerie voice from a man who had been starring at us without blinking.

"Yea, my friend Kat and I are fine, we can take care of ourselves." Who was I kidding? This guy's blank stare alone was freaking me out!

"Well, if you need anything, don't hesitate to ask alright?"

As he talked the fear I felt for him turned into something else, he didn't look scary anymore, it was more like he wanted to warn us.

"Okay." I replied.

Dragging ourselves up, we cautiously sought the assistance of someone in uniform.

"Excuse me, could you tell me where we could get a room close by but inexpensive?"

The man looked at us like we were joking, I honestly thought he was going to start laughing.

"Sure." He said. "Next door. The rooms are $25 a night, no frills ya know."

"I'm sure." Kat said, as we walked away.

His idea of 'no frills' and ours were way off track.

If there was a science experiment on growing mold and the development of funk, this hotel was the main laboratory!

"EEWW." Kat cried. "I don't want to stay here!"

"We don't have a choice but everything will be fine."

Even though I wasn't sure I believed we would be alright I had to keep up appearances for Kats sake.

"Let's pay and get upstairs to see how much money we can spend on food."

Kats response clearly showed her stomach was in control for the time being instead of fear and this is a good thing. It's time to get settled and get something to eat.

There was a short, plump man sitting behind a desk that wasn't quite as broad as he was. His bald head revealed skin that really should have been covered, not only was it discolored but it was peeling. He also had a cigar hanging from his mouth, it was the worst smelling smoke I had ever encountered and I'd had my share of smoke odors. I couldn't help but wonder if he made it himself and entrapped the aroma from the hotel within its casing unknowingly lol, funk on fire … Yuck!

No matter how uncivilized he seemed it was still important that we weren't timid so we pretended as if the surroundings weren't anything out of the usual for us. Stepping forward I used the most adult voice I could muster.

"We need a room sir, for one night at first please." He gazed at us as if we were photographs that couldn't see him. There was no verbal response, just a concentrated stare.

"Did you hear her?" Kat questioned.

All of a sudden, as if he were coming out of a trance he responded.

"Do you girls know what you're doing here? This can be a real dangerous hotel, they call it 'Hotel California'."

We laughed at his comment as if we were in the 'know', when in fact we were really in the dark, we had no idea what he was talking about. Why did adults do that anyway? Why didn't he just say what he meant instead of some phrase that probably hasn't been slang for years!

"That's fine, we'll be alright. We need to get some sleep and we're starving so we'll go upstairs, put our stuff away and go get something to eat." I said. Of course that was the only thing I had the nerve to say aloud.

He sat up, which made me realize he hadn't been sitting up all along, did I mention how creepy he was?

"You girls be careful." He said. His seemingly sincere concern rapidly faded when we handed him the money. This granted us temporary guardianship to an enormous old key on a grimy string. "This is the only key and you need to give it back to me in the morning ya hear?" Holding it for a moment he acted as if it was the key to a chest of hidden treasure.

"Yes sir." Kat said. "We won't forget."

"Thank you." We said at the same time, as we ascended the flight of stairs.

I didn't know about 'Hotel California' but I quickly realized it wasn't a crystal stairway to heaven! Fortunately it at least led us up, I don't want to imagine what laid beneath! There were paper and food particles all over the steps, a gross sight to go along with the rest of the décor. Although I must admit the site of crumbs gave me a minute of comfort, if there was this much food lying around there weren't many rats and roaches? At least I'd hoped not.

Looking for the number on the door was a chore, the smell was awful!

"It stinks!" We said at the same time causing us to finally get out a laugh.

"Jinx, you owe me a coke." I said.

"Yea yea yea," Kat said back still laughing some, "I owe you lots of cokes."

We unlocked the door and had to push it open with our backs. Okay, it stunk and was dirty and dusty. There was a bed against the wall with a blanket that was so thin we could see ourselves through it.

"We're gonna need another blanket or something." Kat said as she started to cry.

"I'm sorry." I said hugging her. "We'll figure it out. I'll go ask that guy if there are any more blankets."

"Okay but you can't go down here by yourself." She said. "Hang on, I'll go with you."

She put her stuff down by the bed and we headed out of the room.

When we first left the room there was a man walking down the corridor. He watched us watch him as we passed each other. He didn't say anything to us so we were afraid to say anything to him and soon he disappeared behind one of the doors.

Before we could even get to the stairs a different man was walking towards us, talking to us.

"Excuse me girls." The unexpected voice began. "Are you alright?"

Kat stopped. "Oh, you scared me!"

"I'm sorry." The man said apologetically. "My name is Greg, what's yours?"

Kats expression changed to a calmer one and she smiled.

"My names is Kat." She said smoothly. "Are you staying here to?"

"Yep." Greg said before turning to look at me. "What's your name?"

"I'm Jenny, hello." I replied hoping I'd sounded as smooth as Kat did.

Greg motioned down the hall, "Do you two want to come down to my room? We're just kicking back smoking some herb and eating. Your welcome to join us I you want."

We looked at each other in relief. "Yes." Kat blurted out.

"Cool." I said agreeably. "Come on Kat, sounds good to me."

We turned and followed him to the end of the hallway. He stopped and reached out to open the door to his room holding it open for us just like a true gentleman would.

"Thank you." Kat said.

"No problem hun." The guys said.

He took each of us by the hand and led us in.

"Go ahead and have a seat on the bed." He offered.

In addition to Greg and the two of us were two other guys with three girls. All of them were talking and sharing a joint. The party stopped momentarily as they glanced up to see that we were joining them.

"Hey girls, what's up?" One of the guy's asked.

"Not much, just checkin out San Francisco."

"Not a bad city right?" He said back.

"We haven't been able to see much of it yet." I said.

"Maybe tomorrow we could show you girls around? For now though here you go." He said as he handed me the joint.

"Thanks, I'd love some!"

Finally, I thought to myself. I can smoke the ugliness of this hotel goodbye. I took a hit and passed it on. We sat there listening to all the guys talk. Observing our surroundings as discreetly as possible, it was apparent that something was going on beyond an innocent gathering of potheads. One of the girls continually jumped up when she was told to get them a beer. It was like watching an owner play fetch with his dog. The guys continuously gave orders to the girls and they obeyed like robots. I hadn't smoked enough to be hallucinating so I looked at Kat to make sure I wasn't the only one that saw what was going on. She gave me a look that confirmed she had witnessed the same thing.

At the same moment our eyes met in secret conversation mode Greg walked over to Kat and grabbed her hand.

"Come on honey, why don't we go or a drive and get something to eat and I'll show you some of the city." He said.

I jumped up. "No, we don't separate, if she goes I go to."

The other man came over to me and tried to pull me toward him, "You can come with me honey. I'll take you to get something eat, we don't have to go to the same place they go to, how boring."

They all seemed to think they were funny and laughed about it. One glimpse at Kat's expression and I knew we were thinking alike. We'd gotten ourselves into more than we bargained for.

Suddenly there was a knock at the door. Everyone froze and just looked at it. Before another word was said or motion was made, it flew open. We really didn't have a moment to think of who he was or why he was doing what he did but he reached in and grabbed Kat's hand, then she grabbed mine and we went flying down the hallway to our room.

"Hurry." He said. "Get in here and lock this door. Don't let anyone in you hear?"

There was no more pretending I could make everything all right. I was completely freaked out and so was Kat. We sat down trying to catch our breath. I looked at the man while he peaked out the door and realized it was the guy we had passed in the hall earlier, I wonder why he would want to help us.

He was still out of breath to. "You girls have no idea where you are do you?"

We both looked up at him, we could see his heart beating out of his dirty buttoned up shirt.

"You could have been killed or raped you know!" He said.

Kat and I both started crying, "You're kidding me right? Who are those people?"

He had us both sit down and told us that the hotel they had sent us to was a prostitution ring and a drug hotel. Nothing else happened here and we were major 'fresh meat' as they would call it.

"You two stay here and don't leave your room or open the door to anyone but me alright?"

We were both scared to death!

"I'll be back in 20 minutes with a pizza and then I'll go see about getting some money for you to eat breakfast in the morning. Maybe you can get on a bus out of here too. Remember what I said, don't open the door and don't leave, I mean it. I'll knock twice then pause then twice again so you will know that it's me."

We didn't want him to go but we were so hungry. He looked back at us one more time before he shut the door.

"Jenny." Kat said. "I can't believe what we got ourselves into, how crazy. I kind of wish we were home where we'd be warm and not hungry."

"Me too." I admitted. "Let's try to get some rest and then we'll eat when he gets back.

"I hope it's soon." She said.

"Yep, me to." I had to agree with Kat. It wasn't just the food, there was something about him that made me feel safe.

We both laid down on the bed and tried to fall asleep but within minutes we heard a buzzing sound.

"Hey, what's that?" I asked Kat.

Kat sat up, "I don't know."

The buzzing sound went off again. We fanatically looked through our bags for something to protect ourselves with in case of an emergency but all we could find were scissors.

"This will have to work." I said.

"How are we supposed to sleep through that?" Kat asked.

The buzzing just kept up so I got up to look for where it was coming from.

"Look Kat, It's like a ringer from the main desk I think."

"Your right, I wonder what he keeps ringing it for, let's go down and ask." She said.

"No, remember he told us not to leave the room for anything." I said in a fearful yet determined voice.

"Your right." Kat agreed.

We laid down on the bed holding our weapon believing that if someone were going to attack us we would fend them off courageously with our manicure scissors! Finally we heard our nock. Two short, a pause and two more short. We both jumped up and opened the door.

"Hi." Kat said. "We didn't think you would come back."

He handed us the pizza and soda. He was truly our angel brought here to save us, in more than one way!

"That's silly." He said. "Of course I was coming back. It's obvious you girls aren't prostitutes and that you had no idea what you were getting yourselves into. I couldn't let them do to you what I've seen them do to so many other young girls just like you two." He said.

"Thank you, thank you, and thank you." We both said at the same time and kissed his face.

"Now you're gonna make me blush." He said sincerely.

We all grabbed a slice of pizza and proceeded to pig out. I'm not sure if being terrified increases your appetite or if we were just hungry from not having eaten all day, but we ate that pizza as if it were our first and last meal.

"Hey." Kat said. "There was a weird buzzing in our room that rang over and over again. Do you know what it was? We figured it might be the man at the front desk but why would he want us?"

"I don't know." Greg said. "But the old man who works here isn't there right now, at least he wasn't when I came up."

I could feel the fear creeping up inside of me and I could see it in Kat.

"Will you go down and check again to see if he's there now?" I asked him.

"Alright, you two stay here, I'll be right back."

"Wow Kat, I'm getting scared, this place is creepy!" I said. What I wanted to say though was that I wanted to go home.

"Jenny." Kat said looking at me. "Can we go home, and would you be mad at me?"

"Heck no, I was just thinking the same thing but I didn't want to say anything or upset you. I'll have to call my mom, I wonder if she would help us get a bus home. I doubt it but we won't know until we try."

We began packing our stuff placing our makeup in its special place and folding our clothes to perfection. Our things seemed more suitable for a vacation in Hawaii than a runaway trip to San Francisco! Once we finished packing we realized how long it had been since our hero/angel left.

"I wonder where he went." I said. "He was just going downstairs."

"I don't know but if he doesn't come back I'm not leaving here until morning because I'm not opening that door!" Kat answered back with despair.

We waited and waited until we finally drifted off to sleep. I woke to see a bit of sunshine creeping into the room through a tiny section of the window that wasn't boarded up.

"Morning." I said to Kat to see if she was awake to. We both sat up rubbing our eyes and stretching and soon realized it wasn't a dream. "He didn't come back, I wonder what happened. Thank goodness he brought us dinner."

"Right?" Kat agreed. "I don't know what we would have done if we hadn't of gotten to eat something. I'm glad you don't mind going home Jen, I miss my mom."

"Yea, me to." I said.

We gathered all of our stuff, quietly opened the door and peeked out as discretely as possible.

"Kay, it looks clear, let's disappear down those stairs." I said.

"I'm right behind you." Kat said.

As we got to the end of the stairway we walked up to the front desk to return the key and decided to ask the man sitting there about the buzzing in our room.

"I was sent out to run an errand for a little while, I wasn't here." He said.

Kat and I looked at each other. "Did you happen to see a man about 5'8" with brown hair?" I asked. "He came down stairs last night to find out why we were being buzzed and never returned. He was a huge help to us last night and we're worried about him."

The old man just shrugged his shoulders as if he could care less.

"I did see two men escort a man by that description out the doors last night. They had beat him up pretty bad, said he had stepped on their territory." He looked down into the mess on his desk and made it clear our conversation was over.

My heart sank to the floor, I knew he had been beaten up for helping us. I grabbed Kat's hand and we walked as fast as we could to the bus depot. Once we entered the depot a sense of relief came to me, a feeling I hadn't felt in the previous 24 hours.

"I'll call my mom and see if we can get home."

"Thank you Jenny, I am so worried about that guy. Dang, we don't even know his name."

"I know, me to, I'm afraid they may have killed him or something. Now I know what that man meant when he said that they call the place, Hotel California, crazy!"

We were in a daze soaking everything in and at the same time, trying to look as if everything was fine.

"Might as well get it over with or we'll never make it home, be right back." I told Kat.

She just smiled and laid her head down on the table still exhausted from our adventures.

In a couple of minutes I was back and scooted next to Kat at our table.

"I called my mom." I told her. "Who called her friend in Berkeley, who called the local police and arranged to purchase our tickets for us."

Kat threw her arms around me and we hugged and laughed, we were so happy to not be stuck here and to actually get to go home! By then the officers were walking over to our table to give us the tickets. I stood up and shook their hands.

"Thank you for helping us!" We both said.

They tipped their hats one after the other. One of them turned back to what he was doing and the other told us to take care and that we were obviously loved and wanted home. That was so sweet and little did he know, something we needed to hear.

Soon we were struggling up the stairs of the bus with our things heading to the back, once again.

"To cool, we're going home, I can't wait." I said.

"Neither can I." Kat said. "I can't believe your mom did this for us. I'm closing my eyes now, see you in a bit Jenn."

I watched her close her eyes and get comfortable. 'Wow, my mom really does love me. I can't wait to get home', I thought to myself.

We slept until we heard, "Chico, we are in Chico. Please grab your baggage swiftly if you have anything underneath the bus so we can stay on schedule."

HER PLACE WAS WITH GOD

As I stretched and looked out of the window, I saw something better than any tourist attraction, my mom's face. The only thing more comforting than seeing her was hearing her say my name. She wasn't the reason I ran away and I really wanted to explain everything to her so she would understand, but my words were never spoken. Life kept going and I went back to school and being me, whoever that was.

The man who helped us in San Francisco risked his life to protect ours, I can't help but to wonder what happened to him, I think about him always!

※

Coming home was pretty much the same as it had been before I left, it was like second nature to look for somewhere else to be.

I called my cousin and found out she had been staying in a small community, Strawberry Valley. She said I could come crash with her for a while, no one would give me a hard time or question me so soon she got a ride to come pick me up and we headed into the hills.

It was such a nice drive but as we pulled into to the little town I started to get nervous, it looked like we drove into a little Indian village. We drove by the homes and then the school where a group of kids and adults were playing basketball, their games stopped and they were all trying to see who I was. It was pretty obvious they weren't too happy about me being there until we pulled up to park and Carol got out. Everyone came up and welcomed her home, me to. We talked while we walked through the school and their little village like town as the kids followed behind us playin ball.

Being in the woods with my cousin, her friends and myself hanging out and talking about anything was the first chance I'd had to take a deep breath in what seemed like forever. It was awesome to not feel like I was in the way or a problem, nice.

They showed me the house I'd stay in to sleep. It was old, big and empty except for a few sleeping area's set up here n' there throughout the house with blankets and pillows.

"Plenty of room for you where your cousin sleeps. Welcome home and don't worry about food, when dinner's ready we'll send the kids up for ya'll." Said one of the men. They all smiled and walked out the door.

I didn't have any blankets so Carol left for a little bit and came back with a warm quilt and a pillow for me, so awesome!

"Here ya go cuz, lets lay out our beds. I really need to close my eyes for a little bit." Carol said, "When we get up I'll get us a bowl to smoke before dinner."

I reached over and gave her a hug, "Thank you cousin, I love you so much. I don't know what I'd do without you!"

"No worries, get some rest now. Everything's gonna be fine."

We got woke up a couple of hours later and it was almost dark outside but I could smell food and oh my god I was sooo hungry! I looked up and saw three or four little ones standing at the door,

"Grandfather told us to tell you it was time to eat, come soon he said ok?"

We both started to move from our warm and cozy place, Carol told them we would be on our way.

We went and joined everyone a couple of houses down and first off which was awesome, the pipe was passed to me. I smiled and thanked the woman that handed it to me and enjoyed smoking then we all ate potatoes and steak. I'm pretty sure it was the best meal I had ever had!

I stayed with Carol for a few days but then I called my mom and she came up and got me, time to go home, again.

Bachmann Hill - Juvenile Correctional School

I was in the 9th grade at Bidwell Junior High, a handful, and in love for the first time. Our first meeting was unconventional to say the least, as was my life though so it all fit. I had been hanging out with Barbie who I refer to as a friend but she was more of an accomplice. We were both angry at the world and hell bent on doing whatever we wanted to do.

A lot of our time was spent drinking coffee at Sambo's on the Esplanade during school hours, but that didn't seem to matter. Leavin home again cause my friend wanted company sounded pretty good to me.

One day Barbie was flirting with a couple of guys in the parking lot. Within no time we were making out in their car, talk about flattery getting you everywhere!

Barbie was in the front seat and it seemed like she was going a lot farther than I'd planned to go. Figuring what was good for my buddy was probably good for me, the guy I was with reached over and pulled me toward him. In one motion he was all over me, he seemed to have four hands and at least two mouths! When he wasn't biting my neck he was sucking it so hard I could barely breathe! He began putting his hands up my top and then decided he'd just take it off and he didn't notice or seemed to care if any of this was something I even wanted, his trying to get my top off helped the blood return to my brain and I pushed him off of me.

I sat up and told Barbie I was leaving with or without her, scooted back to the other side of the car, got my shirt on and flew out the door. I looked back into the car at Barbie and yelled at her.

"Damn, what the heck, you're not going to sleep with him right here. I can't believe you, come on."

She got up and began putting on her clothes, which was apparently more than just her top.

By the time we reached the inside of the restaurant the sound of the car's tires squealing off in a hurry could be heard behind us. I went straight to the bathroom and Barbie went to get us a table.

I was barely in the bathroom door when I looked in the mirror and noticed what dracula had done to my neck. I looked like a walking, talking etchasketch! I had very little normal skin left to show, if it was any longer it could have passed for some kind of rare skin disease. Oh my goodness, I didn't know if I should cry or scream or both!

Placing my hand over it as if I was stretching or massaging my 'stiff neck', I covered it the best I could and left the bathroom to join Barbie.

"Check this out." I showed her my neck.

"Hey Jenny, man, I don't think I have ever had a hickey like that, too cool!

"I don't think so, how am I going to cover this?" I said.

I was thinking about going home but my mom and Geoffrey would see it for sure. In the midst of my being terrified about what could happen I quickly lost all concentration when I looked up and standing in front of me was the most beautiful cowboy I'd ever seen. He was tall with clear blue eyes that were soft as could be with a cowboy hat and boots to match. As I sat dazed he graciously extended his hand toward me, which I realized had a scarf in it.

"Here, put this on, it should help you cover that up."

I could feel my face turning red and blushing. "How embarrassing, thank you." I said to him.

He sat down next to me and never took his eyes off of me. I of course knew this because I didn't take mine off of his either. I was hooked, smitten, as they called it. One thing was for sure, anywhere he went I wanted to go too. It didn't take long before we were inseparable. He always made a bad situation better and never walked away from me willingly. As the days went by we got closer and closer, this cowboy and me. I was 13 years old and he was 18 and we were falling in love.

I was still a runaway but Barbie had pretty much gone home, her parents were used to her leaving now and then. We stayed at her house or on other friends' couches and sometimes slept in a car that Dale had if it wasn't to cold outside.

This time leaving home I had no idea that my mom was worried about me. I figured she was busy with her life as always, but I was wrong. We went to Barbie's house to get some clean clothes and something to eat and were hangin out in the kitchen. Her parents were sitting in the living room watching the news when suddenly a picture of me filled the screen and a voice came next.

"Have you seen this girl? She has been missing for 4 days now and her parents are sick with worry. If you have seen her or know where she might be, please contact the Chico Police Department or call us here at Channel 12 News."

Barbie was in her bedroom about to enter the living room at the precise moment the story aired, Dale and I were still in the kitchen but the entire living room area was visible from where we were.

The moment I realized what had happened I looked at Dale, before another second could pass Barbie's mom turned around and was looking at me. There was no mistaking my photo, it was as if my mom had taken it the day before! Without a word or second thought I hauled ass out the back door with Dale on my heels. Barbie headed out after us and we could hear her mom screaming that she was going to call the police. Great, so much for that safe haven! I wish my mom could have realized that she was making it harder for me to find safe places to be, and that home, wasn't really one of those places. Being on the news just made being a runaway an even bigger challenge! We were on the outside of town so we were surrounded by tons of dead brush. We kept running through the field and in no time the police were on our trail. Flashlights were going back n' forth across the field and finely we found a creek bed to hide in until they gave up and left.

"Man that was close, now what? I hate this hiding stuff, I think I might go home, I can't believe my mom actually went to all the trouble of putting a picture of me on the news. What do you think?"

I couldn't help but try to find out what Dale and Barbie's thoughts were to, I didn't want to get them in trouble.

Neither of them said a word, we just all walked back into town in silence. The irony of beautiful smelling flowers that were carried by the cool breeze did not miss my attention. No matter how insane your life might be at the moment, Chico was always amazing. Finally Dale broke the silence. He grabbed my hand, held my face and looked into my eyes.

"You should go home. You don't need to be hiding like this and not sleeping in your own bed. We will still be together I promise." He said to me.

It was around 2 am and we were almost to Central Park.

"I'm going to find a couch to sleep on you guys." Barbie said maybe figuring we needed to be alone, or just out of sheer exhaustion. She headed toward Chapman Town.

"Here, sit down." Dale led me to a bench and sat next to me.

He slowly reached into his pocket and pulled something out. At first I couldn't see what it was because it appeared to be small enough to fit in his hand. Dale wasn't known for magic tricks, but he did so many unexpected things to put a smile on my face that I could only imagine what I was in store for. My imagination didn't do justice, what happened next wasn't something I had even started to think about, at least not for years to come. When he opened his hands he help up two rings, a wedding band and an engagement ring.

Here I was at the age of 13 feeling like the luckiest girl alive! They were the most beautiful pieces of jewelry I'd ever seen and my heart was pounding.

"I love you Jenny, will you marry me?"

They were perfect and beautiful, both the words and the rings!

"Of course I will, but there is no way. I'm too young and my mom will never agree to it."

"It doesn't matter, as long as you are in my life I can wait."

Wow, this man had my heart like I didn't know a heart could be gotten!

"The only thing now is that you need to go home. Ok?"

He put the rings on my finger and kissed me, I was elated! Hours before this I was hiding amongst dead bushes in the darkness and now the ground had been transformed into the blue sky and I was sitting on the moon. Only love can bring such calm in the midst of such turmoil.

"Ok, I'll go home but you have to come see me tomorrow, you promise?"

He had made my night, heck, my entire life, with one question and two small pieces of jewelry.

"I Promise." He said. Then he walked me to my street and kissed me goodbye.

Floating up the steps to my front door I had no idea what to expect, but at this point nothing could bring me down. My mom answered right away and although she was mad at me, she was relieved. After running from the police n' all I was excited about being home and looking forward to sleeping in my own bed.

Dale had left me with feelings of optimism about the future, our future. My entire body was infused with a wonderful calming feeling I hadn't ever known before.

After that night my life improved immensely. I wasn't punished for my escapade (I never was), and I managed to see Dale regularly being allowed to do whatever I wanted, just as before. My mom was amazing, she even arranged for me to have a sleepover with my friend from school, Dee, after a few weeks of being home. It was a treat seeing how I'd so recently been the lead story on the local news station but other than that, it wasn't odd since we'd both spent the night at each other's houses before. Suspicion didn't set in until she woke us both up at 6 am the next morning.

Un-known to me a field trip had been planned, one in which I needed a suitcase. We got into the car and headed to Booneville, California. It was a tiny hole in the woods, inland from the coast below Mendocino. My days of being the stoner kid at Bidwell Junior High School had just ended. I was in the 9th grade and 13 years old being taken out of school. All this time I thought my mom was just being cool to keep me from taking off, I had no idea she had a limit that could be reached.

She withdrew me from public school system and enrolled me into Bachman Hills, a Juvenile Correctional School. Through the entire process only one thought repeated its self over and over in my mind, my worst nightmare was happening, I was being taken from Dale and locked up at the same time!

Deep down, way, way, deep down, a part of me was happy, my mom had never resorted to such drastic steps to protect me, she really does love me.

We arrived at Bachman Hills and my mom was the first one out of van. She gave Dee the option of going with her or waiting in the car with me. I reassured her that I wouldn't be upset either way, it was apparent that she too was surprised by this whole rendezvous.

An eternity seemed to have passed, but it was possibly more like a few minutes when my mom and a few others from the school approached the van. I smiled at them, knowing I had come up with the perfect plan. After Dee got out I shut the door behind her and locked it along with all the other doors. This was the last stance and I wasn't going without a fight! My mom was going to have to give in and take me home. She and I argued for a little while, but eventually I gave in. It appeared that she had developed a tough skin while I wasn't looking and my usual tactics didn't stand a chance against her new found strength and love.

Now it was time for the inescapable. I got out of the car and was introduced to all of the seemingly 'normal' people that were entrusted with the task of making me a better person. How hilarious, these people didn't even know me, guess they had a manual they used on teenagers like me. The introductions were immediately followed by a grand tour of the property. As much as I hated to admit it, and was sure to not do so aloud, the place looked really cool.

Maybe the long drive, on going introductions and grand tour was all a part of their evil plan to make me so tired and hungry that I'd be too weak to fight. If so, they'd succeeded. The sudden smell of something cooking was making me feel a lot less aggressive and much more agreeable, so much so I am sure I wouldn't do anything to get into trouble if food depravation was a punishment!

Our tour continued and I saw the pool area. At first I could hear the splashing of water, the noise had ceased and all eyes were on me and they started whistling and trying to reach me with their splashing. In slow motion (it seemed), we walked along the huge wooden fence that incased the pool area to the gate.

"Welcome." I heard a girls voice say. "Ignore these boys, you are the new girl so they will mess with you for a while. Let me know if you need help ok?"

"Thank you." I said, happy I was able to respond. My mind was wondering to so many places I was going to have to focus to prevent from losing it altogether.

We'd gone past the pool and walked up a few steps that lead to a wooden porch that connected to an office. It was an adult's version of comfort, the usual suspects, desks, chairs, etc. A man at one of the desks stood up, introduced himself to my mom and shook her hand. He was Bulgarian I was told and had a heavy accent that was hard to understand, he was a little scary. I couldn't help but stand up straighter and knew I wouldn't be causing any trouble here.

The woman that we'd been touring with was referred to as Mooch. Mooch was slang for 'Mutter' which means, 'mother' in Swiss. Her real name was Liz, her and her husband Silas own the school.

Wow, it was starting to sink in that my mom might really be leaving me here. While we stood there in the office Silas spoke, then Mooch spoke and I listened. When they were finished we went out of the office through a door that led into a huge room, it must be the cafeteria I figured and dang I was so hungry! There were rows of tables and chairs and a big kitchen with lots of room for cooking to feed such a group of kids. There were some girls in the kitchen washing the walls with bleach, the smell was strong but at least the place was clean.

"This is our mess hall." Mooch said.

… and as if she knew I was about to give my thoughts a voice about my hunger, she continued.

"We have many meals together here so everyone has to go by the rules at all times. We have dances and swimming with the girls and boys together but mostly girls and boys are separated. The boy's live here on the main property where class is held and meals are prepared daily."

Her accent was like a character from a James Bond movie, which was kind of cool. My many day dreams and fantasies often took me to other countries and meeting people who actually were from someplace else gave them a weird validity.

"This is the quad." She said as we walked out the back doors to a gigantic metal building. "We hold dances here for anyone who has earned or maintained the necessary amount of points. Points are configured by one's attitude and willingness to participate in all projects. This might include cleaning or various other chores and class projects and you can earn trips to the store to spend your allowance. We also have movie nights as well as group sessions to give everyone a platform for the discussing of any issues that may arise."

She finished as she'd started, very professionally and extremely proper and looked at me with a compassionate smile as if trying to quietly reassure me that things weren't as bad as they seemed.

She was so well spoken that her intellect was obvious, but as I glanced into her eyes I felt something that made me believe she was real and even cared. She finally directed her voice to me.

"How are you doing, do you think you'll be ok?" She asked.

The sound of her voice broke the trance she was placing me in with her stare.

"Yes, I think I will be ok." It was a tough response that I could only muster after taking a deep breath.

I looked up to my mom who had been standing next to me through the whole tour.

"Are you really going to leave and go home?" I asked her.

Dee had been following us all along walking behind the councilors.

She walked up and put her arms around me. "I wish I could stay with you, I would if they would let me." We were both working hard to hold back tears.

"Thank you but you need to go home, your mom would kill me." We laughed and hugged each other.

Truth was, this tour thing was starting to work, I was beginning to imagine myself here. Mooch seemed like she might have earned her nickname. Either way, I was thoroughly relieved to see that there weren't any prison bars. I guess my crimes weren't as bad as I'd thought.

We continued walking and soon we were standing next to trailers that had been set along the hillside. There was that smell of pine again and I loved it. It reminded me of Christmas, just imagine, Christmas every day!

The talking and tour continued.

"These are our school rooms, you will have five different classes throughout the day, lunch and of course breaks. While at school there will be no boy girl connection physically at all." Mooch said looking directly at me as she delivered that last statement.

"Yes ma'am." I said, and she continued.

"The girls live up the highway on the girl's property which we will drive up to after dinner and you can settle in to your room. You will have a roommate, everyone has to co-exist so if there are any issues please take care of them in a peaceful manner or there will be house punishments. There are house rules and a daily chore list for everyone. Before anyone goes to the main building chores have to be finished and rooms have to be clean." She gave the impression that that was the end of the well guided, long but not too intimating tour.

I knew there would be rules, at least there would also be dinner. We had come full circle and were standing in the front of the property where we had parked. My mom walked over and hugged me.

"I have to go honey, I still have a long drive and have to get Dee home. I love you and you are going to be fine." She said in her most motherly voice.

"You promise?" I asked and out of nowhere tears came streaming down my cheeks and I buried my face into her shoulder. "I don't want you to go mom, I don't want to stay here. Take me home with you please, I promise I won't do what I was doing anymore. I will be good!"

It was as if I'd reverted back to a five year old and was being dropped off at kindergarten. She held my shoulders and looked into my eyes.

"I love you and you will be just fine. I will call you or you call me as soon as you can and we can write all the time. I love you." She said it as quickly as she could, turned and walked to the van.

"Kay, I love you to." We hugged and Dee and I waved good-bye as they got in the van and drove off.

If there was an appropriate amount of time allotted for a teenager to watch her mother drive off into the distance mine had been reached. A hand gently touched my shoulder and turned me back toward the office. I was introduced to more counselors and no one seemed violent or insane but the idea of being so far from home was depressing. Me, the one that always ran away, was sad to be so far away.

A female counselor instructed me to follow her and informed me that dinner would be served shortly. She suggested I head to the mess hall to prevent being last in line. Mess hall, what an understatement, my whole life was a mess.

How was I going to actually eat? I was starving but so nervous. Then again, I couldn't be known as the new girl that fainted or vomited lol, so I was going to have to figure something out. Thankfully we were having Lasagna, salad and French bread. My favorite meal, ok, maybe there was a God and I was the ward of a new angel who was trying to get the hang of it, yea, that had to be it, I'd seen that in a movie before! Everyone began introducing themselves to me while we ate, most of the girls were all right, and the boys flirted and tried to act big and bad. Didn't they realize we were all big n' bad lol, and that's why we were all here?

After dinner was over it was time for chores, fortunately for me, I hadn't been put on the schedule for anything my first night. We went to the vans that waited just outside the main building. All the girls managed to fill up two of them and we were driven up the highway a short way, it was beautiful and green with grapevines everywhere. When we got to where we turned off we pulled off the road and onto a private path. We parked and a gate had to be unlocked before we could continue up the road. We drove up a steep hill until we finally arrived at the girls' houses. A couple of the other girls helped me with my suitcases.

"Follow me." One girl said. "I'll show you to your room."

She didn't really smile or say much so I just followed, I couldn't stay quiet for long though.

"Thank you, I'm a little nervous." I said.

"Don't worry." she said. "We all are at first."

Finally she smiled, trying to reassure me that I would be fine.

Day break meant I'd survived my first night and with the new day came my first instruction, which was to write Dale a letter. It wasn't a love letter and other than being in my handwriting, it wasn't written by me. Each word was dictated while their eyes watched me like a hawk. In addition to sending this letter, which stated I never wanted to see him again, I was forced to return the rings he had given me. I felt dreadful sending it and couldn't envision how he must have felt once he received it. The only thing I could hope for was that he'd see through it, after all, it couldn't sound like me since they weren't my words right?

As it turned out, he must have known they weren't mine because as soon as he could, he came to the school to talk to me in person and see if I was alright. His plan was a good one, except he had never had the pleasure of meeting my new 'teachers', and had no idea what they were capable of, either was I.

A school dance had been planned and was in the works when Dale showed up. Seemingly a great plan to just mingle amongst the crowd, but they got word of his arrival. They must have felt it would be detrimental to my well being to spend even a moment with him because they crept into the dance and snuck me out! Once outside they placed me in one of the vans and took me up the road to what they called a safe house and told me I had to stay there for a couple of nights for my own protection.

I got the whole story as we drove. Mooch and some of the other instructors accused Dale of showing up at the office ranting and raving and they said he was on heroin or something. They said he was carrying a knife and that he had a gun and threatened to kill all of them if they didn't go get me! Of course I didn't believe a word of it and I was sure they were being melodramatic. Even though I was outraged and knew everything they said was preposterous, the fiasco somehow managed to turn into a blessing, a school trip to Switzerland! Never having traveled out of the country, this was something I was definitely looking forward to. As much as I may have wanted to seem infuriated by the tactics the school used, I had to admit that I was looking forward to a foreign adventure!

Being great at pretending that bus rides were grand adventures, it was an extraordinary realization that I was truthfully going on one! I was a rock star on tour when I ran away with Kat, but this would call for a much higher level of imagination. Royalty? Yes, this time I'd be a princess on holiday.

My mom and Geoffrey had gotten a divorce, I knew she was too good for him. Maybe if he didn't become such a heavy drinker things would have been different but there was a lot wrong in our family and things never seemed to get better. However my mom was able to do it, it happened. I couldn't believe I was being allowed to accompany the school to Switzerland. One thing was for sure, this would be the best 'field trip' I'd ever been on!

Most of the other girls going had more money than I did but it didn't matter. My mom bought me a beautiful gown to wear for the formal event we were scheduled to attend and she gave me $100 to spend. The love of my life was suddenly drifting farther and farther away from my thoughts and if this was part of their plan, I was afraid it might have started to work.

Suspicions about this all being setup to get me away from Dale were quickly confirmed. We were still at the airport in New York when Mooch insisted I send a postcard to him informing him of my trip out of the country. This was no problem (as I let them believe), it was the additional insert of my 'never coming back', that I didn't like. As far as I was concerned they were all crazy, but since they were crazy enough to take me to Switzerland and because I really wasn't given a choice, I went along with it.

Switzerland

Our flight was amazing and Greyhound had finally gotten a run for their money. For someone who thought bus rides were cool, flying was definitely superior. Being so high in the sky was the best!

After bout 11 or 12 hours of flying and getting to watch the movie Rocky, we descended from heaven and landed in the most magnificent place I'd ever seen, Zurich, Switzerland. It was all making sense now, the world was not just the few miles I'd previously traveled, it was massive, breathtakingly awesome and within itself, the grandest adventure that could be lived. Pretending to be a rock star or royalty no longer seemed necessary. Somehow just being me made me feel good.

We had managed to get our things and clumsily exit the plane. We got our luggage then waited and rested until finally a voice spoke that woke me from my own thoughts.

"Ok girls, time to get on the train." Mooch said.

We all stood mesmerized, it was like waking up in a dazzling dream. Never in our lives had we been so quiet, you could hear a feather fall to the ground. We looked around at each other, accepting the fact that this dream is indeed our new reality.

We took a train from the Airport to the village of Bern, it felt like a gift within a gift. We got to see views that were much more intense than they were in the movies I'd seen. Funny, you don't realize how limited your television or even a movie screen is until you've seen the world with your own eyes.

We were picked up in Bern by a farmer and his horse driven trailer. There was plenty of room for us all to sit, we were in awe of our surroundings. The trailer had wooden side rails that had the aroma of a soft, sweet smell.

"Mmmm, smell this Annette." I said.

She smiled that beautiful smile and laughed.

"You're so funny, it's wood silly, only you would consider something like wood

SWITZERLAND

railings wonderful." She quietly giggled at me as she turned to continue enjoying the view.

What was referred to as a road ended up being possibly 10 feet wide, just enough width for the horses to pull us up and around the mountain towards the most exquisite house we'd ever seen!

"Is that where we're staying?" I asked Mooch in shock.

"Yes honey, that's the house we've rented and see that farm to your right?"

She pointed to an enormous barn with several cows grazing out front.

"Every night we'll draw straws and that next morning at 6 am, two of you will go up to the farm and pick up our milk can for the day."

There was no way I was staying quiet with that new information!

"I ain't drinkin that." I said. "I'll go to the store and buy regular milk!"

"That's fine, you can do that but you'll be missing out on something really good and even good for you!" Mooch managed to say while she laughed hysterically.

"That's okay, I'm healthy enough."

Mooch and the others continued to laugh until the top of the house emerged.

"Here we are, your temporary home sweet home." The driver hollered with a smile.

Anxiously, but cautiously we climbed out and grabbed our bags. I dropped my backpack and turned around to see the road we had traveled. Without a doubt what lay behind and before me was the most picturesque landscape ever seen, I didn't even know it existed beyond books and films!

The simplest things were extraordinary, like the small winding path they called a road, the way you could see it rising and falling through the hills. We were completely surrounded by brilliant shades of green. Mother Nature herself had strategically placed perfectly colored flowers as far as our eyes could see. There were Chalets on the hills following the little road down. Not even in a distant dream could I have envisioned someplace so amazing, this place was a masterpiece with God's signature all over it!

"Okay Miss day dreamer, pick up your back pack and let's get organized then we'll go for a walk." Mooch said.

She didn't know it, but for once I was lost in my reality instead of a fantasy.

Knowing that we were about to explore this whole new world our energy was increased. We managed to get everything inside and unpacked in record time. I never thought something of this magnitude could happen to me, I was ready to explore every inch of wonder I could get my hands, eyes and feet on. We were still in awe of our surroundings but couldn't remember the trip up from the train station, Mooch told us it was from jet lag, crazy! So we did a repeat trip up from the train station to the Chalet.

Each of us were enrolled in Bachman for our own reasons and none of us thought someplace like this even existed, much less that the type of lives we were living would lead us to it. We longed to absorb every detail so we would never forget!

The second trip was more majestic than the first. The color green was never my favorite but the green of this grass had almost a fur like quality, also I had never desired to lay on the grass and gaze into the sun but I did now, so awesome! I stretched out in the middle of the flowers and gazed into the heavens. Fortunately for me, I'd just literally been flying through the clouds! That bottomless pit that I'd thought I was falling in, had completely vanished and I was instead resting peacefully and safely on a mountain only inches away from God.

We had all placed ourselves in different spots throughout the grass that was everywhere around the Chalet and could easily hear Mooches voice from inside.

"Girls, we are going to Zurich tomorrow to my brothers Pretzel Factory." We all threw "Ok's", back through the sweet air to her from our spots in the grass.

I loved hearing her speak with her Swiss/German accent. We all got ourselves up and wondered into the Chalet. Mooch was making her hot chocolate with fresh cow's milk and oatmeal that was as sweet as molasses. Bed time was scheduled to follow this sweet meal, but every moment had been so exhilarating, trying to fall asleep so soon would be the hardest task thus far.

"Can we stay up and play a game of hearts Mooch?" I asked.

I knew that all of us were thinking the same thing so I figured I'd put myself out on a limb and ask.

"Sure you girls go ahead, one hour and lights out." She said, giving in to what we wanted, but was sure to do it in a voice that was still in control.

"Yes ma'am, one hour." I said back to her.

"Come on in here and get some cocoa and your food." She hollered, "Be sure to rinse your dishes before you stack them."

She was sure to deliver instructions no matter how many times they'd been said in the past. We giggled at how particular she was, especially when she went on and on about something.

"I love you girls, good night. See you bright and early." She gave us the same response no matter how hard a time we gave her for performing her usual rituals.

"Good night, love you to." All of us chimed together.

The food was as delicious as usual and the cocoa seemed to have something extra. This was real chocolate. I'd had chocolate from Switzerland at home before, but this was completely different. We played a few hands of hearts, spoke on and off about our trip and finally went to bed. We eventually concluded that the sooner we went to sleep, the sooner we would wake up to morning and be able to continue our adventure.

SWITZERLAND

No alarm clocks were necessary, we rose bright and early ready to tour the town. Our first destination was downtown Zurich, this trip was getting better and better. The streets were narrow and filled with people busily making their way from one place to another. The roads were created from cobblestone and had such unique designs, it was built with so much love. It was beautiful!

The pretzel factory was a huge stone building, we parked and went inside its cozy interior. We were led through to the back to a stairwell. One after another a grand room that one would never expect, was revealed to us as we neared the lower level. Everything seemed to be magnified as if designed for royal giants. There was a long table that had proud tall wooden chairs along its side with designs etched in each one. Sitting on one was sure to be the closest that I'd ever come to having my own throne!

"Come on in everyone." Mooches brother said as he broke the trance with his joyous welcome.

Giggling seemed to be the only thing we could think of in response to our surroundings. Another brother made his grand entrance carrying a tray filled with steaming hot pretzels, homemade jam, butter, salt and cheese. We ate until we could no longer swallow. Just as delicious as the food were the stories they shared with us.

We told them all about America, of course we didn't happen to mention the kinds of trouble we had all gotten in there, but it did give me a feeling of belonging somewhere. As glorious as this country was, it made me not only realize that I was a visitor but more importantly that I came from someplace, I belonged somewhere. Along with the brothers Mooches niece had joined us also and we immediately got close. Seems no matter what country we were from we still had so much in common as young girls. She and I exchanged addresses and promised to write each other once I returned to the states.

Once finished we thanked mooches family and left the store to walk through the streets of the city, there were shops as far as we could see.

"Look Darci." I said, "A chocolate factory, let's see if we can watch them making it."

We all found our way into the small, quaint shop and had our wish come true. As you ordered there were windows you could look through into the kitchen area in order to observe the chefs at work. Yum! Swiss Chocolate, could one be enough for anyone … i thought? Totally consumed with the taste and smells of this heavenly delight, we continued on our journey. It wasn't long before we passed a bar.

"Jenny, come on." The girls called out and waving in my direction for me to follow.

"Hey, we can't be in here." My voice, the one of reason? This country was really having an effect on me!

Sure you can, watch." Melanie walked up to the bar. "Excuse me sir, may I have a glass of beer please?"

The waiter turned and smiled at her as if it was nothing for her to ask him for a beer. I began to wonder if I'd fallen into a wonderland, this was absolutely insane!

"Here you go ma'am." He handed her the mug of beer and accepted her payment and turned to us so I walked up to the counter.

"I would like a beer also please." I said sounding all 'old enough' lol.

"Right away." He got my beer and then everyone else's, we were having a ball!

It felt so funny ordering a drink and not being asked for identification or getting laughed at and shooed away! We thought it was pretty cool and convinced the counselors to let us buy some to take to the Chalet, after all we had tons of chocolate to consume, what better than a beer to wash it down.

When we returned to the Chalet we all took everything inside from our day in the city of Zurich and pulled out all of our treasures. Postcards and key chains and chocolate, what a great day we had!

"I'm going to go for a walk, anyone want to come with?" I said.

"Hang on Jenny, we can all go and unwind." Mooch said to me.

"Sounds good." I added as we all headed out the door trying not to stumble over each other getting to the green grass and flowers and trees that covered the hills.

We started down a path that led down a line of tall trees. It surrounded a beautiful open valley with cows and sheep living in the lush of their world. We soon came upon a trough of running water.

"Wow, I wonder if this is okay to drink?" I asked.

"Try it Jenny." Mooch said back to me.

"I don't like water, you know that."

"Try it silly." She said back to me laughing.

While I was tasting the water the other girls reached into the trough splashing me so I got em back, we were havin a ball and cooling off at the same time.

I couldn't believe how good it was lol I hated water and to top it off it felt absolutely wonderful on my face! We kept walking up along the path and along the row of trees that were standing as tall as the heavens, like a protective wall watching over the beauty. We came up to the end of the line of trees and around the bend we found the most beautiful valley of the green grass and all different colors and types of flowers.

"Oh my goodness." I said to myself but out loud. "I keep seeing more and more that is just as beautiful if not more as the last awesome thing I saw, I love it here!"

"Come on girls, it's getting chilly. The sun is going down so we will want to get on inside where it's warmer." Mooch said.

We all followed one another back down the small path, it was about as wide as five feet or so, so cute! Back to the water and splashing our faces and drinking as much as we could. As we started walking again we began pulling one another away to catch up to Mooch, we all laughed and played the rest of the way home.

We ate dinner and went and got our beer out of protective custody and sat in the

SWITZERLAND

back windows of the Chalet looking out over the hills. You could see the other homes scattered out throughout the scene, amazing! We talked, dreamed and drank our beer until all of a sudden someone started to laugh. Then someone else started to laugh and I couldn't help but to laugh with them also. How funny, we were drunk and we weren't in trouble!

"To cool, I could get used to this!" One of the girls hollered out.

"Not." One of the counselors said as they came in from the other room.

"You girls are absolutely the silliest I have ever seen, read the cans of beer you are drinking." Mooch said to all of us.

We all stopped and looked at our cans, 2% alcohol.

"Oh my goodness, only 2% alcohol in this beer, we are not drunk! How funny, it's all in our heads!" I said and some of us starting laughing and falling over.

"I don't know about that, I'm toasted." One of the girls said. "As a matter of fact I think I'm going to get sick." She uttered just before running into the bathroom.

We were all laughing and Mooch worked on getting our attention.

"Ok girls, everybody come in here for a house meeting."

"Hey, I thought we didn't have to do those while we were here." I said.

"Jenny's right." Darci said.

"Very funny girls." She gave me that sweet sideways smile like she had a plan ... "In the morning I want you two, (me and Darci), to go down to the farm and pick up the milk. It's your turn, 6 am sharp, no later you hear."

"Yes ma'am, we hear you." Dorothy and I responded right away trying to sound way more serious than we were feeling lol.

After we were all settled and the sick one rejoined the rest of us, Mooch started talking.

"We are going to visit my brother's school tomorrow and then, after everyone meets and we learn about each other's countries, we will discuss our mountain climbing excursion. We will be hiking in the mountains of the Swiss Alps!"

Her enthusiasm wasn't shared with all of us.

"I can't walk like that Mooch." I said.

"Yes you can Jenny, you can do anything you put your mind to do."

Are you serious ... we were all thinking! The other girls all sat down as if the beer suddenly had no effect on them any longer.

We all sobered up quickly with thought of climbing some mountain, we were just kids!

"Off to bed, sleep tight and don't let those bed bugs bite. And don't forget, we're going dancing day after tomorrow. Now you girls get to bed."

We had totally forgotten about the disco tec, right on, how exciting!

"I love you Mooch, goodnight. Thank you for this trip, thank you for everything!"

"You're welcome honey, everything will be fine." She said.

Mooch always responded in a way that reminded you of her ability to read minds.

"I don't know about that." I said. "I have never been very active, I don't exercise and I know I'm going to get blisters because I don't have good shoes."

"Yes you do," she said reaching into a back under the table. "Here are your boots, try them on."

"You got me boots?" I asked. I don't know how a pair of boots made me feel loved but they did.

"I had an extra pair in case someone didn't have any and I think they will fit you perfect." Mooch said to me.

"Thank you, I love you."

"I love you too, good night honey. See all of you in the morning." She said in the sweetest voice.

We all headed to our rooms, between the hiking trip and the dance it took us forever to finally close our eyes. Another day to come with amazing things happening, I was so excited! Off to sleep we went, all of us with smiles on our faces and in our hearts.

Morning came quickly and right after breakfast we were on our way to the school. The only school experiences I'd had were in the states so I had no idea what to expect, in the back of my mind I figured all schools were probably the same.

I was soon mistaken, this school was like a picture I'd seen of a castle in a fairytale! The interior was so massive there was an echo. Beautiful paintings were placed along the walls that seemed to not only be original, but possibly very expensive. As we walked through the hallways the silence lead me to believe that maybe we'd come too early in the morning. I didn't even hear adults working much less other kids actually attending class, was anyone here at all?

"Elizabeth, how wonderful to see you!" Came the voice of a man who'd walked up to Mooch and kissed her on the cheek.

I guess this meant we weren't alone after all, how did he manage to walk up so quietly in this echoing hall I'll never know!

"Good to see you too, we are all so very excited to be here!" Mooch gracefully responded.

Without hesitation he began the tour with his classroom being first on the agenda. As he walked he gave us our schedule for the day. He must have known we'd be impressed with what he had to show us because once we reached his room he stopped talking and let us take in the atmosphere. It appeared that Mooches brother was a lot like her, he knew when to speak and when to let the silence speak for itself. The room was the largest classroom I'd ever been in. It was brightly painted with incredibly high ceilings. He led us to a section of empty seats and although I'm sure we were trying to match the ambiance by being as classy as possible, we were somewhat noisy and clumsy taking our seats. Before we lost all confidence, Mooches brother chimed in without missing a beat. He made it seem as if we'd been ballerina's who just gracefully crossed to the other side of a stage.

"My kids are excited as all of you are." The man said to all of us. "We've prepared for your arrival by creating a notebook filled with some of our common phrases and words. You girls will be teaching my kids your language also so you'll need to write down common words and phrases that we would need if we were visiting you in America. You all have two hours to get everything finished and then we will talk about the trip we're all taking this weekend. I want everyone to move your desks and sit in front of my students so you can work with each other."

The similarities between Mooch and her brother were crazy! Once we moved our chairs the nervousness seemed to disappear, after all a school project was a school project no matter what country you were in. This turned out to be one of the most enjoyable one's I'd ever been given, which seemed appropriate since this was also the nicest school I'd ever been in. We started practicing the words we'd exchanged which led to lots of fun and laughing with each other.

In between assisting us when needed, Mooch and her brother got to spend some time catching up on each other's lives. You could tell that they really got along. It made me think about my sister and how we seemed to be two strangers living in the same house. Maybe one day we'd be as close as Mooch was to her brother? Who knows, they might not have been so close when they were our age. I couldn't help but wonder how things would have been if life had been different for us.

My thoughts were interrupted with the details of our hike. They basically wanted to insure us that we'd all be just fine. Sounded like something grown-ups say if they believe it or not just to make you feel better about something you have no say in. If it were up to me, we'd venture back to the chocolate shop or walk along the trail, you know, flat ground! We had lunch on the grounds outside of the school and before we knew it our time was coming to an end. This was the only time I could recall a school day going by faster than I wished it would. Not that I bothered to even go to school every day, but if it were like this one, it would have been a home away from. The other kids in the States had no idea what they were missing!

We returned to the Chalet and other than our night out on the town, we would spend the next few days preparing for our weekend hike. We were told that it would be a good time to write home. I couldn't help but wonder if they wanted to make sure our parents had a last word from us in case we didn't make it back! Let's face it, not even a beautiful country can stop the power of my imagination, but in my defense, wasn't hiking something people spent years learning before tackling a mountain in Europe? While one side of my brain was envisioning tumbling down a huge mountain, the other was still in a state of shock that I was actually here at all.

When we all got up in the morning Mooch reminded us about our getting to go dancing, we were so excited. Thank goodness she told us so early in the day so that we had the whole afternoon it make sure we looked perfect for our amazing night out in Zurich, Switzerland!

The whole day was wonderful, we spent time trying on our gowns and doing each other's make-up to see who would do the final work later on. Then we had some lunch and walked back up the path we had fallen in love with and drank some of the amazingly sweet water I was sure would never be found anywhere else in the world. When we came back from our walk the velvety green grass and the amazing flowers called our names and we spread out to find our cozy spot in the mist of it all. Looking up at the blue sky I wondered if Dale was looking at the same sky thinking about me. It had been a while since I had thought about him, good, this is a good thing. Soon Mooch hollered to us that dinner was ready and that brought us all back to reality so we go up and stretched with one last look upwards to the heavens and headed back inside.

Pretty soon dinner was done and our night out was next. Getting ready to go was like a bunch of princesses fighting for the 'most beautiful' contest lol it was so much fun!

After I was dressed and ready to go I stopped by the mirror to look at myself, 'WoW', I thought, I haven't ever looked like this before. My dress fit like a glove, it was a halter top style long dress with a light orange/peach, color material that was so soft, it hung and swayed with my every move. I sure didn't look 13 that was for sure, I will never forget this amazing trip!

To the train and downtown Zurich we went. I couldn't believe it as we slowly walked together through the doors of this place. The lights were flashing through the darkness of the room and we could see the silhouettes of the waiters with their white gloves on as they reached out for our hands, two at a time they led us to our seats at the table that sat in the middle of this amazing room. As we sat they gently pushed our chairs forward and asked what we would like to drink. We looked at each other giggling and blushing I am sure, thank goodness with the lights our blushed cheeks

SWITZERLAND

were the last thing seen.

I started to say a soda when Mooch spoke up. "The girls will all take your house wine and a glass of water and the same for us and a pitcher of soda please."

He was so cute and as we looked around we realized how amazing everyone looked and the clothes they were wearing, wow! I had never seen anything like this other than royalty on television.

We all sat there in awe while we waited for our drinks and soon one by one we were each approached so sweetly, I had never seen anything like it before! This very handsome young man reached his white gloved hand to me and bowed …

"Will you have this dance with me please?" he asked and waited. I reached out to his hand so nervous that I tripped when I stood up lol of course.

"Yes, thank you." I must have been in a dream because from that moment on the rest of the night was a blur. I'll never forget this night for the rest of my life.

The weekend arrived before I could think up any more ideas of grandeur. It was time to face my fears and freezing temperatures, on to Grindelwald to hike the Swiss Alps!

Darci and I helped each other, we took turns convincing ourselves that we could do it. Our journey had finally begun, the mountain was covered with snow and we were covered with layers of clothes, heavy backpacks and big shoes. Once we began walking, it seemed like an eternity. We found ourselves having to help one another up and over the rocks, through crevasses and battling the snow. Whenever we came upon a hill we would slide down using our backpacks like sleds, I must admit that it was a lot of fun. Of course for every hill we climbed, there was another one to conquer. I'd finally decided to give up and just freeze to death where I stood, but Dorothy was smart enough to bring a chocolate bar with her and use it to entice me to make it up the last hill for the day and it worked. If I hadn't already claimed her as a best friend, I did so at that moment!

Once I reached the top I saw a barn in the distance, it was like seeing a mirage and I thought that only happened in the desert. Fortunately, it was real.

"That is where we will sleep tonight kids." One of the teachers told us.

We started back up to finish the distance between our beds and us. We were exhausted and could probably sleep in a snow blizzard right bout' then.

As we got to the barn a few of us peeked our heads in and could feel the heat. "Hey." I said. "It's warm in here. How funny, how can it be warmer in there and so cold out here?"

HER PLACE WAS WITH GOD

"Its easy Jenny, see all that hay? That acts like an insulator and warms the space."

"Awesome, that makes so much sense." I said.

"Ok kids, everyone pick a spot and make a bed out of hay and make room for your sleeping bags and your packs. See you in the morning bright and early!"

No one hesitated getting started and soon everyone was snoring in different languages.

In the morning we headed back down the mountain to where the cars were parked. The trip was much easier than the trip up, thank goodness, and the promise of hot cocoa for us at the lodge helped even more. After a long goodbye to our new friends and the exchanging of phone numbers we all loaded up and drove back to the Chalet for a much needed sleep.

The next morning we all woke to the smell of Mooch's oatmeal and hot chocolate with the reminder that it was time to get our things packed and loaded in the van. We had to say good-bye again, this time to this beautiful place that had been our home for this short time we were here. It felt as if we were leaving a long lost friend. We all were a little sad as we took one last look at the Chalet and the hills covered with beautiful green grass and different colored flowers everywhere. I'll miss the paths we took our walks on but most of all I'm going miss the sweet tasting water, who knew there was water whose sweetness could surpass my Pepsi!

Soon we were off and on our way to the beautiful city called Lucerne. Lake Lucerne was a small city in size, but busy nonetheless. We rented motor scooters and rode around the lake until we were sore. We found a little park on the edge of the lake where there was a chess game set up, a huge one, 24 ft. x 30 ft. or so? The game pieces had to be picked up and walked to the desired spot by the player, I'd never soon anything so cool!

After we enjoyed the city for the day we continued into Yugoslavia (Croatia) for a week of camping in a small village called Savudrija. The campground was beautiful and surrounded by the Adriatic Sea. We spent days camping and even got to spend a couple of nights dancing at this little bar near the campgrounds. I met a man named Boion who swept me off my feet, literally, by taking me dancing for my 14th birthday. I thought I was in love for the first time, again. He was a true gentleman who escorted me back to

SWITZERLAND

our camp and he kissed me, it was a birthday I would never forget. Little did I know that a more memorable reason for me to never forget it was happening while I slept.

Turning over in my sleep was all I needed to wake up again and I realized Annette wasn't in the room. Deciding to celebrate with her, I headed back to the dance floor. She and my new hero were dancing a lot closer than I thought they should have been, I was infuriated! I walked away and went back to bed without being noticed, not that either of them would have been able to see anyone else anyways. When she finally showed up hours later the worst crossed my mind. To this day I'm not sure what really happened that night but I'm sure it's better that way, neither of us ever said anything about it to the other.

Fortunately for me, Mooch had bigger fish to fry, or should I say vegetables to pick, for me to dwell on it too long. We were all excited about going to the beach and spending the day in the ocean. It was wonderful, nothing like the waters back home and the sand was so soft. We all got a lot out of our mountain hike in the snow, but this was definitely more our style. Everyone might not have had heavy boots or shoes, but we all remember to pack our bikinis.

We were playing in the water splashing each other when Mooch pulled up. She wasn't dressed to swim and before we could ask any questions she was calling to us.

"Come on girls." She jumped out of the van and opened the side door. We all looked down at our barely covered bodies and then at Mooch as if she was insane.

"Dressed as you are, yes, bikinis and all, come on, hurry, hurry." As if she could read our minds and respond to our thoughts as usual.

"Where are we going?" I asked.

We all wanted to know, I was just bold enough to ask.

"I have a surprise for all of you." She said.

I didn't know what everyone else was imagining but I was thinking it must be a visit to someone with a glamorous pool, after all, what else were we dressed for?

We drove around for a while and were no longer anywhere near the campgrounds when we stopped in front of an old farmhouse. An elderly couple was waiting outside to greet us and approached the van as Mooch walked around to let us out.

"Here they are, these are my girls from California." Mooch said like a proud mother.

The couple's smiles couldn't have been any larger, they were so happy to see us and their eyes literally gleamed. I had no idea what was in store, but it felt like my grandparents farm. Seeing this couple made me long for a longer overdue hug from my grandma (my grandpa had since passed away).

"Come on girls, this way." Mooches voice was my return to reality cue.

She walked around the main entrance to the back of the farm as we followed.

"There are potatoes in this field that need to be picked."

Her words led to one inquisitive expression from us to another.

"Those faces won't work, I want a couple of you to start here and then two more there and two more down there and we will all meet at the end." Mooches voice carried a lot more excitement than we were actually feeling.

In perfect timing, the elderly couple had reached us. Their faces not only showed their destitute, it was apparent that either we pick the potatoes or they would rot and they would lose their crop. We didn't need any more encouragement. Without saying another word everyone went off into the directions Mooch instructed and for the next four hours teenage girls could be seen picking potatoes in bikinis.

The couple could not have been more appreciative. They thanked us over and over again. We had to admit, being able to help them in what was surely their hour of need, made us feel pretty good. Who knew that helping others would do so much for our own self-esteem? I learned that day that when you help others, you're also helping yourself.

From Yugoslavia we went to Italy, I couldn't wait to tell everyone that we ate spaghetti in a true, Italian restaurant. It was like looking at a picture or postcards, breathtaking, what a beautiful country! The restaurant was fit in a corner of a street filled by cobblestones. On the other side of the road was a stone border that followed the walk all over the city and over the stone border was beautiful water that ran through the middle of the beautiful Italian town. I had only seen something like this in the movies. When we walked in, everyone turned to us and welcomed us into their restaurant and led us to a table big enough for all of us. We struggled to understand them and they worked hard to try to understand us to. We all did the best we could and ordered a full spaghetti dinner with salad and bread. They taught us to swirl the spaghetti with the fork poking into the spoon, turning the fork to twist the noodles around the fork and hoping you didn't make it too big to fit in your mouth, how messy and awesome! We were even invited to dance with them. Mel and Mooch didn't hesitate, we all sat and talked and watched and enjoyed while they tried to teach them how the dance was done, we had a blast!

Italy was more than I could have imagined in a fantasy. The only drawback was the cloud that sat above my head reminding me that it was our last stop before returning to the states. A part of me was looking forward to seeing my mom but I was also a little concerned about the new me running into the old me. It was easy to be someone else somewhere else, but could I pull it off back home?

Instead of thinking about what I was afraid of, I thought about my mom and not being mad anymore, I couldn't wait to get home.

SWITZERLAND

The school planned a dance for us when we got home. It was pretty cool, considering we'd done some summer maturing and had tans like movie stars! It didn't dawn on me how different I looked until one of the boys asked me if I was new.

"No silly, it's me, Jenny." I said with a big smile on my face.

"No way." He said. "You look completely different, you don't even look like a little girl anymore."

"I don't think I am, I really feel like I changed, I don't think I'll ever be that little girl. I know I'll never have an experience like that one again."

We sat there and talked for a little bit and soon I went off with the other girls. Visiting and talking about the one thing we'll never forget, our amazing summer in Switzerland!

Growing Up Into a Teenage Mommy

Soon after we got back from our trip my mom was allowed to pick me up to go home with her. My heart didn't forget about Dale but I had to leave my memories on the back burner. I had no idea what happened to him that night he came to see me at Bachmann but it seemed easier not to bring it up to my mom at all. I didn't want new problems, I just wanted to be home.

The next couple of years folded into each other. I moved in with my mom in Durham and tried to go to high school. I met a couple of friends but still things didn't work for me. Soon I had convinced my mom that I needed to be in town, in Chico. Durham is a small town 6 miles out of Chico where I had been raised and where all of my friends were. My mom had a friend that had a room for rent in town so she signed my money over to me (death benefits from our dad) and I gave it my first shot of bein out and about but doing it the right way...

Since I had my own income and paying my own bills, I could do what I wanted, when I wanted! Well High School ended up being one of the things that I didn't want to do. Don't think I didn't try because I did. I didn't have a locker because they matched me with someone to share a locker with but I didn't know them so that wasn't going to work. School was only about six or seven blocks from where I was staying but since I had to carry my books it turned out to be quite an uncomfortable walk every morning and afternoon. It also wasn't that I didn't want to enjoy being there, but me being who I was, quiet, out of place and not capable of belonging to a 'click', I ended up on my own.

I only kept this up for a short time, within a couple of weeks or less I had gratefully found my friend Laura from Junior High and we started spending lots of time out and about with friends drinking Jack Daniels and eating pizza!

In no time my mom found out what I had not been doing, ie, going to school, buying food, making an appearance where I was staying other than to get a change of clothes and so on. One day I came home and my bags were packed and she was already loading them into her car.

"You're coming home with me to Grandma's in Yuba City to live. We will figure out where you will be going to school once we get you settled. This just isn't working anymore!"

I finished getting what was left and told my mom's friend I was sorry and quietly got into the passenger seat of her car. Off to Grandma's house we went. I still wasn't used to my mom taking charge the way she was, it made me feel good in a way.

I was a little nervous, living at Grandma's house after all of the Thanksgivings and Christmases celebrated there, how wonderful this could be and how peaceful I knew it would be.

I had been in and out of school so much that we decided a continuation school would be the best choice. I hated going to new schools and having to meet new people, I couldn't even imagine actually enjoying myself. I guess like the move, I had no choice, again. My Grandma's home was on the outside of town in the orchards of Yuba City, Ca. and the Continuation High School was even further out so I got to ride a bus to school and home every day and thank goodness we had the coolest bus driver ever. We could smoke cigarettes and weed on our way to and from school as long as when we stopped at our place on the way (a pullout we used), we helped clean the bus out. Our freedom didn't last for long though, within a couple of weeks our wonderful driver was fired. It was so sad and it really hit home with some of us but there wasn't anything we could do to fix things, we felt so bad!

I had never gone to a school that I actually enjoyed and looked forward to going to in the morning, something I didn't expect at all. For the first time in my life I made the honor role, I couldn't believe it! For once I didn't feel stupid, I felt like I was as good as everyone else, like I belonged, something I hadn't remembered feeling before.

I met and fell in love with the coolest and most gorgeous boy at school. His name was Tony, from the moment I saw him I knew he was perfect! We spent time at school together every day and sometimes after school I would go to his house and hang out. We watched tv with his family and sometimes he even cooked me dinner, other times we were most comfortable in his room off the kitchen and he always made me the best chork pocks lol (porch chops), I had ever eaten.

We didn't stay at Grandma's very long, my mom rented a house in town for us and for my one of my aunts. It wasn't long before my cousin moved in with us, so awesome. We grew up together and it was so cool having her back in my life and soon a friend of ours from school moved in with us. Shannon was our age and needed a family to love her and we needed her to be our family.

Our home didn't stop growing there, another one of our friends from school, Marci, was having bad problems at home with her family and she couldn't get to school (how often do you find a teenager that wants to go school? Not often that's for sure). So of course a bed was there waiting for her and tones of love to boot. One more friend of ours didn't have a place to sleep, it was great to see the smile on Wess's face when my mom said he could stay. My amazing mom had opened her home to a group of teenagers and her friend/sister-in-law, all of whom desperately needed her and her love, she stepped in without hesitation and took on her roll of helping all of us!

We weren't close to what people considered a 'normal' family household lol but it was wonderful and it was ours. We spent a lot of time doing things together, we loved driving to the coast to Mendocino, mom had friends there and I felt so comfortable and at home when I was there. One beautiful sunny day we drove into town and parked near the small village market. Everyone got out and followed mom in but I stayed outside by the car to take advantage of bein able to finally smoke a cigarette. I was leaning on our car when a girl walked up to me, she was about my height and age wearing a white t-shirt, levy's boots and a smile.

"Hi stranger, what brings you to my town, do you have an extra smoke?"

I reached into the car and grabbed my pack. "Sure do." I said handing one to her with my lighter.

We were soon interrupted by a guy a bit taller than us as he came up between us.

"Hey it ain't your town sis it's ours. Hi, my names Greg and this is my sister Kasey and you are?"

The look on his face was so very serious but he was so funny, I couldn't help but to laugh.

"My name is Jenny and I'm here with my mom and my cousin and a couple of friends. We live in Yuba City and just came for the afternoon. Their all in the store."

I got out another cigarette and handed it to him, "Do you want one to?"

"Sure." He said.

He took it and thanked me with a quick bow and a smile. "I would never turn down a nice fresh stoggi from the beautiful tourist that just came into town named Jenny." I couldn't stop laughing and he was so cute!

We had all found a spot to sit on the curb and were talking about where I was from and about Mendocino. How awesome that everyone stayed in the store long enough for me to make a couple of new friends, bummer I didn't live here, I wondered if I would ever get to see them again. By the time everyone came out of the store I didn't want to leave. They were opening sodas and lookin around while they put their things in the car and spotted us.

"Hey honey who's this?" My mom asked walking over to me.

We stood up to introduce them to my mom and the others then we hugged and said goodbye. Driving away it felt like I was leaving my home lol and I had only been there 20 minutes or so tops. I was going to miss them, that much I knew.

It was April of 1979, I was 16 years old when I found out I was 2 months pregnant with Tony's baby. I didn't know what to do, I just never seemed to do anything right. In my mind all I could hear was my stepdads voice telling me what a 'fuckup' I was. I really had been trying to grow up and do better and I honestly didn't know anything about birth control. I knew I loved him and he told me he loved me to, so in my heart I knew it would be ok, one way or another.

On a normal day (whatever normal was), our home was pretty busy with the hustle n' bustle of all of us but this hadn't been a normal day to say the least. Having gone to the clinic earlier I had my test in my hand and somehow, an empty house. I was sure it wouldn't last for long so I called Tony and asked him if he could come over. I was so scared, nervous and confused, I had no idea what his reaction was going to be. I know he loves me, he would hug me and tell me that we would be fine, us and our baby…

I fussed around the house trying to make things perfect while I waited until finally I heard the doorbell. We went into the living room and sat down. He kissed me and again I melted and I knew then even more that everything would be fine.

"I have something for you, I love you." I told him and I handed him the paper that the clinic had given me.

I watched his face waiting for the smile I loved so much but I didn't see it, he looked at me and looked back at the paper.

"Really? This is what you had me come over to tell me, that you're pregnant? Is it mine?"

I got up to step back away from him, the look in his eyes and on his face scared the shit out of me!

"Yes, this baby is yours. I love you and I thought you loved me to." I managed to get out.

He was still just sitting there, like he was frozen in time, out of all the ways I thought he might react, being mad at me wasn't one of them, I didn't know what to do or say so I just stood there.

He finally got up and came right up in front of me. "This is crazy and we're both to young! I'm outta here, I'll be back and we'll talk about this."

"Talk?" I asked him. "What is there to talk about? I thought you loved me, you said we were happy and everything was great."

The look in his eyes kept getting scarier.

"That was before this!" He yelled and threw the paper at me and told me that we were over then he stormed out of the house slamming the door. I fell to floor where I had been standing and cried, I couldn't stop.

All I could think of was how could I make the pain stop! He left me, he walked out and doesn't want to ever see me again! I went to the bathroom in a state of numbness and took different pill bottles out of the cabinet, I tried to read the bottles to see who's they were and what they were for but it just got to confusing so I opened up three or four of the bottles and took some out of all of them, I figured if he didn't want me then I didn't want me either so killing myself was the easiest way out!

I didn't even think about what I took being bad for my baby and it proved to make me the sickest I had ever felt in my whole life! I called 911 and then I had to tell the paramedics everything that happened and feeling like the crazy person I was acting like, they took me to the hospital.

Soon my mom and others came to see me and I got better little by little, tests had shown that my baby was going to be ok thank you Jesus!!

Somehow Tony found out what had happened and had to make an appearance.

"I just wanted to see if you were ok, did you lose the baby?"

"No, my baby and I will be just fine, don't you worry about nothin. One thing you always did tell me was that you were a 'free bird', Im sorry."

We looked into each other's eyes for a moment then he turned and walked out the door.

He left and I cried some more, as long as he was gone I knew my heart would hurt but I had my baby, I wasn't going to be alone.

It had been such a long day and an even longer night, we didn't get home from the hospital till 11 or 12 or something. We all went to bed, when we got up the next morning life continued and days went by.

⁓∞⁓

It was another two months before I heard from him again and he was the last one I expected to hear on the other end of the phone when I answered it that morning.

"Hello." I was waiting but whoever it was, wasn't answering, then I heard his voice.

GROWING UP INTO A TEENAGE MOMMY

"Jenny it's me, its Tony." I just sat there, I didn't know what to say or if I should cry or get mad and hang up, he must have read my mind. "Please don't hang up, say something to me. I love you and am sorry I left, I swear!"

I still hadn't said anything and I couldn't believe what he was saying.

"You what, you love me?" I asked him.

"Yes of course I do, you are having our baby and I love you. I don't want to be away from you anymore, will you come down here with me? I have been traveling with the carnival, I'm a Carney!" He said with so much pride. "You can get on a bus and come stay on the truck with me, please?" He asked.

How could I resist, a Carney huh? Crazy but why not I was thinking, at least I would have my love back and we would be able to be a real family.

"Yes, yes I'll come. I'll have to check the busses and see what it will cost though."

"I'll send you the money for the bus." He said. "Call me back on this number as soon you find out alright?"

"kk, I love you." I said.

"I love you to honey." Tony said. "Everything will be ok, you'll see."

We hung up, I figured out the bus fares and got back to Tony soon as I could. He was going to send the money out today so I would be leaving in just a couple of days. So exciting, I was going to Del Mar, Ca.! Now all I had to do was to wait for my mom to get home so I could tell her what I was doing, I knew she might not be too happy.

Much to my surprise she didn't like it, no, but she knew I was going to go with or without her blessings so in no time money was in the mail and I was on my way to an adventure that I thought would last a life time.

When I got to Del Mar it was awesome, I had never been to Southern California let alone a place as famous as Del Mar, Ca. The beach town was absolutely beautiful. There was a cool, crispy breeze with the warm of the sun, I could stay here forever. Tony worked in his tent and I spent the afternoons with him trying to stay out of the way. There was money for us to eat for a couple of days and then he told me that things weren't working out, that he had been taking draws to feed the two of us and he could only afford to feed himself, that I would have to go back home. I tried to convince him I could take a job to but he said that because I was pregnant I wasn't working, so, the only choice he gave me was to go home. He borrowed enough money from his boss to get my ticket, took me to San Diego airport and I said goodbye to him, again. This time he didn't tell me that he loved me. I turned and got on my plane and didn't look back.

The first thing I saw when I got off the plane was my mom's smile. I love my mama, she always makes everything better!

HER PLACE WAS WITH GOD

Summers are hot in Yuba City and the Feather River was the most awesome place to be whether you were young, younger or older. I wasn't showing my baby belly yet and could put on a pair of cutoffs and even button em', slip my bathing suit top on and walla, no one could ever know was five months pregnant.

I stood in front of the mirror looking at my silhouette, there was this tiny little person growing inside of me and I had no clue of what I was doing!

"Hey, Come on ya'll." I said. "Someone go swimming with me, please." I yelled down the hall.

In moments I could hear voices hollerin back. "Yep on my way Jen." Wess Said. He was our buddy and then my cousin, Shannon and Marci joined in unison.

"We pass, we're studying but maybe we'll meet you out there later."

I was laughing getting my things together. "You three need to learn there is more to life than just studying but fine, we will have fun without you."

We all joked and the two of us headed out the door and jumped into his little beater car lol, it always got us where we needed to go.

Pulling up I could tell it was gonna be great. The place was packed so we walked down the pier and found a spot on the edge to drop our legs in the water.

"To cool, I needed this." I said.

"I know huh," Wes said. "Summers here are a killer!"

"Your tellin me, when I was a little girl in Chico we fried eggs on our back porch." We laughed and talked for a while enjoying the water and the people until a shadow started covering my sun.

"Hey, what are you doin?" I asked and turned quick to see two blue eyes that hypnotized me in that one split second! I stuttered until words began to come out as I tried not to show how red I knew my face really was. He was absolutely gorgeous!

"Hi," I said to him. "You're in my sun dude, what's up? Take a seat and feel the water, its real nice today." I smiled and went back to playin with the water trying to hide my smile.

"Hi, my name is Steve." He handed me his hand to shake I am sure but instead I just looked up at his face, his blue, soft eyes so kind and, shoot! I realized he was still holding his hand out so I clumsily shook it.

"Sorry, I get nervous around guys that take breath away like you did. My name is Jenny and this is my friend um um …"

Wes reached down and grabbed a handful of water and splashed me.

"The name is Wess, hi." He said.

We laughed and they shook hands then Steve sat down next to me on the pier. His legs were going back n' forth in the same motion as my own. For that moment it felt as if we were actually one. Laughing at myself I looked up at him and saw him smiling at me.

"You're very pretty." He said to me.

And again, there goes that red face, shoot, oh my goodness I must have been dreaming!

"Thank you, so are you. I mean, you're not pretty, I mean, you know what I mean."

I reached down and swooped up a hand full of nice cool river water and splashed it up at him totally dowsing him!

"That's it, I'm getting you now!" Steve said. He stood up quickly and grabbed me around the stomach, I could feel he wasn't holding to tight so I knew I was ok. I hadn't had so much fun in forever and I didn't want it to end. We threw each other into the water at the same time. I swam down under the pier, up to the other side and back down under to the other side then popped up to see him looking around for me.

"Hey, you had me scared, where'd you go?"

"To the other side, why?" I asked him.

"I thought I drowned you or something."

"No silly not me, I'm a good swimmer. When you grabbed my stomach to throw me in though I realized I need to tell you something, I'm pregnant." I said as quickly as I could.

There I said it, now the silence, the part I hated the most. Well, not as much as I hated yelling. Tony yelled, loud, all the time. Dang, he couldn't share a meal with me without getting mad at me for something, anything.

I looked at him, for some reason I felt I had known this guy for a long time. He sat there looking at me and reached over and kissed me in such a soft motion, then another kiss and another. Then he held my face and kissed my forehead.

"I don't know what you did to me, I just met you less than an hour ago and I want to take care of both of you for the rest of your lives. Is this what they call love at first sight?" He asked. I was mesmerized.

I looked over at Wess. "Kay you two," He said. "I'm gone."

"Sorry dude." I said laughing lol.

"That's okay." Wess said with that 'whatever' lol look. "See you later, be good and be careful ya hear?"

"Yep, eiy eiy sir!" I saluted one quick salute and turned to see this man.

Steve had stood up and was waiting for me to turn towards him, he grabbed my hand and pulled me up to him on the pier.

"Let's go over here where there aren't as many people kay?" He said taking my hand.

HER PLACE WAS WITH GOD

We started walking up and out of all the kids that were playing and screaming in the water.

"Dang, thanks, that was getting too crowded for me." I told him.

"Yea, me to." He said.

We spent the next couple of hours walking and talking and before I knew it we had an apartment together, we were a family (I thought) in the makings. We lived in a little cabin across the street from the drive-in movie theater, it was awesome! He even pulled two of the speakers and ran them up to our roof so we could sit up top and watch movies when we wanted to.

He wasn't always home, he would leave now and then for days on end. During one of his times of being gone I went into labor, 17 years old and alone.

I hadn't had the best medical care during my pregnancy so when they got me settled in to have the baby they realized my blood counts were dangerously low but no one could figure anything out. Everything went ok though and I gave birth to my baby boy Stephen, he was born on October 29, 1979. I knew that naming him after Steve was going to piss his dad off, maybe deep down that's really why I did it. In my heart though Steve was the one that had been there for me through most of my pregnancy, I wish he was with me now.

I was so happy when I got a call from my mom, she had gotten a ride and was on her way over from the coast. Soon after the phone call Steve walked in and sat beside me. His words and promises and sincerity convinced me to forgive him, it was awesome to see the happiness in his face when I picked our boy up out of the crib and put him in his arms.

"You may not be his real daddy but you are the only one he has right now and I am so thankful and happy that you're here with us, I love you." I said to him.

"I love you to Jen, Im so sorry." He said to me, then he told my son how happy he was that our baby was finally here.

Looking into my sons amazing blue eyes and at his perfect skin and face, hands and toes, I knew that he was the most perfect baby in the whole world. He was my son and no one could ever take that reality away from me!

The next day when my mom got there we bout had a family reunion, it was great! My cousins came to see me and a few friends so it didn't take them long before they put me in a private room. We all relaxed while I held my boy and listened to my mom sing for us while she played her guitar, what a wonderful day!!

GROWING UP INTO A TEENAGE MOMMY

When they released us from the hospital we, myself, Steve and baby Stephen, moved in with my cousin. One night Steve and I went to town to go to a movie while my cousin watched the baby. We didn't get to go out much so it was nice to get some fresh air.

After the movie we ran across the main road in town to the am/pm and I called home to check on my boy. We were talking and I told her we were on our way home when Tony and his wife pulled up to the phone booth where we were. She jumped out of the car and took the phone from me and threw me up inside the booth.

I jumped up and looked at Steve. "What the hell?"

In a second Tony was holding me while she punched me, I remember looking up once and could see Steve looking at me. By then I was on the ground again and he wasn't doing anything, I couldn't believe it.

They were yelling and cussing at us and telling me what an awful mom and person I was. Finally they yelled their final obscenities and got in their car and drove off like thugs in downtown Chicago or something! Amazing, I couldn't believe I had just gotten beaten up and only Steve's pride was hurt.

He helped me walk home and when I walked in the door everyone jumped up and helped me get cleaned up.

We didn't hear from Tony again for a while, I couldn't believe what he had done and I had no idea why he hated me so much. I loved him and I know he loved me once to.

What we had, Steve and I, didn't last very long. I moved out of the apartment into a little cabin next to the high school. I had my welfare but it wasn't much and I didn't have any money left after my rent to get food for the baby. I checked the mail one day and there was a check in it for someone else. For days a family came by asking me if a check came in the mail for them and for days I told them that it hadn't. Instead of giving it back to them I practiced signing her name so that I could cash it.

Everyone had been talking about doing it all the time but I couldn't get the signature right for nothing and I felt awful for even trying! There's NO way I could go into a bank and act like this person and lie and cash this lol Oh My Goodness. I put it back in the envelope and wrote a note on it saying I was sorry and put it in the mailbox so she could see it. I put my son in his stroller and we took off walking down the street.

I couldn't do that to her and her kids, I wasn't a thief! Man, something had to change that was for sure.

When I got home I went into our little place and on the table there was note and a $20 bill. She told me thank you that she really needed the money and she understood, I was so happy and felt so much better. I took the money and we walked up to the grocery store to get some food for me and my boy.

⁓∞⁓

I knew I couldn't leave things the way they were so I started looking for a job. I couldn't believe it when I got hired on at the Yuba/Sutter Co. Juvenile Hall. I found the most awesome job! I sat at the control panel, when one of the kids would ring through with a question or needed something, I take the message and find the person they need to talk to.

To cool, my first real job! I was even invited to an office party, which was interesting to say the least. I had to be the youngest person there and really didn't belong, I was pretty sure of that.

We played pool and had a couple of drinks and one of the men I work with asked me to go home with him. I called my cousin to check on the baby and continued with my night. I was 18 and he was probably 40 or 50 lol that didn't last long.

⁓∞⁓

Soon after we stopped going out I met a boy that was locked up and I got to talk to him whenever no one else was around me and the control board. We got real close and when he was released we started to date. He was awesome, he was in a band and was tan with long blonde hair and a collar around his neck for a choker. We loved spending time together but soon his mom found out about me and since I was 18 and he was 16, she threatened to have me arrested for statutory rape if I came near him again …

⁓∞⁓

I ran into Tony one day and we starting talking. Soon we decided to get back together, move in with each other to be mommy and daddy to our baby boy. We also changed his name to what we had picked before he was born, Joshua.

Our home was an old blue stucco apartment, it smelled of moth balls and there weren't very many windows but it had a really tall ceiling.

From the day we moved in the only thing that was good in our lives was our son, I knew me and Tony loved each other once. It seemed so long ago though and the time we shared now was filled with fighting and disappointment.

Soon Joshua and I left and went back to Steve.

Life went on and Steve, myself and the baby went down to Dos Palos to my Granny's for a visit then we got an apartment close by in Los Banos. It was so nice being away from Yuba City and knowing Tony wasn't going to just show up and start a fight. It was a small little town with a park we walked through with the baby as often as we could and our apartment had a swimming pool so the summer heat of California was easily cured.

We were happy for a minute but it didn't last long, we started using acid. There was a poster that we had on the wall, it was a picture of the devil holding a syth and when we got high it was the scariest thing I had ever seen. Steve had changed, he had pulled himself away from me and the baby. Our only income was my ssi and he did pretty much nothing.

The baby and I had gone for a drive one afternoon to visit my aunt and granny, when we came home we were met by a woman and Steve coming out of the bedroom. She ran past me and out the door as I stood there dumb founded, I couldn't say or do anything! He tried to talk his way out of his situation and in his talking I learned that she was a practicing witch! He managed to talk his talk and for unknown reasons I stayed there with him. It was summer and hot in Los Banos but it was always cold in my apartment, I had no idea why but I was getting more and more scared as days went by.

Finally I called my mom and told her I didn't know what to do, Joshua and I were living day to day and I was scared, nothing was right!

I don't remember much here but my mom told me that I called her and told her that if I didn't get out of there now, I might not at all …

She is amazing! Without a vehicle my mom hitchhiked to be with me, it was embarrassing having her there. I was always out of milk for my baby boy, Steve and his friends always drank and ate whatever food I had managed to get in the house. I could tell she wasn't comfortable being there, especially when Steve was there but I had no choice, I thought.

My mom could feel what I had felt all along. "It's cold in this apartment honey and so hot outside." She said to me.

I hugged her. "It's always cold here mom, I really want to leave."

"You will, with me, soon!" She assured me.

I looked over at my son knowing that he was the only good thing in my life. Lying there like the angel he is, sleeping as if nothing were wrong. He was so innocent and trusted me with his everything. I was so mad at my life. I couldn't wait to get out of here, he deserved so much more!!

It took about a week or two but my mom got a hold of my step-dad Geoffrey. He borrowed a truck and came to get us as soon as he could. I didn't know it but my mom had taken the poster off the wall and had taken it to a pastor in town. She told me when we were loading up the truck that they had tried to burn it but it wouldn't burn, the evil was all around it. She tucked the poster in the back of the truck thinking I didn't see her, I did, but I didn't say anything, my mama knew what she was doing. Thank goodness I was being rescued and wouldn't have to be here anymore.

Soon we were off and on our way to a new and safe world, thank you Jesus and thank you mommy and Geoffrey!

Starting Over in Mendocino and Unexplainable Loses

I moved in with my mom into a small little home with a loft, size didn't matter in such a wonderful place. The air and the ocean, the people and the love were all that were important, smiling and feeling good inside was something I thought I had lost forever, I was so grateful!

So sweet my mommy was to run a hot bath for me to soak in, wow, I hadn't done that in such a long time and I never expected it to be anything like this. I followed her directions to the woods in her back yard where I found a hot steaming bath waiting for me. There was an old vanity set up next to it so it looked like a makeshift bathroom, the only difference was that the pine trees and deer were my companions along with the wonderful smell of the Mendocino woods. It was the most amazing bath I had ever taken!

The vacation was soon over and it was time to, um, go to school? lol fine! I had such a hard time with schools I didn't know how this was going to work at all. We did some checking and learned that Mendocino High School had a continuation high so that was where we were heading when we left to go to town. The drive into town was amazing, I love it here. The red woods, the pine trees and the paths along-side the road. People walking with their puppy's down the road into town waving hello to us as we passed them.

When we got into town and found the High School then the Continuation High, I was thrilled to see Greg and Kasey, the brother and sister I had met when we had come through town that last year. They came up to me as soon as they saw us.

"Hey girl." Kelly said. We all hugged and visited. "How are you, no way, you're gonna go to school here?"

She looked in the car and saw my Joshua. "Looky there, hey there little man, my name is Kasey." She talked to Joshua for a minute and Greg looked in at him.

"Well isn't he a handsome little guy!" He looked at me and smiled.

Kasey hit him teasingly. "He looks like you brother!"

He stepped back blushing. "Noooo, not me!" He said fast with a laugh. "Not gonna go there and do that daddy thing that's for sure."

We were all laughing by then, even my mama. I took Joshua out of his car seat and we went inside. They showed us around then took me where I needed to go to get registered, in no time everything was taken care of. I was officially a student at Mendocino Continuation High School, to cool!

***

As I got to know the town, the school and the other kid's, life was starting to get happy again. It was fun going to school and having friends to hang out with and most of all it was awesome being around Greg, we got pretty close after a short time and were inseparable. I did realize though over time that I wasn't the only girl in his life, I called the other women his entourage lol. I spent a lot of time with him and Kasey at their house. Their mom was wonderful to me, she was like a second mom to me and the door was always open. Life seemed to be getting better, with my mama helping me so much with my son and the new people in my world, it felt like I was becoming the teenager I had never gotten the chance to be.

Going to the Community School was cool because I got credits for taking care of my boy and I was able to do the work I wanted to do. I worked in Math because it came so easy to me and I didn't know anything about the other classes. I know that some people think it shouldn't be allowed, that you need to be taught everything but some kids like me can't learn or remember stuff like that.

Don't ask us why cause we wouldn't be able to tell you because we have no idea. But, when I'm doing work I am familiar with or work that is easy to go through then I enjoy doing it in general. Which by the way is part of the reason I never did any work in regular school. I couldn't understand what I had to read or the teachers were always too busy or uninterested to explain it to me in laymen's terms. Biology and History and stuff like that were classes I couldn't even think about being able to learn anything in. I just couldn't understand anything, it was always so frustrating.

The school was built behind the High School but both schools interacted in between each other all the time. The Community School was great. The buildings were built by the students and the faculty that started the school. There were wooden porch like rails with walkways all the around the buildings. There was a recording studio, an art studio and a dance studio. Those were the biggest and most popular areas of study

STARTING OVER IN MENDOCINO AND UNEXPLAINABLE LOSES

for the majority of the kids. They were down to earth, hippies I suppose some would say. To me they were people who didn't think I was supposed to be like all the other people. I was allowed to be me and even though I didn't know who 'me' was, they still loved me. Greg and I spent as much time together as we could. Or I should say I spent as much time with him as I could.

One day and friend of ours, Clue, asked me if I wanted to go for a ride to Ukiah with him to pick up a part he had to get. Well, stupid me thought it would be cool. What he didn't tell me was that we were taking the craziest and roughest road to take to Ukiah, the fastest of course! I didn't want to get caught, my mom would kill me for cutting class n'all. It took longer than we thought in town so when it came time to get to the school we didn't have much time left. He drove so fast on this very very windy road that by the time we got to Mendo I felt sick to my stomach. Low and behold, she wasn't there yet. Cool, that made the rest of the day a bit easier and I told her I didn't feel good cause I ate something bad.

~ ~

It was hard going to school and being a mom at 18, a lot of kids thought of me as the, 'bad girl'. One day at lunch I was sitting by a tree and a guy came over and sat down next to me. We were talking about what was for lunch and then he asked me out. Oh my goodness, I hadn't been asked out in forever.

"Hi Jenny, how are you doing?" He asked.

"I'm doin good, how are you?" I asked back.

"Good, hey, I was wondering if you wanted to go to a movie with me or something?"

I looked up at him and yep, he was really looking at me waiting for an answer.

"I have to ask my mom if she will baby sit for me but I would like that."

His face turned white as a ghost and he stood up. "You have a kid?" He asked me awkwardly.

"Yes." I said. "I have a baby boy, his name is Joshua."

He walked off, he turned around without saying another word and walked away. I sat there and tried to act like nothing had just happened. No one had been listening to us so I got up and walked back to class and sat on the porch and couldn't help but to start crying.

Not everyone in school had the same feelings about me. I had a good group of friends I hung out with at the Community School and would just keep it at that. We weren't always doing what we were supposed to be doing but we always had a good time and we never hurt anyone, at least not on purpose.

HER PLACE WAS WITH GOD

Pulling up to a big group of kids was always cool when you were driving your sisters root bear brown 67 Fastback Mustang. Dru had gone to Catalina Island to work for the summer and I got to borrow her car! I loved this car and other than one more car in town, mine, hers, was the hottest! There was a guy that drove a yellow GTO that thought his was cooler. That coolness faded away though when he talked me into letting him drive the car one night when we were all hanging out. He backed the mustang into a rock in the parking lot denting the rear fender!

There were probably 15 or 20 of us in the church parking lot that night, it was a great place to meet. The parking lot was huge and no one ever complained about us. That night the guys had gotten a cage and were looking for a place to have a party.

"Hey, what about that house up the highway that's being built? We should at least go check it out. Who has the cage?" I asked.

One of the guys spouted out. "I have it but you guys should put it in your car. I don't know where we're going."

Well, it sounded like an excuse but we weren't going to turn away a cage that was for sure. We loaded it up into the mustang and signaled for everyone to follow and up the highway we went.

We found the pull out and parked, got out and walked up the path toward the coast to see what we could find. The house was there alright, we could tell it was still under construction, there was plastic on all the windows and there was wood and plastic n' stuff all over the floors. The doors didn't have the door handles in them yet so we didn't have any problems getting in.

"Hey, go back and get the beer, this is perfect." I hollered.

Next I tried the lights. "Nope, no lights, hey, let's tell ghost stories." I said.

Kasey laughed. "Yea, you are the biggest chicken there is when it comes to scary stuff. We'll see how long this lasts!"

We all laughed and started checking out the house. Soon the beer was brought in and ready for us to drink in minutes. We had fun hanging out, I didn't have a boyfriend but they guys were great and I loved flirting anyways. We ended up in a few different groups. Some were telling scary stories and some were doing truth and dare stuff and the others, well, they decided to check out more than just the beach house.

We could hear them hollerin'. "Hey you guys, come out here and check out what we found."

Everyone grabbed their beers and followed the voices to the cabin a couple of hundred feet away.

"What did you do and whose house is this?" I asked the guys.

STARTING OVER IN MENDOCINO AND UNEXPLAINABLE LOSES

"Check it out." One of the guys handed me a business card.

Mendocino County Sheriff it read. "Oh my God, what are you guys doing?"

I couldn't believe it, they'd made a mess of the cabin and took some wine and food and probably some other things.

"You guys are nuts, this is the Sheriff's cabin where he stays while their house is being built. I hope no one shows up out here. Hey, I don't know about anyone else but I think I'm gonna git home." I told them.

Everyone agreed and started to head back up to where we had all parked.

"Will you have one of the guys get the cage up to the car?" I asked Kasey.

"Got it Jen, I'll be right there." She said and went into the house to make sure nothing was left behind.

We managed to get home that night but the next day we were late getting to school. Me and Kasey pulled up to the Community School to go to class and there were two sheriff cars parked outside.

"Hey, you think we shouldn't come to school today?" I asked her.

We looked at each other and decided to turn on around.

"You got it sis, we should try this another time." Kasey said with a smile. "Let's go see what we can find out before we walk into something.

"Good idea, I agree." Back to town we went where we could find a quiet corner at the Seagull.

A couple of the kids came in after a while and told us that one of the guys had dropped their ROP card from the Community School. Thank goodness he was keeping his mouth shut but they were looking for whoever was driving the brown mustang because it was the car with the beer. We decided to keep a low profile for a few days and thankfully it blew over, we never got into trouble.

I was doing good in Mendocino living with my mom and going to school. I had friends and things to do and places to go. I had a life that made me smile and I had a little boy with the most beautiful blue eyes that always looked up at me so big and full of love, he was my everything, I love him so much!

I was young and didn't know, or want to believe, that people were so mean and so vindictive. Tony had gotten a hold of me and asked for a visit with Joshua. I didn't think anything of it because I wanted Joshua to have both of us, so I said of course. That he could pick him up for a week or two and then either we would come get him or they could bring him home. We had made arrangements to meet at the Seagull, our favorite little coffee shop/restaurant in town.

Greg and Kasey, Joshua and myself were sitting at one of the front tables so we would know when he was here. I looked up and there he was, then her, his wife. She looked at me with that face of unhappiness and anger as always. I couldn't stand that woman, there was just something about her.

Tony walked up to me. "Ok Jenny." He said looking over at my friends with his evil glare then turning his glare back to me. "Why didn't you tell me your friends were going to be with you?"

"I didn't know I was supposed to, why, what's wrong?"

He just held his glare, I could feel it all through my body.

"Come on son, let's get out of this joint." He said.

He reached down to pick up Joshua and told his wife to grab his stuff and they turned to walk out of the restaurant.

"Hey, are you bringing Joshua home or do you want me to pick him up?"

He turned towards me with his face full of anger, laughing at me while he walked out the door. I started shaking, I felt all wrong and I knew it was bad, all bad!

"Oh my god, Kasey, did you see that?" I asked.

"I did, what an asshole! Come on, let's go out there and tell him you changed your mind that you don't want him to go."

We got up and ran out to the parking lot.

"Tony, hey, stop!" I yelled. "Give me my son!"

"In your dreams." He hollered back.

They quickly got loaded up in the car and pealed out of the parking lot and before I could even breathe, they were gone.

My son was gone and I didn't know if I would ever see him again, I fell to the ground in tears.

"Come on girl, let's go smoke." We headed to the beach to our bench, it wasn't going to fix things this time though, I had no idea what to do next.

When we were done smoking I went home and told my mom what happened. I, we, tried to get a hold of him for a couple of days and of course we couldn't. He wouldn't answer his phone and either would his father.

By the next week I received some paperwork in the mail, it was a summons to appear, he was fighting me for custody, I couldn't believe this!

I was in a fog, everything was off, as always …

∽⃝∽

My mom and me were walking our bicycles through the village and I told her that I wished my dad was alive …

STARTING OVER IN MENDOCINO AND UNEXPLAINABLE LOSES

"He is." She said to me.

"What do you mean mom?" I asked her.

She told me about my biological father and how he knew who I was but she raised me as Dodys daughter. She handed me a piece of paper with his name and address on it and told me I could write him. I did, I wrote him and told him that I didn't want anything from him, I didn't want any money or anything like that. I was just so happy to have a real dad, someone that could love me. I sent him a picture of myself and Joshua and told him about us and sent it off with high expectations. Soon I received a letter back telling me that if I ever tried to contact him or his family again he would have his attorney and his friend the district attorney take care of me ... so much for that lol wow, obviously I was as awful as I felt.

Greg, my friend and sometimes boyfriend and I were driving from the bar and we stopped at a friend of his to smoke a joint. It was a small apartment, or space I would call it. Quite sweet though, we walked in and I sort of melted into the surroundings.

There was a small kitchen behind the door as it opened. There was a shelf with knickknacks and tapestries hanging on all the walls. Nothing was left uncovered.

Greg stood up. "Kay hun I'm headed out, call me."

"Will do." I said. He left just like that and I was sitting there.

I was a little embarrassed, I didn't quite know what I was doing or if I was supposed to be doing something or what ... I had no control.

He walked over to me and held his hand out to me. I stood up off the chair I was sitting in and he pulled me to him and then began the most wonderful night of my life. It was almost like i went into like a parallel world or something. This man, such a sweet presence. Such loving and enticing eyes and touch, I almost felt as if I were under some type of spell.

In all actuality, that is all there was to it. We made love until dawn in a magical realm that I wished I never had to leave and when morning came we got up and got dressed. He kissed me and told me he was glad he got to meet me. I melted at his words and his touch again. I left, walked up the street and back to Kelly's house where I would go when I didn't want to go home.

I never saw him again.

I started going out with a guy named Jeff. He was a very quiet man, spent most of his time in the garage at his moms place while him and the guys worked on their bikes, the rest of us hung out and smoked and visited. We all rode together and spent most of our days together.

We weren't together long, then I was with a guy named Kerry. He's such a cute little man, I don't think he was quite as tall as I was, but because of his looks and the leather and the Harley, it really didn't matter. We slept in his camper, never knowing who would show for a game of poker or to smoke or to have a drink. Sharing flirting gestures in public was weird because we didn't have much of that type of relationship, as if we were performing rolls in a play. I usually felt so out of place but I kept with it till he made it clear he was bored with me.

We rode with Kasey and Mat, Gary and Jeff and a couple others. One day we were riding north of Fort Bragg on Highway 101 to Rio Dell to meet up with some more friends that the guys rode with. What a rush for the ego and self-esteem riding into that little town was. There were five or six Harleys and us, two in the front, one behind, two more comin up on the back. As we pull up to the stop sign we all come across the road next to each other.

"Hey guys," I said. "This little town looks deserted."

We all looked around for a minute, then Kasey saw them. "Check it out, right back there." She said.

We looked where she was directing us, there was a little café sitting back off the sidewalk with a handful of older men and a couple of women watching us as if the space ships had just landed on Main Street. We couldn't help but to laugh lol, it was great!

We pulled out making lots of beautiful noise and pulled up to the next block.

"Hey, let me off here." I said. "I'll see if there's a Laundromat so we can go pee."

Kelly agreed. "Ya'll find out where we're going and come back for us in a few minutes kay?"

They of course agreed and we all jumped off the back of the bikes, kiss our man, get a cigarette and they were off. The three of us went to cross the street and saw a few kids standing outside a little store. We lit our cigarettes and walked across to the sidewalk and the boys were so cute and funny flirting with us lol!

We walked with our heads high and our smiles on, to the kids we were what they were told to stay away from lol!

"Hey boys, is there a Laundromat in this little town?" Kasey asked.

Each of them began at the same time, telling us there was one up the block and thankgoodness it had a bathroom! When we came out, everyone across the street in the little café were still turned to the window watching us. We must have been the most commotion they had gotten in awhile lol!

STARTING OVER IN MENDOCINO AND UNEXPLAINABLE LOSES

We were out on the sidewalk waiting for the guys and soon the beautiful rumble could be heard closer and closer.

First around the corner on his scooter was Kasey's old man Matt. He pulled up next to us, tipped his glasses in a hello and we greeted him with a smile. She walked up to the man and the machine.

"Let's go baby." She said jumpin on with ease and down the road they went. Then Kerry was comin up the road and next was Gary to pick up our friend. I proudly met Kerry in the center of the street, his kiss melted me and I slid perfectly into the seat behind the leather I was leaning so closely on. My arms wrapped around him, at that moment I actually felt like that was where I belonged (I think that was one of the only times I felt that with him).

As we drove off I turned and gave a smile and a wave to the kids on the street. The thunder of the bikes was head turning and the attention we brought to the sidewalks was great! They all came out to watch us go down the road and disappear one at a time as we turned up the road to the house we were going to visit.

The people we were visiting were some older bikers, friends of the guys. They rode together before the injuries got the best of them. We spent a night or two and then made our run on back down the coast to Fort Bragg. It was awesome pulling into town, knowing we were back in familiar territory as we followed one another through the streets. The attention that we always drew was so much fun and the men were gorgeous … bikers, Harley's, leathers, strong, sexy and totally in control, we loved to be together!

Finally through town we headed down to the harbor.

The guys were hollering, "Noyo Harbor, back where we belong!" As we pulled into the parking lot one by one.

They turned their bikes around and backed up to the huge, blue garage door that was locked in more than one place, we were back at the Ice House. The doors were opened, bikes were taken in, beers were cracked and joints were rolled. Me and the other two girls began looking for what we needed to accomplish the ritual cleaning of the Harley's once they'd cooled a bit. The guys drank their beers and smoked, began to work on their machines, clean up and replace or tighten or fix whatever needed to be tightened or fixed. We could feel the chill coming on that accompanyies the sun going down and we could hear the foghorn leading in the last of the boats for the day. We closed down, locked the doors then we all headed home like we did every night.

After a short time Kerry went his own way and I hooked up with our friend Clue. He had been a friend of Kasey and Greg's for a lot of years. He lived in a tiny

HER PLACE WAS WITH GOD

community between Fort Bragg and Mendocino, named Casper, with his mom and brother. Riding down 101 you take the Exit to Casper and your closer to the coastline in no time. There are fields with geese and horses and the smell of the ocean is crisp and so wonderful. On the right comin into the little town there was this huge old house made with what looked like a whole bunch of scrap wood. Obviously it held for many years, the inside was beautiful with big hardwood floors throughout the whole house. A twisted stair way led up into where Clue's room was. That is where I spent most of the time so that I didn't feel uncomfortable. I hated being in other people's houses.

I wasn't really living there; I had been staying between there with Clue and then with Kasey and Greg and their mom. He was a tall and interesting looking man that wore his heart openly on his shoulder, ready to except all love given to him. I am sure that his kindness and his soul are what drew me to him. Also though he gave me free coke (cocain), whenever I wanted it and he always fed me.

Out back of the house there was a circle road that surrounded a line of cabins, they rented them to the field workers. He had a goat that was kept tied to a pole in the middle of the back yard. If you forgot and didn't walk all the way around you were usually in for the surprise of your life! This Billy Goat would quickly remind you that it was his space you were walkin in!

A little time passed and we were staying with a couple of our friends. I came in one afternoon and Clue was up on the top loft watching TV.

"Hey." He hollered down. "Hi, I'm up here. Check out the table there."

Without looking he had no idea it was me, what a surprise we all got! I walked over to the table and there were perfectly formed lines of a brownish powder. I thought to myself that it didn't look like any coke we had been doing lately but oh well, it was waiting for me. I snorted it up and headed up the stairs to curl up with him.

"Jenny," He said shocked. "Shit, I didn't know it was you. Did you do any of that down there?"

"Yea, of course, you told me to silly." I answered him laughing.

"I didn't know it was you honey. Shit Jen, you just did a huge line of heroine." He said with the most worried lines on his face I'd ever seen.

At that moment my heart dropped and my ears began to ring and I think he was talking to me trying to explain what I might soon be feeling so I don't freak or anything. Everything was okay for a while. When everyone got home we headed down to Lancing St. in town for a Mendo Burger. After we took a bite or two I looked at Clue and must have been white as a ghost.

STARTING OVER IN MENDOCINO AND UNEXPLAINABLE LOSES

"Damn, I forgot to tell you not to eat." He said as I got up and headed for the bathrooms where I spent the next million and ten years throwing up and spinning and god knows what else! Pretty soon someone came in the bathroom and brought me out to Clue. We were walking out of the restaurant to the car and he had to hold me up while we walked, the sidewalk had decided to perform a dance like a roller coaster ride for me, great! Somehow he managed to get me into the car and drove me to Kasey's. He got me out of the car and up to the front door. I was sloppily hangin on to him so that I didn't hit the mud, I know that wasn't easy for him lol!

Soon Greg came to the door and opened it, he looked at me and then at Clue.
"What the hell dude." He asked Clue. "What's wrong with her?"
Greg went to grab Clue when Kasey came to the rescue. "Come on boys, now isn't the time, let's get her into bed before she starts hallucinating or something."
Thank goodness she took control.
"What did you do?" Greg asked Clue. "Did you do smack with her? I told you not to be doing that shit with her, she hasn't ever done it and I knew she would totally trip!"

He felt awful but it was too late to do anything about it. Clue went home and Kasey and Greg sat up and baby sat me all night, I love them! They got me in the shower even though the snake was there I was sure, got me to bed and took turns keeping me from freaking out. I would sleep for a little while but then the monsters would come flying at me under the bunk, I was on the bottom bunk and they seemed to be slipping through the wooden boards …

Yep, so much for that trip, what a night. Anyways, I don't remember much more, that was the one and only time I did heroin.

Soon it was obvious that when Tony took our son from me I lost track of everything. Wishing I had done things different just didn't seem to do me any good, I was always wrong …

I knew it was time to try to figure things out, court was coming up in Yuba County and I didn't even have an address other than Kelly's moms place so me and a friend of ours from school found an apartment in Fort Bragg to share. I borrowed the money to move in and started looking for work.

A couple of weeks passed and my mom knew I hadn't found anything yet so she offered me one of her cleaning jobs, so awesome! It was an easy job and wouldn't even take long, I thought walking through the home and looking around. Amazing how people with a clean home will pay someone to clean the clean, I didn't understand that.

I found the note about what was to be done when my friend came in and said she was going to help.

"No." I said to her. "I thought you were going to wait in the car, I won't be long."

She didn't listen and kept walking through the home checking things out so I started the work like I was supposed to.

I was done with room one and on the second when she came and showed me her find, some jewelry and some cash.

"Come on Jenny, let's get out of here!" She said heading for the door.

"Oh My Goodness, girl no, I can't do that, put it back and lets take my check and go."

She was in the car and layin on the horn in a second, I couldn't do anything to shut her up but to get in and drive off with the cash and jewelry ... great!

My mom found out what had happened of course so I took the ring to Greg to sell for me, I still needed cash for my rent and court was comin up soon, traveling was expensive.

I finally got the paper work with the court date on it so I went to see Greg, I was hopin there was money waiting for me but instead he told me that the police wouldn't leave him alone so he gave them the ring and the whole story.

※

It was time to get over the mountain and ready for court and hopefully see my boy. If anything in this world was good it was him, absolutely nothing else!

I knew Greg didn't mean for things to happen the way they did and our friendship stayed strong. It was time to leave so he took me to the Hwy 20 turn off.

"Thanks." I said to him. "I love you."

"I love you too, are you sure you want to do this? Do you have your money n'all?" He said to me.

"Yes silly, I'll be fine."

As I jumped out of the truck he reached over and grabbed my arm to pull me back in reaching over to kiss me.

"Now, be careful and call me." He ordered.

I jumped out and shut the door.

"Talk to you soon." I said. "Tell Kasey I love her."

"I will, bye hun." He said.

The truck screeched as he turned it around and headed back towards town. I watched him till he was out of sight and then turned to look up the wonderful road I would begin my trip on.

STARTING OVER IN MENDOCINO AND UNEXPLAINABLE LOSES

Homeward bound, out went my thumb and soon came my ride.

∽∾

The day came, court was here, and nothing was right. I didn't help myself at all that's for sure!

Of course the judge wanted to know if I had settled down so he asked me where I was living.

"Well." I said. "I am sharing an apartment with a friend of mine from high school your Honor."

"What is your roommates name Jennifer?"

"Um …" I desperately tried to remember and holding my tears as good as I could, I told him I couldn't remember her name.

I had no idea what her name was! I couldn't remember her name, I had never felt as stupid as I did at that very moment! The look on his face dropped my heart to the ground.

When Tony got on the stand he told the judge that he wouldn't ever let me have the baby, there wasn't any way in hell, he told him. I thought that was it, he blew it … but again I was wrong.

The time came for the Judge to make his decision, I was handed a handful of paperwork stapled together. I started to read as he started to talk. It was like I was hearing an echo, each time I heard him say something I read the same thing.

Then I heard these words, "The father will derive the mother of the child but because the mother is not stable, I am giving full physical and legal custody to the father with supervised visitation for the mother until another court date is made and an investigation shows that you are ready to take over role of mother again."

Yep, I heard him right. It was awful leaving the court room, Tony and his wife were waiting in the hall for me and he couldn't help but say awful things.

"Don't bother trying to set up visits cause I'll have you hurt before you see my son or take him anywhere!"

They continued to taunt me while I did what I needed to do then I left the court room and headed to the parking lot. I had parked my grandma's car perfectly for a quick getaway (which I knew I would need!) and headed to her arms and cried.

∽∾

Every time I tried to see Joshua, his dad would throw another threat at me and my attempts to see my son got further and further apart.

HER PLACE WAS WITH GOD

We even offered Tony $500 to let us visit Joshua for Thanksgiving, of course he said no and broke our hearts, again. I was sure he would use it against me one day in court.

Finally I had to stop fighting, for the time being, I couldn't stand being mad all the time. I moved into an apartment with some friends in Chico and tried to be me, whoever that was.

We found an add in a magazine to buy pink hearts and black beauties, what a pretty penny we were making from reselling em' not to mention the amazing, 'pick me up', that came with!

◈

Time went by and I learned that Tony hadn't followed through on filing the custody papers. I started calling now and then saying hi and talking to Joshua whenever I could get him to let me.

Life was starting to get normal again lol whatever 'normal' was.

I'm not sure what happened, maybe he needed a break or something but Tony was calling me and offering for me to spend time with our son and that's all that was important. Joshua was with me most of the time and I thought everything was finally getting better. I hadn't used any drugs for a bit other than smoking weed and drinking now and then, I thought I was doing good.

Joshua was about 1 ½ when Tony came to visit and pick Joshua up. He bought some pills from us and I kissed my Joshua bye bye and they were off.

He was supposed to call me in three days for us to set up a time for me to pick up the baby or for him to bring him home but I didn't hear from him. When the fourth day came I called his dad. They totally blew me off, I knew it was going to happen, they were going to take my baby from me again!

Sure enough, that week, again, I was served with a subpoena ordering me to go to court, Tony was suing me for full custody of Joshua.

I went to court and it was crazy. Tony told the judge that when he picked Joshua up that day they had him checked by a doctor and that they found 33% speed in his system. When his wife took the stand, she told the judge that they hadn't been able to afford the test so it was never done.

That really made the judge mad, they ordered us into mediation and said they would make their decisions at another court date. In the meantime, they gave Tony temporary custody and everyone left the court room. When him and his wife came out of the court room he threw her up against the wall and yelled at her about her testimony, it didn't last long, the bailiff came out and separated them and kicked everyone off the floor. I stood there quiet till everyone was gone then asked an officer to walk with me to my car.

※

Finally it was time for mediation and I had to meet Joshua's dad at the court house, this time we were ordered to come alone so it was just the two of us. We were seated in an empty court room at a table along with another couple across the room. We were all told to discuss what we thought our custody arrangements should be.

He wasn't talking to me or looking at me, just sitting there acting like he was reading the paper on the table in front him, although there wasn't anything on it, so I spoke first.

"All I want Tony is to be able to see my son, to be able to spend time with him. I miss him and I know he misses me to."

He quickly scooted his chair back and turned directly towards me.

"Then why haven't you gone along with the court order and visited on your days?" He said with so much anger.

"You threatened me Tony." I stuttered. "You told me there was a hit out on me and that I had better stay away from all of you, that's why!"

All of a sudden he jumped up and pulled a little knife from his pocket, opened it quickly and pointed it towards me looking right into my eyes.

"You want to see a threat? I'll threaten you!" He said with death in his eyes.

I jumped back looking over at the other couple. "Do you guys see this?" I asked them desperate for conformation!

"Yes, we do!" They said and had gotten up from their chairs stepping back not knowing what was going to happen next.

Someone in the hallway had heard the commotion and by the time I was about to the door they opened it.

"What's going on in here?" They asked.

The other couple that was in the room with us told the clerk what they had heard and seen, I was trying to stand as far from him as possible while they figured out what to do.

After we waited for what seemed like forever, they asked him to leave the court house and for me to stay and finish what I was writing for the courts. They warned me to keep my distance and if I needed to bring police with me to help orchestrate my visitation days I should contact them.

When I received the custody report in the mail I couldn't believe what it said, the words brought me to my knees, they were the same words as before ... 'Even though

HER PLACE WAS WITH GOD

the father will derive the mother from her child, we are granting the father Full and Legal Custody of the Minor Child. A visitation schedule will be made through the Mediation Department of the Yuba County Courts'. I couldn't speak, all I could do was cry, for a long time.

I tried to go see my son after that, so many times, each time I was refused, threatened, taunted, and come to find out though, none of the sheriff's in the area wanted anything to do with helping as a civil standby on a custody visitation, great.

In no time he was gone, I had no Idea where they had moved to or if they were even still in town. I couldn't believe he hated me so much he would take my baby away from me.

Things got so out of hand, I felt like I had no recourse until my stepdad Geoffrey and my mom convinced me to move to Yuba City with my mom to Grandma's house and stay there so we could search and find Joshua. I moved and we put an ad in the paper and Geoffrey tried to find him through the utility company's but that didn't work. Finally I got a phone call from a man that said he was Tony's, wife's, cousin and that they were staying with him. It was so heroic I almost fell in love with him on the phone! He had told me that the baby shouldn't be with them, that they couldn't take care of him and that he took care of my Joshua most of the time.

We set up a plan and I was supposed to wait for the living room light to go off then he was going to hand me the baby through the bedroom window. Well, the night didn't go the way it was planned, instead we had a shotgun in our faces and soon the sheriff's, I barely got to hold my son and tell him mama loves him before they told us to go before we went to jail. So, I left my son with him again and could hear him crying for his me but there wasn't anything I could do. I could feet my heart falling out of my body and it hurt so much!

The Downward Spiral Was Sure To Come

I went back to Chico, the one place I knew was my home no matter what. Myself and a couple of others went to visit some friends, when I walked in I saw the most beautiful baby girl in a bassinet. I melted as I watched her sleep, she was so peaceful and oh my goodness, I missed my Joshua so much. A woman came in the room and saw me standing there over the baby starting to cry.

She hugged me and I hugged her back. "Are you alright?" She asked me.

"I'm sorry yes, I'm good, thank you though." I smiled and wiped my eyes. "Is she yours?" I asked her about the baby.

"Yep." She said with the sweetest smile.

She reached in to touch her little hands and gave her a soft kiss. "This is my daughter Sheila Rosemarie. Sheila honey, meet our new friend, um, what's your name?"

"I'm sorry, my name's Jenny and your baby girl is so gorgeous! I hope she wakes up soon so I can hold her."

She reached in and scooped her right up and into my arms.

"Are you sure?" I asked her.

"Of course silly." She said laughing. "She's a baby, not glass."

We both laughed and visited while I held her precious baby most of the afternoon. In no time Leah and I had gotten so close, we were hardly ever apart.

Leah and I were staying with some friends in Chapman Town (small subdivision in Chico), the guys we were with sold cocaine and mushrooms and weed so we never needed for either, to cool, We cooked the shrooms down to make cinnamon tea and then played monopoly while people came in to buy throughout the night lol, we had so much fun and only a few ever knew why we were so happy lol.

There was a knock on the door and I jumped up to answer it, as the door opened I was met by the end of a gun barrel that turned out to be a sawed off shotgun. I was walked or I should say pushed by the gun, back against the wall. I couldn't breath and I couldn't see past the barrel to see the faces. There was a lot of movement and I could hear them going through the rooms in the back of the house then I heard them asking everyone for their money and weed then they asked me but I didn't have anything. After what felt like forever, the gun was taken from my face and the door was slammed shut. I was still against the wall but was able to look around the room and saw Leah and the other girls on the couch crying and went over to them.

"Oh my god I can't believe what just happened!" I said.

We sat there holding each other and the guys came out of the back.

"What idiots." They said laughing. "What luck, we hadn't re-upped so all they got was a gram of weed and whatever cash they took from our pockets, maybe a ¼ gram of blow and they didn't get the money I had hid so far-out."

We didn't quite know what to say to them being so happy but thank goodness the night finally came to an end and we were still alive!!

I found out that if I went to school I still qualified for my benefits from my dad so college bound I was. A new world was opened up to me, for the first time in a long time I felt like I was a real person.

Leah and I got our own apartment and we loved it. It was close to town and affordable and we even had a wash room lol! We each had our own bedroom and our bathroom had a double vanity sink which was awesome for getting ready to go to a party or to get ready for our own, to cool.

I was taking classes at the Junior College in the Paralegal Program and amazed at how much I enjoyed going to school. It has been so long it seemed like since I dropped out of school at the continuation high school in Yuba City. It felt so good to be doing something, I was learning and I had friends in my life that made me smile every day.

One night some of our friends were coming over for a couple of beers and along with the people I knew, there was a man I hadn't met yet. He walked up to me and smiled with this sexiest little side smile I'd ever seen lol and I couldn't help but to smile back.

"Hi, I'm David and you are?" He asked reaching his hand out waiting for an answer.

I was a bit embarrassed and found myself stuttering! No No Jenny, NO stuttering

THE DOWNWARD SPIRAL WAS SURE TO COME

lol I was telling myself.

"Hi David, Im Jenny." I said to him shaking his hand.

He put his hand on my shoulder leading me to the couch and away from the group of people that had formed a crowd inside the door. He sat down and looked at the empty space next to him and looked back to me so I happily, and unknowingly, sat next to him as if I belonged there. Soon his hand was over mine and his lips were on mine to. I couldn't believe I was letting this happen but in the same breath, I couldn't believe what I was feeling. We spent a lot of time talking and he soon learned about my boy I loved and missed so much. He promised that one day we would have him back and we would be a family.

From that moment on, most of our every moments were spent together. Tony was finally used to seeing both of us together whenever we'd try to see Joshua and soon he let his guard down, I was finally able to visit my son again.

A few months went by and Tony was of course, continuously an ass every time we picked up or dropped Joshua off till one day we decided to just not take him back. David had family in Oklahoma and a little gremlin car that would be great on gas for a road trip like that so as soon we got Joshua the next visit, we packed everything we owned into our little car and hit the road. My Joshua was 2 years old then and I felt like I had the whole world all right there with me and everything was finally perfect!

It was almost an uneventful trip, the water pump blew on a Sunday and it just happened to be Mother's Day Sunday lol, nothing was open. We had to use our money for a hotel room and within a few hours David had found a shop that sold him a used pump for a high price but we were up and runnin and out of there by evening. Bummer the guy at the hotel wouldn't give us our money back but I really didn't expect them to. I was happy enough to be back on the road and further and further away from Tony.

We made it to his family's home in Hobart, Oklahoma and rested for a few days and then I went out and found a waitress job while David would watch Joshua. We did ok for a while and then moved to Chickasha. I found a job at the Pizza Hut and it was awesome cause we always got to bring pizza home that was left over when it was time to close up at night. Life had been good, mellow and no problems …

I came home from work one day and my Joshua wasn't there.

"David, where is Josh?" I asked him looking around the room.

He looked at me and looked at the ground. "He isn't here, Tony came and got him."

I fell to the floor in shock.

HER PLACE WAS WITH GOD

"Why David, what happened, what did I do? What did he do?" I asked him, I felt like I was losing my mind! (I have very little memory of when this happened, there were other things going on I can't remember)

David got up and walked over to the window, almost not even hindered by my outbreak of freaking out.

"He's better off with his dad Jenny, its time me and you get to know each other again." He said.

I couldn't believe what he was saying.

"What are you talking about, I thought we were good? I work hard every day and I pay the bills and buy the food, what else do you want?"

He sat down and looked at me on the floor. "I didn't want to be your babysitter anymore Jenny, I want to be your boyfriend, NOT your babysitter!" He yelled to me as close to my face as he could get.

After a bit of our yelling back n' forth and my crying, we calmed down and drove to the sheriff's office.

When we got there I jumped out of the car and ran inside to find Tony and his wife with my Joshua.

"Oh my god Tony, what are you doing?" I asked him.

Joshua saw me and tried to reach out to me almost falling out of his dads arms. I reached out to gather him in my arms and the officer pulled me back.

"No ma'am." He said to me. "I have already seen his custody order and you will have to back off and let them leave with the boy."

I started crying and reaching for him.

"Please, let me see my son, look, he's crying for me!" I sobbed.

"That's why we're leaving, you'll never see him again you crazy bitch!" He said laughing as they headed out the door.

I thought that would upset the officer and he would help me but it was the other way, he told me that if I didn't let them leave they would arrest me.

I fell to the ground, that pain was inside my chest again, I felt like my heart was being torn from inside of me and that my world was over!

Somehow David got me up and into the car and back to our apartment with me not falling apart … as far as he knew.

Life as I knew it at that point was over, everything changed and I didn't know which way to go. Up, down, forward or backward, inside or out lol. They were all the same yet so different … but in my mind there was nothing that was familiar to me, again I was alone.

THE DOWNWARD SPIRAL WAS SURE TO COME

Days got longer and nights were full of fear and the unknown.

By the grace of God I was able to continue living day by day. The fights were constant, if I was cautious, quiet and nice … I could usually get around it, talk my way out of it for that time and maybe the next.

Finally I got a got job at one of the nursing homes as a nurse's aide. It was like a revelation having this new found freedom I enjoyed so much, yet so scared to get to cozy, knowing it may not last long.

After about a week or so his insecurities of my having a job were becoming a fact. I was working a graveyard shift when David came in and found me, told me I should come home with him now. I took him into our break room hoping he would relax and let me go back to work.

"David I can't leave, my shift isn't over for another two hours." I told him. "I'll be home soon I promise."

I reached up and kissed him and he pushed me back.

"No Jenny, you need to come with me now, your shift is over, just come home!" He yelled.

I told him it was time to leave and I pushed him out the back door, so grateful he didn't fight me anymore. A least not there in public lol, at my work of all places.

This went on for a few days, one night he came in walking real quick up to the desk.

"Where's Jenny? She needs to come with me now, there's been a family emergency."

The head nurse and my friend at work were sitting there and my girlfriend Sara came into where I was working to get me, she was so upset.

"What's wrong honey? Settle down before we have to give you another vitamin B shot!" I told her as I got her sit down.

"David is here." She said trying to catch her breath. "He said there's a family emergency."

She got up and we went to where he was. We were getting Sara her shot while David was telling me that my grandma had died. I was in a fog, I was listening and worrying and watching what was going on with my friend and I was trying to understand what David was telling me.

I looked up into his face. "What did you say?"

He reached down and held both of my shoulders as if he were supporting me.

"Your Grandma, your mom's mom died, she had a heart attack and they have been trying to find you."

As he was talking I said goodbye to my friend who had finally relaxed a bit and I told my boss I would be in touch. He just kept talking as we were walking towards the back doors.

"I talked to your mom and there's a ticket waiting for you at the airport."

He held the door open for me as we walked out. I was going as fast as I could, in my mind preparing for travel and in my heart I was broken. I love my Grandma so much, she was an amazing woman and what a sad day this was. I couldn't imagine what my mom and sister and the whole family were going through, all I knew was that I had to get home to them!

Walking through the back field on a short cut to our apartment David's words and attitude changed in a moment.

"Alright." He said. "You can slow down now and just walk with me."

I looked up at him and continued moving through the field as fast as I could.

"Jenny stop, I was kidding." He said. "She's fine, I just wanted to get you out of there and home. That place is nasty and it stinks and I don't like you working with male nurses!"

I was speechless but only for a moment and stopped in my tacks. "You lied … what are talking about, why would you do something like that?"

"Are you deaf? I told you, I hate that place and I don't like you workin with other guys, I saw that guy the other night come out of the room you were in, what were you both doing in there? Huh? Come on are you really going to keep yelling at me?" He said with confusion on his face …

I was so confused myself, I turned to keep walking home. He grabbed my arm and pulled me back throwing me to the ground. I got up and started walking, he slapped me across the face throwing me the other way. We fought the rest of the way home for the next 10 minutes or so, it kept going for days. I thought, I wished … I could die.

I spent as much time as I could somewhere else. I had been staying at a friend's house for a night to get away, visiting and playing with their baby. They were a young couple, our age, to young, but they were happy for some reason and I was drawn to that. Their little 3 month old baby always seemed to give me the peace I had when I held my Joshua. I missed him so much, every day!

I was sitting in the chair in the corner holding the baby and Janet was on the other side of the room folding baby girl clothes and her hubby was in the kitchen makin us some tea, finally a moment of peace.

All of a sudden there was a loud pounding on the door and in came David, he was fuming! He took his hat off his head and threw it across the room to hit me with it and it fell on the baby and onto the floor.

"David, hey you hit the baby you asshole! What are you doing?" I yelled at him.

My friend jumped up and grabbed the baby and the two of them stood in the other room frozen, no one knew what to say or do. He walked across the floor and grabbed my arm and drug me out the door as I fought as hard as I could! He threw me down on the ground, sat on top of me and starting pounding me in the face. As he was hitting me in my face, after each hit he hollered, "I LOVE YOU!" Punch ... "LOVE YOU!" Punch ... "WHY DO YOU MAKE ME DO THIS TO YOU?" Punch ... "I LOVE YOU!" Punch ... again and again and again.

It was evening and starting to get dark but while my head was turned towards the gate I was able to see Mike, Janet's husband, jump in his car start it up, put it in reverse and ram through the locked gate to get help. He had to do it quiet and quick enough for David to not stop him from getting out, he was using me as a threat to anyone that tried to help.

The next thing I saw was a uniform, he shined his flashlight on us and I was punched one last time then the officer grabbed David up and off of me and in a flash he was put the ground, finally!

I was so embarrassed. The ambulance was there in no time and they had me sitting up to clean my face trying to give me a drink of water but even with the straw it hurt too much to keep trying. My eyes were swollen but I could see people all around, all their neighbors had watched everything, I couldn't believe what had just happened. They brought me inside and made me answer a bunch of questions, all I wanted to do was to get out of my friends home. I had brought so much bad to them and I just wanted to go home and be alone, I was devastated and had no one.

My friends wouldn't let me leave, they got me settled and comfortable as they could on the couch and said I was still gonna stay there, I didn't have to go anywhere.

I was so blessed in the mist of such evil.

Of course when its bad lol things tend to get worse, I went to the bathroom and had started my period. Oh my goodness how could this get any worse I thought to myself, I was trying to be quiet cause everyone was still asleep.

Thinking, or expecting I should say, that they would keep David in custody after what happened, I went out to the car to get my tampons. I was leery of opening the door, so I peeked out and checked up the road, I didn't see anyone so I went on over to the car and I heard his voice.

"Hey." David said as he came from around the gate and held me up against the fence.

"Oh my God David let me go!" I yelled.

"No I love you." He said. "I don't remember anything I swear Jenny. It was the alcohol honey I don't even remember what happened other than I am so fucking sore and exhausted! Did you know that they beat the shit out of me? Did you tell them to do that to me?"

I was dumbfounded at the words he was saying to me, I could barely get words out.

HER PLACE WAS WITH GOD

"Are you crazy? Get away from me." I tried to push him away at least enough for him to see my face clear.

"Look at what you did to me David, look at me!"

I wanted him to look at my bruised up face and black eyes.

"I want you to leave me alone."

"I don't know what you're talking about. I love you Jenny." He said … lol. "You're my world, I would never hurt you on purpose, you know that!" He was pleading with me.

"Stop it David, please leave me alone!" I tried to pull away again, every time I did he threw me back to the fence.

I tried to get him to stop by telling him he was going to wake everyone up and get their attention like he did last night but that didn't work either … he grabbed my arm and led me out the gate and down the alley I went with him.

He spoke as if nothing had happened. "Come on, we'll go home, drink a beer and do another hit kay?"

"My clothes and my stuff were back there." I told him.

"Don't worry, we'll get them later."

I followed and did as I was told, as if I were his robot, his punching bag … his love?

Drugs were my sweet escape in no time.

On a night out we were looking for some coke, so I thought lol. We went to one of his friends place and there were probably ten to fifteen other people there. I was so nervous and I didn't know anyone there except for David. He motioned for me to sit in a chair and to wait for him, he stepped aside to talk to his friend then finally motioned for me to follow him. We went into the bathroom and his friend followed us and gave him a small pkg, looked at me and smiled then turned, walked out and shut the door. David locked it and pulled out the spoon and lighter, in my mind I was spinning, there was so much going on in there. All I could do was just watch him step by step while he prepared the syringes, not being able to take my eyes off his every movement. Finally as he was staring up at the needle as he looked at the numbers and clicked it with his finger tip and I saw the little bubble disappear as he finally spoke.

"kk honey a nickel for each of us should do just fine." His words seem to have a smile in them, I love it when he's happy, its way easier on me that's for sure.

He grabbed my arm and I watched as I heard the, 'pop'. It's in, I thought to myself, now what, I love the taste when we shoot dope. But I don't taste that, dang! I looked up and he was almost done with his by then and put everything away.

"David, hey what was that? I thought it was coke."

He laughed as he bulled me up off of the toilet I had been comfortably posted on. "It was 'T', Elephant Tranquilizer. Relax you'll be fine." He said so nonchalant.

I couldn't speak a word and I couldn't see where I was walking, oh my goodness this was awful! He led me to where a group of people were sitting in chairs in a circle and everyone was smoking, I would say a joint lol but no telling what was in it. I tried to sit down and I sat on someone's lap, I got up and tried to sit on the empty chair again and ended up on the next persons lap and that went on for 3 or 4 chairs and laps until I found an empty one. I had no idea why David wasn't helping me, I felt like I was just floating and my legs were rubber. Other than that I don't remember anything until he led me to a bedroom to sleep and I laid there while the walls did some crazy things for hours. Finally, maybe two or three days later we woke up enough to leave.

From there we went to someone else's house and the first thing he did was make a deal and head in to the bathroom with a guy and a girl he was talking to and shut the door. This time I was left standing inside the front door we had just walked through.

There were a couple of older guys and girl that looked like she was about 12 sitting a little too close for my comfort and David just wasn't comin out of the bathroom. It seemed like time had stopped. That was that, enough for me.

I turned and walked out the door and just kept walking, honestly, I didn't even know the name of the town I was in. I was alone and exhausted and had no idea of what to do or where to go. I just kept walking, I had probably made it over a mile when I finally found a gas station with a pay phone but of course, looking through my pockets I realized I didn't have a penny, go figure!

Standing in front of the phone I could see my face in the slightly cloudy, silver like aluminum that the pay phone sat on, even though it wasn't a clear view, I could still see the bruises on my eyes and face and jaw … great, I could feel the embarrassment fill my cheeks as that made my face hurt even worse. I hadn't really paid any attention to anything in so long. Wow, I thought, was I truly grateful to still be alive?

I don't know how I was able to find it lol God I am sure, but in my right front pocket I found a crumpled up little piece of paper that was stuck down in there with my Leah's phone number on it, awesome ! Collect call here you come, suddenly it seemed that there really was someone looking out for me somewhere!

When David and I had left to go to Oklahoma, Leah had left California also and was in Texas but after one phone call, she was sitting with me in the liquor store parking lot helping me plan our escape.

I called my Granny for help and she told me that my Aunt was in Whiteface, Texas. It was a handful of hours away from where we were in Oklahoma but well worth the trip and YaY, my Granny sent us the gas money to get there. We were welcomed with hugs, tones of love and nummy chocolate gravy and biscuits made with the truest love of an okie's heart! Leah stayed the night and headed home in the morning. The next week my Aunt drove me back home to California to my Granny's, her mama's home in Dos Palos. Yum, more chocolate gravy and biscuits and love!

Being taken care of by two of my favorite people in my world was the most wonderful thing I had felt in a long time. I could finally take a deep breath and know that tomorrow was going to be just as good …

Waking up in my bed at my granny's was like being 7 years old again, what a wonderful memory. It lasted for 4 days then there was a knock on the door.

By the time I got out of bed and to the front door David was standing there with three red roses … my granny had a shotgun pointed at his face.

I heard his voice. "Jenny here? Can I see her please?" David said. He took a step back when he realized she wasn't moving from the doorway with the gun.

"I'll blow you up!" My granny hollered. "You leave here and don't ever both my Jenni-pee again you Giggalo!"

To myself I was laughing, she is so cute and she loves me so much!

My heart stopped when I heard his voice again, this time it was so soft with a sincerity I had never heard from him before.

"I came to say I'm sorry, please believe me. I'm so sorry, I love her very much and I want to ask her to marry me. Please help us work this out."

I came out from behind my granny looking at David with tears in his eyes, again.

"How did you find me, and what did you say?" I asked him.

David, trying to keep eye contact with me, me trying to calm my granny down so she'll put the gun down so he could get in front of her.

"I have my ways you know that, will you marry me? I don't have a ring yet but I will get one I promise. I will work hard and we will save up and I will get us a house alright?" He stood there looking so promising with the most handsome smile.

I don't know how but the bad stuff seemed to be fading away and the fear becomes a playful new ground of our relationship. Could he all of a sudden be this sweet, why is he doing this? I love him so much and it hurts so much at the same time. I was thinking so many things to myself not sure of what to say or do. In time of course I did and we were off to run a mission of mercy.

I listened to my granny's and my aunts words of reasoning and their pleads for me to be safe and to let them know if I needed them.

"I love you granny, I love you auntie but I love him to. I will be fine I promise. I'll call you as soon as we get a place and things calm down."

We cried and said our goodbyes and soon we were off, little did I know that the mission included back tracking to Oklahoma and picking up David's nephew and his girlfriend and their puppy to bring them home back to Chico with us.

After we left Dos Palos I got arrested, cited and released at a liquor store in Fresno for stealing a pack of cigarettes and a soda.

On our way home driving through Phoenix, Az we pulled off the highway and found what we thought was a vacant parking lot so David could go pee. Two police cars pulled up, one shined their light on David and one shined their light on us sitting in the van.

The officers came up to us and asked us our names and the other was questioning David. They were running all of our names and in no time David was being thrown up against the wall and handcuffs were bein put on.

I started running to him. "David, what's going on?" I yelled. Another officer grabbed my arm and told us we needed to stay put as I watched him being put in the back of the car.

"You're leaving me here with these kids and their dog and I have no idea what to do or where to go, I need to see David before I do anything." I told him.

I was about in hysterics trying to get this cop to help me but that was just a joke.

"Young lady, there are 11 jails in this city and we have no idea which one he'll be in or for how long he will be there. We'll be waiting for Butte County to come get this one." He said. "They've been lookin for this boy for some time now. You need to get in your van and head back on home where you live."

They wouldn't even tell me what the charges were, I had no idea he had been in trouble or that there was a warrant out for his arrest. They told me they were looking for his brother also who was still back in Oklahoma, I decided to keep that to myself.

With what had to be a miracle, we finally made it to Hamilton City to David's mom's place. At least I had a couch to sleep on and man I was exhausted! They told us he was already in our County jail so to sleep I went. Tomorrow morning is Saturday and I would be able to visit him and finally ask him what the hell happened!

∽∾

I hated being at the jail but I had to get some answers. I was with his mom and finally it was our turn to sign in and hand over our id's. I looked at the name list and next to my name it said Yuba County, I didn't think much about it cause I born in Sutter County and have lots of family there.

It was so good to see him when I finally got to go in. Visiting behind glass got his emotions going, his temper was showing cause he felt bad he wasn't with me to help me. I tried to convince him I was fine and I wasn't alone, I was with his family and I would wait for him. He told me about the charge, I couldn't believe these guys! Him and his brother had strangled and killed a dear in our local Chico dear pens, a felony cruelty to animals charge had them searching and finally catching him after 3 years. Crazy how angry he could get and of how violent he was with me in Oklahoma, and now this. It didn't seem to deter me from him though.

I went to tell David's mom that I needed to use the van and when we were walking back in for David to tell her himself, a woman officer came up behind me right in front of the window where David was for our visit. Grabbing my arm, she turned me around to her.

"You come with me." She ordered.

I jerked my arm down and backed up away from her. "What the hell do you think you're doing? Let go of me!" I hollered.

I looked up at the glass to see him loosin it. I had no idea why they would be arresting me and to do it like this right in front of David in visiting and everyone else there, how embarrassing! He was pounding the glass and screaming so they came in to drag him off to lock up for going off the way he was, what a disaster! I hollered at him while they were dragin him off hoping I could help calm him down.

"Stop David, be careful, I love you!" I yelled to him.

He stopped and looked into my eyes. "I love you to baby, I'll get you out of here I promise!"

The cops were laughing and man did it piss me off! I couldn't say anything though, the ruder I was, the meaner they were to me and to him.

"Im comin." I said to the officers as they were tugging my arm. "How did they know I would be here today?"

They laughed some more, so happy I was to give them such happiness.

THE DOWNWARD SPIRAL WAS SURE TO COME

"We have our ways, don't you worry about that." They said with a smile.

I found out that I had been charged with Violation of a Court Order for taking my Joshua out of state. When Tony had seen in the paper that David had been arrested he notified Butte County Jail that I would be there to visit him. They were waiting for me, wow, of course he did this to me.

Living Life as His Prisoner - The County Jail Was Better

I was in shock, scared and speechless. I had no idea what was going to happen, even though the life I had wasn't all that great, it was all I had and it was mine. Thank goodness my mom still came to visit me in jail and even helped me, she was always there for me.

I spent the day in the Butte County Jail and waited for them to transfer me to Yuba County jail in Marysville. I wasn't looking forward to going to court knowing Tony would be there, his gloating and the way he always looks at me is so intimidating. To see me wrong and in trouble made his day, I don't know why he hates me so much.

The first time I went in to court they released me on O.R., i.e. my Own Recognizance. When we came back for the 2nd court date I was so excited to find out my mom had gotten me an attorney and even more so, to find out we got to court before Tony. That meant I didn't have to walk in to see him watching me with the glare he wore just for me. We were already in our seats so when him and his wife sat down behind us it was easy to know they were there, we could hear their comments about me. I couldn't believe how happy he would get when he talks so mean about me, it really did hurt my heart.

For the first time, someone stood up to him. My attorney turned and looked at them both.

"I am Jennifer's attorney and I advise you to stop making derogative remarks to my client or I will be forced to enter what I have been hearing from the two of you into my case for the judge to read." He said, then turned back around.

WoW lol I felt as if vindication was new and alive! I had never seen this man shut his mouth and sit back in his chair as quick as he did at that moment, even if it was the only time it ever happened. Not much kept me smiling lately but that sure did.

To add to his anger, I was sentenced to only 10 days in custody with time served and probation for Violation of Court Order. When we left the court house I knew he would be waiting outside for me and he was, but since I was with my mom they left me alone.

Sure wish they had Joshua with them, I miss my baby boy.

I stayed with David's mom in Hamilton City for about a week until they finally released him. We moved into a house on Mangrove in Chico. I thought for a little bit that things were changing and getting better but every time I tried to do something right, it turned out wrong.

His sisters invited me to go to the bar with them one night to watch the Chip n' Dale dancers lol, I wasn't one to enjoy something like that and I knew David wouldn't be happy about it so I told them no over and over until they insisted on me joining the party.

"No men are allowed into the party until after the show David." His sisters hollered at their brother as we all started up the stairs to the bar.

I looked back at him, kissed him quickly and went with the girls up the stairs, I turned to see him watching me walk up the stairs then he turned and headed to the downstairs bar with the other guys. In my heart and my mind I knew this night was going to be a bad one.

Drinking my tequila sunrise with my eyes fixed on the table and my drink was my way of keeping my eyes off what I knew I wasn't supposed to be lookin at.

"Jenny, look up girl. You're gonna miss it!" One of his sister's hollered to me from somewhere in the room. Yea right I thought!

Then another had to join in to. "Jenny, come on. Why did you come if you weren't going to have a good time?"

This was so pathetic, I was so mad at myself! I looked up and there right in front of my face just about was this man with hardly no clothes on. His skin was fake tanned and his muscles looked swollen instead of sexy! They had paid him or something I am sure because he was trying to get as close to me as he could. I moved off to the side as quick as I could and sat down where it was quiet.

Finally the dancing was over and all the other women seemed to be happy and content with themselves with their night out, to me it was like a pack of wolves and all I could think of was 'gross'.

The girls found where I was sitting with the quiet and quickly took it away.

"Come on Jenny, let's go find the guys."

HER PLACE WAS WITH GOD

I was readily following behind them to get out as quick as I could and to put an end to such a night. When I finally found David I went up to give him a kiss but instead he jerked his head back, he grabbed my arm glaring at me so I spoke up having a moment of guts with everyone else sitting with us.

"What's wrong David?"

He looked at me and his eyes got huge. "You're a fucking slut! I don't know why I thought I could trust you in a place like that."

His sisters and their 'men', were all sitting there not saying a word. I looked at them knowing someone said something to him.

"What did you guys tell him, that I was embarrassed and didn't want to be there?" I asked them but still nothing.

He jerked my arm and turned my attention back to him. "Don't worry about them, this has nothing to do with anyone but you and me!"

The whole time still keeping a hold of my arm he got up and quickly led me to the street and to the car throwing me around till we finally got home somehow and into the house. He was really mad at me and stayed mad forever it seemed.

I hated always having bruises on my face and my arms. The only thing I had that was mine was this life … my reality.

Days came and went, as long as I did what he told me to do things were better. One day his older sister came to visit, to 'check on me', she said. I wanted to ask her why they let that happen after we went out that night but I was too scared to say a word, especially with David still there. I didn't know how he was going to act with his sister there but soon it wasn't a secret anymore. After we were all inside he locked the door with a new key lock he had put on and calmly walked over to the phone jerking the cord out of wall. I could only sit and watch him but say nothing.

"There, ya'll have a good visit, you can talk in here and I'll be out back. Don't try anything stupid, I know everything you think and do!" He said.

We watched saying nothing while he grabbed his smokes and a beer and headed out the back door locking it from the outside, I felt like a trapped animal.

"I'm so sorry Jenny, we had no idea this would happen." She said to me.

"I told you. I knew he wasn't going to be happy, whatever you guys said to him made him think I'm a slut and he won't let me out of his sight."

"I wonder if he's going to let me leave." She said. It was as if everything I had said went in one ear and out the other. I'm pretty sure the visit was only to see what was going on, not to help me.

LIVING LIFE AS HIS PRISONER - THE COUNTY JAIL WAS BETTER

We looked towards the back of the house to see what he was doing. Of course he was sittin in the chair on the porch smoking his cigarette and drinking his beer watchin me as if he were trying to read my lips as we talked.

"Why don't you wait?" I asked her. "Maybe give me a chance to get out with you? Please don't leave me here." I begged.

"I don't know Jenny, the last thing I need right now is to have David pissed off at me!"

Wow, I turned on the chair I was sitting in to look out the front window for a change of scenery.

"Of course, we wouldn't want that now would we?" I hoped that my words were sarcastic enough for her to hear it in my voice but I was sure it wouldn't have mattered either way.

She knocked on the window to get his attention and told him she had to go. He came in and crossed the room to unlock the front door and let her out. I quickly pushed through the door following her to get out of the house while he was yelling at me.

"Get back here!" He yelled at me.

I had snagged the car keys off the wall on my way out the door and jumped in the car to start it. It wasn't turning over though and I knew I didn't have much time. I looked up and he was standing in front of me.

"Try all you want, I have the coil and you ain't goin no-where girl. How many time do I have to tell you that before you believe me?"

The fighting went on for a while surprisingly so since we lived on one of the main roads in town and it wasn't a quiet street for sure! But as usual, I was alone in my hell and not a sole paid any attention.

Of course that awful day ended as another one began and so on and so forth. We began doing more drugs, cocaine, and crank, whatever was there. We stole gas from cars at night through a hose. Me, always praying I would get caught, but it never happened that way. Soon we moved into a little cabin on the corner of 9th and Pine in Chico.

We were all hangin out, well, David and the other guys were hanging out and I wasn't going to leave and not get some of what they were doin. Especially since I was the one that went through all the hell because of it.

"Hey girlie." Jimmy said with the crooked smile he always had. "You think you can handle this?"

HER PLACE WAS WITH GOD

I jumped up from my chair to the occasion. "Yea Jimmy you back off and go play with yourself, you and David are butt buddies anyways. It's not like you guys are with other girls when ya'll disappear on me. You wouldn't be able to do anything even if you were." I said to him.

Laughing he backed up doing a dramatic dance for me. "Damn David, you got a wild one here huh?"

David was seriously preparing the moment while everyone was razin me so there wasn't an answer for them, just me.

"Here honey." David reached over and pulled my arm across his lap and situated it just how he needed it for a clean hit. Getting the rubber strap he twists it around my arm pulling it tight. I knew what was going to happen and I was fearfully anxious to get it over with. He was tapping my arm looking for the perfect vein, I turned my head. Soon I could hear and feel the 'PoP', as the tip of the needle pierce my vein and I turned to watch. Slowly he pulled the syringe back to see the bit of blood that tells him he got the vein and then so slowly, he pushed the liquid into my arm and on through my body. I could feel my head to my toes become useless and I fell to the floor as soon as he pulled the needle out of my arm.

I could hear him but couldn't respond. "Oh Shit." David said. "I gave her the whole thing, I was supposed to do half of that! Wow baby, you took a good hit, you alright?"

He looked down at me and half ass offered his hand to help me up as I pulled myself up the side of the table.

"I'm fine, see?" I turned a small circle for them and then took my forced seat on the floor while they did theirs.

For quite some time, 6 months or so, time was continuous, it couldn't be counted. David hit me and threw me around by my hair pretty much on a regular basis. I soon learned that if I pounded my head against the wall he would yell at me and tell me how stupid and crazy I was. That I should be locked up in the loony bin, but soon he would get tired of it and leave. That soon became my easiest and fastest out.

My mom lived around the corner and it seemed to be a good place to get money. Usually if I needed cash it was for cigarettes or to go in on the drugs we needed. If she didn't have it or just wouldn't give it me I would scream at her all the way back to my place causing a scene, or not, it really didn't matter to me, nothing did anymore.

Coming home from the store one day our door was locked, I knocked and hollered.

"David, open the door, what are you doing?" But he never opened it. I finally figured out how to get in through the side window, he wasn't there and in his place was a small sweet little black puppy. David doesn't come home for four or five days when he's off on a runner, the puppy was my conciliation prize. Thank goodness I had someone.

My mom named her Amelia after Amelia Earhart because her ears were so big she should have been able to fly. At first I didn't want to like her, she took David's place and that wasn't what I wanted. She grew on me quickly though, she was pretty much all I had and the only thing in my world that made me smile.

Pretty soon my puppy and my mom got pretty close. Whenever David and I fought my Amelia would run away to my moms. I usually didn't realize she was gone until I would see my mom walking up the sidewalk with her to see what was going on. I would tell her a story or whatever it took for her to turn around and go so she couldn't see me the way I was. Sometimes a bruise would be visible on my face or arms or a 'miss' on my arm, I realized one day I didn't even try to hide the big swollen bruise on the bend in my arm.

Having no idea whether it was night or day or the date, I woke up and looked around the room. Nothing looked familiar to me and there was a syringe still in my arm lying to the side. I tried to move to grab it but couldn't. I tried again and again, I couldn't move anything but my head as I looked around the room trying to recognize where I was.

As if someone was looking out for me, a couple of guys that live in our cabins came to see if we were alright, they told someone they hadn't seen either of us for days. I was told that Charles and his friend looked through the windows and saw me on the bed and called 911, they saved my life and they didn't even really know who I was!

All I remember is while I was laying there I saw my mom and her friend standing at the end of my bed then I was carried to the ambulance and I don't remember anything else until I woke in the hospital.

At the hospital they said I was totally dehydrated and was malnutrition also so they hooked me up on i.v.'s and put me in a room.

I was lying there trying to find something to watch on the little tv when David came through the door and it slammed against the wall and swung back shut, I didn't know what to say, I was scared to death and had no idea why he was so mad at me.

"David what did I do? I woke up and it was so scary, you weren't there, then I woke up again and I was here laying in this hospital bed! It's been days, where have you been?"

He had this evil glare that could back a pit off. He walked up to my bed and opened the duffle bag and started to dump it on top of me.

"What are you doing? Stop David, oh my goodness!"

All I could do was cry. Finally as his bag was bout empty of ALL of my clothes, a nurse came running in with security to get him out.

I called my mom and she came to visit me for a bit then it was time to try, again, to get some sleep. My mind was everywhere, my thoughts were numb because life was changing again and I didn't understand why there was absolutely nothing I could do right, I was sure to be a junkie and useless forever …

The next day I found the number for N.A. (Narcotics Anonymous). I called and to my surprise within hours there were five or six people in my room trying everything they had to get me to believe in myself again. The problem though is that there really weren't many times when I did believe, so it wasn't something I knew how to do that's for sure.

They gave me the beginning of my life back and for that I thank God for them every day. When they released me I stayed with my mom for a bit and went to as many meetings as I could until I met a guy that said and did all the right things. He did special things for me, picked me up to go for an ice cream and to go for a walk down town and talk in central park. We would go swimming at the diversion damn in upper Bidwell park as often as he could get the time off work, until I found out it wasn't work he had to get time from, it was his wife and son … I soon learned he had been married for many years and his wife and son were deaf and I was a fool, again.

One afternoon I was at my mom's getting ready to go see Leah when I heard pounding on the door.

"Jenny, hey, it's me, let me in please, we need to talk."

I walked backwards away from the door while I watched and ran into the table against the wall. I knew it was him.

"Leave me alone David, go away." I yelled to him. "There isn't anything here for you!"

He started pounding again and yelling louder knowing I was inside.

"Your there, Jenny please. I love you and I miss you, I need you and I know you need me to, im so sorry for everything." He said.

The noise stopped for a moment, I didn't know what happened then there was pounding behind me on the back window.

"I see you Jenny, I'm going to get in." He yelled at me.

I went into the bedroom but I could hear the window opening and things falling to the floor, oh my God he was coming in the house.

"David stop!" I screamed.

Just then my mom came through the front door and I came out of the room to see her face as she saw David tumbling the rest of the way in the house.

"Get out before I call the police Mr. David Fulton!" She hollered, I was so happy to see her!

He left quickly but looking back at me he told me he would be back and I would be his, not!

On The Road Again

I didn't stay at my mom's long, I soon found myself with Leah getting ready for the trip of a lifetime. We sat at the end of the beds in a hotel room our friends had gotten. The beds sat side-by-side with old torn up mattresses, it wasn't the queen's cabin that's for sure! The carpet looked like a chipmunk was nesting and the smell was something one would have to be able to ignore in the mists of the busy, drug filled life we led. We all sat joking, laughing and flirting knowing it was nothing we would have to make a promise too because we were on our way out of town.

Our friend Rob walked in and sat down on the bed, well bounced lol.

"Hey baby." He said lookin at me then at Leah then back at me. "You're leavin?"

"Yep." I said. "Why?"

"I'm gonna miss you girl." He said looking down and blushing.

Both of us girls started laughing. "No you won't miss me, you'll miss me making you feel like a man." I told him.

"Yep, you guys are just gonna miss the flirtin and the lovin lol, we're smarter than that!" She said patting me on the back, we couldn't stop laughing, he was so cute!

"So, getting back to the matter at hand." I said. "Where do we go to get high before we take off?"

Rob chimed in to that. "I have some for both of you, a going away present so come with me. We'll take my car and go for a drive, how's the upper park sound? Perfect place for a beer and I need to head that way anyways."

Leah started grabbing our stuff. "Ain't leavin nothing here that's for sure!"

"Cool, come on you two, let's get this goin!" Rob said.

I grabbed the rest of what was on the bed and we got it into his car till he brought us back to ours. We jumped in the dusty but warm in a weird sort of a way, car. The ashtray was broken and hangin on by a screw and the lock on the glove-box was stripped out. The material across the top was ratted and left a mess with spiders and their family's right at home. I let Leah in the back seat and I jumped in the passenger seat and swung the door closed.

"Let's go baby!" Leah said with a smile.

Before we headed out too far I knew we were going to stop to get high, yep, the car was pulling into the parking lot of the 20th street Park.

"Ok girls, looks like no one is around." He said.

He pulled out his stash, pulled out the mirror and the spoon and everything else needed. In no time we were all ready to go (How funny, everyone seemed to be prepared for this stuff, guess that just means we're the best at what we do lol ... I thought)

Leah and I sat there and bullshitted and joked while he calmly cooked the perty speed into a perty little puddle in the spoon, I handed him the piece of cotton I had already taken off the cigarette I had while we were talkin and he dropped that into our little puddle, then he carefully placed the tip of the needle into the cotton piece and pulled it slowly into the syringe. We kept talking this whole time as if it were yesterday's news.

"Come on Jen give me your arm, here." Rob said motioning for me to hurry. He grabbed my arm and sat it comfortable on his leg and gave me a squeeze and his sweetest smile. "Now don't move." He said.

"Yea you don't worry about how cozy my arm is silly." I said as both of us girls started laughing again. He's such a flirt but so good at it!

"Just make sure you're careful." I said.

He grabbed his rubber strap out of his pocket and wrapped my arm. Then the little 'pop' sound and then ... hhmm yea baby. That warmth through my body, the taste in my throat, the spin and out it goes. Leah not wanting to watch was at the doors tellin us to hurry so we could head out. Soon as Rob was done with his we were off on our awesome drive through town to the park.

Worry's and fears were gone and excitement for our journey was on!

It felt like I was saying goodbye to Chico in the whole sense of the matter. We had to go see the park, Bidwell Park, one of the most beautiful spots around. When I was little we would have dances at the cross. (There was a tall cross on a small hill up the road into Upper Park. Usually good blue grass type music was played, we played with other kids and ate the picnic lunches our mom made us, me and my sister Dru loved it!)

To get to the upper park we had to turn onto the gravel road and then through the foothills to our own world it went.

The first swimming whole was Alligator Hole and there was a rope tied off of a tree. We would climb up the tree and someone would throw you the rope and up and out ya go. Jumpin in the coolest and bestest fresh mountain water in Northern California! Then the Bear Hole and Diversion Damn. Next up the walk a bit further and over some pretty big rocks is Hell's Kitchen. Once you make it all the way up you could see all the beauty that was there and all the way back down.

The park goes right through town and through the University. In town there is one-mile. It is where they made it a public man made pool with a fish ladder that let the water to go through, connecting from the Chico creek which goes on up the mountain to outside of town. Then five-mile swimming hole. We used to have birthday parties there when I was younger. There's plenty of room for the volleyball nets and barbeques and the water is right there, we used to see how many tadpoles we could collect.

―・―

We pulled over and hung out sitting on the rocks and all of a sudden we looked at each other.

"Jenny." Leah said and looked at me with them big browns. "We forgot about gas money, what are we gonna do? The guys are waiting for us in Colorado, oh my god Billy's gonna kill me!" She said with tears bout to start.

"No, come on." I got up and motioned Leah and Rob to help me get our things together, i.e. the pipe weed soda smokes sun glasses.

"Now for most people that would be a problem." I said. "Not having gas money n' all." I looked at her and hugged her. "Everything will be ok, I bet we can make one phone call and we'll be on the road in no time!" I said. "Let's head to town and git er' done kk."

We joked and talked about our plans while we all jumped in the car to head back to town and our road trip to come.

―・―

In no time our knights in shining armors, Jeff and Peter, were meetin us in the middle of nowhere somewhere near the Sacramento river to siphon us a tank of awesome gasoline. All it would cost us was a hug a smile and a kiss goodbye. Totally worth it and awesome friends!

We could see the lights heading our way. "Hey who's that?" I asked Leah.

We were both lookin and seeing if it was Rob or someone else that might have followed us cause the guys were the other direction.

"Jenny." Leah said looking over to me and laughing. "It's the cops, oh my, kk no biggy, we're just out here talkin right?"

"Yep." I added. "No reason to think anything different I'm sure."

We gained our composure and thank goodness we hadn't gone to pick up Leah's baby girl Sheila Rosemarie yet. It didn't take long and there was one at each of our windows.

"Hello girls, what are you doing out here?" The officer asked me.

I looked up to him and smiled. "We're just sitting here talking."

"Where do you think you are?" He asked me.

I looked at Leah and we laughed. She started to explain to the officer at her window that we had been having a hard time and drove out to the river so we could be alone for a bit to visit. I was doing the same with the officer at my window but soon things went a different way.

"Ma'am," The officer said. "Can you tell me where the river is?"

I looked behind us. "Right back over there somewhere?" I said pointing behind us.

"No, it's right over here on the other side of you. Why don't you get out of the car for me?"

I looked at Leah then back to him. "Ok but I don't know why, i didn't do anything."

"Great." The officer said. "Then you won't mind me throwin your name in here on this little ol' state wide search list, hang on right there honey." He said.

He moved me to one side of his car and walked to the other side to get his radio and started talkin to it.

My mind was going a hundred miles an hour when I realized he was talking to me.

"Jennifer, now, as you know or you should know, you have a warrant out for your arrest in Fresno County. I'm going to have to bring you down to the station and see what's goin on. You can bail from there if you want but we ain't leavin you here that's for sure."

Then he looked at Leah. "Ma'am, you need to skedaddle on out of here and go on home ya hear?"

"Yes sir." She told him. "On my way."

Looking at me worried I told her it would fine and I'd be out soon then I was being put into the back of the car, shit, I thought to myself lol, here we go again.

All of a sudden my mouth began to move and I swear, it did not stop for the next few hours!

I was so spun, I proceeded to tell the cops on the way to the station, everything I was on, how I did it, how much I had done and why lol . The cops were looking in the little window on the door of the booking room and laughing at me cause I couldn't stand still for a second. I was talking to myself and the walls as they peaked in at me. I really thought they were going to call my name but nope, not my turn yet.

"Hey." This guy said as he stumbled in and leaned against the wall. "What are you doing in a place like this?"

I kept looking at the toilet. I had to pee so badly but there was no way in the world I was sitting my bare butt there on that cold metal for everyone to see.

"Hello, someone there?" he asked me.

I turned quickly and looked at his face, he looked so young and awkward to be here. He wasn't really cute and I thought to myself, 'poor guy' lol, and he continued to try to get my attention.

"I'm stuck here forever I'm afraid, will your brother be here to get you out? When you were talking to the toilet a bit ago I heard you talking about it."

"He isn't my brother but he's one of my best friends and yes, I hope he'll be here soon." I told him. "I'm leaving tonight for Florida and I ain't letting nothing stand in my way!"

The guy reached down into his sock to pull a baggie out then handed it to me.

"Here, take this then." He said as he handed me the small bag.

'Shit' I was thinking. "Thank you, I think. Cool, I owe ya one."

The more I thought about it the more perfect it became. I'll be able to get high on down the road a bit later.

"No." He said. "You're saving me here and now so we're even."

I put the bag in my bra and walked to the other side of the cell and waited for them to come get me.

So much for getting right out, they drug the time out as long as they could while letting me make a fool of myself. I was pouring out my truths in every word I spoke and couldn't believe I wouldn't shut up! Thank goodness, before I fell to sleep on that cold fricken hard bench made with cement or something, they were calling my name.

"Russell, up and out." I heard.

"Yes ma'am, here I am." I said jumping up from where I was sitting.

"Roll it up, you've been bailed out."

My heart started to pound, I didn't think he would do this for me, I knew he was mad at me for leaving. When I walked outside the button released door Peter was standing next to the window with his back to me looking out into the sky, I felt so bad for being such a brat.

I walked up to him and put my hand on his shoulder.

"Why did you do that?" I asked him.

He turned to me as if he had been waiting for this moment for a long time.

He held my shoulders and looked into my eyes. "Because I love you and I can't let you stay in jail. When you look at me with those eyes I will do anything for you, you know that."

I could feel the colors entering my cheeks as they blushing began, he was always so sweet to me.

"But you know I am leaving, you know I will jump bail." I said to him.

"And you know that if you are not in Fresno in time for court you will know how mad I will be at you, so, I think you will make better choices sooner or later. I love you ya know."

Walking out the doors toward the parking lot he waited to hear back from me. He looked towards the ground and back up to me. "Yes, I know. I love you to." I said back to him.

I looked up and Leah was there in her car waiting for me waiving her cigarettes for me to come get one.

"Thank you sis, I love you, I was scared our trip was gonna be history!"

"No way, I wouldn't have let that happen." I looked at Peter and gave him a hug.

"Thank you, I will talk to you soon kay?" I said to him.

"Yea, you had better!"

I ran over and jumped in the car. Leah handed me the smokes and I took one out and looked at it as if it were a long lost friend. "Thank you smoke, at least you and my sissy and Peter love me huh!"

I didn't look up but I could hear his tires pealing out behind us.

"Dang, he's mad at me, it's not like it hasn't happened before though lol he is always mad at one of us for something."

"You're so right, he's always upset with us about something." Leah said. "Let's head out." She started the car and threw it in gear and we were off.

I looked in the back seat and saw our princess, Leah's little 3 year old Sheila Rosemarie, all ready to hit the road.

"Sheila honey, make sure you fasten your seatbelt kay?" I said.

"Ok Aunt Jenny, is everything okay?" Her little self asked me.

"Everything is fine, we're gonna go to Disney World, cool huh!?"

"YaY ok!" she got so excited lol. "I'll be good, I promise!" She said.

I watched this very small, petite, most beautiful little girl set herself up so proper with her hands crossed on her lap. Her seat belt up almost over the side of her head because she was too small made me giggle, she was so cute! Her sweet little face would melt the hardest of criminals, that's for sure!

I turned around in my seat and looked out the window as we were leaving town.

Looking over at Leah I couldn't help but to smile. "I love you sis."

"I love you too." She said.

"We're gonna be fine, you know that right?" I asked her.

"Yep." She said to me. "I know, we'll be fine. As long as we are together we will have everything and anything we need!"

Finally life was perfect!

⁓∾⁓

We were out on the highway, cruzin fast down the road and Leah and Sheila were sleepin and it was way to quiet for me. I was getting bored and tired but I didn't want to wake them up.

'Oh yea' I thought, I still have that bag that guy slipped me. To cool! I pulled over on the side of the road but realized I didn't have a rig, damn, kay, I can figure this out. I sat there for a minute dumb founded. I turned the little bottom light on so I could see, used the longest and smoothest key I could find on the ring and dipped it into the whitish yellowish powder lying perfectly in the bag. I pulled it out careful not to knock it off in the dark, which would have sucked! I gently reached it over to my nose and sniffed real hard.

"Oh Shit!" I said, so glad I didn't wake them. Dang that hurts I said to myself. My face started burning, my teeth started aching and I blew and spit out anything and everything I could get out of my mouth and my nose and threw the rest to the ground. That was something else and burned like I had never felt it burn before! I had to get back my composure and get on the road. I could tell it was probably some of the best dope I had done in a long time cause I was sooo wired! Thank goodness some of it got into my system lol. At first I thought it was bad dope, I hadn't done anything but shoot-up for so long …

Soon Leah woke up and took over the driving and laughed at me when I told her the story, I was just happy she wasn't mad at me for throwin it out lol thank goodness her was preggers and not usin!

Driving down the highway we were coming to the mountain pass we had to go over before we got to Norad Air force Base in Colorado. The sun was going down and Leah was driving, Sheila was in the back seat and I had fallen asleep.

When I woke up I realized that we were, ever so slightly, rolling back down the hill of snow we had almost made it to the top of. I looked at Leah, she was frozen with fear.

"I can't stop it Jenny, I can't stop the car and we are going to die now kay?" She said almost in tears.

"Not, get your fingers loose and let go of the steering wheel." I told her, but she didn't let go.

I got out of the car, took Sheila Rosemarie out of the car and just then a bronco pulled up. The man put Sheila in his truck and then tried to get Leah's hands unstuck from the steering wheel. Thank goodness we had almost everything except the kitchen sink in there! I took out speakers, shoes, books, anything with some pressure or substance to it and pushed it under the back of the tires to try to get it to stop rolling backwards. At one point I thought the car was going to run over everything and go over that mountain in this snowstorm! The only thing that seemed to make sense to me was that if she was going to die, I was going to grab onto the car and die with her! I screamed at the top of my lungs.

"Leah, let go of the steering wheel right now or else I will have to jump in the car and die with you because you ain't dying without me, I said NOW! I love you, please!" I screamed.

I don't know what happened, or if it was something I did, the man did or God, but she let her hands fall to her side and the man swooped in and quickly picked her up and placed her safely in his bronco where Sheila had been patiently waiting, such a good baby girl!

As the man and I got into his truck I asked him about the car.

"Don't worry about it." He said. "I'll get it brought over the hill for you."

I couldn't believe he was so nice and helping us so much!

"We don't have any money to pay you or to pay someone to tow it." I said to him.

"That's okay, this one is on the house. Now ya'll load up and let's get you somewhere where you can thaw out ya hear?" He said.

Once inside with the doors closed we were so happy it was warm, I didn't think I would ever feel that again. We felt totally helpless, not knowing what the next minutes would entail we sat and waited quietly to see where we were headed. Soon we pulled up to a small café in what seemed to be the middle of nowhere.

"Here ya go, I already called Sally and you kids are going to be fine here tonight. In the morning you will be able to pick up your car right here close and be on your way."

I looked over at him, he was so calm and content.

"You're going to do that for us?" I asked him.

"Of course." He said. "That's what we do around here. Nice to meet ya'll and remember to be safe." He said.

We got our things and we all said our thank you's and goodbye's, even little Sheila Rosemarie with her beautiful smile on, no fear was to be known by her little self. She had been cuddled in the corner trying to get warm.

"Come on honey." I said. "Let's go get some more heat kay?" She jumped up into my arms. Right then I knew we would all be fine.

People blessing us and helping us like angels. Ones that come into our lives regularly and make things better seemed to be everywhere we went. We clumsily got ourselves and our things through the doors and a woman walked up to us with a big smile.

"Hi girls, how are you doin?" She asked as she welcomed us in. "I'm sorry for your scare, everything will be fine with the sunrise though, it always is."

Wow, it was awesome to want to smile again. With her sweet voice and words that was all we could do.

"Come on in here, I have made up a palate over there for the three of you and there is some soup here for you to eat if you're hungry."

We graciously accepted the sweet offer then curled up in the corner of this lovely smelling place full of love.

We woke the next morning to the best smell of Hot Chocolate; I will always remember that smell I thought to myself, so strong and sweet.

Leah and I looked at each other. "Hey sis, is it morning already?" I asked her.

"It smells so good!" She said to me.

"I know huh! Yum, the hot chocolate smells so good doesn't it?"

"I just said that!" Leah said to me laughing.

"Hey, I smelled it first." Sheila said from under the blanket. We all started laughing and the tension we had felt the night before was gone.

"Good morning kids, ya'll wakin up now? I have some cocoa in here for you and a small breakfast for you to eat before you take off." The sweet woman said to us.

We stood up and stretched. "It smells wonderful, thank you so much!" I said to her.

We all got up and folded the padding up.

"Thank you for everything, you are so kind."

"Come on in here." She said as she led us to the table. "Its Gods work, not mine to take credit for."

Such a sweet woman, I was sure God would bless her for everything she did!

We were eating our breakfast and enjoying the cocoa when we heard a familiar voice.

"Hi girls, did you have a good sleep?" The man from last night walked in and tossed the keys to our car on the table.

"Thank you!" Leah and I said at the same time. "Is it here?" lol again we both asked him at the same time.

"Yep, it's parked outside for you and you don't owe us nothing. We are happy to help you kids. Just get where you are going so that you will be safe and we'll be happy." He said.

"We will sir, thank you so much!" We told him.

He went and sat at the counter to order and we finished the wonderful meal that was made for us then got our things together to head out.

"Come on mommy and Aunt Jenny, we have to git now." Sheila's little voice said lol.

"Thank you for everything." We all told them as we were leaving. We went out and got settled in the car when they opened the door and hollered to us.

"Bless you girls, you be safe now and hope to see you again sometime." They said to us.

We waved to these wonderful strangers as we pulled out of the parking lot and headed back on our way down the summit to the Base.

After what seemed like forever we finally saw a sign.

"There it is, there's the base entrance right there." Leah said.

"Kay, I'll pull in and see if they id us." I said. "I wish we could call or something to let them know we're here."

"I know huh, they should know we are close. We'll see them soon, we have too." Leah said sounding worried.

Sure enough, we were driving ever so slowly creepin round the corner, hoping we would see the guys before the officers saw us. We didn't have any passes for visiting the base or anything and we could barely remember the house number they had given us.

"Hey, Sis, look up ahead." Leah said.

We could see two silhouettes headed up the road towards us. I knew who it was right off the bat. You couldn't miss their, 'strut walk'. D.J. one of my craziest and cutest brother's and Billy was Leah's love. We pulled over to the side of the road and waited for them to get up to us.

"Hey there beautiful, what a sight for sore eyes!" D.J. said reaching into the car to open the driver's door. He picked me up right on out of the car and into his arms swingin me around.

"Thank you for commin and getting us, thank you so much!" He said. "It's so nice to see a familiar face!"

It felt good being in his arms so I decided to just go along with the moment. It was awesome to not have to worry about everything by ourselves anymore, what a relief!

"Good to see you to, we missed ya'll." We both said to the guys.

They scooted us over and jumped in the car, D.J. at the steering wheel and Billy bout sitting on Leah lol.

"Kay, now you can meet Billy's mom and dad. Ya'll can't leave the house though. We are lucky we are not getting caught now. We're not supposed to be out of the home without a visitors pass and I can't get us one because we don't all have id's." He told us. "So, we have to stay here until this storm passes. Till then they have locked the base down. I am surprised you got in."

"We have our ways of getting what we want." I told him.

"Yea, isn't that the truth!" The guys laughed together and made my face turn different shades of red lol i could actually feel it changing. Thankfully in seconds we were parked.

"Okay, that's enough." Billy said. "Let's do this."

We walked up the walk and opened the door. Slowly we went inside the walkway, one at a time.

"Mom, this is Leah and her daughter Sheila and Jenny, the girls I told you were comin to get us."

In came this sweet looking woman, as short as Billy, I tried not to giggle.

"Hey, we are both tall so don't even go there." She said to us with a smile.

"Don't worry ma'am, we won't let your secret out." I told her as we all were giggling.

"Okay kids, you will be sharing this space so keep your stuff picked up and as soon as they open the base you guys have to take off alright?" She asked us.

"No problem ma'am, thank you for letting us stay. We've had a hard trip and will be very happy to have these guys with us so it is all worth it!" I said.

We wandered around looking at the pictures on the wall. Most of them were military pictures, which has always meant so much to me.

"Wow, your whole family is military? That's so cool." I said. All of a sudden tears started to fall. Not sure if it was because I missed my family or because I had no idea how our travels would end up being so far from home. D.J. put his arm around my neck and turned my face to his.

"Everything will be okay, I promise. We have a plan kay?" He said to me. "You girls just hang in there and it will all fall into place."

Sheila looked up at him. "Uncle D.J., why is my Aunt Jenny crying?"

"She's okay honey, she is just happy to see us." He said to her.

"I am too, I love you guys so much!" She said with her sweetest smile.

"We love you to honey." He said hugging her.

We all sat down and picked out movies to watch. As the days went on we were restless as could be!

Then the wonderful day came, six days into the week Billy's mom comes in the house with the message for us.

"Okay kids, ya'll are free to go now. The Sergeant has announced that the base is open." She told us.

We were all hoopin and hollerin, "Finally, we can take off!" I said with such excitement. "I didn't mean that rude ma'am, we are so thankful you have opened up your home to us, you are an angel!"

"I understand honey, I know what it is like to be somewhere and not knowing anyone, it isn't easy."

Billy and D.J. were already packed so they started loading everything into the trunk.

"Don't forget Sheila's toys guys." I reminded them.

"Okay, get your jackets, you'll need them till we get out of the snow." The guys said to us at the same time.

We all grabbed our stuff and got Sheila in the seat belt and jumped into the car.

"Love you ma." Billy said out the window.

"I love you too honey, you too D.J. you girls don't let them be their awnry selves to you ya hear? Make them do what you want them to do." She winked and waved good-bye to us.

"We will, thank you again."

We drove off excited as a group of kids on the first day of school! Soon we were headed to the freeway that was on the map.

"Here we go." Billy said. "Head out this way and we can stop and weigh this up kay?"

"Weigh what up?" I asked.

"Oh yea, we don't have cash but we have the next best thing." He said with his shit eatin grin.

He pulled up the blanket and opened the bags up so we could see the weed.

"We'll sell this at the truck stops. I have a buddy that said he was making bookoo bucks doin this and we will be sure to make enough for gas and grub." He said so proudly.

Leah and I looked at each other and shook our heads. "Guess we don't have a choice but to trust them huh?" I asked her.

"Nope, guess we don't." She said back to me.

We continued to listen to the music of the radio and watch the world as we drove on past it. I was a little scared and felt totally guilty for jumping bail and taking off on Peter. I didn't know what was going to happen but it was easier to just look up with a smile and go along with whatever came our way.

Rubbin my eyes I was sure we had gone quite a few miles. "Where are we?" I asked.

D.J. stretched and looked around. "We are going to make some money for dinner, there's a truck stop right up at the next off ramp."

Billy turned around after hearing us talking. "Right here?" He asked.

"Yea, pull on off the highway. Don't park in the busy area of the truck stop, park off the side over there so I can make some bags kay?"

"Okay." Billy answered. He maneuvered the car through the big rigs and we found ourselves in a lonely, but peaceful, parking space with a little picnic table and a garbage can.

"Perfect, we can stop here for a while." D.J. said.

Sheila peaked her head out of her blanket in the back. "Aunt Jenny, can I go potty?" Her little voice always brought a smile to my face.

"Sure honey." I told her. "Come on. I'll be right back and then I'll help you." I said motioning to D.J.

He tilted his head as if he were saying, 'Okay, hurry please!' And off we went, this little girl skipping along side of me and trusting every step I took.

When we got back the guys were gone and Leah was sitting on the hood of the car with that beautiful baby belly shining in the early evening sun.

"Hey sis, here's your girly girl." I said to her with a smile.

Sheila jumped up inside the car and into the back where she had obviously become very comfortable and cozy with her blankets and her pillow. I giggled to myself, I have always been the same way. If I had my pillow and blanket I could cuddle up and sleep pretty much anywhere!

Leah had been making us sandwiches while I took the baby to the bathroom and handed me one.

"I hope this is made with love because it won't taste good without mayonnaise if it isn't!" I said laughing.

"You know it is honey and I am sorry, I will make the guys go in there and get some mayo before we leave kay?"

"Yea, I suppose I'll survive." I said walking around to the other side of the car. It was dry but full of love.

I plopped myself down and kicked off my sandals stretching my legs up and over the door to fit carefully down in the crevice of the space between the car and open door. It felt so good to stretch!

"Hey." I said to Leah. "When do you think we will be in Florida?"

"I don't know." Leah said as she carefully cleaned up the mess we made with the lunchmeat.

"I do know that next time we are going to have to have to hire a cleaning woman to go with us wherever we go so that we don't have to clean up our own messes."

"aaww lol your so cute honey. I'm sorry, need some help?" I asked her.

"No, I got it." She said to me. "Hey, about what you asked me earlier, I think we will be there in a couple of days. What are we going to do when we get there anyways?"

I looked at her with the question on my mind. "Wow." I said. "I don't know, I suppose try to go to Disney World, that is the only thing I can think of. I would like to drive down on the Keys, I've heard it's absolutely beautiful down there."

"Oh yea," Leah said. "D.J. said for you to stay here with me and Sheila for now, him and Billy went to go do the deed, thought you might be wondering." She said to me laughing. "I hope they make enough money for dinner and some cigarettes!"

"Me too, I hope they'll be back soon, that sandwich just didn't do it that's for sure."

I giggled as Leah turned with a playing pout. "I'm kidding honey, that sandwich was as good as a Filet Minion!" I said to her.

"haha." She laughed lol. "At least we have a minute to relax before we are driving again!" She said to me.

We got cozy and played with the radio until we found a station that sounded good.

Soon the guys came strutin up to us. "Come one girls, let's get on the road."

D.J. handed me some money. "Cool, $45 will feed us for a couple of days and a little gas to!"

Billy was quietly getting everything ready to load up so we could hit the freeway.

"So, does that mean we can buy mayo for the sandwiches now?" Leah asked looking up at him with that 'I know what the answer better be' type smile lol!

"Yes, I suppose I can get you some mayonnaise silly." He laughed and then off we went on down the road to our next stop.

※

One of our stops was at the Mississippi River. We pulled over in a parking area and there was a real long line of people so we went up to check it out. It looked as if people were standing in line to see something. So, we stood there too even though we really didn't quite know what we were standing in line for. Before we knew it we were at the front of the line. Leah looked at the gondola up ahead of us headed out with passengers to the other side of this huge river.

"Hey, what the hell? I ain't goin up there." She stated loudly! "Excuse me, sir?" I could see she was starting to panic on me so I tried to calm her down.

"I love you, its fine silly."

"Are you going to make me go up on that thing?" She asked me with fear in her voice.

"I don't have any choice, look behind you." I said.

We both turned to look, there were people in line one after another after another after another all lined up neatly with a chain to allow a line to form. There were so many people there was no way she was going to be able to get out of this, there was nowhere else to go and she was pissed.

"I swear I will never forgive you for this Jennifer!" She yelled at me. I tried not to laugh but I couldn't help it.

Sheila Rosemarie patted her mommy's leg. "It's okay mommy, we will be with you." This sweet voice said.

All I could do was laugh as quietly as I could but she still heard me.

"Knock it off, you're awful! Take me back kay?" She pleaded.

"You know I can't do that. We're hungry and if we want to eat we have to get up here with everyone else and go across.

I could see the terror in her face as she held Sheila's hand for dear life.

"I'm sorry sissy, I love you." I said to her as we all climbed in.

Sheila sat with Leah on the floor and she could only say a few words.

"Fuck you bitch! Fuck you bitch, Fuck you bitch!" ... lol it was SO hard not to laugh!

Of course we were covering Sheila's ears.

D.J. pulled a joint out of his pocket. "Yes, too cool, thank you thank you thank you!" I said. They lit it and we passed it back n' forth.

What a beautiful ride across the Mississippi River.

We stopped at a couple more truck stops throughout the next few days while we got closer and closer to our no-where land and I was getting restless. Been spending way too much time sitting that's for sure!

"Hey." I said getting D.J.'s attention. "Can I go with you this time? This is crazy, I gotta walk around a bit."

He reached down and kissed me, for that moment, all of my fears and all of my worries went down the highway.

"Come on baby, let's get a few bucks." He said.

I jumped up and started walking with him toward a group of truckers on the other side of the parking lot. We didn't have much luck and were discouraged to say the least.

Feeling a little uneasy about the last guy we had talked to and not knowing if he had called the cops D.J. handed me the two eighths and I turned quickly as I saw the men walking towards us. I slipped them in my pants and pulled my shirt down to be sure to cover them.

"Sir, Ma'am, why don't ya'll come talk to us." They were saying behind us. "Hey, ya'll hear me?"

I turned and got back to the car as quick as I could and stashed the smoke in the back of the car where the rest of it was then woke Leah and Billy and Sheila Rosemarie up.

"Hey you guys, the police are here. Come on, get up!" I said.

I was so nervous my stomach was doing jumping jacks! Leah was trying to get herself out of the back and Sheila too, poor baby, half asleep.

"Officer." Leah said trying to talk while she stumbled getting out of the car and as she stabled herself the officer saw that she was very pregnant. "Is everything alright?" She asked.

They weren't interested in making small talk so we walked to the other side of the car to sit on the hood. Leah jumped up with me handing me Sheila to get her comfortable.

"Sis, now what's going to happen?" I asked her.

"I don't know, I think we should pray huh?" She said to me and we both took her advice and spoke a silent prayer.

The cops had decided among themselves that they were going to do a search of the car to find the marijuana we had been selling in all the truck stops they said. Yea right, only four of em' I think.

I looked at Leah and pulled my knees to my chest. "I think I am going to go to jail." I said as quiet as I could. "I have a warrant out for jumping bail."

D.J. and Billy looked over at me. "You what?" They both said at the same time.

"You heard me, I thought I could make it up later. I didn't think anything would happen and I was wrong. I'm gonna end up hurting Peter real bad." I said. "I didn't mean to do that plus I'm gonna be in way more trouble now."

D.J. put his arms around me and held me. "I don't know what's gonna happen honey." He said to me. "Somehow everything will be alright."

Right then the officers stepped out of the car. "Okay ya'll." One of them said. "I want all of you to get in your car and get as far away from this area of Louisiana as possible ya hear?"

We were stunned, looking at each other we jumped quickly out of the position we had been sitting in and jumped in our spots in the car as fast as we could, waving goodbye we were so relieved for another blessing!

I looked back through the window and they were walking off to their cars talking on and on in their own worlds. I am sure we would have messed up their whole week with all the paperwork they would have been stuck with processing all of us but it just didn't make sense to me.

"Hey you guys, before we take off we should check the front seat for some kind of bug or something."

"Jenny, what is wrong with you?" They all asked me lol.

I grabbed my leather and frantically tossed it out the window on the turnpike. "Those cops searched the front where my jacket was and then they were reaching into the back of the car to search. He laid his hand on the blankets and backed off and instead of finding all of our smoke, he sent us away. I know I have always had angels around me but sometimes it is just too good to seem true."

I settled into my seat and looked at D.J. They looked totally under control, 'how do guys do that', I wondered to myself. I kind of giggled and that started all of them laughin because of me throwing my leather out the damn window lol!

I smiled at D.J. still laughing. "Thank you." I said to him. "I am glad I didn't go to jail."

"Why didn't you tell me this earlier?" He asked.

"I didn't want anything getting in the way of this road trip, it meant too much to me. Everything will be fine now, you'll see." I said. He shook his head and we started watchin the signs on the interstate.

Soon I saw it. "Hey Leah look, that road sign says Disney World!" I said.

She got so excited. "Oh my goodness we are actually into Florida and I didn't even realize it!"

Sheila jumped up in a screech. "Yippppeeeee, Come on guys, let's play, please please please please?" lol she's so cute!

Wow, I can't believe how beautiful it is. It was so clear and bright and shiny, it reminded me a bit of Switzerland, so perfect!

We drove from one huge town to the next. If all of Florida is this big and crowded I can just imagine what New York looks like! There it was, the sign that would lead us to our day of play!

"How are we going to get in there, it costs so much money?" Leah was asking Billy.

Sheila didn't really care how we got in lol, she just knew it was going to happen!

"Here." Billy said as he handed her enough money for her and I and Sheila Rosemarie to get in then the boys went and jumped the wall and we met up inside.

It was awesome, we spent the whole day there. We even had enough money to get something to eat while we were there, we had so much fun. We played all day and realized that no one could ever see the whole place, Disney World I mean, in one day that's for sure!

We didn't have another day to play though so off on our journey we were.

As we traveled through the state I got so excited knowing that I was actually going to get to see the Keys. I had only heard about them, I had never seen anything so picturesque other than Mendocino and Switzerland of course. I couldn't see enough as we were driving, it was as if I were watching TV, it was so beautiful. The colors were bright and clear, the sun shined and people were sitting on their beach chairs along the side of the water's edge as we went from key to key. Soon we were at the end, oh my goodness, by the time we got there it was sunset.

"Here, park over there." I told Billy. Leah and me jumped out and ran up to the dock that was stretched out into the water down the hill in front of us. We plopped ourselves down on the docks so that we could feel the heat of this bath water we were about to totally indulge in as we spoke!

"Come on sis." I yelled as I jumped in and swam out. "It has to be like 75 degrees!"

"Wait for me!" Leah was trying carefully to slide in off the dock.

"Come on silly, jump in and come on out here with me." I hollered to her.

"No, I can't go out there, the sharks will eat us!"

"Not, come on, it's great!" I said as I swam a little further out and pulled off my t-shirt.

It was so grimy from the days of our travels I was happy to wash it, then off came the shorts.

"Kay, take it all off!" I yelled. "See guys?"

They were walking towards the shore from the car. "Ya it's not safe out there." D.J. hollered at us. "Put your clothes on and get back here!"

"What's the matter baby, sceered?" I asked em. "Come on sis, I guess we better go back, it is so nice, I can't believe we're here."

"I know, me too. It is the prettiest place I have ever been. It is as if we were looking at postcards or something, I never understood what 'picture perfect' meant until now."

We swam back to land, dried off lol a little, and put our clothes on to get into the car.

D.J. and Billy had been talking. "Hey guys, let's get some dope huh?" The said to us.

"Shush!" I said. "Where's Sheila?" I looked in the car and her was happy as could be playin with her doll, thank goodness!

I soon figured out the guys had met someone already and they were waiting for us with him in his van that was next to our car. We all climbed in and saw there weren't seats in the back so we settled ourselves on the floor. I had baby girl's hand, I sat down and she cuddled next to me with her doll.

It was getting dark by the time we headed to where ever we were going. By the time we pulled in and parked it was really dark. It looked like we had pulled up to a really ghetto type apartments and there were people walking around everywhere. I was really getting scared so being on the floor holding Sheila was all good for me.

Finally the man in the driver's seat spoke. "Ya'll hang tight here and if I'm not back in 15 take the van and leave." Leah and I kind of giggle knowing he was kidding. He looked back at us and told us he was serious. I couldn't believe what we had gotten ourselves into. There were tones of people, Cajun's, D.J. told me, were everywhere! Pretty much all we could see in the dark was the whites of their eyes and it wasn't very reassuring. He jumped out and headed into the darkness and as we watched the time, I kept a hold of the baby. Thank goodness in a few minutes the man jumped back in with a smile and started up the van and we drove away, finally I could breath.

We drove back to the little trailer park next to where we were swimming, pulled into the parking space and we all got out.

"Come on in, the set-up is in there. Head on to the room then come on out, we'll be out there." He said motioning out the back door.

For a second I wondered where Sheila and Leah were, I looked at D. J. not quite knowing what to do, he took over. He put his hand on my shoulder and led me and set me where he needed me to be. Right then all other thoughts went away. I just sat there and watched him. Looking around the trailer it smelled musty and it was very small, that was for sure. I brought my attention back to the man doing the work. His intense glare into his work drew me in with him. I was watching each step closely, soaking it in. I looked back up at his face, his skin was a soft red with beads of sweat starting to form on his forehead. I reached up and wiped his face off with my hands.

"Thank you." He said to me.

"No problem, I got your back, or your sweat lol, you know that." I told him.

He smiled that crooked smile at me and directed our attention back to the task. Very carefully he had taken the baggie that sat on the table and emptied it out on the spoon that was also conveniently placed on the table before we came in the room.

To myself I thought about how many other people other than us had shot up drugs in this room, eeww, kay, I had to shake that thought! I put my attention back on what D.J. was doing, out of the cup of water, he squirted water into the spoon, a little, then a little more. Soon the white powder was dissolving into cocaine heaven! I was watching how intense he was, I could feel his heart pounding sitting next to me on the bed. Mixing it carefully, he reaches up and pulls a piece of cotton out of the bag that was also on the nightstand as if it were waiting for us. The sweat on his forehead had started to drip down the side of his face so I wiped it off onto my levy's. He picked up the needle, popped the orange cap off and I watched it as it fell to the floor. Very carefully and full of concentration he led the tip of the needle to the top of the cotton ball he had placed in the spoon. He began pulling the plug back as I watched the clear, watery substance go higher and higher into the syringe. He stood it up right and clicked it with his fingers to get the air bubbles out. By this time I can feel my heart pounding, I knew what I was about to do and for some strange reason I couldn't make it happen fast enough. He reached over to my arm and held it tight below my shoulder to see if he could get a vein.

"You actually have a vein from not using for so long, it's been like two weeks or so huh?"

"Yea, cool, it should be easy then."

"I could take care of you no matter what honey, you know that." He said with that smile again.

"Yep, I know you can." I said to him. I sat with my arm stretched out as if waiting for the gift of gold gems. He tapped my arm, saw the vein, yep, that one works, 'I thought to myself.' There was a stick and I opened up my eyes, he drew up once slowly to show we were in the vein and then he pushed the syringe one little bit at a time. I watched it as it was slowly emptied into my arm into never never land. He pulled the needle out and put it in the cleaner and reached over and kissed me. I had begun to sink and melt as if a candle were burning in me but I couldn't reach it to put it out. A warm sensation began at my toes and continued up my legs then on through and past my stomach. The rush went up my chest and into my head and I closed my eyes while I let it use my body as a playground. I could feel it doing things and warming things I didn't know could be warmed.

I fell to the floor trying to get to the bathroom. Thank goodness the trailer is small so of course the toilet was right there. I threw up and cleaned myself up then sat back down. D.J. had already started on his preparations so I carefully slipped past him to get out the door of this trailer that had consumed my brain. I jumped down the stairs going outside, took a deep breath and reached for my smokes. Putting the cigarette to my lips, lighting the lighter and taking the first drag was like a drawn out experience, it had to have been the best tasting cigarette I had ever smoked! My heart had slowed down and the sunset was magical, they skies were orange and red and the water was blue.

As everyone got high they came out and joined us down on the dock, we sat there enjoying our mind loss and played in the water with our feet for hours.

I looked up to the sky and said to myself. 'Thank you Lord for letting me still be alive. Amen."

"Hey, ya'll down there, come on up here." This man screamed down at us. "Come on up here and explain the registration and ownership of this car to me."

Leah looked at me and I looked at her, shit, not our car. Soon we realized it was a trooper so we followed him into a small shack of a police station, at least that is what I thought it was.

"Look kids." Lookin at us over the top of his black sunglasses as if we had been busted. "It looks to me like you don't have much of a choice here. Because ya'll are vagrants here in our state you'll have to sign over the pink slip on your car to me, personally, right away. I advise you to call someone to help you get a way home."

We couldn't believe what was happening, we waited to see what was next.

He handed Leah the phone and told her to call her mom so she did.

"Mom, its Leah. Here, someone wants to talk to you." And she handed him the phone.

HER PLACE WAS WITH GOD

"Ma'am, my name is Trooper Doolittle with the Florida State Police and your children have been found to be vagrants in our state and we don't allow that. Just so that you know, people disappear out here in these parts pretty easily so you need to tell her to sign me over the car and then you need to send them bus tickets on out of here right away."

Wow, we wouldn't have believed it if we didn't hear him with our own ears, it was like a crazy dream lol and bein high to boot, oh my goodness.

As minutes ticked by we signed over the car and to our surprise Leah's mom sent us all a Grey Hound bus ticket home to Chico.

We picked up the tickets and began our journey home. Sheila was struggling behind us trying to carry her back pack.

"Aunt Jenny, are we going home yet?" Her little voice asked me.

"Yes honey, we are going right now. It will take a few days but we will have fun on the bus, you'll see." I said to her with a smile.

"Good, I love you and my mommy loves you." She said to me. "Aaww, I love you and your mommy to kiddo." She jumped up and hugged my neck.

Tucking our bags where they belonged we were finally able to stop and rest.

"I'm so glad we are going home!" I said.

"Me to sis, me too."

D.J. glared at me and Billy looked out the window.

"This isn't my fault cause I have to go to court guys." I said to them, not sure if I was trying to convince myself or them. "It's because they took our car, it's the smartest thing and the only thing we could have done, we had no choice."

"I know hun." D.J. said to me.

He reached over and gave me hug and kissed my face. "It's okay, it was time to go home anyways."

Billy reached over and touched my shoulder as if to say it was alright. "Yep." He said to me. "It's time to go home sis."

Finally we were off and on our way back to California.

We made a stop in Colusa, Ca. and Leah was trying to get some money to make a phone call,

"What are you doing?" I asked her. "We're not home yet."

"I know." She said. "But my uncle lives here and we could probably get some money and I know we could eat. Anyways, I smell awful lol and Sheila has food stains on every bit of her clothes. We need a bath! Please?" She asked batting her baby browns at me lol.

"Fine, only if I can take a shower first and as soon as we get something to eat n'all we're back on the bus home kay?" I asked.

"Kay, I love you sis. I haven't seen my uncle in years, he will be so surprised!"

The guys didn't argue at all, I knew we were all tired and hungry and way past ready to be home.

As we walked up to the house a man in his late 70's maybe came out with his arms open, walking up to Leah.

"Hi honey, is has been so long! How is the family?" He asked as he was hugging her.

"We're all good." She said.

Leah reached behind me and pulled Sheila Rosemarie up in the front of all of us and introduced her.

"Uncle, this is my daughter Sheila Rosemarie and she is 3 years old."

"Hello little miss." He said to her reaching down for a hug. Then he reached out and patted Leah's belly. "Looks like we will have another one soon?"

"Yep, actually, any time." Leah said.

"Come on in kids." He said motioning us into the house.

He told us to get comfortable but I knew I would have such a hard time doing that in someone else's home, how can you get comfortable? I didn't know what to do, I really didn't have a home to go home to, I was thinking.

"Jenny." D.J. said to me. "Where are you spacin out to?"

"Huh?" I looked over to him. "Oh, nowhere, just thinking."

D.J. laughed. "Don't do that no more, you could hurt yourself."

"Haha." I said to him. "So, what are you going to do when we get home?" I asked him.

"Who me?" He laughed while he sat up to light a cigarette. "I think I am going to go get drunk."

"What? I am not gonna drink right now, we can't even afford to eat, how could we drink?" I asked him.

As we were talking I found myself distracted with this guy that had been bustling around the kitchen. He was cleaning, wiping down the counters, sweeping the floor and he was even cleaning the spilled dirt stuff on the floor. Shit, he kept going between the kitchen and the wash room.

Full of energy he was and not bad looking either!

"Leah, hey." I was trying to nudge her without D.J. or Billy seeing me. "Who is that?" I asked her.

"I don't know, I don't think I have ever met him before." She said to me.

"Hey Uncle, who is that guy in there?"

"Danny, just a youngster needin direction so I let him stay here sometimes. Looks like his direction got a bit off course this time huh?" He said shaking his head.

D.J. came up to me and whispered in my ear. "Its okay honey, you can stick around here if you want. I need to get back to Chico anyways, business you know." He said with a wink.

I looked up at his shining blue eyes and that crooked sweet smile of his. "I love you brother, I'll see you back at home." He kissed me and went back to his conversation.

Him and Billy started talking about what their plans were and Leah was talking to her uncle. I was still busy watchin Danny in the kitchen.

I got up and walked up to him while he was at the sink. "Hey, whatchya doin?" I couldn't believe I got the nerve up to talk to him! "My name is Jenny, what's yours?"

He turned around so quick grabbing my shoulders, he scared me at first. "I'm sorry, you startled me." He said.

His eyes were this bursting beautiful blue, I was hypnotized for a moment.

"Hey sweetie, are you alright?" He asked me as he reached out to hold me thinking I was going to pass out or something.

"Yea, I'm fine." I managed to say.

I was so embarrassed, he was so cute and he was so wired!

"Hey, Danny, is that your name?" I asked him.

"Yes ma'am, what can I do for you?"

"I'd like some of what you are doing!" It sounded like I was just making small talk but I was so serious lol!

We both laughed a little. He looked into the other room where everyone seemed to be busy in their own world, reached for my hand and led me down the wooden long hallway into the last room. He shut the door then turned me around to sit on the bed.

"Okay." He said to me looking into my eyes. "Hi Jenny, my name is Danny. Would you like to get high with me?"

And again it was on as I watched his preparation. This guy new what he was doing that's for sure. I watched him get this most serious look on his face. He dumped the whitish yellow powder into the spoon and then there was this chunk that was more yellow than white, he scooted it into the water in the spoon and swished it around till it all dissolved.

"Have you ever done this before?" He looked over to me and asked.

"Yep yep, but you have to do it for me, I can't." I said.

"That's okay, I'll take care of you." He said.

Giggling a little I looked up at him. He caught my eye and winked at me and smiled and went on back to what he was doing. In goes the cotton, then the tip of the needle sittin there suckin up all the moisture in the spoon. I watched as the syringe got fuller and fuller. He held it up tappin the sides of it, again to remove the air bubbles.

"Kay, lady's first." He said to me with a smile.

He pulled my arm out to him and rested it on his leg. I could feel the heat from his body go into mine. Oh my Gosh, this man had my full attention. I turned my head the other way.

"You afraid to look?" He asked.

"No need for me to yet." I said.

I could feel the poke, the gentle pull back to make sure it wasn't a miss, so now it was time to look. I watched the water disappear out of the syringe a bit at a time, mmm, I could taste it in the back of my throat and the heat started at my toes then worked its way up on through my every cell I think.

"You alright?" I heard him ask me.

I was holding onto the edge of the bed trying not to look uneasy. "I don't know, am I?" I asked him trying to laugh some.

"You'll be fine. Just relax while I do this." He said.

I sat back and watched him as he did the preparation for his own.

"Can I help at all?" I asked … I have no idea why lol, not like I'd be able to help in any way!

"Nope, I'm used to this." He said.

He looked at me with his most beautiful blue eyes, reached down and held my face then kissed me. "Do you want to stay here instead of going to Chico?"

Wow, I couldn't believe it. I was really hoping he would ask me that! "You want me to stay here with you?" I asked him.

"Yes I do." He said. "Say yes and we will have a good time, I promise."

"Yes, yes, I would love to take a break before I go to jail again."

"What do you mean go to jail?" He asked me.

"The night we were leaving for Florida I was arrested and Peter, a friend of ours in Chico bailed me out of jail. We still took off though, he's probably pretty pissed off at me."

"That's okay, he won't do anything while you are with me. I'll protect you now." He said so proudly.

"Silly, you don't have to protect me from him, he is harmless, I just feel bad." I told him.

Everyone started movin around so we came out of the room to see what all the commotion was about. Leah and Billy and D.J. with beautiful Sheila Rosemarie were on their way out the door.

"Hey, you weren't even gonna say by?" I said with a pout.

"Of course, goodbye honey." Leah said while she was hugging me. "If you need me you call me kay? I will come and get you whenever you are ready."

"Kay, I am fine I think." I felt myself blushing.

I reached out to her and hugged her whispering in her ear. "He's so sweet! I may stay here for a while."

"You just be careful sister, call me kay?" She told me.

"I will Love you."

"Love you too."

Sheila broke loose from the crowd headed out the door to cling to my leg. "Aunt Jenny, why aren't you going home with us?" her little voiced asked me.

"I will honey, I am just going to visit here a little first kay?"

She reached up and hugged me and kissed me. "I love you." She said and kissed me.

Aaww, "I love you to honey, you be good for your mommy." I said and I kissed her back.

"I will." She said with the sweetest little voice.

"Hey." I said to Leah. "You need to call me as soon as you go into labor you hear?"

"Yes daddy, I will do that I promise." We laughed as they all gathered their selves and their bags back out to go to the bus depot to catch the next bus on back home.

Danny and I got real close real fast. We didn't stay there but for a few days more then we would visit his friends and stayed a night or two here or there on different people's couches and doing dope every day.

He took me to this gal's house in Colusa, Marie. Her kitchen had dishes stacked from one end of the room to the other. After being offered some dope to clean lol, boom, in no time I had the thing sparkling clean and from then on we had a new found relationship, someone else to do dope with.

I was falling in love and I wanted to be happy but I couldn't stop thinking about how much I missed my Joshua, my heart hurt with every beat.

Our drug use got more and more wild. We would set up the rigs and head out on the town, haha, what a town. Keeping the rigs full and ready to use in our pockets made sure we were never without. We would go to the park and when we felt our highs dying down Danny would stop and we would find a spot.

We stayed with Marie for a few weeks but Danny said it was time to go somewhere else so we got a ride to his friend's house.

The man there made me so nervous, he seemed secretive and was making plans with Danny and talking like he was in the mafia or some kind of mob or something. Danny told me he was and I never really believed him but the more I watched what was happening, the more I realized he might be really telling me the truth. We would visit him and stay for however long he needed Danny to be there. He would give us dope to get high, as much as we wanted or however we wanted. Maybe in our coffee or in a needle or whatever our, 'cup of tea' was.

Soon I realized it was more serious than I thought. Danny had some kind of deal with this man, way deeper than I wanted to believe. I followed them one night and I saw the man standing on the overpass of a highway, he was watching something.

I yelled to him. "What's going on, is everything alright?"

"Jenny, you need to git." He said. "I don't want anyone seeing you!"

"Okay, will you have Danny call me so I know everything is okay?" I hollered to him.

"I will hun, now you git!" He yelled back to me.

I left and never got a phone call until I heard from Danny's mom telling me he had been arrested.

I had been staying with one of Danny's friends that I barley new and was so thankful he wasn't in custody for very long.

Danny and I were sitting on the floor listening to music and all I could think about was what I hadn't told him in the last seven days he had been back, I hadn't started my period. I knew I had to say something but I was so scared, I had just lost one son and didn't want to lose another. 'How would I ever be able to do this?' I thought to myself. And getting high lol I knew I wasn't ready to stop that, it was the only way I was able to survive without my Joshua …

He looked up at me. "Hey Jenn, what's up?" He asked. "Seems like your deep into a thought, are you alright?"

I laughed a little. "I don't know, I guess I have to tell you sooner or later but I haven't started my period. I'm never late and I haven't started since you went to jail. So I'm maybe four weeks late now?" I looked at him and his face lit up lol, that wasn't what I expected, especially after the way Tony was when I told him about Joshua.

He turned around to me and held my shoulders looking into my eyes. Oh my god they were such the most amazing color of clear blue.

"You're pregnant, with my baby, our baby?" He asked.

HER PLACE WAS WITH GOD

I had to giggle a little cause he looked like a little boy so excited like he was going to get to go on a candy shopping spree or something.

"Okay, things have to change." He said to me. "No more of that crap for you, you hear me?"

I jumped back and out of his hold. "After what I saw you do with your other baby's mama?" I said to him with an attitude.

Aaww, I felt bad immediately. His head dropped and his smile disappeared, he looked back up at me.

"I guess I deserved that." And he looked towards the floor. I pulled his face up to mine and kissed him. "I'm sorry baby, that wasn't fair and I promised you I would never bring that up again. I'm so sorry!" He put his arms back around me and we just sat there, he held me and we listened to one of favorite songs by Carole King, 'You've Got a Friend'. I wished that moment could have lasted forever.

A couple of weeks went by and I was still using a little, Danny tried to convince me to stop but I couldn't ...

One day Danny had left to run some errands and Marie and I got bored.

"Hey, you have anything left?" I asked her.

She looked up at me. "Yep, a little, he's gonna kick my ass though."

I grabbed her hand and pulled her up to follow me into the bathroom. "I'm gonna stop I promise, as soon as I know for sure that I'm pregnant."

I was sitting on the toilet and she was standing up trying to tie off my arm so she could get a good vein when Danny knocked on the bathroom door.

"Jenny, you get out of there! Your stopping remember? You know you're not supposed to do that crap no more!" He yelled at me through the door.

"I know." I said to him.

"Come on, hurry. I don't want him to see how much I'm doing."

"I know." She said. "Here, hold this." I grabbed the piece of rubber and held it as tight as I could as I watched my shaky hand friend slowly mark the place on my arm as she began the dissent of the needle going through my skin and into the vein. I was sitting there and wow, my head spun and my legs were shaking. I stood up and rinsed off my arm.

"Thank you." I said to her. "Now let's git out of here." We opened the door to the bathroom after everything was cleaned up to find Danny standing there when I walked out.

"I didn't do much." I said, but I was spinnin bad.

ON THE ROAD AGAIN

When I looked him in the eyes I could feel my eyes crossing as my knees buckled and I began to fall so he sat me down. Guess there was no guessing anymore, it was pretty obvious.

We went to the clinic the next day and that was the last time I did drugs for a long time.

We didn't have anywhere to stay that was ours and everyone he wanted us to stay with was using or talking about using, it was crazy. I was pregnant and we were sleeping on one person's couch for a week or two, then another and then another.

Danny was off doing whatever it was he did and everything was the same as the day before until one day when he was gone I left to. I walked all the way to Chico to my mom's house from Colusa lol wow, I didn't even know I had that in me. (Again I know there was more going on with Danny and I but I can't remember)

A Double 2nd Chance

I knew I had to do something different, I had warrants out for my arrest and I was pregnant. I talked to my mom and she went in with me to turn myself in. I had a petty theft and a failure to appear warrant in Fresno Co. and in Mendocino Co. the warrant was for Grand Theft and Concealing Stolen Property. I knew I had a chance of going to prison but I had to deal with it. I couldn't chance being arrested later in my pregnancy and losing my baby, again.

It took about a week but they finally transported me to Mendocino Co. Jail in Ukiah, Ca. Another journey had begun.

I listened while the cops were talking, they were happy they got chosen for the drive to the coast with the prisoner lol how funny. They were actually really nice and even went through a drive-thru to get us some lunch.

When we got to Ukiah I wasn't treated badly at all, everyone was as nice as nice can be in jail. They didn't have loud cell doors that clanged every time they were opened or closed, it was set up like a dorm. So thankful for that because I knew if it bothered me, it bothered my baby to. Everyone had their own rooms with a bed and a desk. Each door had a little window in it that looked out into the common area. There was a row of toilets and a wash room, the doors barley covered the front of the stalls, but it was better than Butte County's metal toilet and sink that was shared by no telling how many other women.

I almost missed being in the Butte County jail, at least there I was home. I was so scared, all I know is I don't want to have my baby in prison.

'Please lord, please don't let that happen to us.' I prayed to myself.

After two or three days I started to fit myself into their routine. The chores were shared and we kept our rooms clean and as long as no one came into the drunk tank or got mad about something at home or a charge, everything was pretty calm. I was on my fourth day of bathroom moping duty when I passed out. After that I didn't have to do any more chores but that got real boring real fast. I turned my attention to the food they were serving. I decided that all the starchy stuff wasn't good for my baby so I refused to eat lol. That didn't last long either cause in no time they had me sitting with the guards to eat my meals. I'm really glad because I was hungry which meant the baby was hungry and it also meant that in a way they cared, that was nice to know.

Finally it was the day of court after waiting about a week. It was a nice drive over to Fort Bragg, I sure missed the coast.

When they brought me in I was so happy to see Kasey and Greg there. I waved and the bailiff motioned to me for no contact so I stopped and stayed quiet like I was supposed to, I so felt like a child but I guess I deserved that.

Knowing that Greg was the one that had told the police everything and gave them the ring along with the five years I was looking at made me sick to my stomach. I wanted to blame him for everything! By the time court was over he had made a different statement and since they didn't have the evidence they thought they had, I was released with time served and a petty theft conviction. Oh my goodness that's so awesome! I wanted to jump up and down and run and hug Kasey and Greg so bad! I missed them so much, their smiles and whispers of, 'I love you, you're going to be fine' we're good enough for the moment, it was so good to see them!

We didn't have to wait long before they transported us back over the hill to Ukiah, sure wish we could have stayed in Fort Bragg longer, it smelled so perfect. I felt like a thousand pounds had been taken off of my shoulders. As I sat down in my room I felt something funny like my stomach was nauseous, then I felt this tiny little butterfly feeling going across my belly hehe I jumped up and hollered.

"Hey you guys oh my god I just felt my baby!" Everyone ran up to feel with me, it was so cool, they made everyone go back to what they were doing and I sat there with this amazing thought of this chance I was getting to be a mom again.

"Thank you Jesus for saving my baby!" I prayed out loud but quiet enough for no one to hear me. I shut my door and laid down, I don't know if I had ever felt so grateful!

It was time to be transferred to Fresno County Jail. I sure wish I had known that we, (me and four others, two girls and two guys) were traveling by, 'funny little plane held together by Band-Aids and bubble gum'!

"Wow, really?" I asked the bailiff. We could see the plane we were going to be flying in through the window. "You expect us to ride in that, is it safe?" I asked him, so ready to have an attitude! We were all talking about how crazy they were when they told us to hush before we had another charge added to our cases! Well that was sweet but I suppose it worked lol it shut me up.

We followed them down hallways out to the landing strip and climbed in, after they put ankle chains on all of us.

"This is so embarrassing." I said quietly. Looking at all of us on the chain gang no words were needed, it was obvious we all felt the same way. I spoke a quiet prayer to myself that it wouldn't be a long trip and that we'd make it there safe n' sound as they buckled us in.

Landing was interesting to say the least and I am sure we were all praying that the Band-Aids and bubblegum stayed put! We were taken off the plane one by one and followed each other as we were directed to the building, embarrassment was becoming something I had better get used to if I planned on being in custody for any length of time, which I wasn't!

It was nothing like the jail in Ukiah, the guards were rude and cared absolutely nothing bout anyone they had in their custody pregnant or not.

I followed orders and kept my mouth shut while one of the guards led me to a closet and told me to pull the mattress down off the pile and drag it back down the hall to my cell. I said a quick prayer for my baby and went to pick the mattress up, the upper bunk really seemed far away. The girl that had been sitting on the bottom bunk got up and pulled it out of my hand.

"Here ya go little mama." She said to me. "I'll get that for ya."

I stepped back in surprise. "Thank you." I told her.

She was as tall as I was with short dark hair streaked with blonde throughout and her face at first glance, looked like a guy but the rest of her showed she was a woman. In my mind I knew I had to let nothing bother me, I was fine and I could do this I kept telling myself.

She got the mattress up there and laid out for me then tossed my blankets up to. "There ya go." She said to me.

She reached over and patted my barley showin baby belly and reached her hand out to shake mine. "Hi, my names Lindsey." She said.

I shook her hand and smiled. "Hi, I'm Jenny."

"Don't be liftin heavy things like that no more while your here with me ya hear?" She said. "I'll help you out, everything's gonna be fine." She smiled a sweet smile and laid back down on her bunk, picked up the book lying there next to her pillow and continued on her own.

I climbed on up to my bed quietly, put my sheet on and slid in to cover myself up with the blanket. I sat there for a bit listening. I could hear one quiet voice singing a song, I didn't recognize the words but it was surprisingly calming. In the cell next to ours were a couple of women arguing over one of them getting a letter from her boyfriend and the girlfriend was jealous, scary how I could hear almost every word. They were living their lives in here so they didn't really care who was listening or who wasn't. Attitudes started to flair and I was relieved when it didn't continue, I would way rather listen to the woman singing.

Finally I started yawning and my baby started movin a little. So awesome I thought, wow, how not awesome … remembering I was in jail. I have to get out of here and be a good mom somehow. I didn't know what was going to happen when this was over but I knew I had to change things. If not for me this time, for my baby. I laid down and curled up under the blankets hugging my pillow and my belly till I finally fell asleep.

Waking in the morning brought back the memory of why I was there in the first place lol I really wish I had done without that soda and pack of smokes, and David to.

Our breakfast was brought to us on trays, man I was so hungry so eatin would be no problem and if it tasted good it would be an extra. It was cream of wheat and lots of sugar packages lol YeS I was good to go!

After we ate I made my bed and laid down and before I knew it I heard them announcing my name over the loud speaker calling me for court, so awesome! I got myself ready which was so easy to do since all I could do was comb my hair and rinse my face. Soon I was led out of my cell and down the hall where I was joined by four other women. The guards had us turn facing forward and in a line and then one by one they put shackles on each of us and ran a chain from each of our leg chains so we were all connected. I couldn't wait to see how we would be able to walk, again I was so embarrassed.

As the group of us were led outside of the jail we followed each other up a sidewalk and then another. While we were walking I looked towards the front of the building, there were others heading into the court house and they could see us as we were heading across the yard to go inside. I had never felt like a true criminal until that very moment, I was so humiliated. Finally we made it to the doors and inside the building still in our single file line. Each of us praying I'm sure, that we don't trip over our own feet and pull the whole group of us to the ground! They led us through the building and then through doors that took us inside the court room and over to the row for us to take our seats.

It seemed like forever before I heard my name again, I had never been more relieved when the judge ruled time served and released me!

What a blessing, God is so good, this I know for sure!

That afternoon I was released and got to walk out of the ickiest jail I had ever been in hoping to never have to do anything like that again!

I realized when they gave me my personal items they gave me the check that Mendocino Co. had sent with me from Ukiah so it was a Mendocino Co. check and

HER PLACE WAS WITH GOD

I was in Fresno! I wanted to panic and cry, I didn't know what I was going to do! The bank was next to the jail so I went in there with the check and explained what happened and I was so grateful when the woman at the counter told me that she knew the sheriff from the jail and had no problems cashing it for me, it was only for like $65 but it was all I had. Now I wasn't broke!

Again lol, I was so lucky. The bus station was a couple of blocks away so on my way I went. Bought myself a one-way ticket to Chico, got some change and called my mommy.

I was staying with my mom and spending as much time as I could with Leah hangin out downtown at Central Park. It wasn't summer yet and the wind and rain made for a beautiful Chico, as always. I was so happy to be home!

I thought about Danny and our baby, I wish things could have been different.

I was 23, almost 24, pregnant with my second baby and didn't get to see my son Joshua who was 6 now, meeting a guy was the last thing I expected to happen. There were five or six of us hanging out and talking about everything and anything. I knew Leah and Billy but not the others. A couple of the guys decided to climb a tree and I wanted to join but when I started climbing I got all kinds of attention lol!

Leah was the first, "Oh my goodness Jenny get down here!" She screamed.

Then Billy and a couple of others hollered also.

"I'm fine." I said laughing. "Like being off the ground is going to hurt me or the baby." I argued.

Then this guy I hadn't met before reached up to take my arm and help me down, I was stuck on his dark brown eyes and skin and the most amazing smile I had ever seen.

I reached out and took his hand and got down. "Thank you." I said to him.

I looked at him and he was smiling that smile again.

"You're welcome." He said. "Look at you pregnant n' all wantin to climb up that tree like a little kid. You don't wanna hurt that baby or you, come on and sit."

So I followed him like a little puppy… lol at least that's what it seemed like.

"My name's John but most people call me Ballou." He said. "And your Jenny right?"

I know I was blushing, I could feel the heat in my face!

"Yep that's me, and this is my baby." I said, patting the small bump that was startin to finally show.

He rubbed my belly and laid his ear on me, on the baby. "Hi baby, I'm your mommy's new friend and I plan on stickin around. I can't wait to meet you." He said.

Talk about meltin my heart, he did!

John and I were a couple in no time, I knew I loved him so much, I couldn't believe how much he loved my baby that wasn't his, but he did. Everything we thought about for the future and our plans were about us and our baby.

It was hard at first, we stayed with some of his friends who ran a stripping company lol that was interesting. Finally we were able to get our own apartment and for the first time in so long life seemed to have some kind of purpose.

John was working doing odd jobs and I was on welfare but it was more than enough to keep us going. Months went by and we continued to be happy. We even loved the same music, country of course.

I was scheduled to have my labor induced on September 14, I couldn't wait to meet my baby. We decided on Amanda Lynn for a girl and Jonathon Drew for a boy.

As soon as he was born the Dr. held him up and he said. "Hi!" With this perfect little voice.

I was lucky my mama and the doctors heard it to lol. I couldn't help but feel sad for all of us that Danny wasn't there, I was so happy that John was.

Days and nights went by while I was slowly but surely learning how to be a mommy again. I missed my Joshua so much, I was so grateful to have my Jonathon and this second chance, someone up above really does love me!

It had been a long time since I had done anything fun that I didn't remember what that meant. One night John and a couple of our friends insisted I go with them but I didn't want to leave Jonathon. Finally they convinced me to go and have fun and our neighbor came and got the baby. Thank goodness his little bed had wheels cause they wheeled him out and into her apartment and locked the door before I could change my mind to bring him home and stay, so off to Cal-Skate I went. As soon as I got there I tried to call and check on him but she had taken the phone off the hook. I was having so much fun and even fell on my butt lol. It wasn't worth being away from my son though so soon I was home and he was in my arms where he belonged.

John and I and our brother Tim and his old lady Alex were going to the run at Beldon. They headed out on the bike and we drove our car but it blew up on our way there. Thank goodness we knew a lot of the people headed up so we were able to get a ride and even get the car there to get worked on.

They announced signups for the wet t-shirt contest and the guys convinced me to sign up so I did lol. Oh My Goodness, I knew a few of the people at the run and I still got up there with the other girls, it was pretty obvious that they were way more used to this than I was. They sprayed down the whole line of women instructing us to turn and pose and turn and pose again lol off with the shirts was next. As I was taking my tank top off I could feel the color rising in my face, I couldn't believe I was doing this, also I wasn't the … sexiest or the best looking!

When they were ready to pick the winner the guy stood behind each of us one at a time for the crowd to yell for their favorites … it was me! Amazing and so embarrassing, I'd never done anything like that before and I was way more conservative than most of the other girls. I won a 100 bucks plus 5 pound of bbq ribs, awesome!

Our Jonathon was about 4 months old when we got a phone call in the middle of the night. Usually those middle of the night calls were bad but this one was just the opposite.

I was in shock as I listened to my Joshua's grandmother on the other end of the phone.

"Jenny, this is Sara, you know, Tony's mom." She said.

"Of course, hi." I said to her. "Is everything alright, is Joshua alright?"

"Well, he is fine but we are not and Tony isn't either. It seems that he was arrested tonight. His wife and him got caught in a burglary and they had the boy with him."

I jumped up hitting John to wake him. "Get up, something happened!"

He sat up waiting to hear what was going on and she kept talking.

"The police brought Josh here with his clothes. Jenny I don't know what to do with this child, we work and we're busy. Can you come right now and pick up your son?" She asked me.

Oh my goodness, I couldn't believe what I was hearing. "Of course, of course I will! It will take me a second to get the baby dressed and we'll be on our way." I said to her. "Thank you, thank you for calling me!"

"Thank you also Jenny, I can't believe Tony! You kids better figure things out before this boy is the one that suffers!"

"I know, it's got to be so hard on him, tell him I love him and I'm on my way."

We hung up and I told John what happened and in minutes we had Jonathon loaded up in the car and on our way to Yuba City. I couldn't believe that in less than an hour I was going to have my boy with me, after all this time and everything we had been through! aaww thank you Jesus for another miracle!

When we got there I had John wait with the baby in the car until I went to see how things were going. They opened the door for me before I got to it and led me into the living room. Up on the counter I saw all of his clothes folded in nice and neat piles of t-shirts, pants, shorts and jammies.

"Hello, are these are his clothes?" I asked. "Where is my Joshua?"

She patted me on the shoulder. "He's down here in the room with his grandpa, he's had a hard night so you guys get him home soon so he can sleep." She said sternly. I understood though, that's their grandson and it breaks their hearts, for their own son also.

I peeked in the room and grandpa was sittin there on the floor with this most handsome seven year old boy, he looked up at me and I fell to my knees. His eyes were the beautiful clear blue I remembered, his hair was a perfect light brown and blondish color almost shoulder length. As soon as I was on the floor he was looking into my eyes and in a moment he was in my lap with his arms around my neck.

He laid his head on my shoulder and spoke so quietly to me. "I know you're my mom cause I have seen you at our house tones of times asking for me and I remember you." I tried so hard to hold back my tears, I didn't want to scare him. "I love you mommy and I'm tired." He said. "Can we go home now?"

I couldn't hold it in any longer. I started crying and rocked him, holding him tight as I could.

"Of course we can, let's get your things and load em up. John's in the car with your little brother, I can't wait for you to meet them both. I love you so much son, I have missed you and I will never leave you again, I promise!" His little arms tightened a little as he squeezed me one more time.

"Ok boy." Grandpa said. "Let's get your things in the car and get you home." Joshua went over to him and hugged his neck.

We headed out and John had already came in with the baby loading all of his things up in the car. They gave us a snack for the kids on the ride home, well Jonathon was a bit young for a snack lol other than the mama but that would have to wait. I was happier than I had felt in so long. I had my kids, both of them and on my way home to a new life!

They said their goodbyes to Josh and to us and we headed on back home, suddenly the word, 'home' had a brand new meaning.

It took a little time but soon it was like I had never lost him. He was my son and I was his mama and we were a family. We moved out of the little apartment that next month into a bigger and nicer apartment. It was so awesome and in the neighborhood I grew up in. It was right next to the Junior High School I went to and we got Joshua enrolled in the same Elementary school I went to also, so cool!

Things were going really well until one day John and a couple of the guys had to go to Oroville. While they were there they saw a friend from town that needed a ride back, they let him put his motorcycle in the back of the truck then him and his friend jumped in the back with the bike for their ride home.

It was a tragedy, something happened and the truck rolled, their friend Johnny was smashed against the barbwire fence and his bike. John held him in his arms until the paramedics came and he died soon after. The other two were hurt pretty badly, everyone got real mad at John but I don't think it was all his fault. Thank goodness they weren't drinking or smoking or using any other drugs. Not only did a lot of people stop coming around us after the accident but he had to go to Prison for 6 months for vehicular manslaughter.

I spent the next 6 months staying close to home and friends until he was finally released. I couldn't believe how much a child could grow in such a short time, I was sad that he missed the crawling all the way to the walkin and then some. Jonathon was 11 months old by the time he came home. I had breastfed him while John was gone and he had been sleeping with me in bed so that had to change right away and my poor baby boy was not happy about that at all! Poor guy screamed for three nights and my neighbors even threatened to call CPS on me at one point, but by the time those three nights and days were over he was a happy camper and sleepin in his own room with his brother and in his own bed, yes!

After John came home and he got a job all of us were able to start enjoying life and thinking about the future. He asked me to marry him and of course I said yes! We didn't have any money and my only income was welfare but my best friend and sister Leah bought our rings and got the dresses together. She even set up the food and everything we needed for our perfect wedding. My Jonathon wasn't happy not being with mommy so he was up in our apartment watching from the window with his auntie.

MINE AND JOHN BALLOU'S WEDDING PICTURE

When we got married Jonathon was about a year old and we starting talking about and planning to have another baby. About three months later I was pregnant and so happy!

Before the baby was born we had to move out of the apartment and into a mobile home we had found. The bus picked Joshua up for school every morning and Jonathon was home with me, life seemed to be 'perfect'. We weren't using drugs or smoking weed and only drank a beer now and then.

It was so awesome when we found out we were having a little girl. John had always loved the name Jasmine and loved the name Nichole so Jasmine Nichole it was! The months went by fast and before I knew it she was being born. Since Jonathon was 3 weeks late and they had to induce me they scheduled Jasmine's when I was 2 weeks overdue lol thank goodness!

I had the craziest craving while I was in labor lol all I could think about was how badly I wanted a hamburger but at that moment it was time for my baby girl to come into the world instead! After just a few pushes she was in the doctor's hands but something was wrong. He seemed frustrated like he didn't know what was happening, the next thing I knew him and John were gone. I screamed until Leah and the nurse came in, they calmed me down and went to find out what happened.

Finally after what seemed like forever John came in with the baby, looked at me and smiled. "Here is your daughter honey, Jasmine Nichole would like to meet her mommy."

I reached out for her and started crying, he leaned over and hugged us both.

"We almost lost her." He said to me.

"What do you mean?"

He pulled the chair up next to me and sat down. "When you pushed that last time and she came out I realized the dr. couldn't get her to cry or breath. He was just holding her like he didn't know what to do so I grabbed her and the suction thing and turned to go in the other room so you wouldn't know what was happening. Me and the doctor sucked a bunch of fluids from her little lungs, her couldn't breathe." He said.

"Oh my goodness I love you baby girl." I said to her.

Holding her I couldn't believe how precious our daughter was, she had the most beautiful brown eyes I had ever seen and this most perfect little face with all fingers and toes accounted for.

It was a busy summer and before I knew it, the excuse I had for not breastfeeding anymore was that I was drinking too much Pepsi, at least that's what I told my Dr. …

Soon we had to move again and found an apartment on 22nd. Sadly enough it fit into our old lifestyle, shooting up and selling speed came like second nature.

To us though we were doing way better than most people that were using and pretty much everyone we knew used. We always had someone on post watching the kids while they played outside with the other kids in the apartments. They weren't allowed to go out of the area we had given them, we didn't want them talking to other kids or anyone about what we were doing and inside they were always watched and or kept in their rooms.

When summer came around we had two accounts with our local ice cream truck guy, one for the kids' ice creams … and one for the dope we bought from him.

We had gotten pretty heavy into drugs and the business in no time. We stayed up nights, kept the house cleaned and since we didn't eat much I was always able to keep food in the house for the kids. In my knowledge of life we were doing pretty good, I thought.

One morning we had slept on the couch like we did a lot so I hadn't gotten dressed yet, I had my jeans on but not my shirt, it was big so I had it over me like a blanket. John had gotten the kids their cereal and set them up to the table to eat and got Jas in her highchair when there was a knock on the door. He opened it a tiny bit and a man was asking him about a car in the parking lot.

He told them it wasn't his and when he went to close it the man stuck his foot in the door a tiny bit and announced, "Probation Search".

Oh my goodness, before I could do or say or even think, they were in our apartment. There was a gun on me, there was a gun on John and there was a gun on each of my baby's at the table. I went to get up to get to the kids holding my shirt over myself when the cop pointing his gun at me told me not to move, I put one hand up in the air and held my shirt over myself with the other.

"Put both your hands up!" The officer yelled at me.

I looked down at my shirt. I don't know what he expected but there was no way I was moving my hand from holding my shirt and I told him so! Finally he had a female officer take me in the other room so I could put my shirt on, of course she found it her duty to tell me what an awful mom I was for being dressed, or undressed, in front of them the way I was.

Thank goodness I have awesome kids and they all sat where they were. They searched the apartment and then they looked over the water heater and gave a big, 'Ah ha', and pulled out a mirror lol and big thing of salt.

I had no idea where the mirror had come from but the officer was about lick it and John hollered. "Its dust and thanks for giving up my hiding place for the salt, she uses too much of it!"

He was laughing and finally I was to, but I knew what was in the hutch and one officer wouldn't quit searching it. I was thrilled when they decided they didn't find what they wanted and left.

I couldn't believe what hadn't happened! It took them awhile to leave our parking lot. They had stopped a friend of ours that came over while they were still outside, they searched her car and sent her on her way. When they were finally gone John went to the hutch where the bag was stashed and got it out. It was only like a gram but enough to have him violated and my kids taken away and me sent to jail if they had found it, we were so lucky!

Of course the first thing we did was to go do what was left, then we got the kids dressed and got Joshua off to school.

I don't know what happened other than pretty much nothing went right for very long at a time. We met Tattoo Dave, he had really good dope and he was amazingly sweet to me and did I say he was absolutely gorgeous? I couldn't believe that I was something he was interested in.

I was with him at his apartment when John came to bring me home to him and the kids. I wouldn't go with him so he almost drove the van through the door, he was so angry. I have no idea other than using the excuse of the drugs as to why I would even do such a thing, I wasn't proud of myself. I thought I was pregnant by him but by the grace of God I wasn't, thank goodness, and my husband took me back as his wife and our kids mama.

PICTURE OF MY JOSHUA JASMINE AND JONATHON

After a month or so went by David called me from Denny's and said he wanted to talk to me. I went to meet him in the rain. He was in his long black trench coat and told me he was leaving, kissed me goodbye, then turned and walked away. I didn't know when or if I'd ever see him again.

Feeling like we had watched ourselves go downhill long enough, we decided to leave Chico. We packed up our kids, ourselves and everything we could fit in our car and drove to Mendocino. We found a campground with space for our little 10 ft. trailer we called home. There we were, myself, John, Joshua at seven years old, Jonathon at three years old and Jas at one. We lived there for a little while and made money from picking mushrooms.

Once I had my aid transferred we were able to move out of the campground. We sold the little trailer and found a little room at the hotel that took the welfare vouchers. It was small and nothing to brag about but it felt almost 'normal' again. John was working at one of the fish places on the harbor and the kids were happy again.

That didn't last long though. John lost his job and so for money he got back into selling dope again. We found a larger trailer to rent and moved from the hotel, soon the parties were often and things were back to the way they were before we left Chico.

One morning I woke up and there were empty Pepsi bottles and beer bottles on the counters with cigarette butts in them and other gross stuff, both Jas and Jonathon were trying to get a drink out of one of the bottles. I jumped up and grabbed them. At that moment I knew my life was really bad but I had no idea how to change it!

Alaska Bound

John called his mom to ask for help and she told him that she was moving to Anchorage, Alaska and needed his help. Meaning, she wanted him to leave the kids and me and pack her up and drive her all the way there. Wow, she didn't want much huh? John left us waiting for him to return. Instead of him returning, I got a phone call asking us to join him in Alaska. He told me that he wanted to live there. There was nothing but trouble for him there in Mendocino and Chico, he wanted a new start on life.

He gave me instructions to sell everything we had. The furniture and anything else that would give me the money I would need for traveling. As time went by things were sold and I loaded my kids and myself in my car and made it as far as Seattle.

I called John, frantically. "We're in Seattle but I don't have the money to get the tickets to get the rest of the way, what am I going to do?"

"It'll be okay honey, we'll figure something out." He said to me.

"How is that? You are in Alaska and I am stranded with three kids in Seattle, Washington!"

"You'll see, I'll take care of it. You stay where you are and I'll call you back in a little while." He told me.

We found a spot close to the phone and got comfortable and waited. Soon it was ringing and John told me that his mom was buying our tickets so we needed to get to the airport.

We were so excited to be able to stop worrying and soon we were on our way through the great big sky. John and his mom met us at the airport, it was so cold. Duh lol it's Alaska! I better get used to this, I thought to myself laughing. His mom gave us a driving tour of Anchorage. While we were downtown on 4th avenue she warned us to always lock the doors and drive straight through, she said the same thing about Mountain View where we found our apartment.

We didn't have anywhere to stay at first so we stayed with John's sister, her husband

and kids for a little while, I felt so uncomfortable. To me, they were way better off than we were and lived in a big, beautiful home. They were nice n'all but it is easy to tell when someone isn't happy with someone else being in their space.

We managed for a couple of weeks and I was about to take the kids and myself to the shelter when my aid was finally transferred, we were able to get into a little apartment in Mountain View. It was a scary part of town but it was affordable and in no time John had got a job at another fishery. Soon his hours got later into the night ... pretty much every night.

***

I was sitting at the table reading the paper when I looked up at the clock, 'Dang, I can't believe what time it is'. I said to myself.

Heading out the door I could see the park on the corner where the kids were playing and hollered at them.

"Joshua, Jonathon, bring your sister in and let's get ya'll to bed."

They all came runnin up the road to me and into the apartment.

"Look you guys." I showed them the clock and we were all laughing. "It's 2 a.m. and it looks like noon." We laughed about the sunlight, then I started to wonder where their dad was.

I hate it when he stays gone at night after work, so many thoughts run through my head.

"Kay my boy Jon, will you go get mommy a diaper so I can get your sister ready for bed?"

He ran to the closet like supper man and comes back to me with a smile and those big blue eyes. "Here you go mommy, where's daddy?"

"He's busy, he'll be home soon I'm sure." I said to him. "Ya'll get into bed now and try to go to sleep, tomorrow we will get something up on these windows so you can sleep easier".

Taking Jasmine into her room I put her jammies on, got her tucked in and kissed her face. I stood there for a minute looking out the window wondering why I left home to go so far away for this, to always be alone just me and the kids.

"Night night honey. I'll see you in the morning, love you." I said to her.

"Love you to mommy." Her little voice said.

Then the boys hollered down the hall. "Love you mommy."

"Love you back, sleep tight."

I waited till the kids were asleep then walked outside and looked up and down the street. 'So, this is Mountain View', I thought. After what everyone told me about this neighborhood I can't believe we're here alone, it's so dangerous here. Gang members walking down the middle of the street, pushin each other around and getting louder and louder as they get closer. The sirens going off are as loud as can be, yep, here they come. There are always police around and someone was shot or stabbed at least twice a week.

I hurried back into the apartment and shut out the lights making my way to my bed.

'Shoot, I guess it will be another one of the nights I sleep by myself, I don't know if I want to do this anymore.' I thought out loud to myself. Finally I dozed off.

Lying in bed I could feel him climbing in next to me and reaching out to hold me. I sat up quickly.

"Oh hell no, are you crazy?" I said to him. "Where have you been all night?"

I looked at the clock, it was 6 a.m.

"Me and some of the guys went to the bar after work." He said to me. "I'm sorry honey, I wasn't doing anything wrong."

I climbed on out of the bed and went to the kitchen to make some coffee. Here it goes again I thought, one story after another. But to my surprise for the first time, he wanted to talk.

John followed me down the hallway. "Jenn, I have something to tell you. Come sit down kay?"

"I thought you needed some sleep, we can talk later."

"No, I need to tell you something, now."

The look on his face began to scare me, he looked so serious.

"What's up?"

"Jenny, I don't love you anymore. I am going to move out with a girl I met at work."

My mind was spinning, my thoughts flew all around my insides. My stomach began to turn into knots and I thought I was going to throw up.

"Excuse me?" I said thinking I didn't hear him right. "Are you kidding me?"

I was holding a big teddy bear he had just given Jasmine for her birthday. I threw it at him and hit him and threw it again and then again and fell to the floor in a fit of crying hysterics. I had ripped the teddy bears arm and I knew my Jas was going to be upset!

Oh my God, I thought. How long? How long have you been playing both of us? There were so many questions and no way to make even one of them come out of my mouth. All I could do was sit there and cry.

I head Jonathon's voice. "Mommy, what wrong with mommy daddy?"

Shoot, the kids, 'damn you John', I thought to myself.

"How dare you do this to us!" I yelled at him. "Go on John, get out and don't ever come back!" As I yelled in a total panic the kids cried along with me.

Of course they didn't understand other than mommy was falling apart and daddy was speechless, that didn't happen very often!

John sat down next to me. "Hey honey, come on. Please stop crying, you're going to get yourself sick."

"You just changed my whole life and you are worried about me making myself sick? You're back-assword and you can kiss my ass because who do you think you are sitting here being nice to me after what you just told me? Get out john, get out now!" I screamed.

"Mommy, are you alright?" Josh and Jonathon were trying to help me up to the couch. "It'll be okay mommy, you'll see. We only need you." They said to me.

I held on to my boys, 'thank goodness Jas was still sleep', I thought while we sat at the kitchen table watching John get his stuff and put it in the car.

"You're taking the car?" I asked him. "What am I going to do for transportation in this city with these kids?"

"You'll do fine, how do you expect me to get to work without a car?" He said. "I'll help you out if you need it."

"No, don't worry." I said. "I don't want to burden you, you just go on your way. We don't need you, we have each other and you don't have any of us. I almost feel bad for you, all you have is some hoochie you found stinkin like fish at your factory. Gross dude, hope you enjoy!"

He threw the last of his clothes in the car getting ready to leave when I heard Jass.

"Daddy, daddy." She said coming up the hall.

"Go back to bed honey, everything is fine." I told her.

"Where are you going daddy?" She asked. Seeing out the door to the car she could see his things. "Why are all your clothes in the car, are we going camping?"

"No honey." I said holding on to her. "Daddy's leaving."

"I'll come back later and talk to you about everything, I promise." He said hugging her.

"I love you daddy." She said. "Aren't you going to kiss mommy goodbye?" He looked up at me and I turned around and went straight to the bathroom, shut and locked the door and hollered at the boys. "Joshua, Jonathon, watch your sister for a minute please."

"Alright mom." I heard their sweet voices saying at the same time.

Sitting in the bathroom I could hear the car pull out of the driveway. Wow, he really did it, he really left the kids and me. I sat there, so many things running through my mind. What am I going to do? Where will the money come from? How will I get the kids into school? Oh my God, this is crazy, I thought as I came out of the bathroom.

"Alright kids." I said to all of them. "Let's get ya'll dressed check out the walk to the store kay? Help your sister and make sure her shoes are on." It took a little time but soon we were off, I had to get some fresh air and cigarettes!

We shut the door to our lonely apartment and began our first walk into the city of Anchorage.

A couple of days had gone by and I decided I had better do something for myself and these kids. We took the bus to the business college in town and as I was standing there with the kids just inside the doors I realized how scared I was. I felt so alone.

I guess I looked like I felt because I heard a voice talking to me. "Ma'am, are you alright?"

"Yes, I am. I don't know what I'm doing but I know I need some help." I told her.

Jasmine was clinging on to my left leg and Jonathon was on my right and my Joshua was sitting sweetly in a chair he had found.

"Looks like you have your hands full." She said to me with a reassuring smile.

"I sure do, I need to apply for the grants and stuff and I need day care for my kids but I really don't trust anyone and I don't know anyone here. Can you help me?"

"Of course we can honey, you sit right down here and we'll get started on the paperwork. There's a lot of it though, are you all up to it?"

It's now or never, I thought to myself. "Yep, let's get this going!" I said with a smile I don't think I had heard in my voice in awhile.

We sat down and I spent about two hours answering questions and signing my life away. By the time we were done the kids were tired.

"Mommy, can we go home now? I'm hungry." Jonathon said.

"Sure sweetie. Just another minute alright?" I asked him and he said back down shaking his head 'yes'.

"Are we all done now?" I asked the woman.

"Yes, close enough." She said. "The rest I can finish myself. Make sure you call the babysitters on the list I gave you and make sure you go meet each of them also before you make your decision. You can't be too careful these days. Everyone has to go through a process of being approved for day care though. These are the ones that are covered through your welfare program. You should have a check coming in a couple of weeks and classes will start on August 24th." She looked at them and smiled. "The kids should be in school by then right?" She asked me.

"Yes, but I think I'm going to sign up for night classes so I can spend the day at home, Jasmine won't be in school for a while. I'm going to go home and check out the referrals you gave me. I hope I can find someone like a grandma or something and someone to help me for evenings. Thank you for everything!" I said as I hugged her and she hugged me back.

"No problem hun, you take it easy now. Everything is going to be alright."

Scary but I sort of believed her. Could things finally get a little better … I thought to myself. I sure hope so.

"YaY." I said to the kids. "Let's see if we can catch the right bus home."

"Mommy." Jonathon and Joshua hollered at the same time. "Look, there's daddy and some lady." They were looking across the street from the bus stop.

"Come on, get up here with me." I said to them. "The bus is here."

I couldn't believe my eyes. This man and this woman in open public right in front of me and the kids.

"Shoot John." I hollered. "Couldn't you be a little bit more inconspicuous?"

I quickly loaded the kids on the bus. By then all three of the kids had seen them and John was turned and watching us get on the bus. I didn't know my heart could sink more but it did.

We found seats and settled in for the journey home. 'So it's real', I thought to myself. I looked at the kids, they all looked so sad.

"Come on guys, we're doing just fine aren't we?" I asked them with a smile.

"I miss daddy mommy." Jasmine said.

All three of them started crying one after the other. I held all of them as the buss took us across town to our humble apartment.

"Come on, let's get home and eat something ok?" I said as happy as I could.

"It's okay mommy." Jonathon said as we were stumbling off of the bus. "I will take care of you."

As I hugged and kissed him I could feel the tears on my cheeks. I wiped them away walking proudly down the street with my kids to our small but private place we called home.

Things were going alright I guess. It was summer now and John and I were doing what we could to be friends which helped with the divorce also. I couldn't keep up with the kids alone so we all moved into a little apartment and shared the bills. John, his girlfriend Debbie, myself and our kids … how sweet.

My drinking got pretty bad. With them there to stay with the kids it got real easy real quick for me to spend all the time at the bar I wanted. I had no idea where my life was going.

I met a man named Mike, we had one thing in common, alcohol. We spent lots of time together drinking until one day I got a call from my best friend and sister in

Chico. Leah was getting married and really wanted me to be her maid of honor. Oh My Goodness I was SO excited! John and Debbie agreed to keep the kids and we figured a way to get my ticket and I was off to California.

When I got home I stayed with Leah and her friends. I even got to go on a couple of bike runs with some of mine and John's old friends from the MMA (Modified Motorcycle Association), that I was the secretary for. It felt so good to see a bit of me I had forgotten about, the 'me' that was happy.

I hadn't seen Peter in so long. It was great when he came to visit Leah and I got to hug him, it was awesome to see a familiar face! In just a couple of days we found out we had to find somewhere else to stay.

It was easy for the two of us to convince Peter into renting a house for us to live in and soon I started going out with him. A short time went by when he asked me to marry him. I really felt bad because I knew I didn't love him that way and I knew I was going to go back to Alaska to my kids. He gave me a beautiful diamond ring and everything I would have needed for myself the kids, he even wanted to pay for my college and my daycare. He would have gotten me a car and anything else I needed but I wasn't comfortable with that. He got upset and hurt when I told him I couldn't marry him and I was giving him back his ring and going back to Alaska after the wedding. He told me I was using him and he got real mad. I knew I had used him but I could have taken his check book and diamond ring to Alaska with me like we had discussed, and not come back but I didn't. I still felt bad, we had been friends for so long.

The wedding was at the Durham Park and absolutely beautiful of course and it was even more awesome when I met Leah's new brother in law. I was pretty sure that I was in love again lol, he left to go home the next night.

A couple of days later I was getting ready to go home and I ran into one of the guys me and Leah used to hang out with, Rick. He was awesome and his smile was perfect and familiar and his heart was gentle, which melted my broken heart.

Next thing I knew we were on our way back to Alaska in his little car that got us to Seattle then we caught a plane the rest of the way.

It was so good to get home and hug my baby's, I missed them so much! John and Debbie and Rick and I were all laying around watching tv one night when there was a knock on the door. I hollered come in without thinking and there was Mike.

"Hi and welcome home, I think." He said. "I thought you might be back so I wanted to come check on you and see how your trip went." He looked at Rick and then back to me. "But it looks like your fine and your home safe n' sound."

I was a bit dumb struck and speechless. "Yep we made it back yesterday." I said.

He quietly waved goodbye and shut the door.

I looked at Rick. "I'm sorry, we had gone out before I left but pretty much the only thing we had in common was enjoying the bars."

We laughed a bit and put our attention back on the movie we were watching.

The summer was almost over and I had finally gotten my financial aid money so Rick and I went out and found me a cute little red car that I so desperately needed. How awesome it was even though it was red lol!

I had gone through the caregivers for the kids and was so happy that I found a woman that treated them like they were her own grandkids. It sure made it easier to go to school knowing they were safe!

I was taking night classes so Rick took us to drop the kids off then drop me off for classes and pick me up.

At first it worked out good but soon he started making it a regular habit of being 20 to 30 minutes late or longer to pick me up and that meant I would be late to pick the kids up to. When I asked him to stop doing that, that I wanted to start driving myself to school so I would have my car, he decided to go back to his wife and kids in California. This I'm sure was a good thing. I know they needed him. He had left his wife so easily, I should have known he would go back just as easily.

Again, other than having John and Debbie at my apartment and my baby's, I was alone.

I started to love going to school, taking paralegal classes showed me I was smarter than I thought I was, I was finally starting to feel alive again.

There was a guy in my classes that was a bit eccentric. He was always smiling at me and trying to talk to me but I ignored him as much as I could. One evening I left class for a minute to go to the restroom to clean my glasses. When I came out he was waiting there for me.

He grabbed my shoulders and put me up against the wall and said, "I think I'm falling in …"

I didn't give him a chance to finish what he was going to say.

I pushed him back. "Don't ever grab me like that again and you don't even know me." I yelled at him. "You need to just leave me alone!"

I went back into class, grabbed my books without looking at my instructor and left as fast as I could to get my kids and go home.

I wasn't too excited about going to class the next night but I loved being there. Of course he was there but this time he came up to me with a necklace in his hand and a sweet word.

"Hi, my name is Bert and this is for you." He said in such a sweet voice. "I'm really sorry, I didn't mean to scare you. Your name is Jenny right?"

I blushed and accepted the necklace. It was made out of hemp with a cute heart on the end and it was beautiful.

"Yes it is, hi." I carefully said in reply.

He helped me put the necklace on and then he gave me a hug.

"I just want to be with you and hangout." he said. "I'm not sure why but I feel something from you and I would just really like to get to know you."

After that we started hanging out a little and to top it off it was awesome meeting someone that smoked weed!

One night after class Bert invited me over to visit. He told me a friend of his was coming by and he wanted me to meet him. I honestly didn't like the idea at first but I really wanted to get stoned and meeting other people that smoked made me finally feel not so alone.

The next day was a Saturday so I had John watch our kids and I went to look for the house Bert had given me directions to. I thought I was going to get lost but it wasn't hard to spot the little blue house.

I sat in my car and waited, I wasn't going to honk and bring attention to myself so I was thrilled to see his smiling face come out his door.

"Thank goodness you heard me pull up." I said.

"Come on in." He hollered.

I got out of the car and we went inside. I could tell he liked me, he kept trying to get me to sit with him but all he was doing was making me uncomfortable.

"I think I'll go. I'll come back and visit tomorrow maybe kk?" I stood up grabbing my things to leave.

"No please don't go." He said, almost alarmed. "My friend will be here soon. He's the one I get my smoke from and I really think you guys will get along great."

He had the silliest and happiest smile on his face I couldn't help but to smile and sit back down. He loaded a pipe and we shared it while were watching TV, it had been forever since I smoked, it was awesome!

I was sitting on the chair when a man walked through the door. He was big and beautiful and all of a sudden my heart started pounding. I'm sure I was blushing, he was gorgeous!

He sat down on the couch and right away Bert spoke up.

"If I can't have you then I want my best friend and brother to have you." He said without a bit of shyness or awkwardness. "That way I will have both of you and the two of you can live happily ever after."

Oh my God, 'What the hell' lol, I was thinking! I couldn't believe what was happening, I was so embarrassed.

Bert came and held his hand out for mine and as if I were in a trance I gave it to him. He led me over to this man and sat me down next to him.

The man looked at me and smiled. "Hi, my name is Big John, and you are?"

"I'm Jenny and this is all really strange." I said laughing and feeling a bit embarrassed. "Im so sorry about this!" I said to him.

He put his arm around me and hugged me. "You don't have to be sorry, here want to smoke?" He handed me a joint to light and that was that.

We started spending more and more time together. It was so awesome when I pulled up to Bert's one day, John was standing on the back porch with two of his girls, Michelle and Jeanette. They were 10 and 12 years old, or close to that and so beautiful! The kids and I got out and the connection for all of us was automatic, it was awesome. He was the most amazing man I had ever met!

I finished the Paralegal program and next was my graduation. John and Debbie, Big John and all the kids were there. I hadn't felt as proud of myself ever as I did that day.

All along we had been living in different homes but being with each other every day so I wasn't surprised when he told me it would make more sense for me and the kids and him to get a place together so we could share the bills and always be together, it was perfect!

Life happened fast. This man and everyone in his life were becoming our family. Not the kind of family I had grown up with; moms, dads, cousins, aunts and uncles and stuff like that but with the man I was falling in love with. Brothers and sisters and nieces and nephews. People that we spend lots of time with. We spent birthdays and holidays together, any occasion was a reason to start a bon fire or to have a barbeque. Bikes, leathers, men and their women, my sisters, life was changing right before my eyes. My kids had more aunts and uncles and cousins than they had ever had before (they hadn't been raised with our biological family like I had), all of a sudden this was their family, our family, and we never had to be alone again!

We found a trailer in a mobile home park right near where Bert lived and our brother and sister, Keith and Karen and their kids Rusty and Sara lived there also lol on Karen Dr.

John's van backed up to the fence meant awesome music along with balloons being tossed in the air by the kids and his beautiful pit girl Shatsi jumpin to the music trying to bite them lol so funny! Him with the food on the bbq and our family sittin around the yard visiting and laughing with kids runnin everywhere. Food and family are the most awesome mix and catching our nephew Rusty and my boy Joshua trying to break into our room on video … priceless lol!

February 14, 1993 - Our Valentine's Day Wedding

Out on one of our crazy nights in the Valley with Keith and Karen along with four or five others, we left the bar with beer glasses up our leather jacket sleeves as we climbed into the van getting ready to go the next bar.

I heard Johns voice. "Jenny, will you marry me?"

I turned around in the driver's seat so I could see Johns face, he was setting behind me.

"What did you say?" I asked him.

"Will you be my wife?" He said again.

I was shocked and excited at the same time, I had no idea he would ask that question!

"Yes, yes I will marry you!" I said to him.

He jumped out of the van and came around the drivers' door. Opening it he picked me up out of my seat and started swinging me around, happiness and love was all I felt! We found the next bar to stop at and celebrated the rest of the night.

We picked the date, February 14 and we picked the place, the old train station in Palmer. There was a kitchen and a stage for the band and it was big enough for our family.

I didn't know how I was ever going to be able to afford a wedding dress, they cost so much. My brother Bert called me and told me to come down to the store right away. I drove into town and met him at the Salvation Army Surplus Store.

"What are you doing brother?" I asked him.

"Come on, come in here and check this out." He said with a huge smile on his face.

I walked from behind him into the store and saw the most beautiful wedding dress!

"Oh my god Bert, I can't afford this."

HER PLACE WAS WITH GOD

"Well, it has a rip down the train but they said they would fix that for you, anyways silly, I want to buy this for you."

I couldn't believe he would do something like that for me.

"You mean more to me than any other woman in my life, I don't get to marry you but my brother does so I get to get you the dress!"

I couldn't keep the tears from running down my face.

He reached over and hugged me. "I love you sis, and this is my gift to you and my brother."

"Thank you, thank you so much!" I said hugging him back.

"Come on honey." I heard a woman's voice say. "Come with me and let's try this on you."

The woman picked up the dress and I followed her to the dressing rooms. "Come on out when you're ready and I'll help you get it zipped up." She said.

"I think I need you to help me get it on, over my head I mean."

"No problem." She picked up the dress and carefully reached over me to guide the dress down around me. I looked in the mirror as we were getting it to set right and I couldn't believe what I saw, I felt like Cinderella getting ready for the ball. Wow, I was really going to marry him, it was actually becoming a reality. I was the luckiest woman in the world!

Going over the plans for the wedding it looked as if we have taken care of everything. The food for the reception was going to be set-up as a potluck. I was so scared that there wouldn't be enough of it. Although I didn't ever get to see the food, I was told that we had a heck of a spread! The band was ready for the day and we had a money tree set up. My sister Anna led the group to make the hall my lavender and white colors, the room was beautiful!

The night before the wedding I stayed the night with my maid of honor, Karine and John stayed at the house with Bert and with his best man Chuck. I didn't realize I was nervous until we were trying on my dress that night to fix the hem and as soon as they lifted the dress over my head and it fell to fit my body, I fell to the ground.

"Are you okay honey?" I heard Karine say. "Come on, let's get you to a chair to rest." She said and handed me a joint. "Thank you, that I can use right about now." We smoked for the next hour or so and then we continued working on my dress.

The next day my mom and her friend came up from California and surprised me, I wasn't sure if she would be able to make it, so awesome! As the time got closer we headed to the hall to get me ready for the awesome day. Myself and the other girls were

FEBRUARY 14, 1993 - OUR VALENTINE'S DAY WEDDING

in the bathroom at the Train Station getting dressed. Me sitting there trying to get my nylons and the garter belt on while I smoked a cigarette trying to stay calm was quite a comical sight lol! I loved John so much and I knew we would grow old in matching rocking chairs!

MINE AND JOHN KARASTI'S WEDDING PHOTO

Finally it was time, a couple of friends of ours sang our wedding song, and instead of the traditional wedding song they sang Love Will Build a Bridge by the Judds, it was amazing!

After the song was done my mom hugged me and laughed. "I would have never expected you to get married to the 'wedding song', you are far from traditional my beautiful girl." She said.

"Thank you mommy, I'm so happy you're here!"

My brother Bert wrapped his arm around mine and stole me from my mom as the cue for me to start my entrance into the crowded room of people. As I was walking I couldn't believe what I saw, everyone in Alaska that I knew was there and it was amazing! You never think that it will go okay or all the people will show up, this time they did. Except for my friend Anna, she led the decorations setup and then got too sick to come to the wedding. I sure did miss her being there.

As we walked I could see John and Chuck at the edge of the stage with Fernando waiting, holding the bible, ready to join us as one. Karine was of course already there, walking ahead of me (which was a miracle in itself, she had been in an accident, hit by a drunk driver a couple of days before and her back was real messed up. She was still there for me and she still stood up for me.)

As we walked Bert looked at me and told me how important I was too him and that this was one of the happiest days of his life to see me marrying his brother. When we got to the front where everyone was standing Bert slipped my hand into Johns. For that moment his hand seemed so large compared to mine. A big man with beautiful long blonde hair pulled back and braided looking as gorgeous as he always did. I couldn't believe my fairytale was coming true!

When the music finished Fernando spoke of how we were put together by God and all of our Alaskan brothers and sisters as a family to be as one. We all stood and listened until he was ready for us to say our vows.

He asked. "Who gives Jennifer to be wed to John?"

"We do." Spoke out my mom and Bert.

I don't think I have ever been happier in my whole life. As if everything in my world led up to this very day, this perfect wedding. We spoke our vows to one another and exchanged the most beautiful Black Hills Gold wedding rings and then he kissed me. I thought my knees were going to buckle underneath me. We turned to face the room, at that moment I saw again how many people were there, it was so awesome!

"I would like to introduce to you, John and Jennifer Karasti." Fernando said next.

Everyone in the room stood and yelled and hollered and clapped and whistled. How amazing! John had to hold on to me to lead me out of the room so that we could take a breath and change our clothes so we could meet with everyone for the rest of the party. I couldn't believe we made it, then and there it felt as if God's love had blessed me with more than I could ever imagine!

"Here Jenny." Keith's sister was standing there with this beautiful, black dress with pleats down the front of the dress and a low back.

"Thank you so much!" I said to her. "I had totally forgotten about something to change into, I was going to put my jeans on."

FEBRUARY 14, 1993 - OUR VALENTINE'S DAY WEDDING

"Congratulations, you two deserve the best of the world and I am sure you will have everything you have dreamed of."

I hugged her and thanked her again for the dress and went to the bathrooms to change. Of course everyone came in behind me, it was so amazing and I felt so special that whole day.

"Okay beautiful." John said. "It's time for me to take off your garter."

I was so embarrassed and could feel the colors in my face. They did the drum roll and yelled like the animals they are lol. After he got the garter I backed off and sat down at our table. John was up on the stage with his back to the crowd and Chuck was announcing that he was going to throw the garter belt. When he flung it all the guys dove for this poor thing, I have never seen so many men look so silly at the same time. Come to find out we had the top of the wedding cake up on the corner of the stage with the band so it would be safe but they kind of all dove on it lol what a scene to see!

"Hey, has anyone eaten?" I asked as Karine came up from behind me.

"Silly, the food is pretty much gone."

"Wow, I wasn't even sure if we had enough food for everyone." I said.

"Yep, all the food tables were full. It was beautiful Jenny, the most beautiful wedding I think I have ever been too." She hugged me and then scooted to where the photographer was setting up.

We took pictures and by then I was ready, I asked John about getting high ...

"Come my wife, and let's indulge." He said.

I followed him out to our van and oh my goodness lol, they had done it up quite well! Peanut Butter on the windshield with lipstick, the inside and outside handles of the doors were filled with peanut butter and whipped cream. It was crazy, I couldn't believe our kids lol. It didn't matter, the world and everything in it was perfect, especially when our brother Keith came outside and gave us some coke to do.

When it finally time to leave we went to the Lake Lucille Inn where we had rented a room and the honeymoon was on.

Three weeks after we got married I got a phone call telling me my Grandma Hoon had passed away. Our whole family was devastated, I had no idea how I was going to be able to get home to be there.

The next day John came home with a round trip ticket for me, our brother Cal had given it to him for me, our family is amazing! I scheduled my flights and was off to see my family home in California, even though going for a funeral was such a sucky way to have to see them.

HER PLACE WAS WITH GOD

I had to leave the kids at home so I wasn't staying any longer than I needed to, a few days later I was back on the plane to go home. After the services were over my sister had to go out of town so we didn't get to say goodbye.

I had a layover in Oakland and when the plane was getting ready to leave I heard them announce over the loud speaker, "Will the woman in the black Harley-Garb, please come to the front of the plane."

I looked down at myself, I don't know what 'garb' is lol I thought, but I have Harley clothes on so I suppose their talking about me? I got up and went to the front of the plane and my beautiful sister Dru was standing there out of breath and in tears.

"I was so worried I would miss getting to hug you good-bye." She said.

We grabbed each other and hugged and cried.

"I love you Jenny." She said to me.

"I love you to Dru, thank you so much for coming here!" She stepped back off the plane.

We continued our goodbyes with tears and smiles until they closed the door for takeoff.

I was so happy and my heart was so full! I couldn't believe how awesome the crew was. They held the plane and even opened the door for us to see each other before my plane pulled away, so cool!

One of the sweetest moments for my sister and me in our lives I think. The pilot and crew were all in tears as they clapped for us, what an awesome day even though we were saying goodbye.

The Talkeetna Blue Grass Festival - Summer 1993

Leaving for the weekend to the blue grass festival meant bringing everything from home including the kitchen sink lol so we had lots of 'stuff'. I was trying to catch the cans of veggies that were falling out of the truck when I looked up and saw one of the many most beautiful sights in my world, all the tarps connected to each other all the way to the end of the camp, five or six camps along each side of two full roads with Harley's parked at every one of them.

I could smell the water as Karen sprayed me to get my attention.

"Hey sis, come on." She hollered. "Get out here with us."

I looked up and Martha was on the other side of Karen with her towels and the bike awaiting her touch, I had mine to.

"Cool." I said. "Time to get greasy, I have extra's if you need em." I said waving my cleaning rags in the air.

I glanced up at the barbeques smoking with an aroma to die for and the coffee smelled even better, the bike wasn't bad either!

It was so cool when we all gathered, hearing each other's bikes, sharing a beer, a story and a bowl. I looked the other way and Karen had Lynyrd Skynyrd blaring, everyone was busy doin their own thing but we were all together as a family.

I would often be nervous with the respect that went with being, 'his'. He likes to keep the control in the open. Very loudly he would voice his possession-ship of me and let everyone know that I did as I was told, I was his. It was known what to do and what not to do. It was as if we had a club, he would have been the president. The club for us though was our family.

"Come." He would say, for me to be by his side.

"Mine is not for you to think or dream about." He would tell any guy watching me.

HER PLACE WAS WITH GOD

We were a great looking pair. Him, 6'2", 350 pounds or so with long blonde hair that reached the top of his butt. Blonde, naturally curled beautiful shiny hair pulled back in one long braid with headbands snug around his forehead. Leather Jacket and chaps that he taught me to put on him. A sensual moment as I perform such a feat as his leathers and there smell, it makes my heart skip a beat or two. Of course, I wouldn't argue it for nothing!

Me, 110 lbs, long brown hair, headband on with silver earrings and a smile. Tank tops and levy's were my normal attire, of course adding the chaps were one of my favorites ... for having clothes on I mean. My black boots and leather jacket topped off my outfits and my sisters were dressed the same. Except of course when we were washin the bikes and our bikinis and cut-off's would do just fine.

I grabbed the soap and the water and began carefully cleaning every nook and cranny of this beautiful motor. I tried not to look up as I was cleaning cause it made me nervous. When I did look up bein bout done, I could see that half our camp had stopped what they were doin and proceeded to watch the three of us shining up these magnificent machines. Of course they had set their eyes on us so as we finished we dance around a bit to the music and gave the boys a short show. It is sure to bring a smile to all their faces and ease any tension.

The guys came over to inspect our work. "Pretty good ladies, we have what you want in the trailer, come on before it's all gone."

It took us only moments to head in for our lines, awesome!

We decided to clean up and get some clothes on to head to the party to listen to their music. I loved blue grass, it seemed to get the beat going on the right track. John was leading everyone down to the party. The younger guys were walking behind us waiting for direction.

"You boys grab the chairs and follow behind us and hustle!" He would holler to them.

John and I roared up ahead on the bike, the wind and the smells of the barbecues, I loved being on the back of his bike. Keith and Karen were coming up behind us on their bike and Fernando and Martha also.

We got down to where the bikes had to be parked and jumped off looking around, the bikers 'Carma Control' were in their full glory as always, to cool!

Walking on down to the gates the bikes sat one by one by one and on and on and on. They were new and old, big and small. Loud and quiet and some being worked on and booths were set along the grassy path. Friends of Johns had a booth for massaging feet, Steve's wife was always so sweet to me but we never really had a chance to talk to each other much. The couple of times we met had been at club gatherings or at a house party but because of the nature of the affairs, woman's conversations weren't meant to be shared by the ears of the brothers.

THE TALKEETNA BLUE GRASS FESTIVAL - SUMMER 1993

We visited for a minute as one of her customers showed up so we said our goodbyes. I quickly caught back up with everyone else. They were working through the crowds of people looking for a space big enough for the group of us to get comfortable. John and all the other guys strutted to the edges to move people as they spread the blankets. We made room for their chairs to be placed for the men and we are settled at their feet as they spread out on the blankets, probably six or seven of them on the ground for all of us. There was plenty of room for the food and for kids. We all placed our personal things in a nice safe spot for when it was needed, i.e. pipe, nummy (weed), bindle and straw, oh yea, and money.

The count would have been incredible, I would guess maybe 12,000 people? Something like that.

It was time to take the order. "One, two, three, no ... you want me to just get ten beers?" I asked.

John looked at me with his beautiful smile. "Good girl." He said. "That'll do."

Me, Karen and Martha fumbled to get the money from everyone to go get the beer run started. The rest of the day consisted of singing with the bands and watching our brother Bert get totally drunk lol. He surprised us, he was always a bit out there when he drank but his intentions were always good. He got a bucket and started on a mission of collecting can tabs for minutes on a dialysis machine for sick kids. He got the people on stage to announce that he was out there and what his mission was and he worked the crowd something fierce! Every now and then though one of the guys would have to go rescue him because he said the wrong thing to the wrong girl or he was going to get his ass kicked for taking a tab from someone's beer without asking lol. How funny. He always seemed to manage, even though we had to baby sit, that's what family was about.

As the day went on we had drank and talked and played and drank some more. Kids were getting tired and cranky and so were some of the men.

"Come on honey, let's get back to camp." John said.

"Yep, let's get out of this crazy crowd. Looks like everyone's been doing too much of somethin." I said as we looked around.

We were surrounded by groups of everyone fully and totally enjoying the choice of music and presence in general. Finally getting everything together we push through to the back of the crowds. I love it, what an awesome place to be. As we were coming out from all the people a group of the kids came running from the water and through the woods to us.

"Hey mom." I heard Joshua's voice holler.

Rusty and Joshua were in the front and Jonathon and Jasmine, Michelle and Jeanette with our dogs Shatsi and Mortique following all of em'. Everyone knew not to mess with our kids, especially with them dogs round!

"There are people swimming naked down there!" they said in shock with stunned looks on their faces.

We tried not to laugh but it didn't work lol.

"They call it Naked Beach, can you believe it?" The kids were all laughing and having a ball.

"Come on guys, back to camp with us." Even with their little arguing about how it would be more fun there lol, they happily followed us back to camp.

As me and Karen were coming up from the bathrooms the kids were screamin and laughin runnin towards us.

"Mom Mom hey watch out dads shooting the scary things, I mean fast things!" They said actin sceered but it was obvious they were having so much fun lol.

We were all laughing and then it 'swooshed' real fast! I looked at Karen and the kids.

"You mean bottle rockets?" I asked.

Then 'swoosh' again and pop pop lol we all ran. Kids one direction and me and Karen jumped into the van until we realized they were shooting em under the van where the gas tank was lol we were out of there! We ended up back at camp doin a line instead of stayin to get got!

As evening came again the music from our stereo sounded strong. You could smell the different odors from each and every barbeque. To melt for were the different smells and the laughter with the fires crackling and groups of people talking (I can hear it as if it were yesterday). We would all eat and share stories of our day, it's so hard to explain … we all just fit so perfectly together.

The partying starts and the firecrackers are set off. The guys hung about 3000 firecrackers around the camp in the trees. John lit the first one and on and on and on it went. This noise was one of the loudest I had ever heard. But to top that, a moment when Karen and I, Keith and John were standing around talking under a tarp (protecting us from the rain) at camp, John pulled my 9 mm Macarave out of his waist and pointed it up and shot it off right next to my ear and as he shot up the water came down bout on my head lol. I tried to get out of the way but my ears were ringin, I couldn't hear much for hours that night. Scared the shit out of me too, that's for sure!

As it got later everyone had pretty much picked which fire they were going to enjoy. If someone needed something they would come through looking and smoke a joint and get another beer. Sooner or later everyone would start quieting down, getting ready for tents and sleep, well, as long as no one was too drunk.

THE TALKEETNA BLUE GRASS FESTIVAL · SUMMER 1993

The next morning while John and I were walking around we found a tent where they were doing tattoos.

"That's what I want, I want my butterfly finished. Everyone always tells me that it looks like a scorpion."

We went in and paid them and they handed me bottle after bottle to drink while the work began. (To cool I thought to myself, a woman doing the work, this would keep John from getting upset about anything) I settled into my chair and leaned back.

"Kay, this is comfortable, maybe it will be easier than I thought." I told Amy, the woman doing my work.

That didn't last for long! As the tattoo needle began its journey, so did the bottle of tequila to my lips. John had left to do something while she was working on me and in the mean time I had gotten chilly so they gave me a shirt to put over my shoulders. About a half an hour had gone by and then another half an hour, I was surprised he had left my side for that long. All of a sudden he came in the tent and was standing over me.

"Where the fuck have you been?" He yelled at me.

My eyes shot open quickly looking up at his face in mine. He was bent over me and yelling and in my face. Talk about a real quick wakeup call!

"Whoooo girl." Amy said quietly.

He kept yelling and I kept trying to explain to him that I hadn't gone anywhere. He said that he had looked in the tent a couple of times and it wasn't me sitting in the chair. I told him I was chilly so they let me put one of their shirts over my shoulders and that I was so sorry. The last thing I wanted to do was to have him pissed off at me!

She was trying to keep my blood from going everywhere, my heart started beating heck a fast and my blood did as told lol, what a mess!

That started one of those nights, one of the nights when he yelled and I followed. I obeyed and he ordered. Damn, I wondered how long it was going to last this time. As always, somehow he figures out that I didn't do anything wrong and he is sorry. As the afternoon went on, things mellowed, we ate and we listened to the music and did lines. Later that night John and I took a walk through the paths of cars and camps and bone fires. To cool, the night was so bright. The festival is the first weekend of August, the sun has begun to descend a little earlier than it had in June but it was still beautiful with the moon shining and lighting up everything around us.

Everyone was saying hello and passing a joint so John would stop and talk and some of the guys would flirt with me. These were the only men 'Carma Control', I can ever remember that were allowed to talk to me the way they did, makin me blush n'all. I love these guys, they had a way of keeping a womans attention that's for sure.

We were walking on the beach over the rocks looking for a place to smoke and we heard someone hollering at us.

HER PLACE WAS WITH GOD

"Uncle John, Aunt Jenny, come over here." It was Day and Cort.

We walked up and a group of the kids that didn't know us were getting a bit nervous, John didn't have any trouble being intimidating.

"You kids stayin out of trouble?" He asked them.

Day came up to me and then to John and gave us a hug and Cort came up to us and did the same.

"I love you Aunt Jenny, you guys getting ready to head out?" He asked as he was hugging me.

"In the morning I think, I don't want to drive out of here without sunlight." John said to him.

"Uncle John, do you want to smoke with us?" Cort asked.

"Sure, but you have to smoke mine too." He chuckled and smiled as we passed one of his beautifully rolled, Matanuska Thunder-fuck joints around.

MMMmm nummy! After we got the kids toasted they all wandered off to do whatever they had to do and we found our way back to our camp.

Lying in our tent we could listen to everything going on around us. It was cool, we could always hear stuff that wasn't intended for other people to hear. I felt bad like I was spying on em or something lol not, specially our kids.

We Live in Houston ... Houston, Alaska That Is!

One beautiful snowy winter night in the Matinuska Valley, there were some teenage girls that knew they ruled it all.

They blasted through the door, our girl was in the lead telling us that Officer Donald was comin in from behind. With that I put the cocaine in the bedroom but forgot about the joint on the table. They came in and sat down while Officer Donald made his way in to talk to us, I reached and picked up the joint as non-chalant as I possibly could. It was obvious that he saw it but thankfully he was more interested in what the girls had been doing. They all came up with their stories and I was sticking up for them to Donald until I realized what had happened. The girls stole the stereo and then walked, in the snow mind you so that there were tracks marking their every step, back to the shed in the front of our trailer. He had followed the tracks to the door of the shed and knocked.

The girls thought it was John. "Go away dad we're smoking." They yelled to the knock at the door.

Of course he opened the door and the girls headed directly for the house with their warning. Talk about close calls? When he came into the artic entry and into the house he walked right past our make shift door that led into our grow room John had built off the entrance, ingenious lol!

It was crazy for a bit but finally things calmed down after they gave back the stereo, and so did the night thank goodness. Better yet, no one went to jail!

HER PLACE WAS WITH GOD

I got a call one day from the Elementary School and they wanted me to come in right away. My kids were always in trouble for one thing or another but both Jas and Jonathon at the same time?

When I found out what happened it wasn't one of the million things that flew through my mind. I soon learned that Jasmine had got caught on the school bus, in kindergarten, trading a bowl of weed to sit next to a boy and Jonathon was smoking a bowl at the bus stop when it got there to pick them up that morning, oh my goodness! As we sat there in the office my heart was pumping so fast. They were asking me who what when where and how something like that could have happened. Of course I told them it was mine and I was addicted, that no one else even knew about it, easy way to keep the problem just on me. They drug tested the kids and sent them home with me. They were suspended for the rest of the week and then it was like everything went back to the way it was and no more questions asked …

One of our sisters and her hubby and their kids were raising dogs and racing in the kids races. One summer they let Jonathon come up and spend time with them to get to know the dogs and help train them and him. When it came time for the Jr. Fur-Rondy they let my boy race! He won the third place beautiful blue ribbon at the Willow Race and the Sportsmanship Trophy at the Junior Fur-Rondy, so proud of him! He was having a really hard time in life and school, it was so good for him. Jonathon, Jasmine and myself spent a big part of that winter in town watching the races, I love them so much for doing this for him!

We had a lot of barbecue's and get-together's between our place and Karen and Keith's and then on to Marta and Mikes or Debbie and Arthur's. Either place, we were always together. Whether it was in the Bronco, the Van the Snow Machine or the Harley we were there.

We drank and danced and played quarters and snorted lines of coke. The most of us resembled each other's attire. Black jacket, vest under the jacket. A black t-shirt advertising the one and only Harley Davidson with snug Levi's held tight by the chaps. The fit is a sensual one, around the waist and down the inner thigh of the leg, he never had to tell me twice to help him with his chaps. Ending with a pair of black leather boots that are as sturdy as the motorcycles they rode. Looking up to the man

WE LIVE IN HOUSTON ... HOUSTON, ALASKA THAT IS!

I'm describing I see the most handsome face and the bluest, clear eyes with stories so deep inside. The headband snug around his head, his long blonde hair is pulled back and braided. As I stand next to him I can smell the leather that covers his whole body, I have to step back to give him the room to straddle his beautiful 1978 FXE Harley Davidson, aqua blue with the shine to match his eyes. The shine sparkles with pride, we had put many hours working and cleaning on this baby. He pulls on his gauntlets, soft leather covering each finger one by one.

He looks over at me. "Come." No other words were needed.

I had already worked on getting my helmet on and my gloves to be ready when he told me to get on, there was no hesitation. We seemed to have it down to a perfection as no others. Stepping up, reaching out with a sturdy hand to hold his shoulder for support, lifting my right leg and holding a stance with the left. My body swings over the bar and the back of the motorcycle with ease as I fit into the seat behind this man in all leather. 'Yep, perfect fit', I think to myself with a smile.

As the night went by the food was eaten in its entirety and the beer isn't spared either. The ones that dare the road would be the ones to make the beer run, hopefully it would be one that hadn't drank anything or at least not much. The fire pit turns into the biggest bon-fire I'd ever seen. Raging heat that mixed with the cold air so that your body didn't know if it was supposed to be hot or freezing.

From inside the house the kids were calling all of us to come inside. Me and Karen and Marta went to check it out. Walking into the kid's bedroom it was quite a comical scene. Our kids all sitting on the top bunk with their shirts over their legs showing their shoes so that they look like little munchkins.

They were rocking back n' forth singing the song, "Everybody must get stoned, everybody must get stoned." lol their so funny!

The kids were always in their own world, their all so good. Even putting up with us they still had smiles on their faces and are always ready to do something to make someone happy. As we started to get to drunk they would make beds all over the living room. Everyone would come in and kiss their kids and then try not to stumble on someone else's while climbing over everyone to get out of the room, then we had to remove Bert because he was peeing out the screen window where the kids were all going to sleep, oh my!

Everyone was so different in their own ways but then again we entwined our lives so that we all seemed to be the same people. In certain ways Keith & Karen's life was a lot like mine and Johns, we didn't talk about what happened behind closed doors. He was demanding of Karen, but her, like I, learned to do what needed to be done before we were told to do it. It seemed to save a lot of heartache that wasn't needed. We were a family and spent all our time together either partying or riding or both. Most of us were pretty bad drunks including my brother Bert. He was always the one wanting to start a fight with the biggest and badest, which was usually Big John.

Some of us would stay up throughout the night, others would find a floor space or a couch and pass out. Some would end up at the bar waiting for the rest of the world to come back around and ready to do some more dope.

We'd get food together and make a breakfast in the kitchen so when the kids woke up we could feed them and start our day right. After we played pool and ate and got impatient we all headed up the hill to another brother and sisters place. I loved being there, her outhouse was made up so sweet. Little flower boxes and bookcases and curtains and it even smelled nice. She was an artist so there were paintings of them and their kids, beautiful portraits. 'Dang, I could never do anything like that', I thought, what a gift to have. None of our gifts could survive with the drugs though, they superseded pretty much anything of any worth in all of our lives.

We played pool and snorted coke until the kids were ready to get home then more dope when we got home and kids were snug in bed.

One night when we pulled in to the driveway John and I were ducking and sneaking into the house. We walked through checking all of the rooms, the children were asleep down the hallway in their rooms. John had me pick them up and bring them into the front bedroom, our room, to sleep in our bed where we could see them to make sure they were safe. He went into the closet and pulled out our two machine guns. I had played with them some with John but they were still intimidating. For some reason my delusions over-took the guns and myself, they were nothing but pure power. I threw the strap of this machine over my neck and held is as if I had been born for it.

"Jenny." He said so seriously. "Don't get out of the sights of the kids. I don't want them to get in and get them." John was yelling in his loud whisper down the hallway to me.

We were pacing the house and looking out the windows. We were sure someone was out there and they had been hiding in the trees and now they are going to come in the house. We were going to kill them before they killed us.

What's My Image?

Such a description, maybe one I've always wanted to speak but could not, always hiding and protecting. Major excitement, all of the me's, I can now share with you. Wow, I've never quite counted the differences.

Me, a smile, a soft word, a kind word.
Me, mischievous, unaccustomed to obeying a rule, doing exactly the opposite of what I was told to do.
Me, disliking a harsh word, a harsh hand, fear and doubt.
Me, exploding with that harsh word spewing forth, unexplained, never understood.
Me, afraid of nothing and everything in the same breath, excepting a challenge, either that or offering my own.
Me, Yes, my favorite. Black leather, silver earrings, my headband, black with purple and red roses with the famous words we know so well, Harley Davidson across my forehead. Making a stand, screaming out loud for everything together.

My head spins and my heart pounds, day by day by night such a thrill, levy's nice and snug, my eagle belt buckle and my leather jacket and boots, my clothes fit every movement of my body, every curve and thought.

I, at that moment, could accomplish anything I set my eye on for our life was an absolute party, barbeque and every day celebration with our music, bars and family!

Fear of the Night

Drugs make the imagination turn into memories of a reality that could have been done without …

After that night things kept going. Day in and day out, some were longer, some were shorter, some were easier to survive than others. Our kids had to figure out how to do what needed to be done, to eat, get to school and everything else they had to do without us pretty much.

John and I headed to town one night, I thought we were just going to see one of his friends or something but instead we pulled up to one of those XXX 'book stores'. I figured he was just picking out another movie …

We went in and I stood there while he held on to my hand, to keep me next to him I'm sure. I didn't look at anyone as I followed him through the store. We were sent into a back room and then to a small room. It wasn't any larger than a closet, there was a tv and video's and a chair. He was working on picking the video when he took some lingerie out of small bag I hadn't noticed he was carrying. He handed it to me and told me to put it on lol in here? I looked around and with no room to change, of course I did it anyways. He turned to watch me while he worked with the movie he had picked out.

When I was done changing into what he wanted me to be, I realized there was a hole in the wall.

"Hey." I asked. "What's this for?"

He bent over to look, stood up and smiled. "It's a peep hole and there's a man in there." He said with a more lustful smile. "Look into it and let him know you can help."

"What do you mean I can help?" I asked laughing and thinking he was joking.

"Just do it." He said.

So as usual, I did what he told me to. As I peeked in and looked around I saw the man, regrettably so he saw me to.

"Go ahead honey, put your mouth up to the hole."

I did ... and while 'that' was happening and my eyes were closed, John's hands and body covered mine. Forcing the escape into never-never land had become my place of solitude.

I begged in my mind for it to stop, I was so ashamed and had never been so embarrassed and felt so dirty.

When it was finally over we got dressed and he led me from the store as if we were leaving the grocery store.

Another night we were driving home from the Dead Dog Saloon and there was a car in front of us. John recognized her as a woman that had been at the bar earlier. He wanted to get her to pull over and for us to do a line but I was pretty sure there was more to it than that.

He flashed his lights a couple of times and she stopped. I got out and went up to her car to invited her into the van with us to get high. She was hesitant but I convinced her and she climbed in with me to join John. He had the lines ready, we did those then he turned the music on and put an arm around her and kissed me and then went to her, then back to me. I looked at her and her eyes were wide as could be and as unsure of what to do and why this was happening as I was. (I knew I could never be enough for this man, there was always another woman whether she was with us or thought about with us or through a movie or magazine).

He unbuckled his belt and put my hand on her breast at the same time so he could watch us while he got ready. We went down to his lap, first one, then the other, then both at the same time. All of a sudden she jumped up and out of the van and got in her car and drove off. He looked at me in that moment, we finished what we had started and went home again like nothing ever happened.

I go to my room and sat on the edge of my bed looking at my clothes. Kay, we're going out tonight, a pretty big party they said. At first I feel nervous like I could go inside the closet, close the door and stay there hoping nobody will want to know where I am. But of course, it doesn't happen that way. He looks down at me with that devious smile and opens my drawers one by one to get a quick glance at what was there to choose from. He holds up a shirt, nope, neckline is too high. Next, nope, long sleeves won't do. I stood up, walked into the bathroom and sat on the toilet for a minute with the door locked. I didn't have to pee but he didn't know that. Taking a long deep breath I flushed the toilet and walk out ready to start the show.

In that few minutes I was gone he had been busy picking out clothes and had laid out a couple of pieces he thought would be appropriate, or inappropriate you could say.

Starting underneath the garter was first, stockings, then underwear that made me blush. I slid them on with a little wiggle that seems to break the intensity, much better. Now to continue and to act coordinated and hook the little thingy's on the garter belt lol. Me standing there only slightly dressed, waiting for him as he picks out a bra.

"Yep." He said with a smile handing it to me. "Here you go."

I stand in front of the mirror turning and looking at the 'me' I didn't know. Tall, great legs, perfect little butt (he always told me), flat belly and up to my breasts. Smaller than most maybe but in the black lacey bra I look just as sexy as the girls in the magazines and video's ...

Taking a couple more glances at the person I was becoming I feel that tinge of excitement run through my body. The sense of doing something that I'm sure I shouldn't be.

"Okay, assume the position." He tells me.

His smile is obvious and being proud of himself is nothing he would hide.

Up go my arms, for a moment I feel like a child being dressed until the mirror is in front of me again. No child here that's for sure! Wiggling and squirming, pulling my dress down over my boobs and then my hips, it doesn't go much further than that. 'Nock ya down fuck ya dresses' are what we call them.

He spins me around, hands me my silver jewelry, each ring, unique in itself. Then silver earrings and silver for my neck. He plays with my hair a bit and decides I should leave it down. Dark, thick, long brown hair with a slight wave and lots of attitude.

Him, a much simpler job of dressing. The levy's out of his drawer, a black Harley shirt, yep, now the chaps. He tightens the belts as the legs fall free. This was my job, pull the two sides together and gracefully as possible I zip up the leg, then the other. I fold his headband, perfect I must say myself. Then he grabs his boots and wipes them a bit, shiny as can be. Finally we're ready to go, whoops, I forgot my shoes. Running in nylons doesn't work very well. Just as walking in heals doesn't work very well in the snow, I could do it, I could do anything! Its winter time so the bike has to stay put in its warm garage, spring never came soon enough.

Jumping into a nice warm van sure felt good after being outside, even though for only a moment or two, we had to let it run for a while to keep it warm. Getting in to a cold vehicle just isn't a good thing to do in my 'nock ya down fuck ya dress'. Vroom, goes the motor and we're off.

FEAR OF THE NIGHT

Pulling up to my sisters' house was always so awesome. The music blaring out the windows and no one caring about the snow on the ground, everyone comes out to great us.

"Hey, there you are." They said. "Thought you'd forgotten your way or somthin."

Lights, Camera and action, here we go. My leather jacket over my shoulder and his on his back we walk around the house. Out back a bon fire from hell was burning beautifully. Big flames to keep minds distracted, everyone swarms around us.

"Here's a beer, here's a drink, do this line, smoke this joint, now let's do another line, it went on forever.

The music gets louder, the looks intensify.

A man would say. "I know who you are, you're his wife right? Man, I'm sure glad he is my friend, maybe he won't want to fight tonight."

As the night passes things turn in to a blur. In and out, compliments and glances, me and my sisters, other women were jealous, other men couldn't keep their eyes off of us. Leather everywhere and men with power.

The night never ends, the next day begins, then the next, and then another, then one or two more days go by. Oblivious of my being, fear becomes my friend and the unknown becomes a playground.

Now I'll close my eyes and hope that when I wake, my breath is still warm. All of a sudden my eyes open slowly, the feel of hands, yep, more than two I can feel on my body.

Without saying anything I say a prayer in my head. 'Help me get through this Lord'. Oh my God, I had to keep my eyes closed. It's over finally and I hear movement around me, music is playing soft and I could hear her tell him goodbye.

What happened in this bed? I don't want to know. So I block my memory by the secrets, but they stay. Oh shit, I have kids at home. I hope their okay, I call them and tell them I'll be home soon. Climbing into the steaming hot shower I begin washing off whatever was there. Maybe to feel clean again.

I loved it when we went out with our brothers and sisters, we were an awesome sight. Same preparations as before but hopefully this time it included boots and Levi's (with a perfect spot for my 9 mm and the dope) on a cold night instead of one of them 'dresses' with heals, lol on icy sidewalks.

Making money was always on the menu and I was his saleswoman. We controlled the place with the dope and the attitude, there was never a dull moment. I wasn't much of a drinker but I wouldn't turn down a tequila sunrise or a baileys n' coffee.

I had a deal set up and met with her in the bathroom and of course after a couple of drinks at the last bar I had to pee, so in the small stall the deal was done while I sat. We

HER PLACE WAS WITH GOD

leave the bathroom and I go back to the table. They were putting a few lines together for all of us then she was on her way.

I sat next to john and he looked at me and smiled. "Hey hun, you do know that's a dude right?" He asked me.

"Excuse me?" I asked him with a look of terror I'm sure. "John I peed!"

All he could do was laugh so I punch him and hard!

"Don't worry." He said reaching to pull my chair next to his keeping it strong where it was so I couldn't move it.

"You're fucking crazy! I can't believe you had me do that without telling me and you don't even care!"

He couldn't quit laughing while he tried to convince me not to stay mad.

"Honey look at me." He said turning my face to his. "She, he, has been like that since I've known her. She lives as a chick and that's all. I wouldn't have let you do the deal like that if I was worried about her at all."

We order our drinks and the music starts on queue. I really wanted to be mad but his control was obvious and respect was demanded. A few of my sisters and myself went out to the dance floor and a brother asks me to dance. John made it clear the answer was 'no', that it wasn't going to happen.

"So take his place." I told him.

He comes to the floor and takes my hand. Holding it he swoops me up as I melt into his arms like I do every time we dance. We fit like perfection, I couldn't help but to give up me, to him.

The other guys that didn't just get a 'no' lol, they gave me the chance to practice how fast I could save leathers, helmets, smokes and drinks in a hot second when the fights would start. They never lasted long that's for sure. Our 'normal' comes back and the night goes on.

After the bars closed sometimes we'd go to one of the after-hour joints, it always made me a bit nervous. They were more of an older and a bit untrustworthy crowd but he always had money to make and for me, a bottle of Cognac was a gift I didn't regret. We called a cab for the ride home, when they pulled up the police did also and even though we were getting in the cab they took my bottle, opened it and poured it out and sent us on our way. Oh My God, I couldn't believe them!

Life continues ... the nights out, the hours at the bars, the party's and the drugs, it didn't go away.

Different nights mixed together, I don't know one from another. There was never

FEAR OF THE NIGHT

a shortage of porn magazines and video's ... including our own. The pressure of his hands holding me where he wanted me to be was a bargaining tool that always won out, I couldn't move. Obeying him left me available for anything used in, on and all over my body with ... for whose pleasure, mine?

One of his favorite nights on the town would be the show we put on for whoever could see in the windows of our hotel room looking over the city streets of 4th avenue. My body clothed in sexy lingerie with his body against mine pressing me into the window. Clothes are discarded and my body is used to show others how our 'love making' is as lustful as one of his movies ... between this man and me.

We would move in different positions or areas of the window depending on where we needed to be, to be seen clearly.

During our drug use and partying I started bleeding and it lasted for five or 6 weeks before I went to the hospital. They did an ultrasound and found out I had been pregnant but the baby was dead. I was angry but relieved that I knew what was wrong. I was sad but grateful, the last thing we needed was another child. This would have been such an addicted baby, poor little thing. And again, what a mom.

Blue Grass #2

The year flew by and before I knew it summer was here and it was time for the festival. We rented a motor home to go in style and for our friends that were getting married at the Blue Grass this year, how exciting! We were ready to go with a dozen cases of Steinlogger, 20 cases of Reiner and two pounds of YuM, Purple Cush.

It was a trip that would surpass no others. When we got to the Blue Grass the 'Carma Control' greeted us with loves and smiles as always but this time they asked John if he would please be nice this year lol.

We parked in the back with a perfectly fitted space for us between all the camps that were being set up by others in our family. So awesome, my mom was even coming up to join us for the day while she was visiting.

Toni was beautiful in her wedding dress and I wore a short, cute white dress with my hair pulled back and braided. They were riding the couple up to the stage as John pulled up to get me. Jumping on the back of his machine it was this awesome man and me riding through the spectators and venders and up to the stage we rode.

Everyone clapped as we took our places on the stage, the wedding was perfect, beautiful and it went off without a hitch!

After the wedding we got on the bikes and rode back to our spots that were waiting for us. Time to get comfortable and to enjoy the music and family until it was time for our performance. Me and my mom got up on the stage and sang a song my mom had written about our lives when we lived in Yuba City and I was pregnant with my first baby called 'Easter Blues'. I was so nervous but it was so much fun!

When we got back to camp everyone was there bringin out the beer and rollin the

BLUE GRASS #2

joints lol huge ones! I went in the motor home to get some of our smoke while John rolled the awning out. As soon as I walked out and under it I hit my head so hard I bout fell to the ground. This continued to happen probably twenty times or more throughout the whole trip. After I hit it a few times John started yelling at me every time it happened. He got mad at me for not paying attention and this didn't stop either. It did make me more nervous though and of course I kept hitting my head. Finally we hung some headbands down it so I would see them but with my sucky vision and his attitude I was screwed cause the headbands didn't work a bit and I had tones of bruises across my forehead.

We loaded up and headed north stopping at Denali National Park. We climbed through the easier part of the mountain, I love climbing the rocks but have a bad habit of getting light headed.

"Jenny." I could hear John hollering to get my attention.

I looked down from the top of the rock I was about to climb and John was lookin at me with that, 'you know what's gonna happen if ya do that' look lol.

"What?" I hollered back.

"Come on down girl."

I smiled and told him to meet me half way. I climbed down, he climbed up and we met in the middle. When he sat next to me and kissed me the wind blew this perfect breeze past us, we both reached up to feel it.

"Look babe." He said. "We're touchin the wind."

It was amazing. We stayed there till the others were hollering at us from the bottom of the mountain. We carefully climbed on down and joined em to smoke as we headed on up the highway.

We found a steak house in a little town called Nenana. There were a few others caravanning with us so we had a good sized group. The first thing I saw when we all walked in together was a beautiful wooden table perfectly long enough for all of us, to cool.

We were greeted by an older man and his wife and treated like kings and queens while we ate a meal fit for the same. Along with the amazing food and company there were pictures on the walls of the planes he flew in WWII with stories to boot.

Our drive continued up to the end of the road past Fairbanks to the Yukon River. We had been traveling for some time were all tired so we stopped at a bar to have a drink and listen to some music. We were having a good time, drinking and visiting but there was a woman that got Johns eye, which wasn't a hard thing to accomplish. I said something to him about wishing he looked at me that way still and shit, he started a scene. He wouldn't talk to me but was obviously mad and looking right through me, I hated it when he did that so I went back out to the motor home. He came in behind me, walked up to me picking me up by my throat holding me up against the closet.

"When will you figure out that I love you and not any other woman? You are my wife and you are who I want!" He yelled at me. "I don't want them! I will look at anyone and you will deal with it!"

He dropped me down and he went back into the bar. I quietly made the bed and settled myself in for the lonely night I had in store. When he came back out to try to get me to come in with him, he was the wonderful, loving man I couldn't get out of my head or my heart.

We parked near the Yukon River for the night and brought the speakers out of the motor home to listen to Pink Floyd 'The Wall' outside, it was awesome.

Heading home after everyone else had gone their own way, we found a rest-stop and pulled in. There weren't any other cars in the parking lot area so we grabbed the sleeping bag and headed to the middle of the most beautiful field of wildflowers we had ever seen. We couldn't see or hear anything other than ourselves and the flowers surrounding us so when we stood up from our 'hiding place'lol, there were a handful of tourists who all started clapping for us, Oh My Goodness such an awesome , wonderful and embarrassing moment!

Our Love Story Destroyed

Nothing ever stayed the same, the good wasn't ever good enough. The truth was always a lie and the way of survival and protection, what happened?

    I left the house with Jonathon pulling him with me as we ran through the woods, out of the subdivision and to the highway. We both had all kinds of sticky things from the bushes in our pants and I couldn't get out with my shoes so they were on my feet to, thank God Jonathon had his shoes on. We came up on a little pond and sat down on the edge to get our feet wet. Looking at my son so scared and so innocent, his beautiful blue eyes looking at me.
"I love you mommy." He said as he leaned on my shoulder.
I put my arms around him and held him tight.
"I love you to baby. I'm so sorry you had to hear that, he wouldn't ever hurt us you know that right?"
He looked up at me again but this time he didn't say anything, he just hugged me tighter. Of course he didn't know that, poor guy. Jas had stayed the night with her God mom, my sis Marta, I'm so grateful she's safe.
"K, come on son." I said to him. "I think we're almost there."
He got up and smiled and we started back on our way, finally we saw the last corner. Walking up to the house I could see the van, I couldn't believe he would leave it for me but that was so cool.
My brother Stephan came out of the house when I went to open the door of the van and Jonathon was already headed in the house to see the other kids.
"Hey brother do you have the keys to this thing by any chance?"

"You can't get in the van yet. Before he took off he drenched it with gasoline." He said pulling the hose out from its hiding place.

"Excuse me." I said in shock. "What the hell did he do that for, he's trying to blow me up now? Shit, how can all of this be so bad that he would want to hurt me and the kids? I just don't understand!"

"Hey sis, here, drink this beer and you'll feel better." Marta came out and snuggled her arm through mine leading me through the house to her bedroom. "Damn baby girl, what's going on? I hate it when these guys go through this, he has everyone on edge!"

"I'm sorry, I honestly don't know. All I know is that I'm sick of him telling me I'm crazy, I start believing him after a while. But im not the one going off the way he does and soaking his own van with gas!"

"Yea yea yea, tomorrow will be another day, you know that." She said. "He loves you, nothing can come between the two of you, and you are our king and queen."

I turned my thoughts to something better. "Yea, i guess. Hey, can I do a line?"

"Come on, it's in the drawer."

Both of us sat down on the bed getting comfortable. Darby, our brother's mom, came to the door.

"What are you guys up to and why ain't I invited?" She said peeking in through the door.

"Get in here and shut the door behind you." Marta told her.

She joined us and we took turns with our lines.

Stephen knocked and opened the door a little. "Hey sis, I checked the van out and sprayed it down for you. Its ok, I already started it so it ain't gonna blow up or anything."

"Thanks, I'm really sorry brother for bringing this shit to your house." I told him and Mart also.

"You're my little sis, stop talking stupid ya hear?" He said to me.

"I hear ya." I said still embarrassed.

"Kay, you guys be good. I am going to take off for a bit. I'll bring you back dinner for all the kids." Then off he went into the wild blue yonder.

My Jas couldn't sleep and wanted to talk with us so we put the dope away and let her join us for a bit. I knew that at 4:30 when the bar closed he would be here, moments later I heard the truck pull up like clockwork. We heard someone screaming bloody murder and a lot of crashing sounds then John came through the door. He looked like something from a horror movie especially with the huge machete he had in his hand. I was so nervous and in shock from what was happening that I couldn't open my mouth to say a word. It was like my mouth was glued shut with the worse cotton mouth in the world! Jas was behind me when he asked me what was wrong, if there was cum in my mouth and now it was his turn.

He started swinging the machete around the room chopping up a TV into the tiniest pieces along with anything else in its way.

There was absolutely nothing I could do to make sure my baby was okay so I hit the wall to brace myself, threw my leather over Jas and started to pray. Every time he flung the machete to one side of us Darby would scream and he would swing the machete towards her which is where Jas was. I wanted to slap the shit out of that woman, I screamed and told her to shut the fuck up! I have no idea how long this went on, finally he put the machete down and was trying to pick me up. I knew if I let him get me off that floor he would take me to the river and kill me.

After what seemed to be forever, the troopers came through the house and were in the doorway with guns drawn on him. He dropped down to the floor with me, still holding tight and telling the troopers that I was having an episode of ptsd. That I thought my ex, David, was trying to hit me and that's why I had been screaming the way I was, Oh my Goodness! They took him quickly out of the house and into custody and somehow my sister took the machete and hid it in the woods and told me to stay quiet. It was all I could do to not say anything to the cops.

I took my rings off handing them to her. "Take these, I don't want them anymore."

She wouldn't take them so I tried to give them to the troopers but they wouldn't take them either so I put em in my pocket. I thought my life was over, I have never felt as devastated and scared as I did at that moment!

The kids all came out of the bedroom and my babies were crying not knowing what to do, it was awful! Jasmine and Jonathon curled up on the couch as close to me as they could and the other kids were told to stay in the other room where they didn't have to be in the middle of the chaos.

John wasn't charged with a felony because they didn't have the weapon, so crazy! I had to go back to the house and couldn't believe what I saw when I walked inside. Oh my goodness, the coffee table had been tossed upside down, it was a glass octagon table and it was broken into pieces and pictures were hanging sideways off of the walls.

I walked into my bedroom and started to cry. My room was about 2 inches, not exaggerating, of glass and everything I owned covering the entire floor of the room. There were holes in the roof where he had tried to throw the dresser out the window. The mattress on our bed had been lifted up and was lying against the wall as if he were going to try to throw that out the window also. My dresser was lying on the box spring upside down with everything thrown out of it and the shotgun was lying on the ground. I picked it up and checked it out, thankfully it had jammed.

Thank goodness no one got shot. I found out that when he was at the house trying to get me to go with him he not only had the machete but he also had a chainsaw, a gun and a shovel in the truck. No telling what he would have done to me if he had gotten me up off that floor that morning.

One of my other sister's said I could stay with them while he was in jail, there was no way I could stay where I was, it wasn't much of a home anymore.

Later we found out that John had called a couple of times during the night from the bar and the guy that was staying with my sister answered the phone and told him I wasn't there and decided he knew something was going on, that's why he came to the house the way he did.

Behind Closed Doors

I look back at what I left and wonder why it took me so long. My God, I loved him so much. Tall, strong, unbeatable image, beautiful long blonde hair and the hottest bike in the Valley. Boy did I think I was bad when I was by his side. The power, the leathers, and my favorite, the looks from the tourists who watched us wherever we go.

I was what Alaska and life were all about. I would walk into the bar, the store, the gas station or anyone's home and everybody would stand to say hello and show his or her respect to this man and me in such attire. I could hold my head high because my reputation was known in a 500 + mile radius from Kodiak to Fairbanks. What else could anyone ask for? It's true, I had brothers and sisters in every town, however, I had something that no one else knew about.

I had a life behind those closed doors that no one would wish on themselves. I had loneliness, fear, betrayal, anger and control. I had drugs and raised voices. I had my sanity tested and found myself curled in a corner fearing for my life. Where did all that wonderful 'image' shit go? I didn't understated. He wasn't gorgeous anymore, he had so much anger that was shared with only me and mine.

I tried to tell someone one day the truth in my life. They laughed and said I was crazy, that he was the catch of the Valley and I was the luckiest woman in the state!

I walked away in my fear all alone. I walked, I ran, I escaped and disappeared to a world I was new to. I left the image, along with my family who said they would always take care of me, except when those doors were closed. I came to a place where the sun shined high, the birds sang, and people smiled. The anger and fear seemed to be slipping away, three thousand miles down the road.

The Beginning of the End

Dena and Bill's house in the woods was awesome and I was so thankful to have a safe place to be that wasn't my disaster of a home. It was off the main road enough for me to feel away from town and it was so pretty, trees everywhere and no boundaries to be seen, all open space. It was all so strange, I hated being in other people's private space, it helps so much that their all so good to me!

Time went by and I continued to try to be useful, I would help with the kids as much as I could and helped clean to of course. We were even planning their wedding, so cool and it was so beautiful there. They decided to have the ceremony outside in the yard.

Soon it was the big day, Dena even trusted me to make their cake and in no time there were red and white streamers everywhere. The dresses were something out of a movie, and the one she had found for me was so pretty! Red and snug to my body, thank goodness I am small enough to fit in her clothes. She's so much more beautiful and happier than me. I wonder if things can ever get better for us …

I knew he was coming but in a way, hoping he wouldn't. I was in the house getting ready to come out when I saw the van pull up. My heart started beating fast and I got really nervous. I had no idea if he was mad or how he was going to treat me and really I didn't want to fight here in front of everyone! Instead of yelling at me he was using a cane to get out and as he slowly walked towards the house he kept his head down looking up just a little to see me in the window.

I went to the door to meet him.

"I don't know why you're here and not home Jenny." He said to me. "What did I do to you to deserve this?"

I backed up a step and ran into the door and lost my balance. I couldn't believe him.

"Are you kidding me, you don't remember John? You came through Marta's house with a fucking Machete and chopped everything up, almost including myself jasmine and Marta and that 'mouth of a woman' that was there!"

He didn't say a thing at first, his head hung down like a wounded puppy.

"I love you, I couldn't ever love anyone else. I'm really sorry and look, your fine." He said like he was proud of himself.

"I have to go, the wedding is starting. We'll talk later." I said.

I left him standing there and took my place with the wedding party.

He convinced me that the best thing to do was to go home with him so I packed my things up that evening after the reception and said my goodbyes. They had helped me get through a real rough time, I'm so thankful! It was time to go home and face the mess with my husband, all I wanted to do was to go to bed.

~~~

We learned that the charges John was arrested on that night were being perused by the DA's office so John and I went to Palmer for him to go to court a few weeks later, our brother Johnny went with us for support.

The three of us were waiting in the hallway for court to start when this woman walked up to me, grabbed my arm and turned me around.

"Are you Jennifer Karasti?" She asked me.

I was startled and started backing towards the door. I was already dealing with John blaming me for all of this against him with the court n'all.

John reached up and grabbed my other arm before I could back all the way outside, "Leave her alone!" He said with his deep voice, my stomach became suddenly nauseous.

They were just staring at me and now everyone in the court room hallway was watching the show.

"Yes, I am." I said.

She stuck some papers in my hand. "You have been served."

I let go of the papers and let them fall to the floor. "I don't know what you mean, get away from me!" I cried.

I was backing up to walk around everyone trying to get to the doors again but they followed me.

"Here Jennifer." The woman said handing me the papers again. "We want you testify against Mr. Karasti."

I was in shock, I didn't know what to do. I took the papers and walked away to sit down with the guy's right behind me.

"Jenny, you don't need to be talking to the judge, they can't make you testify, you're my wife." John said trying to hug me to calm me down.

The woman stepped around to be face to face with John. "It won't stand up in court, we have the recording from the Troopers that were on scene of the attack."

I could barely swallow, my throat was piercing dry and my head was pounding. John told me not to say anything, to not talk at all.

When they called my name I went up and sat in the seat next to the judge. He asked me question after question. I tried to lie, I told him that it was me and that I was crazy, he was just trying to help me. The judge played the tape-recording from the troopers of me screaming and crying. When I heard it I lost all control of myself and had to leave the courtroom until I could breathe again.

The judge sat up and turned to look right at me. "Young lady, I will not listen to anything else you have to say in this man's defense. You are obviously in an abusive relationship and there is nothing I can say or do to help you if you don't want to except it."

They told me I could leave the stand, still court wasn't over quick enough for me! We went to leave the courtroom and John walked off yelling at me to stay away from him, that I turned on him and I was crazy. When we got to the van he kept walking through the parking lot so Johnny drove and I got in the passenger seat. When we caught up to John he started pounding on the side of the van and yelling though the driver's side window to me that I was crazy and I was destroying everything, that it was all my fault.

Johnny tried to get him to listen to him. "It's you John, Jenny's fine. You're the one pounding and yelling and acting like a maniac."

He kept yelling and cussing and screaming so finally we drove off and left him to his war walk.

I was so freaked about everything Johnny drove around and let me talk about what was going on. He let me cry and he just listened. When we got to the trailer John had called already twice then the phone rang again.

I answered it and it was John. "Where have you been Jenny, what are you and Johnny doing?"

"We aren't doing anything, he brought me here, home."

He started yelling at me again, I couldn't even hardly understand his words.

"I'm in the hospital, I had a heart attack but I know your busy, don't worry about coming to see me if you don't want to." He said to me. "I'm fine without you!" Then he hung up.

I couldn't believe the way he was acting. We left and drove back to Palmer to the hospital.

When I got to the emergency room they had him in a bed and all hooked up to wires and hoses and stuff. He looked awful!

"What happened?" I asked him.

THE BEGINNING OF THE END

"Don't worry bout me, I don't need you." And he looked away from me.

I just stood there looking stupid, words barley came out of my mouth. "You can't be mad at me because of what happened at the court house, it is not my fault John, none of this is my fault!"

He acted like he was in pain again and the nurses ran in. They had me leave the room and wait in the hallway, I stopped one of them and asked them about what happened.

"Did he have a heart attack?" I asked.

"Who are you ma'am, we can't give information to just anyone."

"I am his wife, Jennifer Karasti."

"Thank you." She said. "And no, he had an anxiety attack, he will be fine." She turned and walked down the hall.

He was so pitiful and rude towards me. "Do you want me to take your clothes and put them in the closet and do you want your wallet?" I asked him.

I started to reach for his clothes to straighten them out and he yelled at me. "Don't touch my wallet or my clothes, don't touch anything of mine Jennifer!"

That's it, I turned around and walked out of the hospital and across the street to the high school field, I was walkin home!

I could hear him hollering for me to stop so I turned around, he caught up to me yelling and crying telling me how I screwed everything up in court. All I could do was cry, I thought for sure this nightmare would never be over. I looked up at him, he was leaning on the bleachers with the iv tubes and tape hanging from his arms wearing his hospital gown and jeans, unreal I thought. We sat there and yelled and cried back n' forth for over an hour when Johnny pulled up. We both got in the van and while no one said a word, we drove home to Houston.

Days past and nights were long, kids lived life pretty much on their own having to take care of each other and even though it didn't get as bad as it was, it didn't get better either. Walking on egg shells was a way of life, food being thrown at me or out the window was the expected if it wasn't perfect. I don't know how many times a day when there wasn't anything I could do that was good enough, ever. There wasn't anything the kids could do right either. They lived in fear, all of them, every day. I knew it was wrong but I couldn't fix anything for anyone, I felt so helpless.

It broke my heart but I had no choice. I took myself, Jonathon and Jasmine to the airport with money I had been saving and bought tickets to California. It was time for Jonathon to meet his real dad, Danny, and it was time for us to be happy, somehow.

HER PLACE WAS WITH GOD

We were giving our luggage to the woman at the check-in stand and she asked me if I had packed any weapons or anything else I needed to tell them about. I had packed my 9mm macharave John got me for my birthday, I had to tell them. They told me I couldn't take it with me and if I didn't have someone come right then and there to pick it up I couldn't get on the plane. Thank goodness I was able to get a hold of our brother Fernando and he came and picked it up from me. He hugged me and the kids and told us he would miss us and we headed on through the airport to our gate. Awesome, time to go home.

We flew into San Francisco and my cousin Sue was there to pick us up, it was so awesome to see her. She brought us home and loved on us, we really needed the time after everything that had happened. With-in the week my mama came and picked me and the kids up and took us to Mendocino with her.

I missed it here, it always so much like home to me. I love going to my mom's church and I love having lunch afterwards. Everyone brought a dish and we ate potluck, then kids would run in the huge field in the back and play volleyball or other games while everyone visited.

One Sunday there was a visiting pastor. They did an altar call, asked if there was anyone that needed to invite Christ into their lives and with that I was up and out of my seat. The next thing I knew I was standing at the front of the church being prayed over. This man laid his hand on me then started to pray in tongues and stopped suddenly.

"You're still scared?" He asked.

I looked up at him. "Yes, I am." I told him.

I closed my eyes and with his hand still on my head he kept talking to me. "You're going to help other women one day that have been through what you have gone through." He said.

He continued to speak Jesus' love and promises over me and when he was done I sat back down. I hadn't felt very close to God, at all, but it was pretty obvious he was there today and what this man was saying was directly from Him, himself. I just couldn't figure out how there would be anything I could do that would be of any good to anyone.

We had only been back for a week or so and the kids were antsi and hot lol even though it was a beautiful overcast day on the coast so I took them to Big River Beach. Bathing suits n' all they were lying on the beach while the waves came in, covered them and went back out, they were having a ball!

An older couple walking up the beach looked at the kids and then at me.

THE BEGINNING OF THE END

"Aaww they look like miss-placed Alaskans." They said to me and kept walking.

It made us giggle, how funny, if they only knew!

I got my aid transferred and me and the kids found a cute little apartment in Fort Bragg with the beach out our backdoor. My mom's friend sold me his little blue vw on payments so between having our own car and time finally passing, life was getting better. It was easier to smile and my kids were smiling to, thank you Jesus!

I got the kids into school for the last month or so that was left in the year and started working at this cool little bed and breakfast called Joshua Grindle Inn in Mendocino. It's so awesome getting to spend time with my mom and we worked great together.

Having Kasey and Greg and their mom back in my life is so cool after all these years to. Their house was a beautiful wood home in the middle of the redwoods and me and the kids would spend as much time with them as we could.

Kasey fell in love with my wedding rings, black hills gold and absolutely gorgeous and it's not like I hadn't already been wondering if they needed a new home. It was easy to give them to her, she meant so much to me ... like the rings had. She did a blessing over them with sage and prayer and buried them for a time to be cleansed then said they were blessed and good as new, awesome.

Me and the kids went to Willows to visit and for our son to meet his dad. I hadn't seen my boy so happy in so long as he was huggin on his dad and enjoying their dog and his sister and his stepmom. Wow, actually having another families love and help with our kids, awesome! Jonathon stayed the weekend with his dad while Jas and me drove to Chico to visit Leah and go to the Lights parade. Leah was out of town so we went downtown and parked to walk through the crowd and hopefully find a good spot to watch the parade. It was awesome being back in Chico, it will always be one of my home sweet homes.

We walked around the corner and there were a few different people here n' there sitting in the grass. I could feel my breath stop and my knee's start to buckle as I realized David was sitting there, right there! I grabbed my girls hand a little tighter and walked up in front of him, he was holding a baby and there was a small blonde woman, girl, sitting next to him on the blanket.

I didn't know if I was going to be able to say anything, I wasn't sure how or what I felt other than it wasn't good. I had a moment of a thought of pouncing and punching as hard as I could, then I remembered he had the baby in his arms and I had my girl with me.

I couldn't keep my mouth shut any longer. "David, David Fulton, really?"

HER PLACE WAS WITH GOD

The words weren't coming to my mouth but I wanted to tell this woman to take her child and run as far and fast from him as she could go, I felt numb. He looked up at me and his eyes were still so scary but he hung his head low, maybe there was something, just maybe some remorse? I wouldn't ever know that was for sure. I turned quick with my Jas in my hand and headed back to the car as fast as we could go and went and got ourselves a room for the night. The next morning we headed to Willows to pick up Jonathon and on to the coast to our safety we drove.

A couple of months passed and summer was on us, going to the beach with the kids was so good, I loved what we were doing here, whatever it was.

One day when we got back from the beach there was a message on my machine but no one other than my mom, Kasey, Greg and Leah even knew my number. I sat there and looked at the red light for about an hour before I sent the kids out to play so I could listen to it. I couldn't believe it, it was John. Just hearing his voice melted my heart and the tears started. He was so sweet and so sincere … scary.

I waited a few hours and called him back. I had no idea what to say or what he would say but again, when I heard his voice all I could do was cry.

"No honey." he said. "Please don't cry, I'm right here." He laughed and that made me laugh to. "Well, I'm quite a few miles away but I'm right here on the other side of the phone and I love you as much as I did the day we got married."

I wasn't sure what to do, all I could do was stand there crying and listen to his words.

"Come home Jenny, bring the kids and come home where you belong. I miss you, the girls miss you and the dogs miss you." With that we both laughed. "We all miss you. Debbie, Marta and Karen ask me all the time if I've heard from you and when you're coming home, I never know what to say to anyone."

As he kept talking my thoughts were going a million miles an hour, I thought I had it all figured out and all of sudden the figurin was gone!

Choices were made and things changed, again. Jonathon was really enjoying the visit with his dad so we decided he would stay and Danny would fly him home before school started. I'm so happy they connected the way they did!

I couldn't stop thinking about my Joshua, hoping and praying every day that he was ok with his dad.

I gave all my furniture back to Kasey and Greg, quit my job and said our goodbyes. The hardest was saying goodbye to my mom again then having to say goodbye to my Jonathon on our way through Willows, 3000 miles was so far!

When I made it to Willows Danny went over the fluids and checked my bug out to make sure we were safe for the road. He told me to stop at the station where his buddy's work on my way out of town to get the radiator checked real quick. We said our goodbyes and headed through town to the station. They came out and met me, I

THE BEGINNING OF THE END

told them what Danny told me to tell them and Oh My Goodness three of the guys standing there started laughing so hard one of them about fell down.

"What happened, what did I do?" I asked. They tried to stop laughing.

"Young lady." The man said. "Dan just called us and told us you were comin to have the radiator checked. But he didn't tell us you were driving a vw, they don't have radiators!"

They were all laughing and I turned all colors of red I'm sure lol I was so embarrassed and could have killed Danny! I used their phone and called him. I could hear him and Jonathon getting the best laugh ever on their prank and that made my day. Hearing my son so happy was worth all the embarrassment in the world! We laughed some more and I shook their hands then Jasmine and I began our journey north in a car I hadn't paid for yet. Honestly I did feel guilty but I had no other thoughts of what to do, I had to go.

I found one of my Alaska sisters number, Crissy, and was so excited to learn she was living in Seattle instead of Alaska. We stopped on our way through and had a great visit. Before we left her and Jas made us a sign for the back window of the bug saying, 'North to Alaska' in crayon, so awesome! We said more goodbyes and headed back to the interstate.

Driving the Alcan, the Alaska Highway, was one of the most exciting things I had ever done and me and Jas were having so much fun, it was so beautiful! There was a number of us on the hwy at the same time so we all pretty much stopped at the same rest stops to stretch and go to the bathroom and eat n' all. Jasmine was so happy and friendly and loved saying hi to everyone each time we stopped, in no time her had made tones of new friends.

After a few days went by the trip started to turn into more of a mission, getting to John and finally home to the girls. We stopped to eat breakfast and drove the whole day, as the sun was starting to set I glanced at the gas tank and gasped when I saw that there only about a 1/8 of a tank of gas left. Oh my goodness I can't believe I would be so forgetful at a time like this!

"Mommy." Jassy said looking up at me with her beautiful big brown eyes. "Are you ok?" I guess my worry was turning into a few tears and her caught it right away.

"Aaww, yes I'm just fine." I said to calm her down. "Look at this bridge we're about to go across, isn't it awesome?"

She sat forward in her chair looking at the bridge then over to the sides at the water.

"Wow mommy, there's a lot of water and look." She pointed behind us.

By then we had driven across the bridge a bit. I turned around to see what she was pointing at. There was nothing but bridge, water and the huge mountain we had just came through lol oh my goodness, then I looked down and remembered how low my gas was and I got really scared!

HER PLACE WAS WITH GOD

There weren't very many cars on the road but prayed for someone, anyone! I flashed my lights when I finally saw a truck coming towards us. When they were passing us I already had my window down waiting to ask them for directions but I could tell they didn't want to slow down. I waved my arms pointing at my daughter in the seat next to me, when they got up to my window they finally stopped.

"Hi, thank you so much for stopping. I realized I only have a little gas left and I have my daughter and have no idea where we are. I think I'm lost." I said to them trying to hold my tears back.

I wasn't doing very well with that though and by then Jasmine was trying to get to me out of her buckle to hug me.

"No baby, buckle up, I'm fine." I said to her.

I was directing her to sit back down and they rolled their window the rest of the way down.

"Its ok you'll be fine." The man told me with a smile. The woman looked around him out his window.

"Its ok honey." she said. "There's a gas station about ten miles up the road and its almost dark so just pull right up to the gas pumps, lock your doors and sleep right there in your car. They open early and will wake you, their used to people sleeping there so no one will bother you." She smiled real sweet and made me feel so much better.

"Thank you so much!" I told them.

We rolled our windows up cause it was getting dark and chilly and we both headed on our own ways.

We were at the pumps in no time and no one else was there. We locked the doors like they told us to do, cuddled up with each other and our blankets to get some much needed sleep. I love my baby girl so much, she's such a trooper. I freaked out way more than she did!

I wondered where John was right at that moment, if he was looking up at the same stars I was looking at, if he was thinking about me. I just wanted to be back in his arms, I missed him so much and I was so tired.

When we woke up there were cars parked on each side of us and on the other side of the pumps to, so cool! Soon everyone was waking up and moving around so we went in to pay for gas, donuts and juice saying good morning to everyone then headed out with smiles on our faces.

Finally I saw the signs that the border was close, we were closer and closer to John and home. This would be a piece of cake just like leaving the US into Canada, but they had other ideas. I felt like we were picked out to be harassed because I didn't look like the most upstanding mom. I didn't think I looked dangerous or anything like that but they didn't agree. The woman was so rude, when she searched the car she stepped on and smashed almost all of Jass's little toys she had been playing with on the floor.

THE BEGINNING OF THE END

Finally two hours later they let us leave. I was starting to feel guilty like I had really done something wrong. It was exciting to be back on the road and actually in Alaska, what a relief! A few more miles and I found the rest area we were meeting John at, I could see the van before I even pulled in. I was excited and scared at the same time, so much had happened before I left. Jonathon and Joshua were miles away, John and the girls were the other direction miles away and me and Jas seemed to always be in the middle, I just wanted our family together.

I pulled up next to the van, we were both so excited to see him so we quickly brushed our hair in the mirror then jumped out of the car. I peaked in the window and he was asleep so we opened the door and crawled up next to him in bed to kiss his face. He woke up and hugged us, aaww so cool.

We crawled out of the van and while Jas crawled around to see everything John and I talked, well, I listened to him tell me how hurt he was that I left him and the girls. My heart was pounding and I wanted to turn and run back the way I had just came, I wanted him to just love me and to go home so I told him I was sorry.

The three of us crawled up into the bed for a little while and rested and talked and made some plans, first of all lol food, we were all starving. Before I could even think about relaxing he realized my rings weren't on my finger.

"Jenny, where did your wedding rings go?" He was looking at me with such disbelief, I could have just died right there.

I really didn't want to fight anymore and Jasmine had heard enough already and we had only been back together for an hour or so.

So much was running through my mind. "I don't have them."

His eyes were still glaring into mine. "What did you do with them?"

"I threw them into the ocean John. After what you did to me and the kids, we were terrified! We lived through hell because of you and your drugs and this crazy shit!"

I was so confused seeing him and hearing his words as he told me it was me leaving that was destroying our family, not anything that he had done. I knew what I was telling him about my rings was a lie but I really couldn't do this anymore, I couldn't and didn't want to keep fighting.

Finally Jasmine asked us to stop and reminded us how hungry we were.

"Mommy, daddy, can we please go eat now?" She asked so sweetly.

Her big eyes looked at both of us without a bit of worry or anger, just pure love and hunger. We kissed her and each other and decided we would try harder and deal with the rings. We loaded up and got Jas settle in her seatbelt then headed up the road to the little village of Tok and the closest place to eat.

While we ate John told me a story. He said that yesterday when he got where we were meeting he was feeling a bit worried and when he looked up into the sky he saw a cloud that looked like a child crying. He felt something might be wrong with me

HER PLACE WAS WITH GOD

and Jas. That we could be hurt or had died. Then he said that a frog hopped across the highway to him and put his little foot up on his big boot and looked up at him. John looked down at this little guy and he felt reassured at that moment that we were fine, aaww my heart melted. Then I told him about what had happened at the time I found myself and Jas on the bridge in the middle of no-where, almost out of gas and scared to death and it was the same time.

What a sweet message from this beautiful little frog!

Home Sweet Home?

John found us a 4 bedroom house with a garage and a yard just north of Wasilla, much better than being all the way up in Houston. It was so awesome to hug our girls, I had missed Jeanette and Michelle so much and our little princess Chelsea Mae! I still hated myself for leaving without the older girls, for leaving all of them in the first place and for whatever it was that happened to them while I was gone. There wasn't much I could do to make up to them for leaving. Jeanette was really mad, I couldn't blame her though and Michelle tried to understand, they both loved us being home.

Jonathon came home the end of August and soon the kids were all in school, what a wonderful thing! For a while I thought things were changing in a good way.

The bar, the family and the runs, the nights, the party's and bbqs were on and the drugs were as normal as Pepsi and Steinlogger lol.

One night at the dead dog the guys were all up at the bar. Karen had found some left over bottle rockets hid away in a cupboard so we starting shootin em at the bar stools aka lol their feet! It was hilarious, we loved playin and getting em all back at the same time!

We were having drinks and our 'friends', Pam and Mike joined us for a beer then we all went outside to smoke a joint.

Out of the blues she leaned over to me while the guys were talking and asked me, "Jenny, what would happen if I told John what you really did with those rings?"

I'm pretty sure she was pissed off because her old man had been flirting with me all night but that wasn't my fault lol. I couldn't believe this bitch and I couldn't believe I trusted her! Without having control over 'me', my arms swung into action. I reached around to grab her mouth with my right hand, put her to the gravel parking lot and started pounding her with my left hand, that shut her up!

Pretty soon our friend and bar tender was pulling me off her and John was getting Pam up and away from me.

"Come on you two, troopers are pullin in." Carla said.

She turned to tell Pam to go clean up but she was already gone and headed into the bathroom so they led me into the bar.

Someone handed me a shot of tequila and as I drank it I heard someone else holler. "Check it out, the little bitch beat the shit out of the big bitch!"

Everyone was hoopin and cheering, how funny, the craziest things make the night don't they? We were sitting up at the bar when she came on out of the bathroom with paper towels over her face and walked straight out the door and they left. I heard I cut her face pretty bad and couldn't figure out how I could have done that cause I'm right handed. I remembered I had my slave bracelet on my left hand and the ring was a solid silver Harley Davidson eagles head, I must have got her with the nose. I had any drink I wanted bought for me the rest of the night and John still had no idea I had a secret.

The Summer Solstice Parties were always bout as good as the Blue Grass but enjoyably smaller.

Me and Karen and a couple of others loaded up in the van to head down the hill to the bar and get some smokes, thank goodness it was only a few minutes' drive down Pitman to get to the store. Carla was bartending and one of our brothers was sitting at the end of the bar so we all visited for a minute. I asked her for five packs of Marlboro's, she put them on the bar in front of me and a guy and a gal walked in the doors arguing.

The guy walked on behind me and the woman stood next to me. "Hi, hey can I get a smoke from you?" She asked.

I looked at the packs sitting on the bar there and laughed. "Well I can't tell you I don't have any now can I?" I asked her laughing.

I opened one of the packs and handed her a cigarette. The guy she was with must not of been too happy about me giving it to her so he decided to let me know.

"Hey." He said getting my attention. "If you're gonna give her a smoke then just take her to!"

I couldn't believe the nerve of this guy!

Before I could even think of what to say Jerry grabbed the front of his shirt and spoke up, "Do you have any idea who you're talking to?"

HOME SWEET HOME?

lol Oh My Goodness! He started punchin this guy till him and his girl hustled it as quick as they could to the parking lot.

"Thank you brother." I said to Jerry.

"No problem." he said to me. "You girls get on back up the hill now kk and have Big John come talk to me when he has a chance."

I went over and gave him a hug. "Are you alright?" I asked him.

He laughed at the question. "I'm fine, always have been and always will. Anyways, that was ballet dancing lol." He said.

I gave him another hug and we went out to the van. Before I could even get the keys in the ignition a car pulled up behind me and parked. I looked over at Karen, she had already noticed it to.

"Hey sister, what do you think?"

She looked behind the van. "I think he's askin for trouble, way more than he realized!"

I sat in the driver's seat and turned towards the back side of my van, he was parked right there behind us. He pulled up just enough to see me clear as day while I sat in the seat so I grabbed my 9 mm and put it down on the dash where he was sure to see it also. I turned to see his thoughts on that. He left but not of course before he spun his gravel all over Johns van, great, this idiot keeps making it way worse for himself.

Finally we were able to head back up the hill to the party to tell him what had happened and before I could turn around in a circle John and some of the 'Carma Control' were headed down the road to look for this man.

When they came back they hadn't found him. I was hoping he went somewhere safe and would stay there.

The rest of the weekend was awesome! Music, beers, lines and family, what more could one ask for?

When we weren't at a party or the bar we had quite the houseful of family and kids, staying high seemed to be the easiest way to keep up with everything. Our garage was our refuge and it wasn't only lines of coke anymore, I loved smoking it so much more than snorting and for sure more than shootin it.

Life is moving fast and all of our kids had gone through so much in the last year, I would do anything if things could just go back to the way it was in the beginning, but that seemed like a life time away …

All of our kids were angry and confused, it seemed like nothing either of us could do was right or in any way helpful. Our world was out of control on the inside and out, as before, they never said anything as they lived in what we gave them.

I had to do something to keep busy and make some money so I found a job driving cab, lol how funny, I've always wanted to drive cab but never thought it would be in Alaska.

The blue grass festival was on again, man that year went fast. I couldn't get out of my shift so John and the older girls went on ahead to set up camp. I got someone to watch the younger kids and I'd go on up when my shift was done.

Finally I switched from my cab to my bug and then home to the van. I couldn't believe that John had left the girl's supplies and camping gear n' all in the van instead of taking it to them like he said he would lol great, I'll get blamed I'm sure.

I was nervous getting ready, I knew he was going to be less than happy with me so I wanted to make sure I had everything I'd need and what he'd think I needed. Got my leathers, got my money, beer and smoke and the girls things, all I didn't have was a line! That doesn't have to be much of a wait though if I hurry and get up the hill so on the road I was.

When I got there, there wasn't anywhere to park, I finally found a spot way away from the gate. 'Fine.' I thought to myself and started walking.

"Hey Jen, what's up?" One of the guys hollered to me.

"Nothin, just looking for John. Have you seen him?" I asked.

"Um, yea, be careful." He said to me.

I wondered why he said that, so I went to ask his old lady what was up but she was swooped up by a group of people and couldn't hear me.

Kay cool, there's Karen. "Hey sis, there you are. Do you know where he is?"

She pointed to the group on the other side of her. "He's right there."

I looked over and when I spotted him, he turned real quick and caught eye contact with me so I went over and stood next to him.

"Don't Say anything to anyone you hear?" he said looking around back n' forth from one face to another.

"What are you talking about?" I asked him.

I leaned in next to his ear and asked him. "Is there any left of what you had?"

Oh my goodness, he jumped back real quick looking at me like I was his worst enemy!

"What in the hell are you doing here and why did you ask me that out loud?" He said. "There are undercover cops everywhere. Right here, (he pointed at a couple of people behind us) Over there, see, Radical is talking to one right now. He's one of em' you know."

I looked back at Karen. "Are you alright?" She asked. "Your face is white, sit down."

"Dang, what should I do?" I asked her.

"I don't know, Keith is doing the same thing."

"Well, I'm gonna go try to get a high and then get out of here. I still have the girl's things in the van but this is all bad, I probably won't stick around." I said.

"I don't blame you." Karen said. "I wish I could leave to." She laughed. "Right?"

"I love you sister."

"I love you to Jen, and you be careful kay?"

"I will, you to!"

All of a sudden my arm bout jerked out of its socket as John swung me around so we were face to face. "I said what the hell are you doing here and what are you trying to do, send me to prison before the parties even over?"

Spit was flying in my face and my arm started to ache.

"Damn John!" I jerked my arm away and turned around.

He grabbed me again and swung me around. "Now, what are you doing and what do you want?"

I hated it when he got like this, it means he's been drinking whiskey and drowning himself in the crap I can't find!

"Hey, can I have a line and did you miss me today? Driving a cab is so weird and I hated coming out here to meet you by myself."

I looked up at him, his eyes were huge and he was really frantic and irritated. We walked, well, he kinda almost ran, I tried to keep up behind him.

"Hey, wait up for me!"

He was yelling at me and then he walked up to this tree. "Don't talk to this one either, he's the ring leader!"

I followed him quietly to the trailer and up the stairs to go inside.

Some of the other girls were were making coffee. "Hey girl, having a good time?"

I smiled at them and kind of laughed. "It looks crazy out here this year." It was all I could get out.

"Yea it is." One of them said to me. "We didn't know if you were going to make it or not. You're gonna have your hands full with that one, be careful."

"I will." I said. "I'm fine. I'm just gonna go home I think, screw this shit."

"Don't blame you." She said.

I walked back into the room with John and sat down.

He looked up at me. "Now are you going to get jealous because Sue is here? I told you there wasn't anything for you to worry about but you're too focused on yourself to actually believe that I really love you." He said and kept talking. "You don't know how to trust me!"

I was so confused. "I don't know what you're talking about John. Of course I get a little bothered because I wanted to be with you at the Blue Grass and I had to work and come here and you're all tweaked out and think everyone is going to bust you and you wig on me! I haven't been high all day and I just want a fricken line. I did want you, now I'll just get out of your way and head on home."

"Good, you turn and run like you always do." He said. "I don't need you anyways, there are plenty of women around here to keep me warm!"

That stopped me in my tracks, I turned and looked at him, oh my God, I thought my heart was going to break. Again his words left me speechless. I grabbed the dope, grabbed the pot and put the gun in my pocket and walked out of the camper. I didn't look at anyone or say anything.

I could hear him behind me, shit, I didn't want this to happen.

"Jenny, why are you leaving me?" He asked. "Why do you do this? You need medicine that's all, please don't leave me! I'm never coming home if you do this and hey, give me the dope you ain't getting that!" He yelled.

I looked back as his voice changed, it got real low like a growl. He kept yelling and talking so I ducked down between people and headed to the back of the parking area to the van, I was so embarrassed!

Finally after what seemed like forever I couldn't see or hear him anymore. 'Whew, he lost me, what a son of a bitch!' I thought I was talking to myself.

"Are you alright honey?" I jumped bout out of my boots and looked up. It was one of the brothers from 'Carma Control'.

"Yea, I'm fine." I said.

"Do you need help getting to your car?" He asked.

"No, don't. I'm in the van and if he sees you with me there's no telling what he'll do. I'm just gonna leave and keep anything else from happening."

He reached over and gave me a hug. "You know, if he keeps this up we're gonna have to escort him out of here."

"I know, there isn't anything I can do. This is going to have to be up to you guys, I'm out of here." I turned and jumped in the van and it started first time, thank you Jesus!

I had the gun, I had the ounce of dope and I had the bud. I threw the van in reverse to back out hoping I wouldn't hit anyone. I wanted to get past the people so I could wreck the van and only hurt myself.

As I drove I could see everyone having a good time, walking hand in hand, talking and playing music. People singing and puppies playing and little cook stoves set up along the whole side of the road next to where everyone parked.

'Shit, I really wanted to have a good time and this so sucks!' I thought to myself.

Soon I was past the people. I geared up and sped down the road.

Just as I turned to the right there was a trooper. "Yea, break my heart." I yelled. "At least I won't have to deal with that man when he gets home."

I looked in my mirror and he wasn't there.

'What are they doing? Why aren't they going to arrest me?' I thought.

I kept driving, way faster than I should have been on this road. It just kept going though, I couldn't run the damn thing off the road if I ran right into something. Surely God had his hand on me and the van!

I looked up from the road and the trees were beautiful, tears were running down my face and I was having a hard time seeing where I was driving so I stopped on the side of the road. I got the dope and the pot out of my bag, did a fast line, took a hit off the joint that was already rolled and took a drink of my beer, then tried to gain my composure back.

'Guess I better git home now and try to get busy, at least the kids aren't there.'

Pulling into the house I dreamed of it being home sweet home. It hadn't been since not long after the day I came home. I cleaned the house and then my car and was trying to start on the van but Chewy was boucin all over the place. Poor pup, usually daddy takes you with him huh? I wonder why he didn't this time.

"He's having a hard time boy." I said to him. I'm sure that is the only reason, he probably forgot. He jumped up on me covering my face in kisses and more kisses and nibbles. Thank goodness someone loved me. "I love you chewy." I told him.

I could hear the bike comin up the road. Damn, I was hoping he would be gone till tomorrow or something, I hated how he acted like he hated me. I ran in the house and went into our room and started doing stuff. I had to be busy when he got here, maybe he won't be mad, that was a joke.

"Jennifer, I know you're here, where the hell are you?" He yelled.

"I'm right here John, in the room. Why are you yelling at me?"

He came in like he was hitting the door with his whole 6' 2" 300 lb body.

"What the hell, you just leave me whenever you get the feeling, is that it? How can you think that I am that non important that you want to leave me so often?"

"I didn't 'leave' you John, I left the Blue Grass Festival and walked away from you acting like a madman. What else did you expect me to do?" I asked him.

"I expected you to stand by my side, you know you made me look like an ass to 'Carma Control'! You should have been there by my side no matter what!" He screamed.

"You were scaring me John, I had to leave. You didn't want me there, you made it pretty clear I was in your way and you weren't out to have a good time."

"What are you going to do now, leave me again?"

"No John, I'm not leaving you." I laughed. "Anyways, I just want to get high, are you ready to share now?"

"Yeah, I guess, let's hurry up though. Everyone's waiting at the bar for us so get your shit on and I'll get this ready."

He reached over and kissed me with the passion I remembered from before our lives started falling apart.

"There, I told you I love you and I meant it. Now, get ready." He said.

He went into the bedroom to line up some coke and I gathered my leathers and did my hair real quick getting dressed for the part. Quickly we did a line and continued to get dressed to go 'play'.

As We Were

As we stand together, all of us.
Our family grows, strong and sure.
One for all and all for one,
Till that day we stood alone.

We spent our days wild and free,
Laughter and tears along the way.
Who would have known our secrets to prevail?
Our world together as it crumbled and fell.

2nd Time On the Road to California

Being home wasn't what I had dreamed it would be that's for sure. He was still so angry, going to meetings still using and drinking. Working a program but not working a program, nothing was good!

Our kids never had very many clothes even when we lived in Houston, there was never money for clothes for them or for their school supplies. They never had good shoes, the most I could do were snow boots. They had spent so many years feeling unworthy of the love and life, it didn't seem fair, I was so confused! It was like they sat on the sidelines and watched their lives go right on by while they stood there raggedy and unbathed unless I remember to remind them, scraggily hair and dirty hands and faces. Levi's were tattered and too small, my kids wore the same pants day in and day out if they had too. I wasn't a good mom that's for sure.

One of our girls had gotten into some trouble and had been placed on house arrest with a monitor around her ankle. We had been trying to work things out and stay together as a family but it seemed like every day was pressing to make that not happen.

Jonathon found an old pair of pants that one of his sisters had given him the year before. They had been cut to fit his shorter size and he wore them for days before she even noticed them.

She came flying up the stairs screaming. "I am going to kill you! Take off my pants you little fucker!" Screaming and ranting.

I had the kids go upstairs in their rooms.

Our other daughter was in the kitchen trying desperately to ignore what was happening. She kept working on dinner looking at me with those big beautiful sad brown eyes every few moments ... I felt so bad.

Her sister reached around her to the drawer and grabbed a nice big sharp knife. Oh shit, that is all I needed. I fuckin hate knives!

2ND TIME ON THE ROAD TO CALIFORNIA

"I hate you Jenny, I hate you!" She was screaming as she chased me in circles around the house.

Somehow her sister got the knife and covered the drawer. Wow, she was so mad at me and John and the world and I couldn't blame her.

"It is all your fault, you're a drug addict and you left us and it is all your fault!"

Oh my goodness, I had no choice.

I got to the phone and dialed 911. "Come and get this child out of my house right now!" I yelled when they answered.

"Ma'am, what's wrong?" The voice asked me.

"I have a teenage girl in my home going crazy and chasing me around the house. I signed the papers for her to be on home arrest, I want to take away my signature. Get her out of here before someone gets hurt, I have other kids here too!"

"Calm down ma'am, we are sending an officer right now."

The screaming in the background was easily heard as she screamed threats to me and the kids because of the pants.

John wasn't home of course but I had no choice. I'd have to deal with him later but damn, I knew he was going to kill me. Drama was the only thing our family knew, I wondered if I was ever going to have a different kind of life, ever … or if I even deserved anything better?

In what seemed like no time at all he was home. We had calmed down and cleaned up a little, she had thrashed the house and their room was pretty bad to.

When I told him what had happened he was so angry with me and with the kids. He said we stepped in where we had no right. I reminded him that because he hadn't wanted to mess with the court system and the police, I had to be the one to see probation and get her on the program to come home. My signature, not his!

In his anger and to our disbelief, John ordered Jonathon off of the track team, he told him he couldn't do any sports and Jasmine couldn't play little league. I was shocked and again, so confused! For the first time in their lives the kids were doing things they loved and he took it away from them, they had lost so much already. None of this was their fault, they deserved so much better!

The rest of the day was hell for everyone in the house. Johns youngest was visiting from Anchorage, I felt so bad for her, there was always so much yelling and fighting.

Finally John left to go to the bar or something and our oldest daughter and the baby were hiding in her bedroom.

I ran up the stairs to my kid's room to see if they were ok. "Hey guys." I opened their doors slowly, not to scare them. "Are you alright?" I asked them.

As soon as they saw me they ran to me and through their arms around my neck, both of them,

"Mommy, are you alright? I am scared mommy." Jasmine said to me.

HER PLACE WAS WITH GOD

My tears started falling. "I'm sorry mommy, I didn't mean to make you cry." Jonathon said to me.

Telling him it wasn't his fault I slid to the floor with them and held them for a couple of minutes.

Jonathon perked up with his gorgeous smile and eyes. "Mommy look, we are ready to go."

My beautiful, wonderful children had already found their backpacks and their toothbrushes and the clothes and toys they wanted and were packed, ready to go.

My Jonathon didn't hesitate. "Can we go mommy? Can we go back to Grandma and Aunt Leah, please mommy?"

I had never seen such desperation in a baby. I wasn't going to make these kids go through any of this ever again!

Quickly we loaded up our little v.w. car with everything we could fit. The girls knew I couldn't take them with me. Our oldest desperately wanted to go with us but she knew that her dad would have me arrested or worse if I did that, there was no way I could take her. I hugged her and told her I was so sorry, she said she understood, but how could any child 'understand' such chaos?

My heart was so broke for all of our kid's broken hearts! I don't think anything had ever been so hard as to have to drive away while they watched us out the bedroom window.

※

My Jonathon was playing with something but I couldn't see it.

"What is that son?" I asked him.

"It's the garage door opener." He said happily.

"You can't keep that, he'll need it honey."

"Not anymore." He said with a smile. "I'm gonna take it apart and see what makes it work."

So much for that, it's not like I really cared about the dang thing and it wasn't like we were going to ever come back …

Driving down the road so many things were going through my mind, I had no idea where I was going lol this was great! I drove to a friends of ours in Big Lake, a woman named Sam. I had met her when she did leather work for me, she was an older and awesome biker woman.

She was happy to help me and the kids so we hid my v.w. under a tarp while I waited for my money from Danny and his mom to help me with gas and food on our trip home.

It was almost time to leave and needed to go to town to cash a check so I got the gun Sam had put up in the kitchen cabinet. I knew John was looking for me and I wasn't going to let him stop us. What I didn't know was that Jonathon had seen me put it back.

When the trip was ready to begin we said our goodbyes and drove off happily into the wild blue yonder. The traveling was something that my kids and I were getting pretty used to, we loved it.

Getting through the Alaska and the Canada border was only one of the few hurdles of our crazy trip. I had Jasmine's birth certificate but for some reason I didn't have Jonathon's.

I was at the drive-up window of the border crossing office and so close to Canada. "Ma'am, we're going to have to call the child's father to verify that you're the mother and if we can't get a hold of him you may have a problem!" The woman said to me.

Wow, really? I gave them Danny's number and they called him. He verified I was the mom and finally after 2 hours or so, again lol, they allowed us through.

I felt a bit of freedom and finally had a chance to take a couple of breaths. No fear of pissing him off and all hell breaking loose, no more screaming and blaming and kids being terrified, what a relief!

Again, the kids were playing with something but I couldn't figure out what it was.

"What are you hiding Jonathon?" I asked him.

"Nothin mom." He scooted his hand behind him under the blanket and sat like a little gentleman.

"Yea right." I said to him.

I turned and reached under the blanket to the back of the seat and much to my surprise I felt a gun.

"Oh my God, what did you do?" I asked while I pulled out Sam's 9 mm and just about shit!

"Its fricken loaded Jonathon, what do you think you were doing?"

I pulled over and emptied it and put both the bullets and the gun out of the kids reach. I couldn't stay mad at him for long though, the kids had been through so much and he was always in trouble. I was pretty sick of my kids being yelled at.

Being the little guy he was and wanting to take care of his mommy and sister, he did what he thought he had to do. He found the gun and hid it from us to take it with us on our journey home.

I stopped at a little store and got enough change together to call Sam and tell her what happened. She started yelling at me telling me what an awful son I had because he stole from her and that she was thinking about calling the troopers! lol so much for an apology, my son was smart enough to know that we were in danger and he did make a bad choice but his intentions were good, on with our journey we went.

We stopped for the kids to go to the bathroom and look around. The rocky riverbed

HER PLACE WAS WITH GOD

was so cool looking.

"Mommy." Jonathon hollered and I looked up to see what was wrong. "I'm going to pet the baby bears, look at the baby bears mama!" He was yelling as he was running to them.

I bout freaked! "Jonathon no get over here!" I yelled to him.

By then Jasmine was making her way out of the car to follow her brother to the edge then heading down to the baby's coming up to the rocks to see them.

"Both of you get up here now!" I yelled. "When there's baby's there's a mama somewhere and we don't want her mad at us, hurry hurry!"

I was trying to not yell and get them up and into the car then headed on fast as I could without worryin whether the mama was close or not, lol oh my goodness!

We still had a long way to go and my little car wasn't too thrilled about making this drive a second time. We stopped to have a repair shop look at it cause its noises sounded like a band lol they tightened things up and replaced something for thankfully an affordable price and we were back on the road.

We drove a couple of hours and tones of miles when heading around a mountain corner I pushed in my clutch to down shift. It went all the way to floor and stayed there, oh my! There was thankfully a place large enough where we could pull over and get off the road and a little creek right behind where we parked. I let the kids get out of the car to throw rocks in the water, that would keep them content so I could cry without them seeing me. I kicked my car and cried and prayed to God for some kind of angel for me and my kids. It was starting to get dark and a little colder to. I had absolutely no idea where we were other than the middle of British Columbia somewhere.

I was trying to figure out why things always happened the way they did and as if I didn't know that God heard my prayers and He wanted to show me He did, a big rig came down the road and pulled off up past us in the pull over. A man and a woman jumped out of their truck and walked over to our little car and the kids came running from the creek.

"Do you kids need some help?" They asked. "Are you alright?"

I couldn't believe the angels God had sent us!

"Where are you going?" They asked.

All I could do was laugh. "All the way to California."

"We're sorry, we can't go that far." They giggled and we all managed to smile. "But I am going as far as to the next town where there's a hotel. You'll be able to call for help and do something with your car there at least."

Just then another truck came down the road pulling an empty trailer. The man stepped out to the road and stopped him.

He walked up to his window to talk to him. "Sir, could you pull over? These kids need their car towed to the next town. I am going to put them in the cab with my wife and myself but I can't fit that bug anywhere."

"Actually, I was going to get some sleep. We could load the car and ya'll can go on your way and get them kids settled. I'll sleep a while then head on out to meet them with their car." He said.

I couldn't believe it! It was amazing to see one human being helping another in a times like this, God is so good to me! After we got our bags and stuff out of the car we needed they loaded me and the kids up in their truck. We slept and talked for 400 miles or so to the next town.

They pulled up to the local hotel and the man went to talk to the keeper. In no time he came back.

"He's going to give you a room for two nights for the price of one night." He said.

I would have been speechless if I hadn't been so happy! "Thank you so much, that's so sweet!" I said and started crying again.

The trucker and his wife gave us all a hug and told us they would be praying for us and to be safe. The man hugged me again, this time finding my hand to put something in it. I looked and it was money.

"This is for you and those kids, don't forget to eat ya hear?" He said.

"Thank you, thank you so much!" I had never felt so humbled as I did that that moment!

We got comfortable in our rooms and slept without any problems. In the morning I woke and the kids were gone. I started to panic, got up and looked around outside.

"Jonathon, Jasmine." I yelled.

"Mommy." I heard Jasmine say. "It's okay, we're down here." She stuck her head out the door down the hall. "We're having cereal, we didn't mean to scare you mommy, sorry." She said in such a sweet little voice.

I ran up to where they were. "It's okay, are you alright?"

The manager stepped out from the opened door. "Sorry about that, I suppose I should have sent you a note. They were hungry and I wanted to help."

"Thank you, I am not upset." I said to him. "Thanks so much for feeding them."

"Are you hungry too?" He asked.

"No, thank you though, I'm too anxious to eat." I said to him.

With an understanding smile he went back to what he was doing. I kissed the kids and went back to our room.

Soon the truck pulled up with my little bug up on it. 'To cool, now what was I going to do with a broken car on Mother's Day Sunday', I thought to myself. The little auto place was closed so I asked the hotel manager if he knew anyone that could look at it. He had a friend come over to look at it and told me that I had a blown clutch plate, that there was no way they could fix it any time soon. The station wasn't going to open for a couple of days.

I couldn't believe it, of course, damn, I was so frustrated! I cried a bit and threw my fits (in my room in private of course lol), then made some phone calls. Again, Danny had to ask his brother and his mom to help us. They sent us enough money for bus tickets so that we could finish our journey home, I felt so loved! Without being able to wait for or afford the repairs I sold the car to the hotel manager's son for $50 in Canadian money, wow, so sad!

We got our things together, thank goodness we traveled light. I had the bullets and the gun in the purse that Sam gave me before we left and the clothes that could fit in our backpacks and a couple of toys for the kids. I was just happy to have them with me, sure missed my Joshua! Getting on the bus was a like a deep breath of fresh air. We settled into our seats and finally I was able to not think about how we were going to get home and what would happen next.

In a couple of hours we made it to the border crossing from British Columbia into the United States. We pulled up to customs and everyone had to go inside to have their bags looked at and items declared. I knew I had the gun and I didn't want them to find it and think I was hiding it so I spoke up.

"Sir, I have to declare this hand gun I have." I said and gave it to the officer.

He was nice to me and the kids, he said he would run the gun and see what came up. He asked me for the bullets to the gun so I handed him my purse. He dumped it upside down on the counter and not only did the bullets fall out but so did a nice little bit of 'weed shake' that had been left in the purse when she gave it to me. I didn't clean it, I didn't even look inside of it, oh my goodness!

In moments there were officers and dogs around us and I was being escorted away from the kids. They were so scared and started crying.

Thank goodness they let me hug them real quick. "Its ok, they won't hurt us I promise, their just doing what they have to do. Stay with the officers and I'll be right back, I love you!" I told them.

They took me to a room and asked me about the weed and the gun. I repeated the story over and over to convince them I wasn't a drug smuggler or anything like that. I was stripped searched and finally they were happy that I didn't have any drugs or anything else illegal with me. Poor kids, it was so scary for them and they'd been through so much already. It was scary and humiliating for me to, I knew I wasn't a perfect mom lol that's for sure. But man, this bout topped it in all those people's eyes, if they only knew!

When everything was over they led me back to my kids where they had been waiting and of course I was holding the line up.

The officer went to hand me the gun back. "I ran checks on the weapon and it's not reported stolen and it's legal. You may take it and return it to your friend at your convenience if you would like."

2ND TIME ON THE ROAD TO CALIFORNIA

I went to reach for the gun when the bus driver walked in the doors and since the building was so huge and hollow, his loud and pissed off voice echoed.

"Excuse me." He said loudly. "You have had that gun with you on my bus this whole time?"

"I had no choice, my son took it from my friend's house thinking he was protecting us. I found it and declared it here, I am not doing anything wrong."

"There is a sign on my bus that reads, no weapons allowed on bus at any time." he yelled.

'Whoops, I guess I didn't see that one', I thought to myself.

He wasn't finished though. "If you get back on this bus with that gun I'll take it from you and take your children from you in a different country, you'll play hell getting them back!"

What I was hearing took my breath away. Everyone in the whole building was staring at us of course, dang, and I just wanted to get home, anywhere but here!

"Fine." I said and handed the officer the gun back. "Here you go, my kids are worth more than this damn gun is, it's yours."

I just wanted to get out of everyone's sight, so back of the bus we went to finish off our trip home, again.

Down the road some I apologized to the driver, he had been being so rude to me and I felt so bad. I really wanted the tension gone.

Pulling up in Corning I could feel the adrenaline of anxiety building but relief when I saw Danny pull up in his Trans-am, that sure got the kids attention lol.

"Mommy mommy." Jonathon was yelling. "Look at daddy! That's the cool car I was telling you about!" He was so happy.

"Right on honey." I said. It was so nice to laugh again. "I'm just so happy to be home and to see a friendly face!"

We got our stuff and we said our goodbyes to everyone lol, not like we had made many friends.

Danny and Rose were awesome to let us stay with them for a little while. I didn't know how it was going to work or for how long it would work but I was so grateful!

Within days of being home I got sick and was put in the hospital for four days with pneumonia. The doctors told me I had burnt my lungs from smoking to much crack.

One evening we were all sitting around in the living room after dinner watching the news. I was shocked when the screen starting flashing, 'Houston, Alaska Fire Burns

Almost Entire Sub-divion'. The kids jumped up and sat next to me as we watched while they showed pictures of where we lived when the kids were younger. Tears were unstoppable, so sad!

I tried to call a couple of numbers collect to see if everyone was alright, that no one had been hurt but I couldn't get through. Finally I accidentally dialed a wrong number and even though they didn't know me, they accepted my collect call and told me all he could, so sweet.

Danny and Rose and their daughter did so much for us! I knew it wasn't going to last too long though. He was a trucker and up before the crack of dawn and back either days later or late in the afternoon, always with an attitude. They were awesome to me and the kids though and they were clean and sober which really helped me survive all the changes.

Thank goodness summer was almost over, the heat was awful but the kids were finally back in school so I was able to get a get a job in a motel and I was home before they came home every day, to cool.

I started going to N.A. meetings with them, I loved being around people that felt the same way I did about using and not using, what we went through and what we're still going through. I had never seen anyone so happy without bein so high or drunk either, awesome!

I found a program in town that helped me with my divorce papers and actually went through with it. I didn't want to get a divorce but I felt like I was fighting a bull and there was no winning. I was tired of feeling like I 'belonged' to him. When I went into the office there were a group of about ten other women, some had kids with them and some didn't. Some of them were talking about what they had to do to get their kids back and others talked of never getting to see their baby's again, man, I couldn't help but thank Jesus that I hadn't lost these two through all the craziness. Even though my heart broke for their hearts I knew I was so blessed!

After everyone was done talking they turned their attention to me, I could have done without that. Questions were asked and answered and they were sure I should sue John for his Harley and anything else I could think of lol. I told them that you don't take a bike from a man. I finished my paperwork and left in a hurry, back to my own world.

I stayed pretty much to myself other than my kids, Danny and Rose. Danny and his brother made it real clear I wasn't to go out with any of the guys there in the program lol whoops that was the wrong thing to do! On the norm throughout my life, being told to NOT do something usually ended up the exact opposite. Even though it pissed him off, I starting talking to this guy named Ted. He was always nice to me, he would sit by me when Danny and Rose weren't there so we wouldn't be by ourselves.

Jas was so cute in meetings. When everyone would talk they would introduce their selves, "Hello, my name is Jenny and I am an addict." When it came to her in the circle she would say, "Hi, I am an addict's daughter." lol that's my girl!

I really needed someone to tell me good things and to not be judged, but to be treated like a human being. We got real close, real fast. Soon me and the kids started looking for our own place. I was getting aid started so I had a better income and Danny wasn't too thrilled about that but I really didn't have much of a choice. Every house or apartment I had looked at costs so much, even in this funny little town. I couldn't work full time, the kids needed me and half the time I was so tired, I was always tired and it drove me nuts. I hated it and on top of that I was so scared about doing this again, without John.

Finally we found a cute little house to move into and Ted and I spent every minute we weren't at work, together. I quit my job at the hotel and got hired at a local diner for the graveyard shift. I knew it wasn't going to be perfect but the money was better and since my Joshua was back from Texas I was able to get a little help with the younger kids. It was really nice having him around, I had missed him so much!

We dated for a while and talked about getting married, I knew though I would never go through with it. It seemed like the nicer he was to me, the more he bugged the hell out of me. I would go to open my car door and he would already be there opening it for me. It was like that with any door we were walking in or out of, it was as if he were watching my every move to try to help me. It was only making me feel stupid and clumsy though, I guess the nice guy wasn't something I was used to that's for sure!

Soon we broke up and I met another guy at our meetings, Paul. He had a bad reputation for dating all of the new people in our group from the meetings n' all. In no time Danny and his brother were giving me instructions that I wasn't to even think about going out with him ... whoops lol.

He lived with a woman he helped out so that's where we hung out and made meals together, again I got real close real fast. He wasn't as nice as Ted had been though, he had a bit of a mean and 'off' side to him lol something I seemed to lean towards more than I would have liked me to. This one though was a biker, a retired member with his leathers to show ... got my attention.

One afternoon when the kids were in school I was sitting on the floor of my little house going through some photographs I had found in my mom's trunk and there were a bunch of pictures of Alaska. I missed it so much, I couldn't ever stop thinking about everyone I loved there.

I didn't hear the car pull up and Paul walked in. "Hey you, what are you doing?" He asked.

HER PLACE WAS WITH GOD

I looked up and smiled. "Lookin at these pictures from home, I miss it." I told him.

"I'm sorry." He said.

He came over and sat on the floor to look at the pictures with me. He sat back and looked at me all serious.

"What?" I asked him.

"Your family aren't you?"

In my own mind I knew what he was talking about because the pictures were of my Alaska family which includes bikers.

"I don't know what you mean." I told him.

He got up and sat on the couch. "Jenny, I'm serious, you are family aren't you?"

I started putting the pictures back in the trunk, I could go through them later and anyways it was time to get him to change his train of thought! I got up and turned the tv on.

"The kids are still at school, do you want to watch a movie?"

"No, I want you to talk to me. You need to tell me the truth of what happened when you left up there."

I was still looking for a movie and ignoring him.

"You know who I am." He said. "You know I have a lifetime of loyalty to these brothers and if you have left without permission and you are being looked for I may be required to be the one to bring you back."

Ok, did my face look stupid enough at that moment? What he was saying was crazy!

"No, me leaving John was legitimate and I don't have to explain myself to you or anyone else! Anyways he wasn't a patch holder so if you have to know anything, that's all it needs to be!"

Instead of watchin the movie lol he kept talking!

"Don't get mad at me, I didn't realize you were going to put me in this position. If I get a phone call or am contacted about you Jen do you think I won't do what I have to do?"

He got my attention with that! I looked up at him. "And what pray tell would that be?" I asked him.

"I wish you didn't think this was a joke." He said to me.

I could tell he was getting frustrated, there was no way I was telling him about my past or what I had left or what I was headed towards.

"Well, it is pretty far-fetched and anyways I don't know what you're talking about so you are wasting your energy. Take a chill pill will you? Come on, will you take me to Mc Donald's?"

I figured the best way to get his mind on something else would be to lead it there so off we finally went.

A few days later we were making dinner at his place and totally out of the blues he brings it up again.

"Do you realize that if our Chapter received a message that you had left and John wanted you back, gave us the area you were heading and then it got to my brothers, I would have to hold you until you were picked up or I delivered you?"

I was dumb founded. "You have got to be kidding me?"

I grabbed my jacket and went to head out the door to go home.

"Jenny, wait." He said.

"Why, to listen to this crap some more? I thought I had told you enough about my past that you would just want me to be okay. Not ask me a bunch of questions and give me ultimatums and threaten mine and my kid's freedom after I've worked so damn hard to get it in the first place! I'm going home."

Paul turned off the burners and grabbed my arm before I could get out of the house and knelt down on one knee looking up at me.

"Marry me, will you marry me?" He asked me.

I was shocked and didn't know what to say so I said the easiest thing to get him to back off. "Yes." I told him. "I'll marry you."

We talked for a few minutes and I left to go home.

All the stuff he told me about taking me back to John, I wasn't happy with him at all. Can you believe him? He told me that if he had to he would handcuff me or tie me up or keep me in a room till they came to pick me up if that is what he was told to do. What a dork! There was no way I was going to marry this man.

I did a great job at dodging him for the next couple of weeks, even turning him down when he would pull up on his bike and send one of the kids in trying to convince me to go for a ride with him, not!

I ran into an old friend from Junior High, Dave. He was so sweet and wanted to help me and the kids get away from Paul so he moved us to Chico with him. It was nice for a little while, he even let my daughter from Alaska come down to visit. That was so awesome having Michelle in Chico with us, her and my niece Sheila Rosemarie got along great! We had such a good visit but soon it was time for her to go home. It was so hard to tell her goodbye when I took her to the airport, it was hard not to try to fit me and the kids in her suitcase!

I got a couple of jobs and nothing worked, I couldn't keep up with them and Dave was getting madder and madder at me every time, nothing made him happy. I had to quit my job at Chevron because the manager offered me speed to keep the store open for the

HER PLACE WAS WITH GOD

graveyard shift lol that lasted about 3 days then I got so sick. I told the head manager that I quit because I wasn't going to start using drugs again just to keep his store open. They weren't too pleased with that to say the least. They were pretty happy to see me go, so was I.

Dave and I couldn't agree on anything. I was getting calls from Alaska and I was making the calls to. I missed my girls and I missed my husband, whoops, ex-husband. Both of my girls, Jeanette and Michelle would called now and then and we would talk about how they were and how school was going. They told me how much they missed me and wanted me and the kids to come home. Between John, our girls and their sister, Chelsea Mae, and my heart that beat for them with so much love, I was seconds from going back home, again.

One day while Dave was at work I got a phone call. I answered it and it was John, he told me that the lights were still on …

He told me he changed his ways and that he knew he was an addict and didn't want to use drugs anymore. We also talked about some of the trouble he got into while I was gone and that he was going to have to do a couple of years or longer in prison. It was way too easy for him to get so far over his head but it wasn't worth all the questions and fighting, I was just happy to get to go home. He told me he loved me very much and wanted me and the kids to come back and wait for him, it didn't take me long to agree. I broke down crying and soon we were making plans for me to come.

Dave wasn't very happy with my decision or the phone bill I left him so Leah let me and the kids stay with her for a week or so until my money came in. We bought our tickets and got a ride to the airport and we were off.

John told me that when I left the last time he was missing me and wanted to see where I kept disappearing to and why. Him and one of our brothers rode their bikes towards Chico and stopped in Mendocino. They were sitting on Big River Beach smoking a joint (the beach my kids and I played on), when a hippie looking guy walked by. They invited him to sit and smoke with them so he did. John was telling him stories about things that happened between us.

The guy looks at John. "You're not talking about a girl named Jenny are you?"

Wow … what a small world, it was Greg! After that visit they decided to head back towards Alaska instead of going the rest of the way to Chico … no tellin who he could have ran into there!

Third Times a Charm?

When we got home my sisters picked me up and we went to the Valley. Eva was living with Radical and knowing John would be locked up by the time I got home we had already set it up for us to move into her Duplex apartment, to cool. The girls were there with me and the kids most of the time, so much had changed over the years. They had gone through a lot and had grown up way to fast.

I loved being right there, my brother Steven and his wife Patty and their kids lived right up the gravel road and on the other side of it was Debbie, Arthur and Johnny, so cool!

It got kind of boring in my world from time to time so me and the kids got a ride into town to the store and then walked over to a friend of ours, James. He sold the huge tires lol the ones that were as tall as we are. The kids loved being in his truck so he offered to give us ride home and there was no way I was gonna pass on that. The kids were totally busy lookin out the windows lovin the ride and we were talking about me and the kids making it home and getting to move into Eva's place.

He glanced down at the ashtray and back to me and cracked it open quick enough for me to see the bag in it, he closed it and winked and smiled at me. YaY, I haven't been able to do anything since I'd been home, awesome!

When we got to the house the kids jumped out to run and play with their cousins, 'right on' I thought lol, we went inside and pulled the curtains and locked the door. There wasn't any waiting on the preparation of doin a couple of lines, oh my goodness that was great for an attitude change, so was he…

HER PLACE WAS WITH GOD

It was a Saturday morning and I got a phone call from my niece. "Aunt Jenny, I'm getting worried." She said. "I haven't heard from mom since before she went to the party last night, have you talked to her?"

"No honey I haven't, I'm sure her is fine."

"Yea, your right. If you hear from her will you call me?"

"Of course." I said. "Talk to you soon."

We hung up and about five minutes later the phone rang again. I was sure it was our girl telling me the mama called, but that isn't what she told me.

"Aunt Jenny, Trooper Donald called and is coming up to the house. He said something about identifying a tattoo?" She sounded confused and scared. "What does he mean Aunt jenny, what does he mean?"

Oh my goodness, my stomach dropped to the floor, I felt like I was going to throw up.

"Honey, I'm on my way, I'll be there fast as I can."

I hung up and hollered at the kids playing outside and by the time I was ready to pull out they were in and buckled.

"What's wrong mommy, where are we going?" Jas asked.

Tears had started down my face and I hadn't realized it. "aaww, I'm fine honey. We need to get to the kids quick, I'm not sure if anything's wrong yet but when we get there I need you both to stay in the car right where you are ya hear?"

At the same time they agreed. "Ok mommy we promise."

I looked back at their beautiful little faces and smiles, I'm so blessed and I love them so much! I didn't know what was happening but I didn't like what I was thinking.

We got through the subdivision without even getting on the highway. By the time I got to the cross street Donald was coming from the other direction. As he turned up the road toward the house I turned up the same road right behind him and we both pulled into the driveway. The kids were in front waiting for him. I jumped out and went up to them and hugged them while he got out of his car and walked up to us.

"Hi my name is Trooper Donald." We all said hello then he told the kids there was a picture of a tattoo he needed them to identify. He showed them the picture and they said that it was a tattoo that their mom Eve had, oh my. Next he told them, us, that there had been a single car accident and that she hadn't made it … none of us knew what to say. The kids' knees started to buckle and I held on to them the best I could. We went to the ground in disbelief and tears were falling hard. Jasmine and Jonathon jumped out and ran to us trying to hold us, by then they were crying to. These poor baby's, their dad was already gone, they needed their mama and I had no idea what to say or do. Absolutely nothing seemed important, she wasn't coming home.

The rest of the day week and month were all blended in as if it were the day she died.

THIRD TIMES A CHARM?

~~~

They didn't let John come home for the memorial so shortly after that I got a ride with some friends of ours to go down to Kenai to see him, dang why did they have to move him so far?

It was going to be an interesting visit that's for sure, I hadn't seen him since I left. I really wanted everything to be perfect, thank goodness I had already told him I had divorced him in California but my id was still the same, that made the visiting process easier.

I wore a short little dress, one a them 'knock ya down fuck ya dresses' lol, as he called them, one that was sure to make him smile. I left my levy's, belt, top and boots with my wallet and money in them, in our friends car while they were waiting for me in the parking lot. Going in was scary to say the least, I hated going into jails and prisons. Our visit was nice, I was so relieved that we were able to laugh and tell each other stories and cry together. When it was time to leave he hugged me and kissed me and promised things would be better as soon as he got home, I couldn't wait!

After our visit I went back to the parking lot and I waited, and waited, and waited some more. About an hour later a woman came out from visiting and told me that the parking lot would lock down as soon as visiting was over and that no one was allowed to be there, oh my goodness!

'Where had they gone and why would they leave me there like this?' I wondered. I couldn't help but to cry, I had no idea what to do. Another woman came out and asked me what was wrong. I told her what happened and she said I could stay at their place and crash on a chair or something until morning then she could get me to someone else's place that might be able to get me back home. I couldn't believe I was stuck so far away from the valley or even Anchorage.

When we got there I followed her inside. It was a small little place with chairs placed throughout the house. There was a tv on in the little living room and there were others crashed on the couches and the floor. I quietly found an empty chair and closed my eyes wondering if there would be any way I could sleep. I heard some commotion so I looked up and couldn't believe it, the woman that had given me a ride was standing over a gas stove with a burner lit, she was trying to light a crack pipe, I could have died right there n' then. I turned around in my chair and closed my eyes again, this time as hard as I could. In the morning, which didn't come soon enough, the woman apologized for what I had seen, if I had seen it she said, and she took me to another house.

I waited in the car and soon she came out with a woman, a man and two kids following behind them motioning for me to get on out of the car. I stepped out and they came up and gave me a hug.

"We're so sorry you got left at the prison. That happens more times than you would think." The woman told me.

We laughed, well they laughed and I tried to lol, man, I couldn't wait to get home! They were so nice to me. They fed me, gave me a change of clothes and let me use their phone to get a hold of the Valley and a ride home.

It was quite an eventful weekend and I was more than thrilled to finally get back to my kids and to find my clothes.

Things were pretty hectic after Eva was gone so me and the kids made plans to move out of her apartment. I wasn't happy about it, a little nervous actually. I decided we'd have to find a place in Anchorage. I had a car, which was a necessity for livin in the Valley but without John home it was really hard with all the kids livin so far from everyone and everything.

I found a little apartment in Mountain View close to the kids school and the boys and girls club, it was right down the street, so awesome. One our brothers lived just a couple of roads over from me which was awesome and he had the best smoke in town. Him and John had always helped each other out and even though he was still upset with me for leaving, he was happy I was home and trying. It was so nice having someone to hang out with that didn't mind, and even enjoyed, my kids hangin out with us to. He smoked with me every day and helped me whenever I needed something, what a blessing we lived so close to him.

I didn't think I could get close to anyone, our family had each other and we were pretty sure we wouldn't ever need anyone else. When I met our neighbor's Betty and her daughter Amber they were soon so important to us, to me, my sister and best friend! They were definitely the hugest plus about having to be in the city, I don't know what me and the kids would have done without them.

Soon my Michelle moved in with us and our families were inseparable until John got out of prison.

When he got home we stayed at the apartment for a few more weeks until we found a mobile in Spenard. Moving in we learned we hadn't picked the best area of town lol, again. I walked the kids to their bus stop one morning and there was a woman dressed like, well yea lol, dressed like that. The kids asked me why she was dressed that way so early in the morning when it was so cold. I changed the subject and just kept doing that as many times as it took until their bus got there. Great, prostitutes on my kids bus stop corner and right around the corner from our house. I thought Mountain View was

THIRD TIMES A CHARM?

bad, which it is, way more violence but this was something I hadn't even seen before.

Wow, John and I with our kids was so awesome, I missed our family so much! Both of us being clean and sober was new, we both quit smoking weed to. John worked in the garage doing auto repair jobs hoping to open a shop soon and I got a job working in one of the Alaska Gift Shops downtown. For a while it seemed like our lives were back on track. He worked, I worked and kids went to school. We even sat around and watched our old favorites on tv, mostly wrestling.

On New Year's Eve we didn't go out and party, that was a first! We stayed home with the kids, lit candles and watched movies all night long. Jonathons bed was in the living room, he had already fallen asleep before we blew the candles out and went to bed, Rowdy puppy slept with him so he jumped up and claimed his spot.

We were woke up in the middle of the night by his barking and the heaviest smell of smoke I'd ever smelt! We both jumped out of bed as fast as we could, got the kids up and out of their rooms and outside. John worked frantically and got the fire out before it reached the curtains and burn the whole place down. We called 911 and they came to make sure the fire was out and took us all to the hospital. Thank goodness we were all alright, we were coughing black stuff for a couple of days but it stopped soon.

We had someone washing all of blankets cause the smoke was so nasty. We figured out that the candle on the television hadn't gone out all the way when we blew them out that night so little by little it burned through the plastic and the tv. They said that after washing the blankets that were on Jonathon's bed five times it was still coming out with soot in the water. We asked Jonathon about what happened that night. He said that Rowdy woke him up a couple of times messing with him so he pulled the blankets up over his head so he could sleep. Oh my goodness! He did that on purpose! If he hadn't of covered his face and had breathed in all that smoke he could have been real sick or we could have lost him! Rowdy was our Angel and he saved my boy, so amazing!

After five months or so things started to change, not to something that I didn't already know though. Things were back to me being the awful person I had always been, the 'wonderful family bliss' feeling, didn't last very long, with us nothing seemed to.

He starting telling me that the girls think I don't love them and that since I already left twice I was sure to leave again. That I didn't even know them anymore because of everything they went through when I would leave with Jasmine and Jonathon. That they weren't as important for me to take care of also.

I found out the when I left both times, he left to. He was gone emotionally, physically and mentally so our girls were left without him or me. Thank goodness the baby had her mom but the other girls were on their own and even if I had known then, there wouldn't have been anything I could have done, except to have not left in the first place. That was it, everything was my fault!

Pretty soon there wasn't much of a moment where the fighting wasn't happening and I ended up losing my job trying to get back n' forth. I applied at a gas station for something closer to home and was so excited when they told me the job was mine. I just had to take a drug test and pass their background check. I was sure there wouldn't be a problem, it's the first time in my life since I was 12 that I hadn't smoked weed in six months and I hadn't been in trouble with the law in years, except for two tickets so I knew it was mine. I went home waiting for the call and was so disappointed when they told me I didn't get the job. I didn't pass the background check and I tested dirty for marijuana. Oh My Goodness you have got to be kidding me!

Unreal, I felt betrayed by my own body. John and I hardly had a good moment between us or our family as a whole. Even though we were both clean and sober it seemed to me that it was like a dry drunk for him. He was angry and blamed me on a daily bases for more than one of the million things that happened.

Sometimes he wouldn't have sex with me, he would tell me that he didn't want me to be back with him if it was just for our sexual relationship ... lol Oh my Goodness, I couldn't believe he was saying something like that! I questioned my every decision for the last how many years?

I started going to my Miss Betty's house to do laundry and smoking with them. There was no way I would have been able to put up with his crap without smoking, I had to have something that was mine. He was driving me crazy being so mean to my kids. He had always been mean to them and I never had any say over it, I was never strong enough to stop it.

The craziness was never ending for all of us. Jeanette and Michelle's only knowledge of our lives was that it was great for a little while and then it wasn't. It got bad and then it got worse and when I left it became worse yet. The more that happened over the years, the angrier our kids got. I don't blame them at all, they are beautiful young girls whose lives were thrown upside down from the git go without none of us as parents having it together enough to make it better and I regretted it with all of my heart!

One afternoon it got way out of hand, one of the girls were mad at Jasmine about something and called her a 'little bitch' right in front of us. I looked at her, I looked at John and he just kept staring at the tv. Jas sat down for a minute while they argued then she went on back to her room. I was so mad, I tried to let it go but we argued continuously. It was the same as always, John using me and the younger kids against him and the girls, how I hurt them.

After a few days of this I could tell my kids were having a really hard time and they weren't happy. As far as John and the girls, there was nothing the kids or I could do that was good or right. One evening I could hear Jonathon crying and found him and Jasmine in the bedroom.

"I want to go home mommy, I want to go back to Aunt Leah." He said to me.

"I know honey, I know." I said.

I didn't know what to do other than to hold him, it didn't seem like enough to comfort him though. He needed something to hold on to, to know that it would be okay, soon.

I reached down and put my arms around both of the kids and whispered to them. "I have a plan you guys, do you want to leave?"

Their faces were covered in smiles that exact moment and both of them starting asking at the same time.

"Will it be the last time, will we have to come back?" They both asked me.

I hugged them as tight as I could. "No, we don't have to come back. Now you guys don't say anything, I'll have to figure things out."

I left the room and went on with the evening.

One of the girl's friends was over visiting so after Jonathon was feeling better, the two of them went outside to sweep the shop for John. They were talking about how everyone was fighting all the time and how bad things were getting again. My son, thinking he would understand after what they were talking about, told him that we had figured out what to do, that we were leaving and going home to California.

He came right into the house and told our daughter. She came into the living room and began making snide comments under her breath to me. Finally I asked her what was wrong and she told us that Jonathon had told Jason that we were leaving. John was right there.

He stopped what he was doing and starred at me. "What is this, you are going to leave again?"

I talked a lot and kissed some butt and finally convinced him I wasn't going anywhere. I went back in the hall to use the bathroom but the door was locked so I knocked.

"Who's in here?" I could hear my son. "Honey, let me in." He came and unlocked the door, ran back to sit on the toilet and cried.

I put my arms around him to love on him, poor guy, damit, I hate it here!

"It's okay honey, everything will be okay." I told him trying to calm him down.

"I'm so sorry mommy, I didn't mean to tell our secret, it just came out."

"I know, it's okay." I dried his tears and hugged him a little tighter. "I love you, we're going home soon I promise and there won't be any more secrets. I'm so sorry son!" I told him.

HER PLACE WAS WITH GOD

When I woke up the next day I knew we were done. I wasn't going to put my kids through this for one more day. The morning passed, John left to run some errands and the kids were in school. I got all our stuff loaded up in plastic bags and hid them in the trunk of my car. When John got home he went to do some work in the shop and the girls called saying they were at their friend's house so when Jonathon and Jasmine came home we quietly made our escape. When we got to my Miss Betty's apartment they hid my car for me, I was hopin to be able to drive home in it. That would sure make the planning easier but of course he found it lol and me, duh!

The knock on the door wasn't unexpected but it still stopped my heart for a second, he blamed me for so much. I had to keep strong and keep my heart cold. I didn't want to show him how much I really love him and how much I hate everything bad that happened to us.

From the bedroom I could hear his voice, he sounded like he was giving orders to be let in but in a strange and calm way. Betty must have been so nervous. I know I was scared and nervous also. That was just it, I was tired of always being scared and nervous!

I was sitting on the bed when he came in, he was so big standing over me. He reached for my hand and sat next to me.

"Why are you leaving, again?" He asked me.

I closed my eyes, said a prayer and took a deep breath. "John, I can't let my kids live in fear and with so much anger around them anymore. Their lives have to be different and the only way that's going to happen is by me making it happen.

Looking into his eyes I could see his tears and honest confusion and I could feel my tears running down my face. This had been going on for way to long, I knew it was over but it was the hardest thing I'd ever had to do. I could feel a part of my love for him was gone, I had to protect myself and my baby's. I could feel something inside me that said I was going to have something so much better one day, I knew it was the end.

Our discussion went on for a little bit. One question, one answer, another question then tears and more answers. I told him he couldn't threaten me and he couldn't follow me. He couldn't promise me anything and he couldn't make me feel like everything was because of me ... I was done.

We stayed with Betty and Amber Lynn until my money came so we could get a flight to Seattle and a bus the rest of the way home to Chico.

Saying goodbye seemed so much harder this time, we had gotten so close. My family was my world and they were a part of that. I knew I wouldn't be coming back like before, I could feel in my heart it would be different this time. I had to make something happen for us, something happy and something that would last.

Pulling into the bus depot I felt so loved seeing Leah and the kids waiting there for us and the first thing I smelt was Chico in the Spring. The blossoms were all over the Valley and they must have been in full bloom cause the smell was almost as wonderful as Leather, Coffee and Christmas!

Dave and Leah had gotten together after I left and I knew he wasn't going to be thrilled about me and the kids bein in town. We got our stuff loaded into the car and sat there for a minute talking and hugging.

"Don't ask me why I did things the way I did, all I know is that it was time to go. At this moment sitting with you sister, I have no idea where me and the kids are going to sleep tonight." I told her.

She grabbed my hand and kissed it. "You will stay with me whether Dave likes it or not. You are my sister and there is no way in hell I'm going to let you sleep in a car or go to a shelter!"

The kids were having fun playing in the car while we talked so it wasn't too easy to get them to settle lol, we did it though of course and headed 'home'.

We spent the time between the bus station and the house figuring out what we were going to say. Dave and I had a bad parting and we were pretty much telling him he had no choice but to like me being there or he could go somewhere else. Leah and I had always been there for each other and I am so happy and lucky she was ready and happy to help us now. I honestly didn't come home with intentions of making things hard or weird for him or to piss him off. I was uncomfortable also and real scared of going to a shelter with my kids.

Jas had passed out by the time we got to the house, it had been a long trip and she was so tired. I brought her in and she curled up on the couch and slept for what seemed to be days. Pizza was the best celebration food so we bought three or four of those huge Rico Pizza's and by the time she finally woke there wasn't any pizza left. Poor thing, she was so upset so we went and got her some as soon as she was ready.

I had put these kids through so much, I know it was just a pizza but anything that brought comfort to them at that point was something worth investing in. Jonathon was so excited to be home, he missed his auntie and cousins so much. It was so nice to see the fear he used to walk around with gone from his face. He seemed to be carefree and thankful to be where we were no matter what the situation. I was so lucky to have such wonderful and happy kids. I sure miss my Joshua, I can't wait to let him know we we're home!

The house was pretty crowded but I knew it was going to be and it's not like I was in any position to complain that's for sure, I'm so thankful that we had a place to sleep and eat! I wasn't going to put the kids into school when we got there but I didn't realize that there were still like three weeks or so of school left. Anyways, all the other kids were in school and mine would go nuts here every day without them.

Let's see, we have mine, Jasmine 11 and Jonathon 13 and Leah's kids are Jesse 5, Felicia 6, Mathew 7, Charlee 12, William 14, and Sheila Rosemarie 16 and Dave's son was 8, whew! I don't think I forgot anyone. Then of course myself, Leah and Dave lol, love it. My niece Tracy and her baby girl were there most of the time to so yep, we had quite a full house!

Me and Leah loved going to a bar called the Wild Hair, we drank too much and played a lot of juke box music and pool. We always wondered if we'd run into some of the old crowd from the mma, but it never happened. The only one I found was our friend Terri, they had his picture on the wall and I found out he had passed away years before, how sad!

One night at the bar I met a guy named Big Fred. In a couple of weeks it was pretty easy to see that our relationship was based on him being infatuated with me, the biker chick that left Alaska. He bragged about me being from Alaska to his friends all the time and spent most of his spare time at the bars, he was a member of a local club for men.

For him, it was the Alaska and the biker thing. For me, he was a big man, close to the size of the man I had just left 3000 miles behind me but he had a softness I hadn't seen in a man in a long, long time. I also really enjoyed not living with him but spending time with him at his place and going home.

Other than that it seemed like his nights at the bar and drinking were his favorite hobbies and past time which seemed to get real old real quick for me.

We went to have a drink at one of his friends' houses one night on the outskirts of town somewhere. I had never spent time with him with his other friends before so I wasn't very comfortable. He had a bit too much to drink and told me that if I ever left him he would kill me lol I tried to not cause a scene, he sure said the wrong thing! John had said that to me before, 'never again will a man talk to me like that', I thought to myself. I didn't throw a fit in front of his friends. They showed us where we could sleep and I curled up to myself ignoring him all night. In the morning I told him I didn't want to see him anymore. The words he chose for me just happened to be the wrong ones to use. He used every excuse available, it just didn't matter.

It Took My Breath Away

The sound, the power, more so, the excitement,
Yes, my heart, it's pounding, and there, the man,
He's big, he's strong and the smell, it's his leather.
The rumble is his Harley … beautiful, so beautiful!!
As I reach out to hold the seat, I throw my leg over. Yes, a perfect fit.
Me on this seat as he walks over and straddles his monster machine.
My body lies against his back, against the leather and his strength
This is only the beginning, where does it go?

Such a world, it changed you know.
New people in our lives,
More men in leathers as they too rode side by side.
Me, always seeing the smiles in their eyes

Suddenly I understand, a bit of control I suppose,
Only a selected few, so so few can hold on so tight to such power.

Can you … Have you?

The memories, they tend to slip … not far though
The pounding of my heart, almost as loud as the bikes that rumble by.
Such a longing, such a need.
Will it ever go away?

I pray forever not

The First Days of the Rest of Our Lives

Danny, Jonathon's dad, was happy we were home. I knew he wasn't sure if I would stay but I really had no thoughts of going back to John. It took a bit for him to believe me but when he called me about a house he had found for me and the kids, I knew he was giving me the benefit of the doubt. It was his friends place so I didn't have to go through a bunch of whoopla or anything to get in thank goodness. It was small but for me and the kids, absolutely perfect!

I finally got enough money to move in with my aid check and Leah loaned me the rest that I needed, we were finally going to have a home. It sits on the West side of Chico, aka College Town. I couldn't complain, it was a roof over mine and the kid's heads. It's a small house that sits behind a larger home closer near the street, so cute! Walking in there's a small, long living room then go left into the kitchen, through the little kitchen to a back hall with two small bedrooms and a bathroom. It was kind of awkward but it was comfortable and I didn't have any bad feelings about it, to cool. I was so thankful that the owners were willing to work with me. Danny helped me with some furniture and me and Leah gathered things together. I started over again, one last time.

After spending so much time in Alaska, Chico and summer were two things together that just didn't go well for me. It gets up to 115 degrees sometimes and with the little water cooler I have that doesn't work, it seems even hotter than it really is.

Jasmine and Jonathon spent most of their time at the one-mile. I grew up spending my summers there also and the upper park. Over the years though the weed and beer turned into heavy alcohol use, way too much dope, gangs and violence and the ages had gotten way younger, it breaks my heart. My kids didn't know any different so they fit in like putting on a velvet glove.

Thank goodness I had Leah and her kids, whenever her and Dave had problems they would come to their second home, so awesome. If it wasn't for her I wouldn't have our little home or anything, I was so happy to be happy again! I didn't like being by myself anyways. I knew some of the people that live next door to me from my past and there was a guy that lived behind me in some cabins. His daughter is sweet and he's nice, just a little creepy lol. My kitchen is real small and the only little window in it looked right into his kitchen window. I enjoyed his company and I am so thankful that he could get me stoned with the ritual, ~ wake and bake ~. With everything I had gone through I truly did appreciate him getting me stoned in the mornings. After we smoked, I'd leave and go back to my little house and drink a cup of coffee sitting in my little front yard.

Everything seemed great until one day he was just upright weird to me, time to find my smoke somewhere else. His daughter and Jasmine went to school together so at least she knew she had a friend close by.

The kids were new in school and town, thank goodness they didn't have problems meeting people, especially when they had a chance to talk about being raised in Alaska and it's always a great conversation starter.

Jonathon made friends quick, (most friends the kids made this next few years are children of all the people that I did dope with years ago or were apart the same world, crazy) he enjoyed being out and about to much though. I got a phone call one night from the Police Department wanting me to pick up my son. I get there and of all people sitting there waiting for her son was David Fulton's brother's, ex-wife. Right away she starts talking about David n' all. After about two hours they brought the boys out, I could have picked anyone else to have to be there with that night! Time went by and he was arrested again. This time for hanging out on top of the old Senator Theater roof with another friend from a local family we knew when we were younger (lots of us back then had been up there also). Yep a small town Chico is, it seemed like I'd been gone forever but the same people seemed to be everywhere … doing the same thing.

In no time Jonathon was growing up and so handsome, Jasmine was getting taller and more beautiful every day. She isn't the little girl she was in Alaska but she's still my baby, not liking her room being in the back of the house her made a little room behind our couch in the living room where I slept. She moved her mattress and used crates for a small bedside table, her books and toys appropriately placed.

"I love you mommy and since we don't fit on the couch together anymore this will do." She told me.

Looking at my kids, I know that everything was worth bringing them to a better place.

JONATHONS STORY ABOUT LIVING IN ALASKA

~~~

In no time my kids were well known by the police station, probation officers and the juvenile hall so we didn't go through just one or two probation reports, probably four to six of them between different kids at different times. I was so confused when they asked me about our back grounds, our lives we lived before now. I hated telling them about our drug use and, our life style and where the kids were before I brought them home, I had to do it more than once.

Some of them were choosing paths I was really worried about, hanging out with gang members, being violent with lots of attitude, things I thought they knew better to stay away from.

One day at the probation office I told them I didn't understand why my kids were acting out this way. He read through the files and asked me about our life in Alaska and how the kids and myself described it in all of their reports.

"Well," I said. "We're a family, we were there for each other."

"Did you ride with the 'Carma Control'?" He asked.

"Not always and some of them yes, but they were like family. John wasn't a patch holder."

We sat and talked for a bit and soon I realized the way we had lived our lives in Alaska, is the way my kids are living their lives now, the only way they knew how ...

As summer kept up, our little house ended up being a pretty busy place. The people that lived next door partied all the time and my kids spent a lot of time with their kids. They all smoked but they did the other crap to, I hated knowing it was so close to us all the time.

Some nights I couldn't sleep because there would be like five or six teenagers from next door all sitting up on top of their metal roof frying on acid. Of course Jonathon and Jasmine loved it (there seemed to be no way for me to keep them away from everything I wanted them to stay away from).

After I went out with Frank I figured I was better off without a man around. My kids and I had been through enough and mean men seemed to be everywhere.

Big John called a couple of times and was always high on pain pills or drunk. I think secretly I waited for those calls, maybe it told me that someone still loved me or something but hearing his voice on the phone always threw me off. I dreamed that things had been different and everything happening was a dream. Then he would remind me how messed up it was when he would tell me that it was my fault our girls were having such a hard time.

He told me. "I don't want to make you feel bad or anything, that isn't why I called. But you know if you hadn't of abandoned them things would have been different."

What? Oh my god, I was always so amazed at the martyr this man played.

"Kay John, I have to go." I would tell him and hang up.

Leaving him in Alaska and sitting there in my small living room 3000 miles away, again, I felt like I did the other two time I left. Questioning myself over and over wondering if what I did was right and even if it wasn't, how could I ever go back after everything that had happened?

So much had been said and so many things had happened. Then I do a rerun through my mind and in no time I remember that what I did, I did for my kid's lives and I will never regret it! I knew that somehow, in time, things would be easier. I wasn't quite sure if I could do it yet. I was pretty sure that John was sick of me leaving and coming back even if he was part to most cause of it, I could understand that. I know how much of a yoyo I have felt like for so long, I am sure he was feeling that to.

I even got jealous when I found out who he was seeing and going out with or sleeping with. Then he would tell me that none of the relationships he has mean anything, compared to knowing the perfect love, ours, there will never be a love so perfect. That's usually when I would stay away from his calls for a while. His words made my heart ache so much, I couldn't listen to them, my heart is broken too.

HER PLACE WAS WITH GOD

My kids were still spending most of their time with their friends at the park, in all actually, I had no idea where they were. I was either home by myself or at Leah's house until I met Todd. He was way younger than me and he really got along with my kids, everyone else teased me and called him my boy toy lol how funny. I'd never had one of them before lol.

In a short time he was there every night and pretty much staying with us and soon I got sick with pneumonia, again, and was in the hospital. I didn't have anyone to help me with my kids so he stayed with them for the week I was gone. When I got home they told me he hadn't been there most the time, just in the morning to make sure they got to school and to maybe get them something to eat. The summer had been so long it seemed and the kids had been through so much and now they were pretty much taking care of their selves on their own.

I never paid any attention to the directions on the medicine's they sent me home with and when I left the hospital they sent me home on 40 mg a day of Prednisone. I took it every day and before I knew it I had gained like 60 pounds. I don't think I had ever weighed this much in my life except for when I was pregnant.

I started to notice my Jonathon coming home in really nice clothes, new hat and sunglasses. He always told me that someone gave it to him and I would always believe it. Him and his cousins were spending a lot of time on the streets at night but I had no control. Jasmine spent a lot of time at the 'zoo', an apartment complex that was alive, so to say, and kickin when I was young also. She got caught up in the drugs and the party's real fast.

One night the highway patrol even woke us up early one morning pounding on my door looking for my oldest boy Joshua. I hadn't seen him in a while, thank goodness he wasn't there!

I really thought that coming home would help my kids, not make things worse.

Finally summer was over and school started, at least I would have some idea where they would be, this is a good thing. It's amazing how beautiful and colorful Chico is in the fall, in Alaska it was white and cold. I was so happy to be home but I was still so torn, my heart was in two different places, 3000 miles apart.

Todd didn't work, of course, and I had no idea what I was doing in life other than surviving for my kids so we broke up on Halloween night. I walked all the way to Leah's cause my kids were there getting ready to go trick or treating, way more fun than what I was doing!

A week or so after he had been gone, the kids and I were woke up by the police knocking on our door at three in the morning looking for him. He was a suspect in different burglaries, oh my goodness! How was I so blind to leave this idiot boy in charge? Thank God he wasn't there anymore and my kids are alright! Men, boy's lol? NOT …!

I was on Financial Aid aka welfare, so when I was better after being sick for so long they told me I had to start their welfare to work program. K, 'I can do this' I thought to myself. My kids go to school all day and there's a bus I can take a few blocks away so I did it. I took the bus every day at 7 in the morning and then home again at 3:30 hoping that Jasmine and Jonathon were doing alright and made it home from school. Usually I found out that there had been a fight or something had been stolen, if it wasn't one thing it was another.

I was really excited though, the program was at their office learning how to handle interviews and how to dress for them and all that good stuff. It was nice to actually be doing something in what seemed like the first time in my life but I knew I had accomplished a lot. I was a certified paralegal in Alaska, that in itself is worth being proud of!

It was Thanksgiving and again away from John and the girls. I didn't know how I could survive this, I hated being alone. If it weren't for Leah I truly don't know what I would have done, thank goodness for family. We had a huge group and it was great but even better than the good food was Rick being there too. We knew each other from Junior High and he had gone to Alaska with me in 91.

After that day he came by to hang out, we'd watch a game show or something, maybe a movie, it was really nice to actually 'talk' to a man. That was all I was interested in though, I wasn't looking for another reason to turn on the roller coaster …

HER PLACE WAS WITH GOD

> Started 1:30 pm
>
> Jenny; 12-12-98
>
> The feelings I have in my heart for you are hard for me to explane sometimes. One day they just came out and wanted to stay, because I had you on my mind and felt as if I was missing you. Even after hearing you say that you didn't want a relationship my heart stoped for a moment started back up and sent a message to my brain. And this is it "If we can get her to smile and be happy again that's a step in the right direction." "So don't give up ever because that's when you miss her." And the more I missed you I sadder I felt, even others say that when I've been around you it shows.
>
> So what do you think of just makeing each other smile and being happy. And see what of our lifes we create together."

RICKS LETTER TO ME

He came over one day, then the next, and the next and always one day turned into the next day until every day I was looking forward to him coming by. It was so weird having a man around me that didn't have one sarcastic or mean word to say or look on his face. I kept pinching myself, I couldn't believe it was really happening.

He's so cute, such a hillbilly mountain man. All I had to do is mention to him I needed something for my apartment and the next day or so he would show up with whatever it was, it was like Christmas every day. One day he had left to go back to his dad where him and the kids had been staying and came back real quick. I was laying down on the couch and he came in, took my hand and slipped a silver double-heart ring on my finger. He kissed me and told me he loved me and left. I thought I would die right there! I was so happy and so not sure at the same time.

I didn't believe much from a guy, words were so easy to come by it seemed, but the day he put that ring on my finger I knew my life was going to change again.

Things were always good and we spent a lot of time together. When the kids and I got home I pretty much quit cooking. Between Willows and now Chico my kids enjoy microwavable foods and mac n' cheese or Mc Donald's of course lol. In no time I was cooking for him and my kids and then I was cooking for all of his kids also and remembering how much I loved it. Ricks kids are, Mary 11, Tina 9 and James 8 then mine, Jonathon 13 and Jasmine 11 lol, what a group! My Joshua, 19 now had moved to Willows, met a girl and they were are having a baby, I'm going to be a grandma!

Mine and Rick's lives were pretty entwined now so he talked to my landlords about the house in front of mine that was for rent. Before we knew it, it was Christmas Eve and with a lot of paint, lots of repairs and tones of love he made the house a palace for our family's to move into. The kids had gone through so much already and they all really deserved good things to happen for them. All our Tina wanted for Christmas this year was their own home.

Grandpa covered the kid's eye's and drove them around in the dark a bit to get them confused about the area of town they were in, then brought them to their new home.

"Kay kids, look now." Dad hollered to them.

The kids were surprised and so happy, they ran through the house and hugged all of us over and over. I have to admit it was probably one of the most wonderful Christmas' any of us had in a long time.

I didn't know how it was going to be okay through the holidays without John and the girls. God knew what he was doing though, mending my heart and mending Rick's and all of our kid's hearts at the same time, how amazing!

It was quite interesting getting everyone settled, there were so many of us but it really did work. Jasmine, Mary and Tina shared the front bedroom, James had a room and Rick and I had a room. Jonathon and our brother Charles that moved in with us stayed in the two rooms in the back house. It was awesome having both places but Jonathon bein back there didn't last long. He was sneaking out at night and having girls over, every time Charles and Rick would tell me about something Jonathon did I got so mad at them never realizing that they were telling me the truth and my son was not, whoops! Jonathon moved into the room with James in no time that's for sure lol!

Rick and Charles worked full time driving for a local thrift store and I was going to school at Butte College for the Alcohol and Drug Studies Program. I didn't stay in the program long, the classes I had to take were at night and I hated being away from home and the kids in the evening like that. Parking at the campus was awful, the only place I could park at night was way up away from the campus and it was too dangerous to walk out there so I volunteered to work in the office for a drug and alcohol rehabilitation program.

I left at lunch one day, my second day there to go home for my break. I had taken one hit off of my pipe when I heard a door shut out front. I looked out the window and saw two Sheriff's walking up to the house so I went out to the porch to meet them.

"Hi, what can I do for you?" I asked.

The officer looked around me into the house. "We're looking for Stephen Russell, have you seen him?" He asked me.

"No, I'm his mom but he doesn't come around much."

The officer was still trying to see into the house from the porch. "I smell marijuana, are you smoking?"

He was pushing past me and walked inside to find the smell was from me.

"So, why don't you go ahead and show me where your weed is and what you were smoking in."

Another officer came in also and they proceeded to go room to room to see what they could see. Next thing I knew they had found my little plant I was growing. It couldn't have been any bigger than bout six to eight inches tall. The first officer came back in the house with the other one behind him carrying it.

They went through my bedroom and found our metal locked box in the bedroom, they were so funny lol.

"Where is the key to this lock? Does your boyfriend have it on his key chain?" They asked me.

"No, no one has the key, there isn't one." I said.

He went and found a crowbar on the side of the house and took the box on the porch and smashed it till it opened. It took everything I had to not laugh, I mean, he was putting so much work into opening this tiny little box. He found the two ounces of smoke and $40 which to them would constitute sales and of course let's not forget the felony cultivation charge for my six inch experiment. Unreal, they acted like they were displaced ghetto cops or something.

"Okay ma'am." The one officer said to me. "Turn around and let's get these handcuffs on you. You're going to have to go down to the station, you are under arrest for cultivation and possession."

I had my purse on the floor because I had just come in for lunch and had planned on leaving for work again.

"I need to put my purse away and call my kids or one of em at least so that they'll know where I am."

"Sorry but you're not going to make any phone calls." He told me while they walked me out the door.

They left the door open and left my purse sitting in the middle of the living room.

When we got to the Sheriff's substation they called Rick's probation officer. The dates weren't updated in their system so they thought he was on searchable probation still. That thought didn't last long, he's been off probation for a while, what dorks! I

THE FIRST DAYS OF THE REST OF OUR LIVES

couldn't believe what was happening, oh my God, it had been years since I had been jail! I made it through waiting for everyone else getting arrested, there had to be like 2025 other people being booked. At least there was a payphone and a bathroom, thank goodness!

I called Rick's dad collect and told him what happened, not crying was the hardest thing to do. I was so worried about the kids coming home from school with me not being there. I couldn't believe that after all the things I did in Alaska, I'm here and in trouble over this.

Sitting on my bed I knew I wasn't going to be able to keep to myself for long, it had been so long since I had been in custody. I knew I had to do this even though I was nervous and my heart was beating a thousand beats a second. The whole thing didn't seem as bad as I thought it was going to be. The worse was the humiliation while being searched, looked over, cleaned and dressed appropriately in the beautiful orange jumpsuit they give you and the whole time feeling like you are being looked down on by everyone that looks your way. Then into a cell with the women. One girl Tina, I knew from when we were kids and there were others. She told me she was there for dope and that she wasn't the only one. She told me a few others from our past that were there also, all for the same thing. It broke my heart.

She invited me out to the table with her and the other girls (there were two cells with two beds in each for a unit. The open area for the four of us had a table a tv, a payphone and a cold metal toilet and sink) I knew I had to play nice no matter what I thought, I was lucky I knew someone in my cell.

I sat down next to her and started up conversation. "Hey Tina, long time no see."

She hugged me and kept her arm around me. "This is Jenny girls, she's cool, no problems and I can't even believe you're here! What happened girl?" She asked.

"You wouldn't believe it, I have been clean for three years now and I end up here over a little bit of smoke and a tiny little plant, their acting like it was a full-fledged garden!" I told her.

I couldn't stop the tears while I was holding my head in my hands.

"This is crazy, I have been out of trouble for so long."

"Its ok honey." My friend Tina said. "You'll be home in no time."

She stood up behind me and started rubbing my shoulders to get me to relax. At first it was nice and was starting to work but soon I realized that her touch was meaning more than just helping me relax so I thanked her and slipped out of her hands to make a phone call.

"Thanks, I feel better. I know jail isn't the best place to lose it but I suppose it will have to do." We all got a laugh and I dialed grandpa's hoping to talk to Rick.

It felt good that he accepted my collect calls and I was so happy that Rick had stopped by his dads at the perfect time that I called.

HER PLACE WAS WITH GOD

"Hi, I love you!" I said, and started crying again.

"I love you to honey, don't cry, everything will be ok." He said trying to calm me down.

"I can't even see a judge till Monday and its Friday night, which means I have to spend three nights in this place before I go to court. They could have waited till Sunday or something!"

We both tried to laugh, I could hear in his voice that he wasn't happy either. "We'll get you an O.R. at court on Monday and you'll be home in no time." He told me.

"This is crazy, they were looking for Joshua and there I was takin a hit off my pipe, dang! Now I'm gonna lose my job to."

"Don't worry about it, you'll find something else, you know that." He said.

"I love you, we better get off your dads phone, can I call you tomorrow?"

"Yea, I'll come over round 4 so call between 4 and 5 in the evening k? I love you, don't forget that!"

"I know, I love you to honey. Bye bye, tell the kids I love them k? Are they alright?"

"The kids are fine honey, I'll make sure they eat and all that good stuff, now stop worrying ya hear?"

"K, just make sure to tell all of them that I love them and I'll be home Monday and to be good. Love you honey, talk to you tomorrow."

"Love you to, try to relax?" He said trying to calm me again. "Good-bye hun, talk to you tomorrow."

"I will, bye, talk to you then." It was so hard to hang up the phone.

I did though and then went and laid down on my bed for bit and tried to make myself fall asleep. I figured if I slept the whole time I was there it would be Monday morning in no time. It didn't work of course, which was fine. At that point I was ok being where I was other than missing Rick and the kids.

In no time it was Monday and a group of us went to court. I didn't really mind going, what I hated about it was having to come in through the 'in custody' door from the back of the court house in an orange jumpsuit, it's just the right 'style' to catch everyone's eye.

Such a relief when I saw Rick and his dad in the back. I waited my turn and sat with my attorney and did what I was supposed to do. Thank goodness I got my O.R. I was more than ready to go home that's for sure.

After all of us saw the judge they loaded us back up and took us down to the jail, perfect timing for lunch (or not), yippee, does a girl great for a diet! I got all my stuff cleaned up and packed and was ready to go but hour after hour no one came. The system is awful, I wasn't called out of there until seven that night.

Dad was outside waiting for me when they let me out the door. Rick had to go back to work so he had been there all day long waiting, I felt so special!

"Come on kiddo." He said to me with that smile. "Bend over so I can kick you in the ass k?"

"Yea yea yea dad, I know. Thank you for being here for me." I reached over and hugged him and kissed him on the cheek and we went outside. We got in the truck and he drove me home.

A week or two later I got a call from the kids teacher at school. They had been talking about their mom being in jail and one of them brought a leaf to school so she wanted to meet and talk. All of our kids were raised around weed so I wasn't too surprised but then the Sherriff called also and told me I needed to work on getting my prescription if I wanted to avoid any more problems … now I had to figure out how to find a doctor.

When I met with their teacher. I felt like I was on trial at first but as it turned out, she actually really did care. They had a handful with our group of kids and it would take someone with a big heart and tones of understanding and patients to keep up with them.

She wanted to know about our past and our today, my health and our family. I'm sure that knowing more about our lives and the kids she could understand them better. We had Jonathon in the 6th grade and Mary and Jasmine in 5th grade and Tina was in the 3rd grade and James was in the 1st grade, whew!

<hr />

With the years my kids had been in school in Alaska they never got shots or saw a dr. or a dentist much. There was a dr. that was giving all our kids shots at the school so I asked him if they took new patients. He said no that they were full but since Leah is my sister, my family, they let me make appointments for me and the kids, YaY, we had a real Dr.!

Within a short period of time and a couple of trips to the doctor's office and the lab, I had a grip of diagnoses and specialists I could have done without.

The first was Chronic Hepatitis C. My Dr. did a biopsy and could see I had been infected with it for over 20 years (the culprit sure to be the dirty needed I waited for with David behind four other people in this old ran down cabin with no electricity or water).

I have a rare blood disease called Hereditary Non-Spherocytic Hemolytic Anemia

I have Retinitis Pigmontosis, RP is an eye disease that causes tunnel vision and blindness.

I have an Arrhythmia (Bradycardia)

HER PLACE WAS WITH GOD

I have C.O.P.D. Emphysema and Allergies
I have Anxiety and PTSD

When my Dr. told me I had Hepatitis C it was so scary and he seemed so off. He told me the diagnosis with a very professional type voice and told me he had to report me to the health department. Before I could ask him much more, he left the room and a nurse came in behind him. She told me he just really has a hard time giving news to patients sometimes, he does care about us. I knew that, I'm glad to know he wasn't disgusted with me. Honestly I thought I might have had Aids, a lot of the symptoms matched and I was an ex-iv user and other things so I don't know why I got upset, thank goodness it was what it was.

I left the office, got into my car and lit a cigarette and sat there smoking it. All of a sudden I realize there might have been way more to why I couldn't ever keep a job or keep up with any kind of sports or anything like that. I always thought I was useless and a screw up or a 'fuck-up' as my stepdad had always called me. Wow, maybe I wasn't all of those things after all? Tears started falling, I couldn't believe what was happening, really Lord? Hepatitis C? I felt so dirty!

I drove to Leah's and knocked over and over again. Leaning on her door I slid to the ground crying until I realized I was in public making a spectacle so I went back to my car and drove home. I'm really glad the kids weren't home yet, Dale (Rick's brother and the cowboy my mom sent me to Bachmann Hills to keep me away from when I was 13) and Rick were watching tv. I came in and sat down and told Rick that we needed to talk. He turned around to me and I told him what the dr. told me. I started crying again and told him I'd pack mine and the kid's things and we would move if he wanted us to. That I didn't want to hurt the kids or put him or anyone else in jeopardy.

He came over to sit next to me and loved on me, both of them told me, no, that I wasn't going anywhere and that I was home where I belonged!

I made an appointment and went to see my cal-works worker at the employment office and with her help I applied for SSI. I had really been trying to do something to earn my own living. I have been on welfare most of my life and not proud of it. I had no idea what I was going to do financially with my kids growing up and me not being able to keep a job. It took about a year or so and being denied three times before I was granted it by the judge, it was like a million thousand pounds off of my shoulders. I couldn't stand the thought of Rick and Charles having to be my only way of survival for myself and my kids, what a relief!

I had a real hard time dealing with the diseases they told me I had. No matter how bad I felt about myself or no matter how many times I called myself a 'mutant' Rick would hold me and tell me he loves me and none of us are going anywhere. We'll get through it one day at a time together as a family, he's is my Angel sent from God!

THE FIRST DAYS OF THE REST OF OUR LIVES

I went to see my Joshua at a rehab one afternoon and while we were visiting a man came up to him to show him some tattoo drawings he had done.

This man seemed so familiar to me but I wasn't sure so I pulled up the sleeve of my t-shirt to show him the cover-up tatt work he had done on my shoulder. "Excuse me." I asked him. "Does this look familiar to you?"

He looked at it then to me, his face went from confusion to realization and he smiled. "Jenny?"

He came around the table and hugged me, we were both in shock and so happy! I had thought about him, tattoo Dave, so many times over the years and didn't expect to ever see him again. How awesome that he was alive and healthy!

Then and Now
Written for Rick

Today, so different than yesterday was.
A love I can trust, a love that is true.
Our family, you and me, our children, sweet as can be.
Days into nights, nights into days.
So much more to learn, so much more to soar than ever before.
Your eyes are so sure looking into mine,
A promise to the future, I never thought I'd find.
Knowing a love so strong and true,
I can't wait to grow old with you

I love you the Whole Wide World!!

Is That a Rainbow God?

It seemed so crazy, sometimes out of hand, every day was an adventure in one way or another. I was always scared and unsure, worried I couldn't do this. The craziness was with the kids and I. Since Rick worked so many hours, his introduction to whatever had happened that day usually ended up in yelling and someone being hurt or mad when he got home at night and a high percentage of the time we didn't find out about whatever happened till a couple of weeks or months down the road.

There were so many kids that arguments were a given, some days were good and some days were awful, I had no idea how to be a good a good mom. The hardest for them I'm sure, were mornings after a big fight, which happened often. They would still have to go to school and usually that would lead to something happening there also.

My guilt was on me constantly, every time something crazy happened I blamed myself for what all the kids had been through. So much had happened and after us changing our lives around almost overnight we didn't realize how much harder it was going to be for them. I had so many regrets. The kids fighting was an 'always' thing, and yelling, screaming and crying was something I could SO do without. I hadn't ever done this clean and sober before, all I could do was to always yell back, it was so hard for all of us. I felt like such a failure, I couldn't figure out the fix for anything!

It was bad when it was just me, Jasmine and Jonathon, Joshua also when he was at home but to be responsible for someone else's kids? I was so afraid of myself, the only thing that ever shut my Jasmine and Jonathon up when they were standing face to face screaming at each other was to slam their heads together. It worked and I knew, obviously, I couldn't do that to Rick's kids. Now what I was going to do? Even putting them on the wall or in a corner ended up being an ordeal, I had to be the worse mom in the world and the most Evil Step-Mom with capital E, S and M!

My kitchen was off and out of the way of the living room so when thing got too much for me I would head there to clean or cook something or both. I would sit on the floor hugging my legs and cry. On the amazing moments he was home and found me there, no words needed to be spoke. He would kneel down to put his arms around me and rock me while I cried until I could breathe again. Wow, thank you Jesus!

Finally time was passing and life was becoming something worth waking for more every day and before I knew it months turned into a year. By then everyone was scattered throughout the neighborhood and Chico. Keeping track of them was a chore in itself but so totally worth it! Life was like I used to dream it could be. We got up in the morning, made coffee, got kids up and dressed, fed and off to school then Rick and Charles would head out to work.

I cleaned the house and loved on our Karma kitty that Jonathon had brought me when he was a kitten. I really was happy, I don't think there had been a day that went by where Rick was mad at me or yelled at me or looked at me with a mean look or anything, every moment was a miracle. I didn't even know a man could NOT get mad at a woman lol or at me I should say, there had to have been something I did wrong, but nope, never!

The dynamics of our kids had become amazing and colorful, like pieces of a rainbow flying in all different directions!

The kids were busy in their worlds and I really needed something to be busy in to. I found out about California Department of Rehabilitation and made an appointment, I was so excited! I didn't know what was going to happen but I heard they had helped a lot of people so all I could do was to try. My case worker was awesome, we met for a while and talked about my life and what I had done, what I hadn't done lol and what my dreams, wants and needs were. It was so awesome to sit and talk with someone that really cares.

We decided that going to Butte College was a good thing and since I loved to type and was good at it, I decided to go through the Medical Transcription Program. Their program was amazing, they covered my gas, my books and my tuition and even bought me my very first computer.

At first I was doing really good, it was so basic but harder lol if that makes sense. I had to take other classes to like medical terminology and a biology class, I barley passed those but I did it. I couldn't believe I could still learn, so cool! I also took an online Creative Writing class. I had written poems years ago when I was high but they were always so crazy lol and of course were soon lost. I had so much fun in this class though, the poems I wrote seemed to be so much a part of who I was, or had been, so awesome!

I got through the semester and realized I couldn't keep up with how many tapes had to be done to go to the next level. I was getting warn out and more and more tired so I had to drop from the program and I was so sad. I loved what I was doing and I hated never knowing when I would feel great and when I wouldn't. When I was sick it could last for a day or for 3 to 4 days if I got real busy or stressed.

IS THAT A RAINBOW GOD?

Even thought I couldn't stay in the program any longer they let me buy the computer from them for fifty bucks, so awesome!

⌒∽⌒

Sitting in my room at my computer I felt like I was where I belonged, I hadn't felt that in a while. I was gathering my poems and posting them to a site I found, stories.com. I put what I wrote there and others would read it and comment, wow, real feedback. It was awesome having strangers tell me what a good writer I was, I had no idea!

As I sat there one day I heard a voice over my left shoulder. I turned to the left and didn't see anyone so turned to my right and still didn't see anyone. I could hear the kids in the other room and rick hollerin at James for leaving his tools out in the rain and then I heard it again.

This time, it was still over my left shoulder but much clearer and louder. "Jenny, it's time to write your book. The name of it will be 'Her Place Was With God' and it will be your financial freedom."

I kept looking over my shoulder and then the other side again but still no one was there, it had to be God! I knew it was time and I knew its name, now all I had to do was to figure out how to get started.

I spent weeks writing stories. Stories off the top of my head, story after story after story. All of a sudden it seemed to come to me so easily, I had no idea I was a writer let alone that I would enjoy it. As time went by I started checking out writer sights. I thought I should look and see if there was a way I could actually hire someone to help me with my work. It's not like I could pay much in the beginning but the finished product was a promise from God, that I knew for sure.

After a few days of searching I found a cool site, moonlighters.com. I read through whatever I could find to read. I was scared about having to talk to strangers about my work and what kind of reactions I would get from other writers.

I wrote a small introduction about myself and put a menial price of $100.00 a month + extra's for future publishing n' all of course. With the research I did I found out hiring a ghost writer or someone to do what I needed, to put my stories into, 'readable form', can cost up to thousands of dollars. Not that they aren't worth it because they are. If I could afford them, it would be well worth the investment.

I registered and posted myself on the site, then went back to check it out. I was happy with what I had done but was scared, excited and exhausted in the same breath. Time to shut off the computer and take care of dinner or something. I shut it down and went to smoke with the guys.

We got busy and I didn't get to the computer for a couple of days. When I did I couldn't believe I had already gotten five emails on my post. Wow, so awesome to see what they said. As I read them it was obvious how people were so different than others. I read them all and shut my computer down for a bit and when I went back that evening I had gotten ten more answers to my posts. Oh my goodness, first I printed out each response. Some were positive and some were pessimistic, some changed my meanings and some just didn't understand at all.

I knew that I couldn't make this decision on my own, I had to give this one to God. I prayed and began going through all the responses and threw out the ones that gave me that, 'I don't know' feeling. When I was finished I sent a copy of my short, 'Behind Closed Doors', to the ones that were still in the running. I knew that from sending that piece of my work, I would get someone's attention. Within a few days I had heard back from most of them. There were little things that helped me weed through the prospective writers and it ended up being so simple, it was pretty much a given. By the time I was done I had one piece of paper in my hand.

We connected right away and made all the work and financial decisions. It's so exciting to get started, really get started! My first assignment was my bio, which would give her an idea of who I was and where I had been. Then she sent me a list of questions and from there with my answers the story began to be written, one small memory at a time made story after story. My new journey had begun.

Another Sad Good-Bye

There was so much happening with so many different lives in such a small space, as time went by it got better and better.

Rick worked fulltime and kept food on the table and bills paid. I was constant with my emotional break downs of insecurity's and medical problems, not thinking I could be a good mom to all these kids. Charles worked hard and pitched in on the family's finances and beer drinkin after work, especially on Friday nights when Skip would come out to play poker. Charles and Skip became Uncles to our kids and brothers to me and Rick and added to all the kids with their own independent worlds. We found this perfect connection that kept us together and somehow got us through year after year. We're going through different stages but in the long run we've come to depend on and love each other so much!

I was in the kitchen thinkin about what to make for dinner and heard the phone ring.

"Jenny, it's for you hun." Rick hollered from the living room.

I came in and he handed the phone to me. "Thank you." I told him, but I could see the concern in his eyes.

"Hello?" I said.

"Hello, Jenny?" I heard.

"Yes, who is this?"

The man sounded as if he had been crying. My heart stopped as I realized it was John. All of a sudden I got scared and tight inside. I looked up at Rick, he smiled, kissed my cheek and headed back to what he was doing. I went into the bedroom and sat at my computer desk.

"What's up John?" I asked, trying to sound as calm as I could.

"You have to come home, we need you here. Arthur died and the family needs you now."

I know I heard what I did but I think I was numb … oh shit, he said Arthur died. I felt my stomach drop and tears started coming.

"Oh my God, I'm so sorry." I managed to say.

"Jenny, please. You'll come home right? You know that this is where you belong." He said to me.

"I'll come home for the funeral and for Debbie and the kids and I'll come home for you and the girls but I'm not coming home to stay." It was so hard to talk while I tried not to cry.

Sweet Arthur. Debbie and Arthur had been together since they were young. They have been so close for so many years. Author was like a father/brother to John and like a grandpa/uncle to the kids, Jasmine adored him! When she was 4 - 5 years old I would take her over to Debbie and Arthur to watch her for me. As soon as she got there Arthur would give her the remote to the tv and tell her she could watch whatever she wanted. He loved her and always spoiled her. How sad, all my nieces and nephews losing their dad, and my sister Debbie, Oh my goodness, he was her one and only forever, I couldn't imagine!

It seemed like all those years from the past were being ran like a movie in front of my eyes, the people, the family, the love and the insanity. It took me a second to snap out of it.

"Okay John I will come, I'll figure it out somehow. There isn't much I'm going to be able to do." I told him.

"You just need to be there for Debbie, she's your sister and Marta is falling apart so she isn't going to be much help and the girls have all the kids to take care of and Karen won't be able to help from Oregon."

"I know, its okay. I'll call you back as soon as I have a schedule for the flight."

"We're not going to make the service day and time until we know when you'll be here so figure it out right away and get back to me kay?" He asked.

"Kay, tell Debbie I love her. No, never mind, I'll call her myself." I told him.

"Goodbye Jenny, we love you and I'm really glad you're coming home. Thank you." I could hear him starting to cry, it broke my heart.

"You're welcome John, I'll do what I can but I told you, I'm not staying." I reminded him.

"Talk to you soon." John said quickly and he hung up, at least I hoped he had cause I started crying.

I wasn't much at handling death and I didn't understand it and the pain and loss that went with it. I knew when I left that some would die, their lifestyles called for it.

ANOTHER SAD GOOD-BYE

Those night time phone calls and never knowing who it was going to be next is what scared me the most.

I sat there for a little bit trying to figure how this was going to happen. I didn't know how Rick would feel about me going to spend time with John and the kids and my family there. He knows how much I love them and miss them but this could be pushing it maybe?

Right then he came in and sat down and held me. "It's okay honey, I know you need to go to your brother's funeral, here is $1,000 from Charles and I'll add to that. Book your flight and we'll get you to the airport."

I could feel my heart growing so big it barely fit in my chest anymore! "I love you so much, you are so good to me!" I said grabbing him and hugging him so tight!

I wish I could have stopped crying but that didn't happen any time soon. I can't believe how much I'm loved and that they understand my heart so well. Not being asked or expected to separate my lives, sometimes I wasn't sure if it was real ... God is so good to me!

He asked if I was alright and loved on me some more then left the room. Once I was able to gain my composure back I picked up the phone and dialed Debbie's number.

"Hello." The woman on the phone said.

I was sure it was Debbie, there was such emptiness in her voice.

"Debbie?" I asked her.

"Yes." She answered. "Jenny is this you?" She asked and broke down crying.

She was so sad, I wish I were there to hold her. "I'm comin honey, I'll be there as soon as I can."

"You're going to make it? I'm so happy, I wasn't sure if you would be able to. I don't know what to do, there's so much that needs to be done. The services, the money, the food, the people." Her voice started to fade out.

"Debbie, sister, I love you. Everything is going to be alright." I told her. "I don't know what help I'll be but everything will be ok, I love you so much!"

"I love you to, you're really comin?" She asked me.

"I'll be there as soon as I can get a flight booked out then I'll call you when I get into town. Is Cassie or Jamie or Kelly home?"

I could hear her hollerin. "Jamie, Aunt Jenny wants to talk to you."

I could feel the hustling and bustling going on in the room while I waited for Jamie, I felt so helpless.

"Hi, are you coming home Aunt Jenny? My mom needs you, I wish Karen was here to."

"I know honey, I'm sorry. I'll be there tomorrow night I hope. Do me a favor, help your mom kay?"

HER PLACE WAS WITH GOD

"I will." She said. "We set the appointment up with the funeral home guy and I guess we're going over there later today." I could hear the hurt in her voice, poor thing.

"I'm so sorry baby, your daddy loves you. You know that right?"

"I know, I miss him so much already. It's just so strange knowing he isn't coming home, it's not right." She said and started crying.

I had no Idea what to say. "I love you, tell your sisters and your brother and Courtney and Day that I love them and everyone else. I love you to sweetie, so much!"

"I love you to Aunt Jenny, see you soon." She said to me and the phone hung up.

I sat there for a bit then went to find Charles to hug him so tight and tell him thank you for his softest heart! I could already feel the anxiety and fear that overcomes me like it always does when I begin a trip back in time to my world and life in Alaska. Knowing I had to change roles and be the 'wife', the mother, sister and auntie to my family I missed so much. It was so hard to know it was just a few days I would have with them then I had to leave them, again, to come home.

I had the money for the ticket so I got right on it to book my flight then get back to Debbie so they could make their arrangements and I started packing. I was so sad, scared and nervous all at the same time, and excited. I missed everyone so much and couldn't wait to hug them.

Jasmine peeked in the bedroom. "Hi mom, are you alright?" Her said in her sweetest and most quiet voice.

"Yea, I'm fine honey." I said wiping the tears off my face.

She came into the bedroom and stood in front of me.

I could see the tears on her face to. "I'm sorry honey."

She fell in my arms and cried. "I can't believe he's gone mommy, it just seems like yesterday he was giving me the remote and laughing at everyone who tried to take it from me. He was so good to me!" She said while she cried. "And I can't believe I can't go with you."

"We can't afford it baby, im sorry." I told her.

"I know mom, I'm ok. I need to be here anyways to help Tina out with the house while you're gone." She said as she wiped the tears and stood up tall and strong.

"I'll only be gone for like four days k?" I said.

Tina came in and hugged me, then Mary, James and Jonathon. "We're sorry your sad mommy." They all told me. "Everything will be fine and the house will be just fine while you're gone so don't worry k?" They told me with their beautiful smiles on.

I hugged all of them. "I love all of you so much, you mean the world to me! I'll miss you and think about you the whole time I'm gone. I'm so blessed and have the most awesome kids!"

I melted while they all kissed and hugged me. "K, I gotta get in gear." I told them.

"I have packing to do and all that good stuff. I'll call you when dinners ready k?"

As they were heading out of my room they all hollered back at the same time. "Ok mom, love you mom. Bye mom, see you in a bit. The same goes for me mom, love you!" They all told me.

I was so lucky to have so much love, even with something bad happening I could see our family's had become one, I'm so blessed!

∽∾

Getting off of the plane I held my head up high. I knew I couldn't do this without crying, I wondered how I was going to handle this trip. It was the first time I had been back since I left. I had gained quite a bit of weight too. In all my life I hadn't ever weighed any more than about 110 pounds and now I weighed 180. Man, somehow I had to do this with my head high that's for sure. All the people, all the memories, good and bad.

I got off the plane and found my way through the station and down the escalator to the luggage pickup. How amazing, I love this airport. Every time I'm here it feels like I am home but then every time I am in Sacramento airport I'm finally home also. I was watching the bags come out of the luggage shooter and head for their never ending circle as they await their people to thankfully find and rescue them. I looked around to see what kinds of people were there and saw my Michelle coming through the doors that go to the parking lot.

She's as beautiful as ever! "Hi Honey." She came up and we hugged, I couldn't believe how much she had grown up.

She wasn't a little girl anymore, she's a beautiful young woman. I couldn't wait to see Jeanette to. I was nervous about that, she blamed me for a lot of what happened. I suppose it was easier that way, I understand I think. It sure hurts though, i wouldn't have ever left our girls if I had any other choice.

We got my luggage loaded in her car and headed for town talking the whole time. It seemed like I had been gone for so long.

"I'm sorry I had to come home for this. I wish it could have been something good, a wedding a birthday, anything but a funeral!" I said to Michelle and looked up to her.

I could see her getting sad. "I'm sorry honey, I didn't mean to bring it up. I'm sure you've been having to deal with your dad and everyone else. I love you so much."

"I love you to, it's been so frustrating."

"I'm sure it has, thank you for picking me up."

"No problem! Do you know where you're staying yet?" She asked me.

HER PLACE WAS WITH GOD

"Not really, everything happened so fast. Marta said I could stay with her and Debbie said I can stay there."

"Why don't you stay with us, I don't want you having to worry about where you're going to sleep." She said with her most beautiful smile.

"I'm only going to be here for 3 nights so I shouldn't be in your way much."

"You're not in my way mama." She said.

Aaww I love her so much!

"I'm glad you're here, I miss you." She said looking at me with the little girl face I remember.

"I miss you to, I'm so sorry honey. I miss you and your sisters and your dad all the time."

We only let ourselves be sad for a little bit and before I knew it we were home.

The next morning Michelle brought me back out to the airport so I could pick up my rental and then drove out to the Valley to see Tammy and Brian. I missed them so much! I hadn't seen John yet, I had just talked to him on the phone before I left California.

I was surprised when he found me at Tammy's. "Hey Jen, phone hun." Tammy covered the phone so he couldn't hear her and whispered. "It's john, have you even talked to him yet?" She asked.

"No, not since I've been here. It's ok though, no worries." I told her.

I took the phone but man I was so nervous. I hated feeling so outside of myself, lots of that was changing from one world to another in a 24 hour period.

"Hi John, what's up?" I said.

"Hi, why haven't you called me?" He asked me.

"I didn't know where to call you at. Anyways, I came up to see Tammy and Brian and my other Tammy. Are you alright?" I asked him.

"Yea but Debbie needs you, I thought you were going to be with her."

"Of course I'm going to be with her, John. When I talked to her this morning she told me there was a house full of people and they were already drinkin. I'm going to stop on my way down the hill. And anyways, why are you talking to me like this?" I asked him.

"I don't mean to be loud, I'm sorry. I just don't know what to do and I really want to see you." He said in a nicer and quieter voice.

"Are you in town?" I asked him.

"Yes." He said.

"Why don't I come back in and we can all go to breakfast, is Jeanette with you?" I asked him.

"Yea, I've been letting her crash here, it's better than her bein on the streets."

"Good, k, ya'll git up and get ready then."

ANOTHER SAD GOOD-BYE

"kk, bye." He said. "Jenny, hey. I'm really happy you were able to come."

"Me to, talk to you in a bit." I handed the phone back to Tammy.

"Dang, I just don't want the drama and stress." I told her.

We laughed and smoked a few bong hits before heading back down the hill.

"I'll be back up later after the funeral, I love you guys!"

"We love you to, love you Michelle!" They hollered to us as we headed out.

Tammy and Brian had been there for Michelle and Jeannette when John and I weren't. They helped them a lot when I left and John went off the deep end, they got a big part of the craziness of our family falling apart. One of the million things I feel guilty about … (I also found out later that John had threatned them and their family because of helping during some of the 'bad times' as he had also done to others that tried to help me, they weren't happy about it to say the least.)

We decided not to stop at Debbie's on the way down so I called her. We were going to be comin back out for the reception after the service in town later. I really wanted to be able to do more and to be there for her and the kids but they had already been drinking and doing whatever. My life changed when I went back to California and I like it. I enjoy going to bed happy and waking up happy, I hadn't ever had that and it wasn't something I was willing to give up any time soon. I was so scared of my mind space and what it was going to be like seeing everyone again, I should be excited.

It's so awesome getting to spend time with Michelle and now with Jeanette and their dad. I had a million different thoughts going on in my mind and my heart was racing when we pulled up to his apartment.

"Are you ok mom?" My sweet Michelle asked, she has the most beautiful smile.

"Yep, I'll be fine honey." I got out of the car and held my head up high while we walked up to his house.

The stairs were old and went down about five steps to what probably had been a basement. Michelle knocked and opened the door.

"Hey you guys, are you here?" She said walking in.

I followed her in and shut the door. It was dark so I followed her through a room into another then through some sheets hanging as a door into a bedroom.

"Dad, are you here?" She asked.

"Yea, I'm here. I didn't know you were going to be here so quick." I heard him say.

"We came all the way from the Valley, it's been a good hour dad. Come on, where's Jeanette?" She asked him.

"In the other room, I can't get her to get up. You go try." He hollered.

Michelle went back in the room we had just came through. I looked at John lying there, for the first time in years he didn't seem so intimidating.

"Hi, remember me?" I asked him.

He turned around with a spin. "Oh shit! Jenny, hi, I didn't know you were there."

I turned around as he got up to put his sweats on. "Not like you never seen me dressin before huh?" He asked with a laugh in his voice.

"No, but, that's ok. You decant now?"

"Ha, that's not a word ever used to describe me!" He said laughing. As always he found himself quite comical.

I turned back around and gave him a hug and sat at the table. There were a couple of photo albums so I started going through them.

"Hey." He said. "Don't take no pictures out of there!"

"Don't worry bout what I'm doing and get ready to go k?"

When the girls came out of the room Jeanette came over to me. "Hi Jenny." She said hugging me.

I wanted to cry. "Hi Honey, I love you so much."

"I love you to."

As they got ready to go we flipped through the pictures, I was stopped in mid-flow by one of my favorite 'good' memories! A picture of John and I sitting on the tailgate of a truck. Him kissing my cheek and me with the biggest smile on my face. There was so much love in that photograph.

"Nope." He startled me with his voice directly over my shoulder.

I jumped and his arms went out to catch me. "Hey, it's ok, it's just me. But no, you can't take that picture."

I sat up and took a deep breath, it was so weird being in the same room with him. He stepped back a bit and I finally found words.

"You better get ready to go cause I'm hungry. I want a copy of this picture before I leave, I love it." I told him.

We tried hard to get them out the door so we could go eat, it took a bit … I was happy to be here with everyone but it really seemed to be such a shame to have to be there because of one of our brothers dying, I hated that. Breakfast was nice, we managed, the four of us, to sit and have idol conversation very lightly touching on things from the past. It was alright, no one was getting their feelings hurt or anything, I'm so happy it was going so well. Every now and then the radio in the restaurant would play a song that of course had to be one we shared in memory and he would sing to me, with me, then we would act like nothing happened. He tried to say he was sorry a couple of times. Memories were flashing in front of my face as if I were in a theater, I really wanted the movie to be over and for life to continue.

We made it through breakfast and went to John's mom's house so we could spend a minute with Jeanette's baby Alexis, her's so beautiful! Grandma was pretty loud so the visit didn't last long. I'm glad I got to see my granddaughter but sad that our girl had to leave in tears feeling so bad, she's so torn and having such a hard time. I couldn't let myself feel responsible for this to.

ANOTHER SAD GOOD-BYE

We took them back to the house and left to go get ready for the funeral, God I hate going to funerals!

Pulling into the church parking lot was almost overwhelming, I talked to God for a second and sat there taking it all in. Bob, Stephen, Johnny, Keith, Debbie, the girls, and the more I looked the more people I saw.

"Wow, it's now or never." I said.

"I agree." Michelle said.

We got out of the car and walked up to the crowd, all my brothers and sisters I missed so much. I could have killed my brother Steve!

"Hey Jen, give me hug sis." He picked me up and hugged me tight. "Are you pregnant?" He hollered out.

I macked him hard. "No I'm not pregnant, I'm healthy, no dope you know?" And turned a circle for him lol.

It didn't matter though, one after another I was crying and hugging everyone I missed so much.

I heard a scream from the other side of the parking lot, my sister Marta was running towards me. So small and fragile she was, her black leather jacket rubbed against mine as she slid into my lap and we both hit the ground in tears.

"Jenny, I need you, I don't know what to do!" She was sobbing and drunk and couldn't have weighed 75 pounds soaking wet.

"I'm so sorry honey, I love you."

"I love you to Jenny, Karen's gone, you're gone and now Arthur is dead. What am I going to do, why is everyone leaving me?"

"We didn't leave you, we love you." I said trying to calm her down but we both sat there and cried. "I'm here for you right now."

She laid in my arms in the parking lot while I held her and rocked her for a bit. After a few minutes we calmed down enough for us to get up, she was so upset. Karen and I had both left at the same time, poor thing, her and Debbie and all the craziness we left them with.

John came over and helped me up. "Come here, someone wants to say hi."

I couldn't believe it. "Hi Radical." It was all I could do to keep from cryin again. "I love you brother and miss you!"

He hugged me. "Hey sis, miss you to. How are you doing?" He asked me. "You look good, looks like your clean I see?" He turned me around to look at me not being paper thin.

HER PLACE WAS WITH GOD

"Thank you, yes I am!" Man did that feel good to be able to say!

Marta and the others were starting to wander into the church. So amazing seeing everyone, it was like a family reunion.

I wasn't sure where I was supposed to sit or anything so I stood off to the side. Next thing I knew John came up and stood next to me, then Michelle and Jeanette. I looked up and there was my brother Bert.

He grabbed me whispering. "Sis, I love you so much, you're here! I can't believe you're here." He said. "Look at you, your right where you belong!"

He grabbed my shoulders and stood me back next to John. John took my hand like it belonged to him, as if I were playing a role in that movie or a play that everyone expected me to play out …

I looked around the church, a lot of the people I recognized. It seemed like I had been gone just a day and it had been three years. In through the doors came a tall slender woman, the dress was a gothic design, black gown with a veil. As she lifted the veil and removed it from her face I could see it was my niece, my heart got real sad real quick. The young girl wore white face makeup with black eye makeup and lips.

I walked up to her and put my arms around her. "I love you honey, I'm so sorry."

She hugged me back. "I love you to Aunt Jenny." She said. She was so sad and looked so empty inside.

I stepped back and went back over with John and the girls.

John took my hand again. "Thank you, she needed that. See, you are needed you know." I looked at him with a sarcastic glance as to tell him to 'knock it off'. I was thankful when the pastor started talking because attention was moved elsewhere, as did my hand.

After the sweet and very tearful service we were all meeting out at Debbie's. I took Michelle to her car cause I knew that if I was to get out there with everyone I needed to be able to leave whenever I wanted to.

My heart was pounding as I pulled up to the crowded gravel driveway. I found myself a safe place to park where the exit was accessible for me at any given time I needed it.

I sat there deciding how I was going to do this when I saw my brother Bert headed towards my car. "Come on girl, git on out here and get a beer. It's been sittin here with your name on it and its bout to cry you know."

"Yea yea yea, give it here then and give me a hug." I said laughing.

He let me shut my door then picked me up and swung me around.

"Here you go, how are you?" He asked me. "You look good sis, I missed you so much!"

"I'm good, the kids, me and Rick, his kids and Charles are all doing well." I told him.

"And these people are?" He said with his sarcastic self.

"These people are my family. You would love Rick if you met him, could you ever imagine me never being yelled at?"

He looked down towards the ground. "It's what I would have wanted for you." He said.

"Well, he has not been mad at me in the whole 2 years we've been together. So now what do you think?" I asked him with my smile on.

He hugged me again. "Good, kay, now, let's go see everyone."

We walked up the drive to the trailer, everyone was saying hi and lots of huggin was going on. Little Mike and Marta, Glen and Teresa, Keith, Bob, Bert and John, Joel and Debbie and all the kids and Steve and Johnny and and and Chuck and Lucy and Martha and Fernando and dang! I found myself a safe spot on the porch with my sisters, it was like old times sitting there watching the guys be themselves lol!

Drinkin green beer for their brother was something they had no problems doing, they drank and ate and drank and puked. Then as they drank some more I realized I was sitting there watching the exact same scene I remembered from before, like a Dejavu! How funny, at that moment I fingered it was time for me to head out. I knew I wasn't going to stay long, I was gonna go on back to town. My flight left tonight and I'm so excited to be on it, I miss Rick and the 'happy-crazy/sanity' of my other home so far away.

After saying all my goodbyes and crying even more, I made it to my car.

I had almost made it out when Bert caught me. "Hey girl, where are you going? You weren't even going to say goodbye?"

"I tried, I have been saying goodbye for a half an hour and I didn't know where you were."

I figured I would get out of the car and give him a hug until I realized that wasn't what he had on his mind. He reached in my car window and planted himself on my lips, I thought he was going to swallow me!

I managed to push him away from the car. "What the fuck is wrong with you?" I yelled at him.

He stood up and stepped back with this awful look on his face. "I love you, John loves you, all your brothers and sisters love you! This is your family and this is where you belong!"

I couldn't believe him. "Don't tell me where I belong, you can't say that! You can't expect me to go through all that shit all over again!"

HER PLACE WAS WITH GOD

He kept yelling at me. "This is your family, this is where you belong no matter what!"

"You're fucking crazy Bert, you don't know what happened. You weren't there, you never got to see what went on behind the closed doors!" I yelled back at him. "I'm out of here!"

I got ready to back out and hollered to him. "I love and miss my family every day, don't ever talk to me like that again, good-bye!"

With that I drove away and tears flowed down my face. I drove on up about a ¼ of a mile and pulled off the side of the road to dry up my face before I got on the highway.

✦

'Dang, I'm glad that's over', I said to myself and God. So happy I get to go home. It was so strange how it turns out, when I'm not here I can't hurry and get here fast enough, when I'm here I can't wait to leave but then a part of me is torn when a sister hugs me and asks me to please stay, please don't leave again, that hurt my heart on so many different levels. I didn't leave cause I wanted to, I didn't have a choice with my kids' lives, our life and death decisions. My choice was life, love and being happy.

Knowing it wasn't my responsibility for what was going on with John, there wasn't anything I could do but walk the other way, which I did with my head held high. I called my Tammy and told her I loved her but I was heading back to town and had to catch my flight home.

"I understand honey, it must have been crazy I'm sure." She said.

"It was, it is. I'm just happy to be going home, other than missing everyone, I love you!"

"I love you to. You get home and let us know when you make it there safe." She said to me.

"I'll call you guys from the airport. Love you bye bye."

"By hun, we love you to."

We hung up and I continued drivin down the hill to town to meet Michelle.

When I got there the kids were runnin round. "Hi grandma, love you." Davin hollered while he continued on his run through the house.

"Love you to honey." I said laughing, I love my grand-kids so much.

"Hi Jenny. Hey, dad called." Michelle said to me from the kitchen. "He wants you to call him."

I sat down with her at the table with her. "K, I'm not sure if I'm going to see him before I leave."

"That's up to you mom, whatever you do or don't do is fine. I'm going to miss you,

ANOTHER SAD GOOD-BYE

it's been nice having you here."

"Aaww thank you, it's been great seeing you and your sister and the kids and your dad to. I'll miss you so much, I miss Rick and the kids to."

"I bet." She said and hugged me.

We sat there and talked for a while and pretty soon she handed me the phone. "Are you ready to call dad?" I love her so much!

"Yep, this I need to do."

We had a good conversation so I'm glad I called. Of course I would miss him and the kids and our family but I didn't regret my choices, this I was sure of.

Me and Michelle and the kids spent the evening together and then went to the airport. Saying our goodbyes always sucks, I hate walking away from my kids. I love them so much, there isn't a moment in a day when they aren't in my thoughts and my heart.

Finally home where I'm comfortable and where I truly belong, my mind continues on the trip back in time to Alaska and the question of where I belong. Where should I be or who should I be and how should I be that person, lol which person ... an emotional jet lag maybe??

Finally, days, weeks and months go by and things start getting back on track.

The man that loves me, my kids, my sisters and brothers and nieces and nephews, yes, this is what I'm talkin about, a happy life.

Where Did I Go?

Me, the me I can't find stuffed somewhere in my heart where only the aching empty feeling reminds me of what I used to be, who I used to be. Sometimes not understanding the ways of the world or how I was allowed to let such chaos be a part of me and other times longing for the craziness of that chaos. I sat at his feet while my sisters were at their man's feet, doing whatever we are told to do. Always longing to hear the loud rumble of the bikes coming together and the sweet sweet smell of leather. Yes, we took control, the quiet people looked at us in disbelief. Us, their women, our men, brothers and others, they wonder about our deepest secrets, wondering what we lived and stood for.

Days in days out, one by one, then another, never ending. Never alone, always together we share our nights and days as one.

The me I miss from time to time, bringing my past for judgment. My world will never be the same and today my heart still peeks in and remembers, quickly stepping back though, knowing that those years are no more forever.

Michelle and Jereme's Wedding - September 2002

Every day living with Rick and all of our kids as a family amazes me. Life was so busy there wasn't a moment to spare and time went by as quickly as a thought crosses your mind.

I was so happy when I got the call from Michelle telling me that her and Jeremy were getting married and she really wanted me there. Again though, there wasn't any way I could afford to bring the kids with me. I felt bad, I know they miss their sisters so much but they were pretty busy with their lives here in Chico so thankfully they weren't upset with me.

Arriving at the Anchorage Airport is always as exhilarating as the time before and the time before that. Maybe it's the whole aspect of traveling but most of all getting to see our girls I love so much! I got myself to the luggage thingy and just when I found my bags I saw Michelle. She had a big smile on her face headed right for me.

"Hi Jenny, hi mom." She said. "How are you doing?"

It was so nice hugging her, like a part of me that was missing got temporarily put back.

"I'm good honey, I'm so happy for you and Jereme and I bet Davin's happy to!"

"Thank you, it's been pretty amazing and yea, he's such a big man in his little suit. It's so cute, I can't wait for you to see him!" She said with her beautiful smile.

We were walking and talking and tryin to keep my luggage together lol.

"Dads all nervous, said he don't want to give up his baby girl."

"Aaww of course he doesn't want to, that's sweet." I told her and I could see her blushing, she's the cutest!

"He wanted you to know he was looking forward to seeing you."

"How has he been?" I asked.

"He's ok I guess, he still lives where he did the last time you were here."

"Hopefully I'll have a chance to visit with him for a little bit."

By now we had reached the doors of the airport to the dark but wonderfully cool garage. We got the car loaded and between the laughing and crying a bit and talking we were on our way home in no time.

I was so nervous, I knew this time though that I was stronger and it wouldn't be as hard. It's always nice being able to stay with Michelle and Jeremy. They never argued and if they did it wasn't around anyone else. When we got to Michelle's I got my stuff put up and laid down for a while, it was 2 am and Davin was nowhere close to being interested in going to bed. It was cool though, my daughter Chelsea was at Michelle's also, she spends a lot of time with her, so awesome! Davin played between the bedroom (I was sharing his room with him), and Chelsea, Michelle and Jeremy out in the living room so he was yellin and playin most the night and I still slept like a baby.

The next morning was nice. We had time to get me out to the airport so I could pick up my car and go see a few people. I was hopin to find Marta but I wasn't sure who was doing what or how anyone was so it was a total hit and miss. I knew my Emma and Steve would be around so when I headed out to the Valley I would give them a call. Thank goodness for cell phones huh? Just then I heard my phone ringing from the floor of my car, obviously where it had dropped. Cool, no lost phone, I thought to myself!

"Hello." I said waiting to hear who it was.

"Hello, Jenny?" My heart kinda dropped to my stomach, I never knew how things would go with us.

"Yes, hello." I said, acting like I didn't know who it was. "Who is this?"

"Me, it's John, how are you doing?" He said.

"Good, I'm doing good. I couldn't find my cell but when you called you found it for me, thanks."

He laughed a bit. "Cool, it's nice I could do something good for you huh?"

"Thank you, don't be that way John." I told him. "So, what's up?"

It was so strange hearing his voice, it always throws me for a loop.

"I was hoping we could visit a bit before you left town after the wedding?"

I wasn't sure what I wanted to do, I knew I wanted us to be ok. "Sure, of course." I told him.

I had planned on not being here long, I didn't want us to spend too much time together. I just wanted us to have a good visit with no problems and no one being blamed for anything.

"I hope I can find the wedding, I have a map and Michelle gave me directions so I should be fine."

"You better. Everyone's going to be there, my mom and Alexis and Jeanette, Chalsie and Melissa is here to, it'll be nice with us all together." He chuckled. "Except my mom of course, she hasn't changed much so excuse her mouthy ways. I just hope her and Jeanette can handle the day without arguing."

Hearing him and knowing I was there in the same town seemed to make my brain stop … it took me a moment to think of something to say lol.

"I have to go to Walmart and buy a dress, the one I brought doesn't fit." I told him.

"What?" He asked. "Don't worry bout it, your beautiful and always will be as far as I'm concerned."

I could feel myself blushing and the last thing I wanted to be was uncomfortable laughing and visiting with him, I had to figure out how to be ok with me and our visit.

"Thank you." I said laughing. "It doesn't help my size difference any. Hey, I'm getting ready to drive and I haven't figured town out yet to not pay attention."

"Kay, I'll call you in a couple of hours and make sure you find us, the wedding is at 1. It's nice to talk to you and hear your voice Jenny."

I hesitated a second. "Yours too, talk to you later." Damn … dang, I mean. I hate having my heart torn between two worlds and lives.

Driving through the city to the store I realized it obviously wasn't Chico lol, that's for sure. I had to remember how to get there, Anchorage was huge and I never did know it all real well. Most of my time had been spent in the Valley when I was here. I never was much of a city person. I finally found it and of course, not knowing which directions the one ways went and the ways in and out of the store and through all the people traffic lol, it was quite comical!

It was so hard to find something nice cause I felt so big compared to the 'me' I used to be. Thank goodness I finally found something I liked and got into line to pay for my dress. Now I'm hoping I wouldn't get lost looking for my car in this huge parking lot.

I found my car and headed on out to the highway towards the Valley. I called Tammy and Brian and they were getting ready to come to town so we made plans to meet and I headed on up to Steve and Emma's. I love them so much and love our visits. I could only stay a little while and it was time to git back to town for the Wedding. I was excited for the kids and I was so excited for myself getting to drive to the Valley no matter how few days I was going to be here.

I found my way back through town to Michelle's to get dressed for the wedding. Thinking about not knowing who was going to be there wasn't helping me stay calm that's for sure. I did know though that Tammy and Brian would be there and all the girls, Melissa too, Johns daughter I hadn't even met yet, so awesome!

When I got to the house it was much calmer than I had expected. "Hi mom, how was your morning?" Michelle asked and gave me a hug.

"Hi honey, it was good, I love driving out there. If I hadn't of gone now I wasn't sure if I would have had another chance before I had to leave tomorrow. Did you and Jeremy need me to keep Davin for you tonight?"

She blushed, so cute! Her and Paula had been doing makeup and music was playing and Davin was dressed most handsomely in his three piece tuxedo.

"No, we're fine. We're taking him with us down to Homer. Jereme's got a game down there comin up soon so it'll be perfect."

"That's so awesome! I better go get dressed."

Michelle was grabin Davin and heading out the door. "Kay, love you, see you there. You have your map?"

"Yep, no worries. See you there, love you to honey." I said.

In a matter of what seemed like seconds the house cleared out to just me, myself, and my luggage. I took a deep breath, sat down and looked around at Michelle's pictures. I love looking at family pictures. Thinking about everyone that might or might not be there and everything that could or wouldn't happen, I got dressed and found my map and headed to the wedding.

I only got turned around once but I made it, oh my goodness I was so nervous! There were a few cars there, I was a little early but wanted to get in and get my video camera set up. I haven't worked a video camera in forever but the kids really wanted me to bring the wedding home to them so I had to give it my best.

I heard a sound then a voice. "Jenny, hi."

I turned around quick and about spilt my water and hit my head at the same time!

"Hey, don't do that!" I said. "Oh, hi." I said. Words were barely coming out of my mouth and John was so handsome standing there in his suit laughing, I could have smacked him!

"It was always so easy to do that to you." He said still laughing. "Like when we would hide in the back of the hallway from you and then me and Jonathon would jump out at the same time."

"I hated it then and I hate it now!" I told him. "You know you guys could have given me a heart attack many times!"

SO funny he was lol. Thank goodness him making me laugh brought my words back.

"You look nice." I told him.

"Well thank you, you do to."

We were standing there talking and we heard a car door shut. We turned around and Debbie was walking up to us.

MICHELLE AND JEREME'S WEDDING - SEPTEMBER 2002

"Hey Jenny, I was hoping you were going to be here."

"I wouldn't have missed it." We hugged and we all talked.

Debbie and her new man Shane and my niece Jamie, me and John. Wow, it was like a flashback or something all of us together.

I finally saw Tammy and Brian getting out of the car.

"Hey, there's Tammy." John turned to head inside. "So." He said. "We don't have much to say to each other."

He turned around to me. "Save me a dance yes?" He said, then he winked, smiled and walked away.

Great, there wasn't any way I was getting on the dance floor with him. My heart was pounding and I could feel my palms starting to sweat.

"Jenny." Tammy hollered and then again. "Jenny, over here."

I turned around and hugged and kissed Debbie. "I'll see you guys up there in a few, I love you!"

"We love you to, you look so good!" She said to me.

I laughed a little. "A little bigger than needed ya think?"

"Not, are you on drugs?"

"Nope." I said proudly.

"Well then, what do you expect?" She said with the most beautiful smile.

We hugged and they walked up to where everyone was gathering and I went over to join Tammy Brian and Mackenzie.

"Hi honey, I love you so much!" I said hugging Tammy. "Look at you!"

Tammy was a bride's maid and her dress was so pretty!

"I love you!" She said.

We hugged and laughed and I couldn't believe how beautiful Mackenzie is, wow!

"Alexis is here too. I just hope everyone is good, I know Jeanette needs to see this beautiful little girl, I couldn't stand not seeing her either!" She said to me.

"Hi Brian, miss you!"

"Miss you to kiddo, you look good!"

"You to, I'm really glad you guys are here. I have no idea who's going to be here today."

"You'll be fine, stick with us." He said with his smile that always made me feel better.

We all went inside and were quickly shuffled out back. I grabbed my camera and headed for the perfect spot. I couldn't believe all the people, some I knew and some I didn't.

Behind another camera I saw a face I recognized. "Hi Gabe, how are you doing?"

He peaked out from behind the camera but didn't smile.

"And hello back to me?"

He stood up and starting out he was sarcastic and upset. "You just left, you left him for no reason! You promised you wouldn't leave again and you did. Now look at everything that has happened, look at all the crap that happened to him!"

Excuse me? Oh my goodness my blood was starting to boil! "And you are mad at me after everything everyone has been through including me?" I asked him trying not to cry.

I was dumb founded and didn't want to make a scene so I turned to walk out of the room.

"Jenny, wait, I'm sorry." He grabbed my arm and turned me around to give me a hug.

By then I was crying, he's lucky I don't wear makeup anymore!

"I'm sorry." He said. "You hurt a lot of us when you left."

"Yea, well it pissed me off a lot and hurt me also having to leave, so, isn't that the same?"

"K, a truce?" He asked sounding as sincere as he could. "I have pictures to take and you have a camera to set up. I love you and it really is good to see you! I know John is happy to get to see you." He smiled and looked across the room. I looked where he did, John was across the room watching us. "He loves you ya know."

"Yea, I love him to, always will. That doesn't mean I'm in love with him."

I headed out to set up my camera saying hello to everyone. Shirley, John's mom and her new husband and the kids, everyone looked so beautiful. The wind was light and the hills were the most beautiful green covered with beautiful colored flowers as far as you could see over the hills. Wow, I was standing out on the grass videotaping the hills in front of us in awe. Alaska truly was one the most beautiful places in the world and I missed it so much.

K, that's enough reminiscing. I made myself turn around to all the people and begin to do the best I could to place my camera where I'd get the best video for my kids at home. They would have loved to come with me. Jas really wanted to see Melissa, she spent some time with her when she had come up last year for Christmas. It was nice they had made friends, I wish I could have been there for her and the other girls more. It breaks my heart every day.

The people started settling and the music starting playing. I found my spot out of the way and kept myself quiet and busy. The Wedding was so beautiful but our Michelle was even more beautiful! Davin walked out and then out came all the girls, their silky lavender dresses flowing in the breeze. Behind them came John walking out of the building with his arm linked with hers. In a flash it seemed like the years flew by my eyes like a photo album page after page after page. It seemed like just yesterday she was in junior high!

Before I knew it everyone was clapping and people were moving about, my body

MICHELLE AND JEREME'S WEDDING - SEPTEMBER 2002

finally starting to relax. I sat down to gather my camera equipment while everyone else around me was moving out and away from where they had all been settled. It was great, I sat there and watched everyone walk towards Michelle her dad and Jeremy and his beautiful Hawaiian family that stood so proud as they were greeted by all the guests. People were taking pictures everywhere, one of this mommy's favorite part of the day, pictures and memories I could bring home.

I managed to find my way out of the outpour of people.

"Jenny, Jenny come here." I heard.

I looked towards the voice and saw our girls. "Jenny its Chelsea and Melissa, come here."

"Hi girls, how are you doing?" I got up to them as quick as I could and gave Chelsea a hug and turned to Melissa.

"You're Melissa aren't you, you are as beautiful as I thought you'd be." She was Johns double just like Michelle and Jeanette and Chelsea are. "You look like your father."

"Yea, I know I'm gorgeous, everyone tells me that." She blushed and looked down.

I reached out and gave her a hug. "How are you doing, are you alright?"

"Yea, now that I'm here with my dad, well, I've been staying with my grandma but we fight a lot. Grandma fights with everyone." That we all agreed on!

We talked a bit and when I went to walk away she asked me, "You're going to stay here and go back to my dad and be my mom right?"

She hugged me and I hugged her back. "No honey, I'm going home early tomorrow morning."

"You are home, you love my dad and he loves you and you're perfect for him. You're the only one." I looked at her and smiled.

Trying to keep tears back I kissed her cheek and kissed Chelsea's. "I'll always be here for you as your mom, I love you and your sisters like you were my own. I'll see you in a bit."

"Hey Jenny." Melissa hollered and I turned around. "Will I get to see you again?"

"aaww of course honey, I'll come by your dads this evening so we can visit k?"

She turned around to sit with her sister. They were wearing dresses their grandma had made for them, they are both so pretty! "Alright, love you mom, see you later." She said to me as they went back into their own beautiful world.

I could feel my heart aching and was thrilled to find Tammy and Brian on a table in the cafeteria part of the building, quickly I found my spot with them.

Brian smiled and made me feel good like he always does. "How ya doin kiddo?"

"I'm ok. It's like I'm in a time warp machine or something."

Brian put his arm around my shoulder. "If it wasn't for you needing me I wouldn't have come you know. Tammy didn't need me to come with her for this shindig, I knew you were going to need support and so here your support is. I will be right here as long as you need me to and when you're alright, we'll take off and head back to the valley. Tammy has to be in a bunch of pictures and there's food, you hungry?"

I had to think about it for a second and then I realized I hadn't eaten all day. "Dang, guess I better eat huh?"

"Duh." He said and we all started laughing. "Come on, let's eat." We all got up and headed to the two long tables full of enough food for anyone to fill up on!

Looking around I tried to see who I recognized. Annette, Chelsea's mom, was always so sweet to me.

"Hi Jenny." she came over and gave me a hug. "Do you remember my husband Dave?"

"Hi, of course she does." He reached out to shake my hand.

"How could I ever forget the work you do." I told him. "You're a great ivory carver artist. I know I said that wrong but I think you know what I mean lol."

"Yes I do and thank you."

We talked for a minute and I found Tammy and Brian again and got back to the food.

"Hey, let me in line with you, I'm starving!" I told them.

We got our food and found a spot at the table with Annette and her hubby.

"I'm glad you were able to come Jenny, I know you mean the world to Michelle and the girls couldn't wait to see you."

"Aaww thank you, I couldn't wait to see them to. I can't believe how good you've been over the years Annette. You know, no matter what was going on you always worked with John and me, you never told our Chalsie she couldn't be with any of us."

"Thank you, that's nice you told me that. I'm sorry you won't be staying, the girls miss you ya know."

"Yes, I miss them to. I miss all of our family and I miss Alaska itself."

We all ate and visited for a bit.

Everyone was still eating when I got up to put my plate in the garbage and Gabe came up to me in hurry.

"Hey Jenn, John would like you to sit with him and talk."

It looked as if he were waiting for an answer or waiting to escort me where I was instructed to go. How funny, still following orders after all these years.

"Hang on, let me get something to drink."

"Kay, hurry up though." He told me.

lol I couldn't believe it, 'one of these days things will change', I thought to myself.

I walked up to the table where John was sitting. "Hi beautiful." He said patting the seat next to him motioning for me to sit there. "Come on and sit with me, we haven't been able to visit yet."

"Ok, I'll sit for a minute. I can't stay long, I have to get ready for my flight tonight."

MICHELLE AND JEREME'S WEDDING - SEPTEMBER 2002

He turned to me as if I startled him.

"What do you mean, your leaving tonight?"

"My flight leaves at 1 am I think, something like that."

"I wanted to spend some more time with you, maybe go to dinner or something?" he said.

"I'll have to wait and see what happens later. I told Melissa and Chelsea I would be over tonight so we could visit, I'll see you there of course."

"That would be nice, you know she really wants you to stay."

"I know, she told me. I wish I could do more for her and all the girls. This is real hard." I could feel tears welling up in my eyes and the last thing I wanted to do was to start cryin! "Hey, I'm gonna go find Tammy, I want to get some pictures of Mackenzie and Alexis while their together, amazing isn't it? Their so sweet."

"I know, Jeanette is so torn up, she having a real hard time Jenny. You know, if you came home she would have a mom again and maybe she would have a chance." I couldn't believe what I thought he had just said so I didn't say anything at first but then had to ask. "What did you say?"

"You heard me, you should stay." He said bluntly.

"I have to go John."

I went to stand up to go when Gabe came up to us. "Kay kids, how bout a picture?"

John grabbed my hand. "You can sit down long enough for a picture with me."

"Fine, a picture." I sat back down and Gabe took his picture.

I hugged John and turned around to walk out from behind the table. I heard John start to say something, I hoped it was going to be something nice but I was wrong.

"There Gabe, take a picture of the back of her head as she's walking away, it's her favorite pose."

I stopped to turn around to look at him, I couldn't believe the gall of this man.

"Are you kidding me, your somethin else! I'll see you when I come to visit the kids this evening and it's the kids I'm coming to see!"

"Yes, fine, I got it. Sorry, didn't mean to make you mad."

"Yea you did. Shut up John, I don't want to talk to you."

I walked away pissed. Got my soda from the table now abandoned and found Tammy and Brian in the other room with the kids.

"Hey kiddo." Brian welcomed me with his smile and hug.

"Hi, he is such an ass!" I spouted.

"And should I guess you're talking about Big John?"

I tried to laugh as I sat down but I was trying to hold back the tears to. "Yes, he always finds a way to be so fricken rude that in an instance I remember why I live in California and fell in love with Rick and changed my life and and and ..."

HER PLACE WAS WITH GOD

Tammy came over and gave me a hug. "Its ok honey, we're here for you and we love you."

"I love you to." I said and told them what happened.

"We're sorry, yea, he hasn't changed much."

"I'm just thankful I'm going home tonight, other than missing my family here so much."

"We know honey, you need to be home with your hubby and kids. You'll be back up here with me and the rest of your family soon enough, I have faith!"

We sat there and talked for a bit then I saw Gabe comin up to me.

"Hey Jen, John wants you to know that him and Michelle are going to do the father and daughter dance soon and then he wants to dance with you before you leave."

I sat there and waited for him to keep talkin. "Did you hear me?" he asked.

"Yea." I said, I couldn't stop myself from laughing. "I don't know how long I'll be here."

"You have to stay for Michelle's dance so just chill." He said.

He turned to go back to John and I took a deep breath and went outside to smoke.

"Hey, I thought you didn't smoke." Tammy said to me.

"I don't but I am today and maybe tomorrow." I told her.

"So, you gonna dance with John?"

I didn't say anything at first, Tammy's beautiful smile makes everything ok for me. I'm going to miss her so much.

"No, I can't. When we used to dance, which we did as often as we could, it was so real, so close and personal. I can't be in his arms like that, it would be to nice, I would remember how good it could be. I don't need to be reminded, I know how good it could be, I also know that the bad was enough for me to not want to do it again, ever."

"I understand and don't blame you, it'll be alright." She told me and hugged me.

"I'm gonna grab my camera and stuff and head on to town I think." I told them.

Brian and Tammy had been getting Kenzie ready to leave to. "Yea, we're gonna head out. They just took a bunch of pictures, we had to stay for Tammy to be in them but now we're out of here." Brian said. "Come on girl, we'll walk out with you and take a couple of bong hits before we leave, sound good?"

"Sounds good to me." I said finally feeling like I could smile again.

"Me to." Tammy said, so off to their car we went.

Looking back behind us as we crossed the parking lot, which was huge, I figured it wouldn't be long before someone else came out of the building. It was so weird seeing so many people I hadn't seen in so long.

We were sitting on the car smoking when John came out the doors. "Jenn, over there." Tammy said pointing towards the building.

MICHELLE AND JEREME'S WEDDING - SEPTEMBER 2002

I looked up and saw John. "Damn, I don't want to argue with him, I just want him to be nice."

"Want us to tell him to leave you alone cause I will!" Brian said, he's such a love to me, even after all the chaos and problems he caused them for helping me in the past.

"No, I'm ok." I told him. "I'll be right back."

I walked towards him and he walked out through the parking lot towards me.

I could hear him hollerin at me. "Hey, you were gonna sneak out on me I see?"

When I got to him we just stood there, a bit uncomfortable I'd say.

John spoke first. "So, you're going to just leave?"

"Yea, I'm tired, I have to catch my plane tonight so I'll go get things together and get my car back to the airport n' all."

"I was hoping to spend some time with you before you left. I want to take you to dinner."

"I'm sorry, I'll be by in a couple of hours to visit with the girls and you if your there."

"It's not exactly what I was hoping for, but I guess it will do." He said sarcastically. "I know, you'll come see the kids but not me, I understand."

I know he was playing and trying to make small talk, I hate it when he acts like I owe him something!

"I have to go John, see you in a bit?"

"Yea, I'll be headed home here pretty soon. People are starting to pack things up and all that good stuff."

I walked to my car and put my stuff inside. "I'll go find Michelle and tell her I'm gonna go." I told him.

"I'll go with you." He said.

I didn't know what to say. "K." That was all that came out lol what a dork I must have sounded like!

I wandered off and found Michelle and everyone and said my goodbyes and headed back to my car.

"Jenny." His voice startled me and I jumped. "You scared me again!" I yelled to him.

"Sorry, well, kind of." He said laughing. "It's been real nice seeing you and getting to spend time with you."

Again I wasn't sure what to say. "You to John, talk to you later."

He turned around and started to walk towards the building to go in and turned around. "Bye Jenny, see you tonight?" He asked me.

"Yea, see you tonight." I told him.

He turned back and went inside and I headed back through the parking lot to Tammy where they had been waiting for me.

I kissed them and said goodbye. By then they had gotten everything loaded and were ready to get on the road for their long drive back to Willow and I was about ready for my long trip home. I couldn't wait to be with Rick and the kids, Charles and Skip and my sisters and the kids so off to Chico I'll go.

I knew that Michelle, Jeremy, the kids and others would be back to the house soon and I wanted to get there to get changed before everyone got home so I hauled butt and made it through town without getting a ticket.

By the time the kids came home I was packed and all my stuff was loaded in my car. I was going to come home and clean for her but everything was pretty much already done so I cleaned up Davin's room a bit while I was packin. It seemed like the time I spent there went so fast, I couldn't believe it was already over.

"Hey mom, I'm so glad you were able to be here!" Michelle said as she came into the house and hugged me.

"Me to, I love you so much, I would have been so upset if I had missed this perfect day."

"You left before you and dad danced, he was bummed."

"I know, there wasn't any way I could dance with him, it would hurt too much honey, I'm sorry."

"No, I'm sorry. I knew that and I love you and I know you love us. It's going to be ok, whether you visit or move home you'll be back, you'll see."

"I have no doubt in that, there's no way I can stay away from you and your sisters and the baby's!"

We sat and talked for a bit then everyone else came home. Soon we were all eatin dinner and enjoying the evening.

I found a quiet place to rest for a few minutes before I went back to town and found my notebook in my bags to write a letter to John I had been needing to write. I had to tell him how I felt about a few things, well … maybe more than just a few.

When I was done I got everything together to go see the girls.

"Hey hun, I'll be back before I go to the airport, I need to go to your dads and visit with him and Chelsea and Melissa for a little while."

"Alright, drive careful and call me if you get lost or something." She said laughing.

"Right?" I said laughing now also. "I wouldn't be too surprised, you know I can't get around this city without getting lost and going in lots of circles."

"You'll be fine, see you in a bit and tell the old man to be nice!" She said while she hugged me.

"Will do, talk to you soon." I said.

I went to my car and headed to the other side of town to Mountain View.

Getting across town was easy, remembering which street he lived on was something

MICHELLE AND JEREME'S WEDDING - SEPTEMBER 2002

else. I always got the streets mixed up so I had to go up and down each street till I found the right one.

Damn, there it is. Finally I saw the bike parked in front and you can't miss that, wow, she is still just as perty! A beautiful Aqua green/blue, pretty and proud she sat there. It had been so long since I'd seen this baby. I was standing there spacin out on the bike when I realized that the girls had seen me, 'I better go in' I said to myself.

I found my way through to where they lived in the basement. I could hear John but couldn't see him yet.

"Hi Jen, come on in, I'll be there in a minute." I heard him holler.

Chalsie, Melissa and myself sat down at the table and started going through pictures. "I know that picture I want is still in here. I'm going to take it this time even if he tells me no!" I told them.

"I don't blame you, I'll get it for you." Melissa said.

She's such a sweet heart, all our kids are. I'm glad he was able to be here for her.

John came in from the back. "What are you doing? Don't take any pictures out of there you guys!" He said in a loud voice I remembered well.

"John I really want this picture, it's one of my favorites."

"Mine to." He said while he closed the photo album. "Anyways, how have you been? I wasn't sure if you would make it over here after the wedding and the busy day. I'm glad you did though."

His little place was cluttered and crowded but comfortable. He had one of the dinosaurs for a computer and his frogs and Harley pictures everywhere. Me and the girls sat on the bed and talked about Alaska and California and everything else we could think of to talk about. Totally out of the blues Melissa said something about John still waiting for me to come back to him and that he still had my wedding dress. I looked at him confused.

"Shut up Melissa!" John hollered.

The look in his face brought back memories so I figured I had better just keep my mouth shut cause I didn't want him getting mad at her. Wow that was weird. I'm sure my dress burned up in the second fire when the trailer burned down in Spenard after me and the kids left. It was so hard to sit there and keep my mouth shut but I did.

We visited for a while then I told them I had to go. "I love you kids and I miss you."

Melissa gave me a hug and then Chelsea gave me a hug. "We love you to, we wish you could stay though, dad does to you know."

"You two are so sweet. I love you but I love Rick also and he's in California with all the other kids, I have to go home."

They both looked at me with that sideways glance. "Ok, I'm going to my other home."

HER PLACE WAS WITH GOD

Chelsea jumped up by me on the bed. "That's more like it." She said with a smile. "I love you mom and will miss you."

"I love you to honey, both of you and I'll be back and visit soon."

I got up to get my stuff together and John handed me a head band. A huge one, one exactly like the other headband I had lost in the fire. I couldn't believe it but he had bought it for me at a yard sale.

"Hey John, you know I got the other one back to."

"What do you mean?" He asked.

"The guy that lived behind us had it in a bag of stuff. When I pulled it out I saw it was the big white one with Harley Davidson on it just like the black and purple one that you got me. Isn't that amazing? I can't believe that God gave them back to me! Anyways, thank you!"

He smiled and gave me a hug. "I don't want you to have to loose things, it sucks and anything we can get back is a good thing."

I picked up the headband and my purse, keys and jacket then said goodbye to everyone.

I could hear John as I was leaving. "Hey, Jenny, what do you think you're doing? You can't just leave like this."

"What do you mean, 'leave like this'? I have to go get my stuff packed up and get my car and me to the airport John."

He sat in his chair looking at me with the eyes that for so many years managed to get me to do pretty much anything for him.

"I wanted to take you to dinner and visit some more, just you and me."

I gave him a hug, turned around and walked towards the door. At first I could feel my heart beating real hard. I decided to give him the letter, I wasn't sure though.

"Here," I turned back around and handed him the letter, he took it but just looked at it and then looked at me. "You know I can't talk to you about how I feel so I have to do it this way, you'll have to read it."

I felt like I was trapped, like I needed to run if he got up as I was leaving. I turned to head up the stairs and out the door as fast as I could when I realized I didn't have to hurry or run ... there's nothing he can do to me anymore!

Outside of the house I was stopped again by the most beautiful blue FXE Harley Davidson that had not only his blood sweat and tears in it, but mine as well.

Sitting in my car I started to cry so out of there I was.

I drove a couple of blocks up to another road and pulled over to call Michelle. "Hi Mom, what are you doing?"

"I'm just leaving your dads, he's so awry!"

She laughed, hearing her made me feel better. "You're telling me? Yea I know huh." She could always lighten my anxiety in a second! "Why don't you come on home and eat barbequed burgers with us before you have to get on the plane k?"

"K, sound good, I'm on my way. Hey, thanks honey. I love you."

"I love you to mom, its ok. He does it on purpose you know."

"Yea, I know. I just wish it could stop hurting."

"I know, I don't know if it does but I know that you're ok so don't let him talk to you in a bad or weird way, nothing like that."

"Nope, I won't. He got weird once but it was when I was leaving so it's fine. I think he still has my wedding dress though, I thought it burned in the fire."

"Huh, I don't know, I thought it did to, crazy."

"No worry's, it just seemed so weird." I said.

"Drive careful mom and see you soon." I love hearing the girls call me mom, I love being mom!

"I'm going to swing by Marta's and see if she's home then I'll be right there." We said goodbye and hung up.

Heading through the crazy city of Anchorage I was hoping I wouldn't get lost. Soon I found Marta's place but no one was home. I was bummed I didn't get to see her and some of the others but I was happy to be going home soon, now it was time for kids and food.

I made it back to Michelle's and ate dinner with her, Jereme, Davin and a few of their friends. Such sweet kids they are. Newlyweds, happy and loveable on their wedding night at home with their son and their closest friends and family, what could better!

I hate goodbyes, I'm glad I have my car, at least no one else will have to deal with the airport traffic and all the people just to get me there, It makes it easier all the way around. Soon I was loaded up in my car and saying goodbyes and kissing and hugging everybody.

As we said 'see you soon' and I drove away I could feel the tears welling up in my eyes. I looked up to heaven. "Thank you Lord for this wonderful trip, thank you for my Michelle and all our kids and for Davin and Jeremy and for John and everyone."

I was so happy and excited to be going home but I also felt like I was walking away from a home, a home and family I missed and love so so much!

Come Dream With Me

Who were you in my dream?
The one that stood by your side.

What did you hear?
I heard you tell me you loved me.

What were you wearing?
Beautiful shining black leather that caught your eye.

What did you want?
I wanted you to ride with me throughout all eternity,
I wanted your undying trust, love and soul.

Why were you hiding?
I was told we were wrong for wanting the things we strived for. The drugs entwined with sex and insanity, the weapons, the anger and everything behind those closed doors. The only way we knew to live our lives.

Who was with you?
My brothers, your brothers, our family, all of us as one.

Where were you going?
To the highest mountain top to touch the wind, don't you remember? You touched it to.

Why did it end?
God had to take you from me so you could continue living. Your guardian angel came to me and begged me for your life.

What would have happened if I hadn't of left?
I would have had to bury you along with my heart … I had to make it stop.

What did you learn?
I learned that our love for excitement and terror wasn't enough to keep us alive and safe. I learned that all the empty spots inside of me couldn't be filled by keeping you as mine.

MICHELLE AND JEREME'S WEDDING - SEPTEMBER 2002

Do you miss me?
With every beat of my heart and every breath I breathe. Wishing and praying every day for the memories we shared to not mean so much to me. It doesn't happen though, it doesn't go away. It will never go away. I will love you for the rest of my life

… Ditto

Sometimes the Colors Fade … Will They Get Brighter God?

Days, weeks, months and even years went by. Kids are growing up and every morning I can't help but to smile and tell Jesus thank you. There isn't a moment that passed that I wasn't in awe of how He is transforming my life. It was still hectic of course lol with our group of kids, 'The Brat Pack', dad had named them and there's never a dull moment.

There were some problems with the property we were renting and the owners told us they had a lot work to do on the house, so, it was time to move. Wow change again, I so don't like change!

Rick and Charles were still working fulltime and I have my SSI and kids were doin what kids did. At first we started looking for a home to buy using Charles' loan. Things fell through with the place we found in Los Molinos then we were blessed with a beautiful, huge home in Durham! We were renting instead of buying but it was so worth it. There were 3 bedrooms with a big room built on to the garage for a 4th bedroom, 2 bathrooms and a huge back yard, we were all so excited!

It ended up being a really hard move on all of us. We had accumulated so much in the last five years we were living there and I wasn't any help with the physical work. The kids and Rick and Charles worked so hard for a couple of weeks getting us moved from one home to the other and finally it came together.

Since Rick and I got together there wasn't once that he raised his voice to me or was rude to me. There's nothing I could cook wrong for him or anything I could say or do that equaled any type of dissatisfaction in his eyes or heart. I wait daily for something to happen and it never did until after we all got moved in to the new house. He was so stressed with the move and working all the time like he did, plus we had the boys in and out of prison and the juvenile hall and kids on and off of probation and parole. He was nice to me but he wasn't nice to the kids, he was yelling at them all the time. There wasn't anything our kids could do right and I had dealt with that for so many years it was like fingernails on a chalkboard to me.

I had finally had enough and we fought for a bit and I took off. I drove up to the park and parked and cried. I figured that sooner or later someone might worry about where mom was and he would come look for me but no, he didn't. Finally I drove back home and feeling like an idiot I started another argument. It didn't last long thank goodness, soon we talked and he promised to mellow out.

Things finally started to calm and in no time I realized that as he quit yelling at the kids, I had also. All through the time we lived on Pomona things were so out of hand and I was so new at being a clean and sober mom. I yelled with the kids back n' forth on a pretty regular basis every day and mornings were horrific for the most part. We had three girls and two boys that were teenagers and at home, most of the time. With Rick and Charles and all of the kids getting ready for school and work at the same time there was always a problem or two or three or more. It was still the same now that we're in Durham but there was way more space and kids had grown up some.

Still over the years I've been writing and waiting for my writer to get my work into story form. It always keeps me busy whenever I didn't have a houseful of kids and their friends, there was never a dull moment in our home.

I started feeling worse and my sick days were more frequent and longer, soon I realized my health problems weren't going away like I wanted them to. My Dr. decided that it was time for me to do treatment for my Hepatitis C. The thought was scary and I knew I would be alone a lot of the time. Rick and Charles worked all the time, Jasmine had left home and Jonathon and Joshua were gone and Tina Mary and James were young and busy with school and friends.

An ordeal in itself was having to use a syringe to take my medicine. They told me I had to bring needles and vials with the medicine home with me and give myself shots lol OMG that wasn't going to happen so thank goodness my nurse let me bring it in to the office every week and she gave them to me, it was either that or I wasn't going to do the treatment. Having the syringes in my house was really bad for me. I didn't have a yearning to use, it was just such an icky dirty feeling that I had from it. 'I hate being the sick mutant that I am and it's because I was a useless junkie!' I said to myself often.

The medicine hit me really hard. I spent my days in my room throwing up and feeling awful. Rick tried so hard, he brought me anything I needed or wanted when he was home and he held me when I needed to be held. The counselor at the kid's school was amazing, she stepped in and helped with transportation whenever needed and more, she is such a blessing!

HER PLACE WAS WITH GOD

As the months went by I got sicker and I went from the 180 lbs. down to 130 lbs. Rick, Charles and our friend Skip were always around in the evenings. Rick would do his best to get me out of my room to visit and to smoke so I could feel better and maybe eat but it never worked much.

Something happened with me being sick and not able to be there for him, I almost lost Rick. Very little time passed and he was fixing what was cracked … thank God it wasn't broke!

My Dr. stopped my treatments cause my blood counts were getting to low, I was always to tired and weak. I really do hate being sick all the time, if it wasn't one thing it was another when it came to my body. The only thing good that came out of my treatment was that I lost so much weight lol YaY!

With me getting stronger and mine and Rick's hearts getting strong again, life at home was finally getting back to normal lol, whatever that was. I wanted more though, I didn't like being his, 'girlfriend', I was his wife in all sense of the word so I asked him to marry me.

Me in a tie-dyed dress my mommy bought me and him in his tie dyed shirt and jeans with our kids sisters brothers nieces and nephews we were married at Wild Wood Park in Chico, such an awesome day!

Finally being able to call myself his wife and him, my husband made such a huge difference in my heart. From him, I really needed the commitment he always promised that he had to me and all of our kids, so happy that our family was coming back together.

I can't imagine another loss like that in any of our lives, what a blessing true love and forgiveness are, I love my family so much!

MINE AND RICKS WEDDING PICTURE

There is a Happiness in Me

There is a happiness in me which lives in spite of all the days of pain and misery that sometimes I recall. A little joy whose roots are deep and keep on holding on, even through the times I weep they are solid as a stone. There is a happiness in me that's near to having wings and I'm convinced it's sure to be each time my angel sings. Sometimes I feel it's not enough, this meager bit I give and that this life is not where I should live. I hunger for a different kind of place than where I have been, not comprehended by the mind, with not a single sin to mar its pure perfection, to detract from all it is, and so in that direction my feet must follow His. Because this happiness in me was planted long ago to shield me from the things to be, while I remain below. God cut my earth-bound mourning's, and granted I should be attuned to heaven's voices … through his happiness in me.

Answered Prayers and Lessons Learned

I was sitting at our computer on some of my favorite websites. Let's see … there's Orbitz.com, cheaptickets.com, cheapflights.com, Continental Airlines, Alaska Airlines, American Air Lines, Expedia and on and on and on. If they had a price for a flight to Alaska I was saving the page or acting like I could buy it. I searched through the hotels and flights and rental cars then add up my trip. I can't go without a car, I tried to ask around and pay someone for letting me use their car while I was there but no one had an extra vehicle.

    I actually have no idea about when I was going, but I do know that when I finish my book I'll be back n' forth throughout the year. For this trip I wanted to go and sit down and talk to everyone and tape our visits. You know, when we're sittin around talking and different people come into the conversations then one story reminds someone of a story and then another story and before you know it there are hours of memories. When I went up for Michelle's wedding I spent some time with Steve and Emma and the kids in Big Lake and had gotten into quite a conversation about our lives and the party's and bbq's and this n' that lol. I'd of given bout anything to have a tape recorder goin at that moment. I wanted to spend a little bit of time with everyone, without that I didn't think my story would be as in-depth as I thought it should. I couldn't get it off my mind, I felt obsessed. Every day I found myself online looking for a flight that could magically become mine lol. I even asked my writer for help on my trip, the obsession was getting worse. I prayed and prayed for months, it seemed like years!

    It had been a good morning, I was drinkin a cup of coffee picturing myself sitting with my Tammy that lives in Willow, Alaska when the phone rang.

    "Hi Aunt Jenny, I love you." It was my niece Tracy.

    "I love you to, what are you doing?"

    "Well, I was wondering if you would like a ticket to Alaska."

    There was a pause for a second but it felt like a really long time, I felt like I was inside a hollow tunnel. I wasn't sure if she had just said what I thought she said but was really praying it wasn't a trick or a joke.

"Aunt Jenny, are you there?" She asked me.

"Um, what did you just ask me?"

"You heard me right, would you like a trip to Alaska?"

I could feel the tears starting to come out of my eyes but I didn't want to cry because I still wasn't sure exactly what she was saying to me.

"Did you really say that? Did you just offer to give me a trip to Alaska?" I asked trying to contain myself!

She starting laughing. "You're so silly Aunt Jenny. I love you and I want to give this to you. My brother was supposed to use the tickets to go on the fishing boat but he can't leave now. I have these tickets and their nonrefundable and who else would I give a trip to Alaska to?"

My tears started flowing. "Oh my goodness, you're serious? I don't even know what to say honey, you just gave me my trip?" I had to ask again.

"Yep, only its train and plane, it's out of Chico on the train and then you fly from Seattle to Anchorage. I think we can change the dates, not sure but we'll finger it out, I love you."

I couldn't stop crying. "I love you to, oh my goodness, are you sure about this?"

"I'm sure Auntie. Its ok, everything's going to be alright. You get your thoughts together and give me a call here in the next couple of days. You can come over and we'll change the reservations to your name and the dates for you k?" She was trying not to laugh lol I was so emotional. "You go and calm down now, talk to you soon auntie."

I was speechless lol. "Love you so much and talk to you soon." I told her.

I hung up and sat there in awe, i felt like I was going to explode!

It took me a bit to pray and thank God for letting me go. I knew I had to go, it was just on Gods time not mine right? I keep telling myself that but I don't seem to listen well. When I was done praying I found my phone and called Tracy back and told her exactly how amazing it was that she is giving me this trip. I was in shock for quite some time I think. Then on to call Jas and Tina and my Leah and my Mommy and my sister Dru and and and anyone else that would listen to me.

Finally it was time to change the tickets into my name so I went to see Tracy. She was on the computer and we were visiting and talking about when I wanted to go. Dates, times, etc, at first I wasn't paying any attention to what she was doing, a friend of hers had come in and invited me to smoke with him so we went on the porch and smoked a joint while we talked about the flight and the train schedules. When I came back in I realized she was entering her credit card information.

"Hey, what are you doing? I thought these tickets were already paid for?"

"They are, we just had to do some changes that's all."

"Honey, what did you do?" I asked her.

"It's no big deal, I had to buy the tickets again cause I found out that nontransferable meant I couldn't change anything but I still got a good deal and the train doesn't cost to change it."

I went up and gave her a hug, I couldn't believe what she was doing for me.

"Why are doing this?"

"Do you think I would give you a gift and then tell you that you can't use it cause the dates can't be changed? I don't think so. I love you, you are my favorite aunty and I would do anything for you."

And again I started to cry and we sat there while she hugged me. "Thank you so much. You give me something so wonderful and look at the wreck I am!" We both started to laugh. I can't believe I actually get to do this. Next May, beautiful long sunny days, no ice on the roads and longer hours of sunlight, it's gonna be perfect, you're perfect!" I told her.

"I love you Aunt Jenny, there we go, it's all done." She said and printed out my flight and train schedules and hugged me goodbye, I have an amazing family. Unreal, it was all ready, everything was set, wow lol I can't believe I'm really going! I miss everyone so much and I know not everyone is too thrilled about the work on my book but I also know that without them I wouldn't have the same story.

Again I am in awe of God!

After Rick and I got married Jasmine and her boyfriend moved home and her was pregnant with our grand-daughter Kelsey Mae.

It had taken me so long to stop being a bad mom, to quit yelling and screaming and losing my control. I was so scared I wouldn't be a good grandma but when this most beautiful baby girl was born and laid in my arms I knew everything was going to be ok. Having Jasmine, her boyfriend and the baby living with us wasn't easy at first but it was worth it. I wouldn't change it for anything and thank goodness she was born before my trip! Also Jasmine had been going to Oroville Adult School and was going to be graduating and her birthday was coming up to. I sure hope I scheduled my trip right.

Everything was good, knowing I was going back to my other beautiful home to work on my book and to see everyone I missed made me so excited. I couldn't wait to see the kids and my sisters and brothers and even though I was nervous as heck I was still looking forward to seeing John.

One evening I got a phone call from him, he always calls in the middle of the night so I didn't answer but we listened to his message on the machine. Rick is always so good about him calling.

The next morning I called him back, always curious ... I listened as he told me how happy he was and how proud of himself he was that he had made it through detox and was on his way that night to Tacoma, Washington to stay with our brother Steve.

Then he had to say it, he told me he never needed another love in his life because he had the best love there could ever be and there could be no other to match it. Right then I felt that old feeling of control creeping over me, I felt like he still had that hold on me, the hold I had worked so hard to get rid of. Then he said, 'Now, don't go and play rabbit with your man like you did with me.' lol Oh my goodness, whatever I thought, he is such an asshole! Quietly I began to cry to myself, I didn't want him to hear it in my voice and I didn't want to feel whatever feelings were there, everything was echoing around me like I was in a tunnel. Most important though is that I'm happy for him and proud of him that he found the strength to do something good for himself, maybe he won't be the next to die after all.

I told him when I was going to be in Seattle for the day before I could catch my plane while I told him about my trip. He said we would defiantly get together the day I was there, they would ride to Seattle and pick me up. Steve had a bike for him to ride till he got on his feet so we could go ride and maybe I could get an extension on my ticket so I could stay longer ... not, that wasn't going to happen! We said goodbye and I hung up my phone. How could I ever think or even entertain the thought that he or anyone would be worthy of my losing everything in my world that means anything to me. His voice was so sweet, he sounded so calm and sure of himself, like he used too before things got bad.

A better idea, I got a hold of a friend of ours that had moved there and we made plans for them to pick me up, how awesome!

Soon it was time for me to leave to catch my train, I was actually going to Alaska! I wouldn't have ever been able to afford this trip, our brother Charles loaned me money also. He always helped me and the kids with money without expecting anything. Just being happy to get some of it back from time to time and knowing he was able to help one of us, his heart is huge. He knows how important my time in Alaska is to me, so amazing this is really happening.

It was so exciting going to the station and waiting for the train. It was so hard to envision myself actually getting to go to Alaska and getting to actually see all the babies and getting to be Grandma Jenny but soon the time was at hand.

HER PLACE WAS WITH GOD

Of course the train was scheduled to leave at 2:30 a.m. so we sat there from 1:30 a.m. to 3:30, almost 4 until the train finally showed. It was grad night for Chico State so we passed time listening to the parties and watching the funny drunk people walk from here to there and everywhere, I was still so excited waiting for my train.

Finally lol, the train pulled in and Rick helped me put my bags on the top stair inside the entry way and kissed me goodbye. He climbed off the steps and before I could tell him goodbye again the train was pulling away from the station. Waving and blowing kisses I found myself alone. Wow, okay, here we go! I was able to finally find a spot to put my luggage. I was hoping we could check them to go under the train but since Chico is an un-manned stop I had to have them on board with me. I made my way up the little stairs trying to find my seat and the conductor looked at my slip and directed me where to sit. After being clumsy and getting my bag up over my head I sort of fell into my chair, looking around I was hoping no one was actually watching me fall and stumble and hit myself on everything lol!

I was seated with another woman that was from Chico also. I don't know why the conductor thought that meant anything, but he had said since she was from Chico I should sit with her. Well, right away it was obvious that she didn't want any company.

She sat up looking at me, almost in horror. "Wouldn't you rather sit up there or over there?" She pointed to another seat. "That way you will have more room to stretch out."

"He told me to sit here, I don't know if it is a good idea to go against the conductor." I told her.

With that she got up, took her stuff and went to the open window car, the viewing car where you can sit and watch the scenery as the train chugs away.

It's pretty cool actually and I was happy when she got off in Eugene. Now I don't have to deal with her for as long as I thought I would, for hours and hours and hour's lol! There were two men setting across from me. One snored up a storm and the other smiled at me sweetly. I smiled back and tried to get comfortable. I felt so strange like I didn't belong, I don't know how to act in public by myself. Don't get me wrong, I love traveling. I finally got up the nerve to find myself a Pepsi and the bathroom, once I figured that out I was good. The men sitting across from me were very friendly. They offered me a banana and I accepted, then they showed me all the food that had been prepared for their journey. Tones of fried chicken, sandwiches, chips, sodas and juices. Obviously they were truly loved by the women in their family, so cool. They joked with me and kept me smiling when I was feeling nervous or out of place, almost like they could tell.

Riding on the train is way cooler than flying. Getting to see the little towns tucked into the green woods along the mighty railroad tracks, it was mesmerizing to say the least. Finally we were in Seattle. I called my friend earlier and had let him know we were runnin late, we ended up not getting back to his place till like one in the morning. The kids had gone to bed already but his girlfriend and her baby were waiting up for us. We shared a nummy hard lemonade, they went to bed and I fell asleep on the bed they had all ready for me.

I woke bright and early the next morning with energy to sell. Dangit, there was no way they were going to wake anytime soon and I was going stir crazy. His television set up is more than I could understand. He is a computer and electronic specialist and with five different remotes I couldn't even change the channel on the tv lol so, I decided to try to make some coffee, that would relax me for a little while. I went to the kitchen trying not to be nosy looking for the coffee pot. I turned it towards me so I could see how it worked and I realized it was one of those fancy types of coffee makers with a cappuccino machine, it was way to early for to be able to finger that out.

Safeway was behind their apartment complex so I decided to walk over to the store to get a cup of coffee. That would pass some time but thankfully the kids woke up and soon had woke up their dad, hehe, they helped me. It ended up I didn't have to walk to get coffee. It had started to sprinkle which sucked but they made me coffee and breakfast. His girlfriend was very sweet and I'm glad Frank and the kids were doing good. We've missed him and the kids being in Chico.

It took a while but soon they were ready to hit the town. Me as impatient as I am, was very excited to get to see Seattle for the first time. I suppose I have been to the airport a few times but it's not the same as driving the city streets and seeing its famous sights. We went to a huge building, it's a childrens learning place with cool hands on things for kids to do and a whole floor of different types of food to choose from and the Flea Market was cool. They have a fish market where they throw the fish as they prepare it for the customers, they perform like a show and it's even been on tv lol and it stunk something awful, but we had a good time. By then I was getting tired though, it was early still but late enough for them to take me to the airport.

Yes, time to travel some more, so excited and so nervous in the same breath!

Getting all of my luggage together and into the airport was quite comical. Never, ever ever will I travel with this much luggage ever again. Dang, I can't believe how clumsy I looked, I suppose it wasn't just looking clumsy, I was definitely clumsy! I went straight to the check-in so I could get my bags out of my way. Next was the excitement of the security search. Man, I was nervous. Not like I had anything illegal on me, it's just one of those things. They made me throw away my lighters and x-rayed my bag. Then they padded me down and swabbed my carryon bag and my purse. All I could think of was if I had put smoke in them or not but they were bought new for my trip and I'm sure they were looking for residue of anthrax and explosive powders n' all. Once I got through security it was pretty cool. I had hours to wait but at least I was at the SeaTack Airport ready to go bye bye. When I walked into the upper level it was amazing! It looked like a huge mall, at least one section of a mall. There were shopping stores and coffee shops and five or six different places to eat. At first I panicked thinking about how many people were in the same area I was in but then realized that everybody there had gone through the same searching procedures I went through also. So then I was able to calm down and find a place to relax.

The room is amazing. There's a huge wall that's all glass facing out towards the runways and where the planes landed and took off, too cool. I found a table with some chairs where no one else was sitting, pulled out my notebook to get started on some writing. The people around me seemed to keep my attention though, there were so many different kinds of them. Families and business people and teenagers traveling somewhere for a trip, maybe it was a sports team or something. There were dads traveling with their kids, moms with babies to take care of and absolutely every different kind of person you could imagine. Soon I realized that there was no way I'd be able to write so I started making phone calls. I was so nervous I figured my family would make me feel better and as always, they did.

The excitement of travel has always been one of my favorites. Sitting on a plane in the middle of two people who don't want to talk or even look at the other people near them is not lol, thank goodness for free Pepsi and headsets with music and a movie. A kinda funky movie but I suppose it was cute. The new cartoon movie of Little Red Riding Hood and along with all that good stuff it was only like a three or four hour flight so I hopped it would go by quickly. I think I even had a chance to close my eyes for a minute. When I woke up I was craving another Pepsi but before I could find the stewardess the captain was announcing it was time to land. So, the Pepsi would have to wait and the getting to go pee wouldn't lol.

I called Michelle to tell her I was there, she was as excited as I was. Wow, here we go, this is amazing, getting to see my kids and my sisters and brothers and towns and streets and homes I remember, too cool!

I managed to get my bags off of the turn thingy, oh yea, it is called the luggage carrousel lol. I had a big bag with my laptop wrapped up in my blanket with my pillow. I can't believe how heavy it ended up being. Then I had my smaller bag packed with my clothes n' all, my carry-on bag and my purse. Dang, never again will I travel with so much luggage I reminded myself again. I carefully got everyone of them on my shoulders where they belonged and headed outside. I was waiting for Michelle when I saw her walking around the other cars and groups of people to find me. I picked up my bags and walked as fast as I could to her.

ANSWERED PRAYERS AND LESSONS LEARNED

Hugging her made me realize that I was really there. "Honey, I missed you so much and you look great!"

"I missed you to, I am so happy you're here. The kids are asleep so at least you'll be able to get some sleep. They are so excited to see their Grandma Jenny." She told me with such a beautiful smile.

I was still thirsty so asked Michelle if we could stop at the store on the way home. We got my bags loaded in the back of her truck and drove and talked all the way home.

"Oh yea, honey, can we go the store?" We both laughed cause we totally forgot, we were having such a good visit!

"I'm sorry, of course." She backed out of the driveway. We went up and around a corner to a little market so I could get a bottle of water and a Pepsi then home we went.

Jeremy had the couch all made up for me when we got there, they made me feel so welcome. We sat up and visited for a little while and then went to bed. Well, they went to bed and I changed into my jammies and curled up on the couch. I had been going and going and going and I had been so excited and nervous and unsure about everything that when I laid my head on the pillow, I realized my mind wouldn't stop. Shit, a million different thoughts and people to see and things I wanted to do ran through my mind as if it were the new Indy 500 roadway!

In what seemed like a moment I opened my eyes to see the sun shining through the glass doors. I had done it, I was here! I heard someone in the other room, my daughter Jeanette was coming in to the kitchen to make herself some coffee.

That got me out of bed! "Hi honey, how are you?"

I jumped up to hug her and she hugged me back. "I love you." I told her.

"I love you too." she said. Just hearing those words from our girls made the whole trip worthwhile.

We talked for a little bit and she went downstairs to get ready for work. Michelle and Jeremy's home was real nice. It was a town house but when you walk inside you go up stairs to the living room area with the kitchen and a bedroom and a bathroom and then down stairs to go to the other two rooms and another bathroom. Jeanette had been staying with them and my other daughter Chelsea, picks Michelle's daughter up from day care and brings her home and watches her every day while her sister is at work (YaY my Michelle and Jereme had the most beautiful baby girl, Keaira, I'm the luckiest grandma!). I am so happy that after all the years and all the crazy stuff that happened, they still spend as much time together as they can.

Jeanette left for work and I made myself a cup of coffee, standing there looking out the sliding glass door was breathtaking. You could see the mountains in the distance, we were in the 'Anchorage Bowl' they call it. Wow, it's as beautiful as I remembered it was. I said my prayers and enjoyed the air for a little while. I knew the next days were still unknown, the fear of that tried to creep in but instead I took a deep breath and started planning my strategy.

Soon the kids were movin around and getting ready for their day. Watching Michelle's calmly ran home made me so happy, I missed her so much. We loaded up and took Davin to school and then Michelle took me to the airport to get my car. I finally found the rental area and waited my turn in line.

I handed the woman my reservations. "Hello, can I see your Driver's License please?"

"Yep, no problem." I said opening my wallet. "Shit, I mean shoot! I'm sorry."

"That's fine, are you alright?" She asked.

"Yes, I don't have my driver's license, I must have left it at my daughters."

"You do know I can't give you a car without your license right?"

"Of course, I wouldn't expect any different and wouldn't have even asked. I'll be back, thank you." I said while I walked away from the counter.

Trying not to cry I moved over to some chairs in the lobby, thank goodness they were there. I was carrying my purse, my jacket, my travel bag with pictures and everthing else. I had begun teaching myself to maneuver without falling lol, it wasn't easy to do with the amount of luggage I thought I needed on this trip!

I called Jas. "Jasmine, tell me every things going to be okay before I freak out! I can't find my driver's license." I told her in a panic. "Michelle just dropped me off and isn't answering her cell and I'm at the airport trying to rent my car."

"Calm mom, calm, take a deep breath, everything is fine. Where do you think it is?" She asked me.

"Probably right inside the top bag. My dark blue jeans are right there and it should be in the back pocket. I spose I can get a cab and go get it."

"No, stay where you are for a minute, I'll call her and call you right back." She said.

"Kay, I love you and thank you."

"Your welcome mommy, I love you too."

I sat back and straightened my purse up. I had pretty much destroyed it looking for my license. I felt like a total idiot cryin n' all. I was afraid everything would go bad and here I was 3000 miles away! Not, I know better than to think that way.

Finally my cell was ringing. "Hi mommy, I got a hold of Michelle and she is leaving in five or ten minutes to bring you your license kay? She found it in your pocket."

"Yay, thank you so much! I kept missing her when I called, Cool! I love you honey."

"Love you too mommy, go outside and wait for her and call me when you get your car kay?"

"Okie dokie pokie, bye bye."

I gathered up my bags and headed back through the airport to where Michelle dropped me off and sat down to wait, I have the most awesome kids!

I figured I had better use this time and make some phone calls, I know Marta's waitin so I'll call her first.

"Hey sis, how are you?" I asked her.

"I'm good." She said. "You're here, where are you?"

"I am, I'm waiting at the airport for Michelle to bring me my driver's license so I can pick up my car. You want to go to breakfast with me?"

"You bet! I can't wait to see you!"

"You too, where do you want to eat?" I asked her.

Marta was as excited as I was. "How bout Gwennies? I know you remember where that is, it's across the street from the Harley Shop."

"Yep, I know where that is." I said. "How about a half an hour? I have to head on up to the Valley after we eat."

"Alright see you there, love you Jenny."

"Love you to sister, see you in a little bit." I hung up the phone feeling so good inside!

I looked up and there was Michelle's truck, yes! Such a sweet smile always on her face. She gave me my license, I gathered my bags again and headed back to the rental area. I waited my turn and this time I handed her my debit card and my driver's license.

"Will a P.T. Cruiser be alright ma'am?" She was reaching over the counter to hand me the keys.

"Are you sure? How much more will that cost?"

"Nothing, it is the only compact car we have left."

"Then yes, it will be fine."

I signed the agreement and headed out to find my car. Finding one little spot in a thousand spots wasn't easy but not hard enough for me to give up that's for sure! I kept walking looking for my number and finally I found Thrifty Rental's section. There we go, matching numbers and dang, there sat an absolutely beautiful Red P.T. Cruiser.

To cool, great car! I felt like a little kid with a new toy. 'K Jenny', I said to myself. 'You can do this. Your work starts now, no hesitating and no backing out.' I looked around the car before I started it. I didn't want to drive it till I had figured it out a bit. I loaded my bags in the back and tried to roll down the windows but there wasn't a handle or a button or nothing. No way can I drive a car without the windows down, that would totally suck. I looked around till I found someone working with the cars.

"Hello, Ma'am, can you help me I hope?"

"What do you need?"

"I just rented this car and I can't figure out how to roll the windows down." I felt so silly.

She reached in the car and showed me the switches. Get this, they were in the middle of the console on the dash in the middle of the car, right lol, like I would have ever found them there?

HER PLACE WAS WITH GOD

"Thank you so much." I told her

"You're welcome, have a good day." She told me.

"You too."

Cool, I started the car and rolled down the windows and on the dash the mileage on this car was 8 miles. Ha, not for long, that made me laugh lol!

Sitting in my car for minute I said a prayer. "Thank you Lord. Here I am, I'm so nervous. Driving this car, having my room, having a plan. The whole thing is amazing, I still can't believe I'm here. I am so blessed and it is all because of you! Please help me drive, please keep me calm while I get to visit everyone I can find. There are so many people I want to see, I don't know how I am going to have enough time to do this so I will let you lead Lord. Thank you Jesus, Thank you for this day. In Jesus' Name, Amen."

I drove out of my parking space, out of the parking building and on to town. So hard to believe I was driving in Anchorage and on such a beautiful morning too. Right away I saw Minnesota Dr. I was scared I wasn't going to be able to remember how to get over to Spenard to the resteraunt. It took one turn and then another and dang, walla, I did it! There it was, the famous Gwynnies and the Harley Shop.

I pulled in and found a parking space, I didn't see her anywhere waiting yet so I called her cell. "Where are you at?"

"I'm almost there. See you in a minute, love you." She said.

"Kay, Love you to." I told her and hung up.

I parked my car and cleaned myself up a bit. I was so anxious, it had been years since I had seen her. I didn't see her at all when I had gone home for Michelle's wedding so it had been since Arthur's funeral that I had seen her last.

Soon her was pulling in so I grabbed my purse and the pictures, locked up my car and waited for her.

"Hey you!" I hollered as we both started towards each other hugging and crying.

"Let me see you." I told her still holding on to her. "You look great and I miss you so much! I'm so happy we get to spend some time together!"

"Me to, I miss you. You look good to."

"Thank you, I am good. I had wished that Rick would come with me, maybe next time."

We were laughing and talking as we walked in and were led upstairs by the hostess to get our table. Both Gwennies and the Harley Shop had been in the same spot for 100 years. The gold miners spent lots of money in this restaurant when it was just a little café like place. We were seated and we talked and we talked and then we finally ordered and then we talked and talked and talked some more!

When we were done we decided to go drop Marta's car off and she could go with me to the Valley. I wanted to spend as much time with her and my Miss Betty as I could. I couldn't check into my room until after three in the afternoon so I had plenty of time to make some stops and get lots of hugs!

Marta told me she had called Cal and we were supposed to go and get him to go to the Valley with us. I wasn't sure what she was plannin and started to get nervous.

"Hey sis, I don't think I want anyone else going with us. I have too many places to go and things to do. I had planned on us going to see them for hugs and then during the week to."

"Ok." She said. "Let's drive over there so you can say hello."

"Cool, we can do that." I said.

She didn't have to know how nervous I was. If she couldn't feel it then it probably meant that things hadn't changed much for her … I wish her and the rest of my family here were as happy as I was.

She gave me directions to a trailer court and we drove through till we got to his place.

"That's Keith's car I think, I did't know if he would be here or not." She said.

My heart was pounding but I was again both nervous and excited! I had heard so many crazy things my brother had been involved in, the dope had really messed him up bad. We got out, knocked on the door and waited but no one was answering so I turned around to leave when I heard it open.

I was already off the porch so couldn't see who it was and he stepped out. "Hey girl." He said when he saw me.

"Hi Cal, how are you?" I stepped up to the porch to hug him.

"Are you going to the Valley?" Marta asked him. "We're going for Jenny to see a few people and for the drive."

"No, I can't go nowhere." He said. "The wife, kids and Keith are here. He flew in early in the morning."

We walked over to my car so I could show it off and get ready to go. I had just got into the car hoping to get Marta ready to go when I turned around and Keith was standing there. I didn't expect to see him, or I was scared to see him, somethin like that.

I jumped back out of the car and looked up to see his face. He still looked like my brother but I could tell he wasn't the same.

When I reached out and hugged him he kissed me and swung me around. "Damn brother, I missed you so much! You doing okay?"

"Bout okay as this old man can be huh?" He said laughing and joking.

"You like my car?" I asked him. "To cool, they let me rent a P.T. Cruiser!"

He jumped in through the window to look inside and my heart dropped. Knowing how crazy my brother was, I wasn't sure if he was gonna jump in and want to take off in my rental or get out and be a nice brother like I needed him to do.

HER PLACE WAS WITH GOD

"120 miles an hour huh?" He laughed and asked me. "Want to check it out with me?"

"No no no, come on, can't do that. I wouldn't be able to cover the insurance!" I said laughing with him.

"Who said I would hurt it?" He said with his smile that was both playfull and scary lol.

He got out and we visited for a bit then we got back on the road.

First stop was to pick up my 'package' of smoke! I knew I'd still have to get some more but I didn't want to be totally out when I got here.

I called Miss Betty and Amber Lynn, they told me to meet her at Wally World (Walmart), in Eagle River. I was sure that this journey would prove to be comical as I hoped we could find the store, to the highway we went.

Pulling in the parking lot I saw her by the other doors. I parked and we met in the middle to hug and laugh, hug and cry, I love it! Me seeing all these important people I miss so very much, so awesome! In just a minute Amber and Will and the kids pulled in so I could give her a hug too. The kids are so beautiful, just like their mommy and daddy. Miss Betty, Marta and I all wandered inside so I could buy a couple of things then we headed to the house for some coffee and time with my sisters, my niece and her kids, how awesome!

I missed driving on dirt roads, everything off the main roads are mostly gravel and directions are never easy to follow. Miss Betty was with us giving directions thank goodness lol!

"Kay, right down there to the right Jenn and then another right into the parking lot and go ahead and park right up there in the shade." She pointed up to the edge of the gravel drive.

I could see the pool, slide and other toys waiting for the kids to play on them.

Amber Lynn wasn't home yet so we sat in the yard and had a ball goin through everything in my package I picked up on our way there. There were Betty Boop shirts and a Betty Boop Levi Jacket for my Miss Betty and some cake pans I had been collecting for her forever and some other odds n' ends. Next of course, Bob, aka my Bob Marley stash can, had been waiting for me patiently.

I held up Bob and smiled. "Here we go, just what I needed." I said.

We smoked a little then put everything from my package away then tucked it nice and safe in my car.

Amber got home a few minutes later with the kids, I couldn't believe I was actually sitting here with her, my Miss Betty and Marta. I thought about them and missed them every day when I was home, now here we are visiting and laughing, so awesome!

Soon I had to say goodbye and Marta and I got ready to I head out to the Valley. I was so excited, just the drive alone was worth the whole trip!

"I love you honey." I told Miss Betty.

"I love you to Jenny, call me when you get to your room k?"

"I will, I will call you as soon as we get back." I said getting into the car to head the rest of the way to the Valley.

We talked about everyone and everything. Just being with Marta was like stepping into a time warp, I suppose that was how most of the trip would feel. First on the way was my brother Bert, he was staying at our sister Debbie's house. The last time I had seen him was at Author's funeral also, just like the last time I had seen Marta, what a hard day. Remembering which road was Williwaw was interesting lol, by the time I found the right turn I had plenty of other drivers pissed off at me I'm sure. Driving up the gravel road I continued through my time warp, I remembered it well. Pointing out where my brother Johnny's girlfriend lived and then on up to the trailer.

He came out of the trailer and waited on the porch, a tall man with a healthy belly and a full face of hair. Next I saw the most beautiful pit bull, Rowdy. I still wish to this day that when I left John the last time I had taken my puppy with me, I regret that decision.

I parked the car and jumped out. "Hey brother, how are you?" I asked him.

When we met in the middle of the driveway he picked me up and swung me around. "Hey sis, I love you so much!" He said with a huge smile.

"I love you to brother. You look great!" I told him.

To see the tears on a man's face because he missed me made me feel so loved! Rowdy wasn't shy about telling me he loved me either. I sat on the floor with him while he kissed me over and over and over again, he was so happy to see me, I was crying in a moment. It was so hard to leave everyone I loved here and it was hard to be back knowing I was going to leave again. We talked for a bit then Bert and I drove up the road to pick up my niece so we could visit for a little bit also.

"It is so awesome to be here, how bout a bit of California?" I asked and I pulled out my BoB Marley can handing him a joint to light.

"Yea, right on!" He said with that smile. "Thanks sis, what a way to wake up in the morning huh? Your beautiful face and a joint."

We sat and smoked, laughed and cried. I have a hard time saying goodbye but with how many people I wanted to see I needed to get going.

"Hey, I need something, you said something about being able to get me some smoke? I need an ounce kay?" I asked him.

"No problem sister, call me later." He said.

"I will, love you." I told him.

"Love you too sister." He said.

We waved goodbye and drove up the road to see another one of my niece's then we went into Wasilla. The next stop, my Tammy's work to surprise her. It was so cool driving through town. It had been so long since I'd been there, so many memories.

"Hey, there's the Mug Shot Saloon. Remember the nights there?" I asked Marta.

"Ya, remember when Little Mike tried to steal all the pool balls and cues?"

"I do and I remember falling down the back stairs trying to get to the van." We laughed and talked as we drove on by the bar.

It took a bit but I remembered where Tammy worked. It took forever because they had built so much onto our little town it all looked different.

"Come on sis." I said to Marta. "I'm so excited!"

We walked up to the counter and asked for Tammy. "Can I tell her who is here?" The woman asked me.

"Jenny from California, and thank you."

"No problem." And she walked back through the office.

The next thing I knew my Tammy was runnin through the office, out the door and into my arms. "You're here!" She said so happy. "I didn't know when you would be here and here you are, I missed you so much!"

"I missed you so much to!" We hugged and cried and laughed.

I couldn't stay and visit with her long since of course she was still at work but we made plans to meet Friday night.

We said our goodbyes again and headed to the parking lot.

"I better call Tammy and Brian and let em' know we're on our way." I told Marta when we got back in the car.

Marta and I were having a ball visiting everyone. My other Tammy was waiting for me and by the time we got up there it was about one or two. I was so happy to see her and Brian and the kids. My granddaughter and all the kids were doing so good and looked awesome, I'm so happy for them. I wish I could be there and be a part of the everyday worlds though, I missed all them so much!

We smoked and visited then the girls sang for me, their so smart! I love spending time with Tammy and Brian. Tammy is always there for me and her voice I love so much!

"Okay honey, I love you." She said. "You tell Rick that we want you two living up here with us. You know we have room for you to build a house or put up a trailer."

"I know, I love you too. I want to be here too but I have so much to do still. I need to get to work, tomorrow I have to start talking to others and tape our visits."

The space there we walked around was huge and beautiful, in the back are the train tracks and you can see Sleeping Lady Mountain in the distance.

We kept talking and walking. "That's what I'm doing during this trip, workin on this book of mine. I wish I knew how it was going to turn out, if I can really do what needs to be done." I said.

"You'll be fine honey." Tammy said. "I have faith in you. All you need to do is to

ANSWERED PRAYERS AND LESSONS LEARNED

stay focused and pray and you will be led."

She hugged me and I started crying. "I love you Tammy, can I come up later?"

"I'd be upset if you didn't." She said with that beautiful smile.

"Kay, see you soon."

"I won't say goodbye Jenn but I will see you this evening."

The girls ran out to us. "Can we walk you to your car grandma Jenny?" The kids grabbed our hands and we headed out to my car.

The girls hugged me and Marta then we got into the car and headed back down the hill. My most favorite Mountain in the whole world!

As soon as I sat down in the car my phone was ringin. "Hello." The sweet voice said. "Hi, it's Michelle."

"Hi honey, is everything alright?" I asked her.

"Yes, we were wondering when you were going to be back. Chelsea is waiting to see you before she goes home. We barbequed burgers and hotdogs, do you want something to eat?"

"Aaww right on, I can't wait to see her and I would love a burger. It will be a little bit though." I told her. "I'm leaving the Valley now and after I drop Marta off I'll be home. Ask Chelsea not to leave kay? I love you honey."

"I love you to mom, see you in a bit. Are you okay getting home?"

"I have your directions, I can do it I promise." We laughed and hung up.

Soon we were on our way back to the city.

Talking all the way home made the drive go by way to fast and in what seemed like a few minutes we were at Marta's.

"I'm so glad you're here Jenny."

"I'm glad I'm here too, it's been so nice getting to spend time with you!"

"I wanted you to see the girls but their busy right now."

"That's okay, I'll be back. Im going to go have dinner with Michelle, Jeremy, Jeanette and the kids then go check into my room. I love you!"

"I love you to sister." She said. "See you soon." We waved good-bye and she headed up the drive way to her place.

I loved driving through Anchorage, even if I had to turn around once or twice lol I knew I could make it home.

I'm so glad Chelsie hung out till I got there, she works early in the morning so she wouldn't have been able to stay much longer. I love getting to spend time with my girls and family, a yummy dinner was a plus!

After we all ate and visited a while Chelsie went home and I loaded up my stuff to go to the hotel. Michelle didn't want me to go to a hotel but she understood. For me, everything with my book to do with Alaska was so emotional and going to see everyone the way I had planned to, lol there was no way to know what might happen.

"I love you honey."

"I love you to mom, you call me if you need me and I can't wait to see you again. Oh Yea." She said. "We'll be leaving to go camping tomorrow night or the next so if you can't reach me we'll be at Big Lake."

"I will I promise, have a good day at work and yes I will, see you out there if I don't see you sooner." Hugging again I knew I had to let go and get into my car and drive away, again, I hate doing that.

Back to Eagle River, a little town 15 miles north of Anchorage headed towards the Valley. Pullin into town I tried to remember Miss Betty's directions to look for my hotel. I was thrilled when I saw the sign and happy to see it was a nice place, I can't stand an icky hotel.

I got registered then went back out to my car to get my bags, it was quite a chore getting everything together but I finally did it. I made it up the elevator, found my room and dropping everything in my arms I tried my key to open the door and it didn't work. Okay, let's try this again. I slid the card again and still it didn't work. I bout started crying till I realized how silly I must look standing there freaking out the way I was so called the desk instead.

"Microtel Inn may I help you?"

"Yes I hope. My name is Jennifer, I just checked in and my card isn't working in the door. Can you help me?"

"No problem, I must have put the number on the card wrong. You can come on down and get another."

I tried to sound calm. "No, I can't do that. I just made it up here with all my stuff and I can't do it again. Will you bring it to me please?"

"Sure, I'm sorry." He said. "I have a customer so as soon as I'm done I'll be right there."

"Thank you." I said and sat on the floor with my bags. I took a deep breath, 'everything will be fine', I told myself.

In just minutes the guy came out the door that led to the stairs. "Thank you for coming so quick."

"No problem, try this one." He said handing me another card.

I slid it through the door lock and walla, the green light opened the door that time.

"Have a good day ma'am."

"You too."

He headed back down the stairs and I pushed, carried and dragged my bags into the room and shut the door. I looked around, cool, nice and clean. I have a tv, a clean bathtub, a phone and a bed to sleep on. There's even a little bench to sit on under the window, so cool. I curled up on the bench and smoked the rest of the joint we couldn't smoke earlier. Miss Betty and Marta don't smoke much plus I hadn't smoked in three days because of traveling so getting stoned was a very easy thing to do lol, to cool.

I stretched across my bed thinking I could close my eyes for a bit before I headed back out. Well, one moment, another moment, then another moment passed and that was it. I sat up and realized that I was totally by myself and I didn't know how to act. I miss my family something fierce, I don't know what the next week has in store for me but I do know I'm blessed. Thank goodness for cell phones lol I text the kids and called home to hear Rick's voice, aaww everyone made me feel so good.

Closing my eyes wasn't in the cards for the evening so I cleaned myself up a bit, straitened out my bags and decided to head back out to the Valley. When I came down stairs the guy at the desk was talking to someone about when they closed the side door.

"I'll be coming back late, which door should I come through?"

"The front will be open, we close and lock the side one at 11 p.m."

"Thank you, have a good evening." He said.

"You to." I said back then out to my beautiful red PT Cruiser I went.

Back in my car and back out to the highway, one of my favorite places to be other than with my girls or up at the top of the mountain with Tammy and Brian and all the kids. So exciting it was going to Steve and Emma's to visit, I hadn't gotten to see them yet. When I got to Wasilla I called them and they told me to call em when I got to Johnson Road, it was right before the Big Lake turnoff. Okay, I should be able to find that huh? Again, my amazement of driving through the Valley, to cool! When I found Johnson Road I started up the gravel road noticing that it seemed so familiar.

On up the road a bit and a bend or two, I passed a road off to the left that was the road where Marta lived the year that John attacked me with the machete. Yep, I'll just keep on goin! That made me a bit nervous, at least I recognized where I was huh? I called them back and they gave me directions on up to their place. Pulling in I was so excited, it had been so long since I had seen anyone. I was trying to get my purse and stuff together when they came outside.

"Hey girl, look at you!" My brother Steve said.

I got out and hugged him and Emma then we all went into the house.

"I can't believe you guys are here, you both look so good!"

"You look good to honey, God is awesome isn't he?" My brother said.

I love it when my family could easily talk about God, it showed me that I am not the only one out of all of us that knew there was more going on than the drugs and the crazy stuff! We talked about how life was going and the work I'm doing on my book. I'm amazed at how many people were excited about my book instead of the opposite,

I love knowing they believe in me!

"You guys smoke still yes?" I asked them.

"Oh yea!" My sister Emma said. "Actually, Steve doesn't smoke anymore."

He sat up to explain to me. "I have to take different meds for pain management so the smoke kinda gets in the way."

"Good for you." I said.

Emma is so sweet and funny. "Now, that doesn't go for me!" She said laughing. "I'll smoke with you."

"Cool, I have some smoke we grew in California."

I pulled out Bob and took out a joint to smoke. "Can we go outside and smoke? It's so nice today."

"Yep." She said. "That'll be fine."

We went outside and sat on the porch while we smoked the joint and talked. Being there with them was so very heart warming. The pull I was having was so strong.

"I can't believe how beautiful it is here Emma."

"It is isn't it? You know we are buying property, fixing it up and building a home then reselling it. It's nicer if there is a house already on the property, it leaves you with much less work."

There was a place across the street for sale too so we walked over and looked at it. It was inexpensive and so cute and right by them. (It ended up being sold before I could even think about it though.)

That's okay, by the time I'm ready for something like this I will be able to pick what I want and where I want it.

It was so nice to have a friend, a sister to talk to, I had missed her a lot.

"I really want to be here sister. I love it here and I can't stand California in the summer. It was fine when I was younger but now it seems to be totally unacceptable!"

"Probably cause you were here for so long your body changed to the weather."

"Yea, I think so. The heat there never bothered me, even when it got as hot as 115 degrees!"

"Dang, no way!"

"Unreal huh? I can't deal with it now. All I do is hibernate under the airconditioning and never go out and about unless I have to, you know, shopping, appointments and that stuff."

"Well, we are here and we love you. We would be thrilled to have you and Rick out here! We're going to be selling this place to you know. There is a sauna out back and a huge dog pen and about 2 acres to boot." She said.

We walked around the house and they showed me the property and their dogs. Three beautiful babies that were very spoiled, just like ours are. I had been there a while and was feeling it was time for me to be going.

ANSWERED PRAYERS AND LESSONS LEARNED

We went back into the house and I got my purse and stuff.

"I need to come back and spend some time with you guys and take some pics too."

"Cool, we'll be waiting to hear from you. Hey Jenn" Emma said. "I was wondering if you would let me do something with you. I'd like to pray for you and anoint you with this oil."

Emma read the bible verse to me that explained the oil and the ingredients in it.

"I would feel very blessed for you to pray over me, thank you!"

The next few minutes were my sister and brother praying over me while anointing me with the Lords words and oil. Talk about feeling like I belonged on the top of the world, nothing could be better! So nice to listen to Steve speaking the words of the bible but more so, knowing he understood what he was saying.

"I am so happy you guys can pray and study and listen to God. There were so few of us out of that mess that could do something like this."

We talked a little longer, hugged and then I drove back out the gravel road. I missed that, pretty much all the roads were gravel unless they were a main street, even lots of businesses were on gravel roads.

I figured I better call Tammy before I came out, it was about 8 p.m. by then but still light outside of course, to cool!

I stopped at the end of the road to get a soda and make my phone call. "Hi Tammy, it is too late for me to come and see you?" I asked when heard her answer the phone.

"No, honey." Her said. "Not at all! Are you coming now?"

"Yea, I'm at the Big Lake turnoff."

"Kay, see you in a minute, you alright?" She asked me.

"Yep, I'm great."

"Good, the kids are waiting for you so hurry." She said, I love hearing her voice. "Love you." She said.

"Love you to Tammy."

We said good-bye and I headed away from the store.

Back out on the highway I past Cherry Lake Subdivision and then the Houston Lodge singing, "Hooston, Hooston means that I'm one step closer to you, do do do do do do … Houston, Ak baby, not Texas." I laughed at myself.

∽∂∾

I had some crazy memories from the Houston Lodge. 'I don't remember all of them though' lol, I thought to myself.

One year on my birthday we had all been camping and stopped in at the Lodge for some coffee and cocoa for the kids. My brothers little Mike and Bob were at the Lodge having one or two or three.

"Hey little sis, happy birthday!" They both hollered to me as they stumbled across the room to us and attached themselve's to John and I for a hug.

"Love you sis, love you brother." They said lookin back n' forth at us both.

"Hey, where's your birthday cake?" Bob asked.

"We didn't get a cake this year. That's fine, camping is way better than birthday cake, you know that." I told him.

Him and Mike kept jokin around and the next thing I knew I saw a look in his eye lol,

"Brother, what are you doing?" I asked.

That crazy and loving smile said it all. He pulled his pants down, bent over and stuck the end of the sparkler between his legs and lit the end of it. I couldn't believe what I was seeing lol Oh My God it had to have been the funniest thing I had ever seen! We worked on covering the kid's eyes so they didn't have to see what we were seeing, it was fricken hilarious!

"Happy Birthday to you, happy birthday to you, happy birthday dear sister, happy birthday to you!" They both sang with such happiness and love lol!

A memory I'll never forget, I am truly loved lol …!

Another memory is when we went to the Lodge for a Halloween Party one year, so cool. I never knew how to do anything with my hair or with 'me' other than the basic look and the clothes, levy's and tshirt. My sister Karine was awesome though and worked magic! I wore a sexy black witch dress and she teased my hair lol. I had only seen that on tv when I was a kid and had no idea it did anything other than cause a lot of knots and then the makeup. I couldn't believe it when I saw myself in the mirror, I wasn't one to 'pretty up', but I was a knockout that night. I almost didn't want to go but I'm glad I did, it was a fun. Some people lol, even family, didn't even recognize me at first. Karine won the costume contest with her upside down man, it was awesome!

On up the highway till the strait away leads right into their driveway on the bend in the highway. I love it! Pulling in I could take a deep breath and knew I was somewhere I belonged and loved.

Up on the porch the girls were waiting for me. "Grandma Jenny, hi, you came back to see us?" They both said with such sweet little voices.

I gathered my things and headed to the house. "You bet I did and I'll come back as often as I can while I'm here."

"What do you mean, while you're here?" Their both so curious and sweet.

"I live in California, I have to go back next week."

The girls had come down to me at the bottom of the stairs and were walking up with me and with Tammy.

"I don't want you to go, you can stay here?" They were asking me.

"I love you sweetie. Both of you but no, I can't stay here. At least not right now."

Tammy stepped in. "We want her to though! We love you Jenny, you are our family and you are these kid's grandma. You and Rick can come up you know."

"I want to so bad, I don't like the heat at all, it's miserable. I was just talking to Emma and Steve about this also. It didn't bother me when I was a kid but it sure does now."

We were in the house by now and sitting down to smoke. "Hey Brian, how are you doing?" I said giving him a hug.

The girls were right there to talk to me. "I can sing, you want to see?"

"You bet I do!"

They both put on the sweetest show for me. I'm so thankful these little girls have Tammy and Brian to love them the way they do.

We walked around the property talking and laughing. The girls were playing so I pulled my camera out to video tape them, they loved it. They jumped in their little car and drove on off with instruction for me to follow. So we did, it is so beautiful with the train tracks in the open now since a lot of the woods burned, that's sad though.

Tammy was trying to convince me to move up on the mountain with them. She told me we could call the station ahead of time when I needed to take a train from Anchorage to the house in Willow and they would drop me off at the bottom of the hill from the house. I videotaped the property showing it to Rick and telling him that this was where we could live. It even has its own driveway with immediate Highway access, cool huh? 'One of these days', I told myself, 'one of these days'.

Tammy and Brian's boys, Joey and Dustin and their families live with them also. It was fun videotaping Joey while played on his little scooter he fixed up and the kids playing.

Soon it was time for me to head home, well, back to my room to see my Miss Betty for a minute before I went to bed. So trippy being on my very own schedule, I liked it but I missed Rick and the kids a lot. I was looking forward to the drive back down the mountain. As soon as the kids saw me getting my purse and camera together they voiced that they would walk me to my car and ran up to us and grabbed mine and Tammy's hands.

"By Brian, love you and see you tomorrow."

"Love you to kid, be good." He said with a smile.

"Always."

We walked out to the car and I hugged em all again then got in my cute little red

P.T. Cruiser. I waved goodbye to them and driving away the tears fell. It was so hard to leave, I love being with them.

When I got closer to Eagle River I called my Miss Betty to pick her up so we could spend some more time together. She was at her daughter's house so I went there to see her, after all the directions and me getting frustrated n' all of course lol. After we visited with Amber and the kids, Betty and me sat in the car and took a couple of hits so I could relax. Being stressed over the, who, what, when and where lol … I needed it!

"I'm worried about you honey, are you going to pick up Marta?" Betty asked me.

"No, not tomorrow. She is going to go out with me Friday and Saturday to visit the guys. We have to find Bob and I'm supposed to go see Glen and Rick. I saw Keith but I want to see him again if I can."

"Well, call me when you get back to your room kay?"

"Of course, I love you. I will be fine I promise."

"You better, I need you and so does everyone else here and in California!"

"Yea yea yea." I said laughing as we hugged and kissed good-bye.

I got lost leaving their subdivision, at least I was on my way to find my hotel. Thank goodness it was only down the street and around the corner, to bad I hadn't figured that out yet lol.

When I got back to the hotel I sat in my car in the parking lot and called my sister Marta to say hi then I called my sister Lucy. I couldn't wait to see her. I wanted to see all the kids too, I didn't quite know how I would make that happen yet. My brother Chuck passed away a month ago and they have had to go through so much. They are one of the strongest families I will ever know that's for sure.

"Hi Lucy, how are you?"

"I'm good, how are you doing?" She asked.

"I'm fine, getting ready to go to my room and see if I can sleep at all."

"I bet, your mind must be going a million miles a minute!"

"It is, I have so many things I have to do and so many people I have to see and half of them I still have to find. Marta knows where pretty much every one is im hoping, im looking for Radical to."

"Yea, he was at the funeral." She said in such a quiet voice.

"I'm so sorry sister. How are you and the kids holding up?"

"We are fine, we are strong and are sticking together."

"You're stronger than I would be! I know we can't meet till Saturday or Sunday but do you want to meet for coffee in the morning before you go to work?"

"That early, are you sure?" She asked.

"Yep, I miss you so much and I'll be going out to the Valley first thing in the morning anyways."

"Cool, I'd love to! Do you remember where Geoffrey's is?"

"The brown building in the Carr's parking lot?"

"Yep, that's it."

"Kay, what time is good?"

"Can we meet at 10?"

"Yep, 10 it is."

"Love you Jenny."

"I love you to sis and can't wait to see you. It's so good to hear your voice, sometimes I call the cell just to hear Chucks voice."

We both laughed a little, it was good to hear a happy sound come from her. "Yea, I do too." She said.

We said goodbye and hung up then I gathered my bags and started the trip through the parking lot and up to the hotel to my room.

I think it was about 11:30 or so by the time I got there. I cleaned up my bags and put my clothes away in the dresser. It was a perfect little room and I loved the little bench underneath the window. I smoked a joint and called anyone I could think of till I realized what time it was. I had to remember also that everyone at home was an hour ahead of me lol, whoops!

Next I tried Amber Lynn's to talk to Miss Betty.

Amber answered quiet, I could tell I woke her. "Hello?"

"Hi honey, I woke you, I'm sorry."

"No, I'm still up, it's okay. Are you alright?"

"Yep, I'm good. I just wanted to tell your mom I love her and good night, you too of course."

"She isn't here, she went home earlier. What are you doing up this late missy?" She asked with such a cute tone! "If you don't get some sleep my mama's gonna kick your butt!"

"I'm so loved! I finally got back from the Valley. I'm gonna try to get some sleep. My mind is going a thousand miles a minute and really hoping I can make it stop."

"You try kay? We love you and we're worried about you."

"I'm fine, no worry about me and I love you to. I'll call you guys in the morning."

We hung up and I laid there to see if I could think about sleeping lol. I had lost my charger and couldn't keep my phone charged by just using the car charger so I decided to go for a drive to Wally World to buy a new one, no better time than the present huh? I loved walking through a store at night when no one else was there. I was looking for a tank top my niece Tracy had gotten at home, a tie dyed purple tank and it was so cute. No way would I have expected anyone to know my name 3000 miles away from home at midnight in Eagle River, Alaska huh?

"Miss Jenny, what are you doing?" I heard lol.

I turned quick to see sweet Amber. "Hi honey, you scared me."

HER PLACE WAS WITH GOD

"Didn't expect to see anyone you know huh?" She said laughing.

"Not really." I said while we hugged each other.

"I'm just looking at shirts and need a charger for my cell. I couldn't sleep so here I am."

"When you leave you go to your room and get some rest alright?" She instructed in a most loving way lol.

I saluted and kissed her goodbye then walked back to the electronics. Where of course they didn't have the charger I needed. I went ahead and got myself some shampoo and conditioner and toothpaste n' stuff then went back to the hotel.

It was so nice and peaceful at one in the morning and light outside like dusk time. A few people were out here and there doing this and that and me enjoying every second of it.

I woke early, so awesome. I got out of bed and remembered the continental breakfast I read about. I had never seen a real nice one in a hotel so I guess I just have to check it out. In my frog jammies and my tie dye tank top I headed down in the elevator to embark on my day.

There were a few people there so I waited my turn to stay out of the way. I don't do well around a bunch of people I know, let alone a bunch of people I don't know. Cool, there was a shelf of different kinds of dry cereal and oatmeal packages with bowls and all kind of things to add to it. There were bagels and cream cheese, bananas and there were muffins, banana nut and blueberry. There were even waffles and jellies, syrup, coffee and orange juice and even apple juice. When everyone else went on their way I went in closer to check it all out. My stomach wasn't as hungry as I wanted it to be. I knew I was nervous about what the day would bring, anything could happen from this moment on. I made myself a bagel with cream cheese and tried to take a bite but it didn't go well with me so I quickly tossed it in the garbage while no one was looking, I hoped. I poured myself a cup of coffee and a cup of orange juice, put a couple of muffins on a paper plate and headed on back to the elevator. I gotta say that the orange juice was the one thing I couldn't get enough of. By the time I got to the room I had to turn around and get more orange juice. I came back up again and curled up on the bench under the window and ate my muffins and drank my coffee and juice then smoked a joint.

So beautiful, looking out the window I could see the mountains around the little town. People everywhere, I love watching everyone. I finished drinkin my juice and coffee and smoking and jumped in the shower to get ready for what laid waiting ahead.

ANSWERED PRAYERS AND LESSONS LEARNED

Let's see, gotta be just the right thing. I had lost enough weight since the last time I saw anyone, sooo happy about that! It gave me a good feeling to know I looked nice and healthy and I could hold my head up high to everyone I saw, absolutely everyone, I was ready for the world!

I sat at the bench under the window and talked to God for a minute and said a morning prayer. "Thank you Lord, stay with me today. I am yours Lord Jesus, thank you for the day and for your protection. In Jesus' name, Amen." And I was ready to leave.

Passing others in the hotel I made my way through the halls out the side door to the very pretty and red P.T. Cruiser in the parking lot. I had finally figured out how to work the alarm lol, thank goodness.

I stopped at the gas station to fill up and to get some more orange juice but theirs wasn't as good as what I had at the hotel lol water works. I had plans to meet Lucy for coffee but it was way early so I figured I would go to the Harley Shop in Wasilla first and then go out and wake up my brother Bert. I needed to spend some more time with him and if I was lucky he would have my smoke. He was staying up from Geoffrey's Restaurant, perfect!

My drive to Wasilla was every perfect thing I needed it to be just like all the other times I've gotten to enjoy the drive. I would have been fine staying in the Valley the whole time but the hotels cost too much. It took me a minute to find Williwaw Way again. It was still the same of course, to cool. On up the gravel road to Debbie's trailer, I pulled in the gravel drive and gathered my things up. I figured I'd leave my smoke in the car, I only had one joint left and was hoping Bert had some more for me.

'Dang, I hope he's up, I suppose I should have called.' I thought to myself. Bout that time Rowdy came out the front door to welcome me.

"Hey boy, hi honey." I told him as he bounced around licking me and trying to knock me over, he's so cool. It was aweosme how happy he was to see me!

"Hey sis." I looked up and Bert was standing on the porch.

It was so good to see him looking so healthy. Full face of hair, happy belly and happy eyes that shined when he smiled. I missed him!

"Mornin brother, did I wake you up?"

"Yep, but there isn't anyone else I'd rather wake me in the morning that's for sure!" He said with his silly smile.

"Haha, silly."

I went up and gave him a hug and we went into the house to sit down. Rowdy was still lovin on me while we talked about my trip.

"Do you have any smoke for me by any chance?" I asked him.

"No, not yet, I have to go up the road to get it still. I have a couple of bowls we can smoke though."

"That'll do for now, I only have one more joint left and I'm way too far away from home to run out that's for sure!" I said laughing.

He got up and went into the other room and brought the bag and his pipe to set it on the table and took Rowdy outside to put him on the runner.

We were talking and smoking when we saw someone pull up to the front of the yard.

"Who's that brother?"

"I don't know." He got up and looked out the window.

About then I looked around and saw I don't know how many cops coming into the yard from all sides of the property.

"What the hell Bert? Oh my God!"

I grabbed my purse running out to the porch throwing my hands up into the air yelling, "My name is Jennifer Russell I live in Durham, California!"

The officers had big guns and didn't look to be in much of a good mood. Shit, I couldn't believe this!

One of the officers grabbed my arm and pulled me over by my car. "What are you doing here?" He asked me.

"I just got here night before last, I have my ticket and everything."

"Whose car is this?"

"It is my rental car. I have the paperwork, what is going on?"

"And you don't know?" He asked me.

"How would I know? I told you, this is my brother. I've been in town for two days. I came out to visit my brother and this is the welcome I get?"

I was trying to see what was going on around me when I saw they had taken Bert into custody, he was in the back of a patrol car.

There was a lot of ruckus going on and I heard Rowdy going crazy, I looked up to see officers with huge gun barrels pointed at his head.

"No no no, don't shoot my dog!" I screamed and went to run out to him and the cop grabbed my arm and pulled me back. I kept screaming, "There is no reason to shoot him, he will listen to me please don't shoot him, I can tie him up for you!"

At first they ignored me but finally one of the other officers gave them instructions to wait. "Go ahead, tie him up." He told me.

I ran up to him quick as I could. "Come on honey, I'm sorry this is so confusing for you." I was so pissed and hurt and crying now to!

I grabbed his collar and watched the officers scatter here and there. "Go ahead and tie him up to that bench by the trailer." An officer told me.

I realized that Bert had him on a runner in front of the door so of course he wouldn't let the cops inside, they were going to kill him.

I would have died if they would have shot him! "Come on Rowdy, you can lie

ANSWERED PRAYERS AND LESSONS LEARNED

down here. You'll be fine boy, I love you."

I told them I didn't have anything to tie him up with so I sat and held him for a minute until one of the officers brought me his leash from inside the house.

"Here you go." He said to me.

"Thank you." I tried to be polite but it was hard, they were so rude and scary.

I put the leash on him and got him tied up to a table against the trailer. "There you go, you be good. Someone will be over later to get you inside kay?" I hugged him and walked back over to my car where they were all at.

"Just so that you know we are here on a raid so all the vehicles need to be searched." One of the offerers said to me.

Well, that made me start fidgeting. "Alright, then, you will be searching my car?"

"Yes ma'am, is that a problem?" They asked looking at me sideways lol.

"No, not at all but I am a legal marijuana 215 patient and there is one joint in my car."

There, I said it. My stomach was in knots and I felt like I was going to throw up. I couldn't believe what was happening, the only thing I could think of was going to jail on my trip and not being able to make it home by my scheduled flight time. Being stuck 3000 miles from Rick and the kids, oh my God, this was a nightmare!

"Ma'am, I need you to show me where the marijuana is."

"It's right here." I went to the car and opened up the console and took out Bob and opened it and handed him my joint.

"That's okay, you can destroy it yourself."

"Are you serious?" I asked him.

He stepped back and laughed at the moment or at me most likely. "I sure am. Anyways, you'll be able to get more." He said snickering.

I had bent down to empty out the joint into the gravel. I looked up at him and looked around at the other officers there. 'Why don't you just come with' I thought to myself ... 'I don't think so' lol oh my goodness!

They got a kick out of it and they were all being so sarcastic, all it did was frustrate me even more. I got up and got my purse to show them all of my paperwork. My prescription and my 215 Patient card and letters from my doctor. I showed them my car rental paperwork and my return airline ticket.

"You know, your California 215 license don't mean shit here." He said to me.

"Excuse me?" I asked him.

"Nope, you may be legal there but Alaska doesn't recognize another states laws because ours are different."

I had no idea what might happen next, I had to make them understand! "Sir, I had to leave home and come up here to work on my book I'm writing. When I leave home my diseases don't stay at home, they come with me so in turn my medicines also come with me."

The more I explained the nicer they seemed to be to me. "I suppose your right." The one officer said. "Still, you better be more careful about who you spend time with."

"This is my family, I have to see them no matter what their doing or where they are." I told him. "So, I'm almost afraid to know what all of this is about."

"Well, put it this way, we're are all DEA and Federal Officers."

"You're telling me that this is about dope?"

"Yes ma'am." He said. "That's right."

All of a sudden I could feel the anger welling up, I was so pissed!

Another officer came over to where we were talking. "Your brother wants to talk to you."

"I don't know if I have anything to say to him." I said.

They led me over to him and opened the back door of the car so he could talk to me. "Sis, I'm sorry. I need you to go into the bedroom behind the dresser and get the house keys. I need you to watch the house till you can get a hold of Cassie or someone and Rowdy needs to be let into the house and fed n'all."

"And you expect me to do this? Your wrong, how dare you!" I yelled to him. "I ain't gonna take care of any of your crap Bert, none of it!"

One of the officers stepped up closer to us. "You can come back in a couple of hours if you want and let the dog back into the house and lock it all up."

That made me laugh. "What in the hell would I come back here for?" I asked them.

I looked back to Bert. "I don't know whats goin on here but I do know that you lied to me and you put me in some major jeopardy this morning. Why would you do this to me? Wow, I can't help you brother, I'm outa here!" I told him.

I looked up at one of the officers and told him I wanted to slap him so bad! lol he told me to go ahead then all three of them turned away, so I did, it felt great!

I turned and walked back over by my car. "Can I leave now?"

I figured they were probably done with me. I hadn't paid enough attention to know what they took out of the house but I am sure it was enough to charge him because they had no intension of him getting out any time soon.

"Hang on, I think so." The officer walked over to the others and had a pow-wow, finaly they decided that they didn't need me. They took all my personal information and told me I could leave. 'You don't have to tell me twice' I said to myself as I got into my car. I backed out between all the undercover cars then headed back out the gravel road and lost it, tears started to flow.

All of a sudden I heard a voice over my head ... "Something is going to happen to you while you're here if you're not careful."

ANSWERED PRAYERS AND LESSONS LEARNED

Okay, it wasn't a request or a thought I told myself, that was a word of warning from God and I heard it loud and clear! I was so scared, everything that could have happened ran through my head over and over and over again.

As I was driving back to the main road I called Jas, she had tried to call me while the raid was going on and they wouldn't let me touch my phone. "Mom, what's up?" I started cry as soon as I heard her voice.

"Mom, what's wrong?" She asked me.

It was so hard to talk. "I was visiting Bert at Debbie's house and he was raided!" I said through the tears and panic.

"What? Mom are you alright? I've been trying to call you."

"I know, the DEA were there and wouldn't let me answer your call."

"Are you driving and crying?" I could hear it in her voice how scared she was for me and with her being so far away, neither of us knew what to do.

"I'm fine honey, I am driving away from Debbie's down Williwaw. I'm supposed to meet Lucy for coffee up at the restaurant right now."

"Mommy, you need to stop the car, pull over kay?" She said to me. I missed her and wished I was home at that moment!

"I can't, I'll stop when I get there. I just don't want you to hang up kay?" I told her still crying.

"That's fine mom, take a deep breath kay?"

"Yep, I'm trying." I tried to calm down. Deep breath, deep thought ... no, no thoughts!

"I'm fine honey, I'm just freaked out." I told her what happened the best I could and then realized I couldn't remember how to find Geoffrey's.

God was with me though, next thing I new I was driving into the parking lot. "I'm here now." I told her. "Hang on, let me find a parking spot."

I sat the phone down while I parked. "Hi hun, im back. Now all I need to do is to stop crying."

"You will mom, I love you so much. Is Lucy going to be there?"

"Yea, she will be here any minute now. I'll call you back kay."

"You promise?" She asked. "And you'll call me if you need me right? I love you!"

"I will honey, I love you to." I told her.

We hung up and I started to cry again.

I called Marta to tell her what had happened, at least tried to. "Marta, hey Bert just got raided at Debbie's while I was there."

She just started screaming. "Marta, hey, listen to me, I need to tell you this!" I tried to tell her. She kept screaming louder. "I can't talk to you while your screaming, you have to stop or I can't talk to you! They almost shot Rowdy but I got the cops to let me tie him up by the house. Bert had his runner blocking the front door."

HER PLACE WAS WITH GOD

"What!" She said screamin more. "They shot Rowdy?"

"No sister, they were going to but they didn't, he's fine. I am not though and Bert is in custody." She started screaming again so I hung up my phone. So much for that huh?

Other people were walking past me in my car to go into the restaurant, I felt like an idiot sitting in my car being hysterical. I hate drama but at the same time knew I couldn't make it stop.

I had to do something, I felt like my mind was a whirlwind and it wouldn't stop!

I called Lucy's cell phone to see if she was still meeting me. "Hello, Lucy?"

"Yea, it's me, are you okay? Why are you crying?" She asked me.

"I was in a raid at Debbie's just now. She isn't there, Bert was."

"What? You've got to be kidding me!"

"I wish I was, then I could stop crying and enjoy my time with you! Are you here yet?"

"I'm getting out of my car right now."

I looked in my review mirror. "There you are, kay, see you in a minute."

I hung up, got out of the car and ran over to her to hug her. "I can't believe that the first time I get to spend time with you I'm this upset and crying, I'm sorry!"

"No honey, its okay. I'm glad I was here and we were able to meet. Are you hungry?" She asked.

"I don't think so, I haven't even had much coffee yet this morning." I said laughing. "Can you believe it?"

We helped each other in our visit I hope, we spent about an hour talking laughing and crying until she had to get to work. We said our goodbyes and she headed out while I called my Tammy and Brian. My stomach was killing me, I really needed to sit and smoke so I could relax but they weren't home yet.

One of the kids answered the phone. "She told me you would be calling and was hoping to be home by now. Are you alright?"

"I'm ok, just having a really hard morning and need to see her. I'll call back."

We said good-bye and I hung up. I tried calling Steve and Emma, they were home so I headed up to their place. When I got there I told them what had just happened, we smoked and talked and walked around outside. Finally I was a bit more together, at least I didn't feel nauseous. It's awesome knowing that God was there with them and with me. Obviously it's His plan He wants me to follow and not my own, we prayed yesterday, not only prayed but they anointed me with oil. I know He is with me, with us!

Their phone rang and Steve went in to answer it. "Hey Jenn, its Marta and Cal." He told me. "They want to talk to you."

"Hi, what's up?"

"Nothing, we're on our way to the Valley. We have to get a hold of someone to take care of the house. Have you made any calls yet?" Marta asked.

"I'm not doing that sis, there's no way I'm taking responsibility for this crap. I told you the first day I got here that I knew I could be putting myself in some bad situations but there's no way im going to allow myself to get caught up in the drama.

"That's okay." I could hear Cal say in the back ground.

They were talking back and forth, it sounded crazy and I couldn't understand them at all.

"Here, Cal wants to talk to you." Marta said to me.

"Hey sis, I'm here with Marta for a bit, she's pretty upset."

Obviously they were already drinking, she was drunk when I called her earlier, that's why she was screaming the way she was. Makes me so sad.

I finally got out words. "I'm pretty upset to."

"You alright?" He asked me.

"I'm fine I spose. I have to go."

"Here's Marta, love you sis." He said.

"Yea, love you to." I told him then he gave her the phone. "Hey Marta, I have to go."

"Kay, call me?" She asked.

"Love you bye." I said hoping my sarcasm wasn't as loud as I was feeling it!

I was supposed to pick her up Saturday morning to go out to the Valley to help me get everyone's stories on tape, I was so excited. Not to sure about that happenin anymore after the raid and hearing what God told me, no telling what would be next!

After that phone call I needed another smoke, I hung up and got one out of my car.

"Hey, I thought you said you didn't smoke cigarettes?" They asked me.

"After that shit happened I wasn't strong enough, I went to smokes and Pepsi's, at least till I calm down this will just have to do."

We laughed and walked around the lot a bit, it's so beautiful!

"I need to be up here, I need my girls and grandkids in my life, I need you and Steve in my life, I need Tammy and Brian and the kids in my life and the rest of our family, and I want to be on this mountain that takes my breath away!"

I could feel my heart pounding. I missed Rick so much and the kids and I knew I was going home, it was still going to be one of the hardest things I've ever had to do, leave this place and these people again.

"Hey Jen." Emma said. "After us praying over you yesterday and everything that happened today, what are thinking now?"

Sitting there it wasn't hard to figure it out. "I'm done, I don't have to do this. God doesn't want me in jeopardy to get more stories for my book, I have everything I need. I do need to make it home and on time and in one piece, I just have to re think all of this. I heard him, I heard him clear as day! God told me word for word, 'Something is

HER PLACE WAS WITH GOD

going to happen to you while you're here if you're not careful.' I know now there are certain people I'm not going to be able to see either."

"That's right." My sister Emma said. "You know what kind of things went on up here back then, a lot of its still happening and it's gotten worse. It's sad but true."

I could feel tears coming on. "I know, I miss everyone. I miss our barbeques and the bone fires. I miss the runs, the bar and our rides. I don't think I need to be pushing myself and putting myself in danger though. This is it, this is my last chapter!"

We talked for a while and Steve and Emma started tending to their sweet garden. I watched in awe, such love for theirselves, each other and God, I love it. They reminded me of Rick and me, just wanting to love God, each other and our kids. To wake up in the morning with a smile on our faces and our hearts and to go to bed at night the same way.

I figured it would be a good time for me to make some phone calls. The sun was out and it was nice and warm so I was able to walk up and down the road while I talked to my Miss Betty.

"Hi Honey, you're not going to believe what just happened! Remember when you wanted me to slow down and I probably wasn't going to be doing that?"

"Yea, of course." She said.

"Well, I was in a raid this morning at Debbie's place with Bert and I had an epiphany. Have you ever heard of that before? Where something, life, all of a sudden makes sense?" I asked her.

"I think so, are you alright?"

"Yea, I am now. I'm so pissed off at my brother though, I can't believe him. I would kick his ass if I could right about now but I got to slap him. I'm done, I'm not going to chase after stories like I was."

"What do you mean? Are you going to chill out and spend some time with the ones that need you?" She asked with a sound of relief.

"Yep, that is what it means. Seeing them the way I was going to could have and most likely would have only broke my heart or worse and I don't want to hurt their hearts either."

"Good, im so happy!" Miss Betty said. "I'm not glad about what happened, how scary! I'm glad you will be able to enjoy your trip now."

"Yea, me too. I love you." I told her.

"I love you too."

"I'll call you tonight kay? I'm not sure when I'm gonna pick you up yet. I have to talk to Marta later and see what happens with our plans. I pretty much think there won't be any plans other than Monday at the barbeque. Hey, have I asked you yet if you would go with me?"

"To what, the barbeque?"

ANSWERED PRAYERS AND LESSONS LEARNED

"Yes, please?" I could hear her sigh and laugh like she would.
"Of course, I wouldn't let you do that by yourself. I would do anything for you."
"I love you, thank you!"
"I love you to."

We said good-bye then I called Rick and Jas to check in and I had to call Michelle and tell her what happened. They had already gone camping though so I'll wait and tell her when I visit them at camp. Finally it was time for me to head on up the hill, at least I wasn't hysterical anymore, thank goodness!

We said goodbye, prayed for the day and I headed back out the gravel road to the highway. I called Tammy but she hadn't gotten home yet. I was so frustrated, I couldn't believe what that happened. If I had known he had anything to do with dope at all I wouldn't have been there. I was dumbfounded, I could have lost everything! That's what kept running through my mind. Me, having to stay and having to borrow money to bail out of jail then postpone my trip home, which would cost. Then keeping my rental car somehow and that would cost to. I would have to stay with someone because I wouldn't be able to keep my room, what a mess.

'Kay, I'll stop' I told myself over and over again lol, it didn't happen that way and I'm fine. Not only am I fine but I am able to take a deep breath now and slow down … I wish it would hurry and get to my mind though, the breath I mean!

I drove on up pass Tammy and Brian's till I found a pull out on the other side of the road. I figured that way it would be easier to pull out into traffic when I was ready to leave. It was Memorial Weekend Holiday so there was a lot of people on the highway. I pulled off the road and found a good radio station. My note book was always in the right place at the right time.

I started on a page and wrote more and then more and then more on a real small notebook. Two pages this direction, three more the other direction. Six or seven more in a backward but orderly fashion with notes directed for a move or a thought added in stretched around to a blank area on another page. Man, I sure hoped I could read my notes later! I cried for a while, I yelled a little bit and I prayed and wrote a lot. After what ended up being about two hours I called the house again but she still wasn't home. That was okay, I wasn't done yet. I wrote a bit more and finally got it all out, man, what a feeling. Like a thousand pounds lifted off my shoulders. I got out and smoked a cigarette and thanked God for me being able to even be there. I decided to give it a shot and head down to the house. If they weren't there yet then I would just go back to my room or something.

I was so thankful to see the car when I pulled in. My Tammy hugged me and we talked for a bit and smoked and then I headed back down the mountain.

So awesome, I finally got to the room and curled up on the bench under the window. The next thing I knew tears were falling down my face. 'It's okay to cry' I told myself. I can't believe what had happened. I couldn't believe Bert. Marta too, I realized she was drinking like this all time and it broke my heart. I don't want to lose another sister to alcohol or to anything or anyone else!

I made a few phone calls and finally got my Miss Betty and Amber Lynn on the phone.

"Do you have time to visit? I need to just relax and enjoy you and the kids."

"No problem honey, come on over." For the next couple of days my hours were filled with driving from Eagle River to Willow and back and as much around Eagle River as I could manage without getting lost. I loved spending time with my Miss Betty, Amberlynn, Will and the kids, I missed them so much!

The next afternoon me and my Miss Betty went to visit my other Tammy, her life was happy for her now also. It was to cool driving up to the house and seeing the top of the ranch style red house roof which meant I had gone the right way. When we pulled up into the driveway she was outside waiting.

"Look at you driving a P.T. Cruiser, how did you swing that?" She asked with the most beautiful smile.

"Would you believe it is my rental? They said it was the only compact car they had left so I didn't figure I could tell them no."

We laughed and I got out of the car and we hugged and talked. I introduced everybody, Tammy and her daughter, Miss Betty and Tammy's boyfriend who was doing something right because she seemed as happy with her world as I am in mine and that was to cool! It was nice to know that out of all my family here there were some that hadn't lost their hearts and or minds to the same extent as others.

We had an awesome visit but I was happy to go back to my room but more so dinner, I was finally getting un-stressed and hungry!

We went down to the gas station to get a soda so I figured I would check my bank balance before we headed to my room, being so far away from home I was scared of screwing up my finances. Low and behold I am glad I called, my account was short $186. I called my bank back and they told me that it was my hotel that had withdrawn the money. I called the hotel next and told them that they needed to check into this problem and I would be there in about 30 minutes.

I ended up making a huge deal out of something that all figured its self out in the long run. I'm so thankful that mine and Betty's relationship is strong, otherwise it might not have survived and that would have broken my heart!

Next thing I knew it was Saturday night and coming up on Monday was the barbeque. I hadn't seen Fernando and Martha yet, i was so nervous about who was going to be there. So many of us were gone or dead or still using and I had no idea who I would see. I sure hoped that Keith was coming, I missed him. Glenn and Rick were supposed to be there but they must not have made it in off the boat soon enough and Bob and Crissy were going to be there to I hoped!

Monday morning I went on out to the Valley before I picked up my Miss Betty, I had to say way too many goodbye's. I had pretty much given up on the fact of bringing home smoke after what happened at Bert's but I couldn't stand being out anymore. On my drive to Willow I stopped at the Harley Shop coming into Wasilla, I was so happy I was going to be able to buy shirts for the guys from Wasilla on it instead of Anchorage like usual. I love going into Harley Shops but this time I was a little bummed. I started to look around when I went inside and a man at the desk asked me if I needed any help.

"No, not right now. I'll look around a bit." I told him.

"Alright, but Sherri will help you if you need it."

"Okay?" I said with a question.

As I started to walk she was walking where I was going like she was worried I was going to steal something. Unreal, I didn't say anything to her lol, I swear, someday I am not going to be afraid of confrontation! I continued to walk around while she played my shadow till I managed to find the three t-shirts I liked for Rick, Charles and Skip and went on my merry way.

I stopped by Carr's grocery store to try the cheese sticks I always ate before I left, they had the best deli in the Valley! I continued on my way and went on to Brian and Tammy's. Visiting there with them I feel like I'm home and there shouldn't be anywhere else to have to go, one of these days.

While we visited my soul seemed to be longing for what was there. I could have sat on the mountain side listening to the creek and the birds and train and the kids playing for hours. The calm that seemed to enter into and become part of me was something I truly didn't want to walk away from.

"I love it here Tammy, I really do want to be here, and we can pull a trailer in or build a cabin till we find a piece of land or something."

"You know it, I want you here to, and you don't have to leave now you know." She said with her 'for sure' smile. We laughed and cried and walked around the lot with the girls. I videotaped the kids in there motorized car while the boys played on their motor bikes they got out of the garbage and fixed up, cool huh? I had to do one last video to show Rick where we could live and the beauty that came with it.

We went on back into the house, I knew this was going to be the last time I saw Tammy before I had to go home. I felt so sad but so happy to be going home, always so torn in half and feeling like I should be both places and with all the people I loved at the same time.

Brian gave me some smoke and a little pipe to use. "What should I do with it when I leave? I won't be able to take it with me and I won't be able to get it back up here."

"Don't worry about it kid, go ahead and use it and give it to someone or something. It's not a big deal and you have to have something." He said and winked at me.

"Thank you, you made it a little nicer for the next night and afternoon, to awesome!" I said.

It was the end of the Memorial Day weekend and the 'Carma Control' had been on a run up past where we were towards Talkeetna and Denali on a run. A group of them had passed us on the highway on our way out to the Valley on Friday and now they were on their way back to Anchorage. Me and Tammy and the girls took my video camera and went out to the end of the drive way to tape them for a bit and took a couple of pictures of us by my car then we said our goodbyes.

"I love you Tammy, I will miss you so much!"

I hugged her and the girls hugged our legs. "I love you to, keep your head up high and keep workin on your book hun and you'll be back in no time!"

I had to get out of there before I started crying and I couldn't drive.

Driving down the Parks Hwy it felt as if I were saying good-bye to another old friend, the bikes were stopped at the little store and driving on pass the Houston Lodge brought a smile to my face. Lots of memories around here that's for sure. Next I passed the famous Cheri Lake Subdivision, then pass the turn off to the Houston High School and Junior High where the kids went to school.

Beautiful trees, woods and country homes and on pass the Big Lake turn off. I always loved looking at the fireworks stands, they were pretty cool. Had a couple on one side of the highway and a couple on the other. Big money of course but big fire danger these days. Next is Pitman Rd, the Dead Dog Saloon and across the street a gas station, a video store, a little café and a couple of other offices. Along the gravel of the parking lot of the Dead Dog they had cleaned up the whole lot and had built some small log homes and had sold them and rented them to people to live in. To cool, no more wasted space. It used to be full of old junk cars and stuff like that. It felt so strange knowing I wasn't going to pass all of this again for some time.

My phone ringing brought me back to reality and I could see Marta's name on the caller id. "Hi honey, what are you doing?"

"Hey sister, I'm going to go to Fernando's for the barbeque, you want to ride with me or meet me there?"

"I'll meet you there, I have to checkout of my hotel and grab Miss Betty, she's gonna come with. I'm a bit nervous." I told her.

"Its going to be alright, everyone is looking forward to seeing you."

ANSWERED PRAYERS AND LESSONS LEARNED

"K thank you, I can't wait to see them to. Talk to you later, love you."

"Love you to, drive careful."

I found my way into Eagle River to my room, I didn't want to rush my packing cause when I did that I usually would end up leaving something important and that really sucks. So I took my time and got things loaded a little at a time. It sure would have been easier if I didn't have to be on the third floor. Oh well, all's good. Soon the job was done and I smiled at the people at the desk, gave them my key card and headed out to my car.

Once I got everything organized I went and picked up my Miss Betty. I'm so glad she's going with me, getting to spend more time with her makes the short trip from town to Eagle River and back more than worth it. When I pulled up she was waiting for me outside and Amber and the kids were waiting to.

"Hi pretty lady." She said to me. "I'm going to miss you, I love you." Amberlynn said to me as I was getting out of my car.

"I love you to." I told her while we were hugging. "I'll be back soon I promise! I don't know how things are going to turn out in the long run, only God knows that but I do know that I can't live without Alaska and everyone I love up here being in my world. I have to come back, I can't be away for to long."

We sat and talked for a minute while we played with the kids. 'I'm really going to miss them.' I thought to myself.

"You sure you don't want to go with us?" I asked her.

"Me and these kids? Nah, I won't do that to your brother." She said laughing.

We said goodbye and Betty and I headed out back to the highway.

I never realized how quick the trip from there to town really was, it's not that far at all. We talked the whole way and when we got to town I called Marta but she wasn't answering her phone so I called Fernando.

"Hi brother, what are you doing?"

"Hey sister, I'm good. We're waitin for you to come eat with us you know."

"Yep, I'm on my way. Will you give me directions and do you need anything?" I asked him.

"Right on and thanks for asking. We need a loaf of French bread, can you pick it up?"

"No problem." I told him.

I found my pen and notebook, got the directions then headed to the store.

How funny, as we pulled into the parking lot it was so weird. I had worked over at the Kmart that used to be next door to the grocery store and we lived across the street in the trailer court before we moved out to the Valley. I hadn't been in this area in a long time. We found the bread he needed and then we managed to find Fernando and Martha.

Marta was just pulling up too, I realized she was trying to talk to me from her car but my window wasn't down so I got it rolled down quick as I could.

"Whats up?"

"Hey, Keith and Brenda and the kids all need a ride. Can we take your car and go get em?"

I didn't even think about it and the words were falling out of my mouth. "No way, I can't have him in my rental car if he's messed up, is he?"

Marta smiled and looked down. "When isn't he?"

"Yea, no, I can't do it. Ask Martha, she might help. I think she's in the kitchen."

"Ok, thank you sister."

We both parked and she went inside to find another ride. We got out of the car with the bread and my Pepsi and I turned to Betty.

"Oh my goodness, I'm excited and nervous at the same time." I said. Betty got out of the car coming around to give me a hug. "It's gonna be great and I know you can't wait to see everyone."

"I know and you're so right, I can't wait! It's just been so long." I said.

Just then Emma and Steve pull up so I waited for them to get out of the car.

"Hey sis, I'm glad you're here." My sister Emma said. "We wanted to pray with you before you left and I didn't think we were going to get the chance, Praise God!" She said clapping. She's so beautiful and has the most awesome smile.

She got out to hug me then got some things out of the car. Steve was getting out on the other side so I went over there for a hug.

"Hey brother, I'm really going to miss you both."

"We're going to miss you to, you'll be back though. You have a life here, we all know that. I'm just glad you showed, we weren't sure and we wanted to pray with you before you left."

"You guys are so sweet, Emma told me that to. I love you so much."

"We love you too little one, let's find the food huh?"

As we all headed up to the yard I felt like I was walking into a past life, I couldn't believe it. I knew they were all going to be here, it was just so trippy to see everyone.

Fernando and Martha and the kids, they were so grown up and gorgeous. These girls had the cutest leathers when they were younger lol SO cute and bad to the bone! Their youngest, oh my goodness, Fernando had told me about their trips to the Junior Olympics, she was in Taekwondo, so awesome! I was hugging one person after another, my sister Lucy and all the kids were there to. It was sad to see Lu without Chuck, we didn't talk too much about him, mostly about the kids.

Inside was Martha and their son. I hadn't met him yet, he hadn't been born when I left. He was like 10 years old or so, it was all so sir-real seeing the kids grown up.

"Hi Martha, how are you?"

ANSWERED PRAYERS AND LESSONS LEARNED

"Jenny, Oh my goodness." She said coming over to hug me.

Keeping tears back wasn't one of my best attributes. "I love you, I can't believe how big your kids are! I miss you and Fernando and all of them so much."

"We miss you too, you comin home?" She asked while we sat down to talk while she made her salad.

"Soon, waitin to finish my book and then I'm going to buy a place out in Big Lake by Emma and Steve or up the hill past Willow, I love it out there."

"Yea, these kids wouldn't let me live that far from town." She said.

"That's ok, I'll always come visit and barbeque!" I was having such a good time. "I better go walk around a bit, my Miss Betty is out there, her came with me."

"Kay, love you Jenny, see you in a bit. The salads done so whenever Fernando barbeques the burgers you guys can eat."

"Love you so much Martha and I'm so glad I'm here." I told her.

"We're so happy you are to." She said with the sweetest smile. "You know we think about you all the time, your missed and loved. Don't forget that."

"Thank you sister, I won't, I promise."

I went out to the yard to sit by my Miss Betty and soon Marta and Martha were heading out to pick up our crazy brother. I really wanted to see him, I miss him so much.

"Jen." Steve hollered. "We're gonna take off, Emma doesn't feel good, gotta git her home. We want to pray with you first though."

"Kay, here I am." I told him jumping up from my chair.

Putting our arms around each other I could feel the love I missed so much from my family here. Even though there was so much insanity and craziness, there was always the family love and at moments like this it was stronger than ever!

STEVE AND EMMA PRAYING OVER ME BEFORE I LEFT TO GO HOME TO CA.

HER PLACE WAS WITH GOD

"Thank you Lord for our sister Jenny, we bless her trip home and her family where she is living in California. We will continue to thank you for the finishing of her book that will bring her home to us Lord. Keep her safe and keep her warm and strong. In Jesus' Name, Amen."

I could feel the warmth of theirs and God's love from my head to my toes. "Amen." I said.

"Amen." Emma said also.

As tears fell we said goodbye and hugged. I hated saying goodbye, I hated having to leave these people I love so much.

"I'll see you and talk to you soon I promise."

"You better, we love you. Bye honey." Both of them said to me.

Everyone said their goodbyes and they headed out.

I sat down and felt numb then Fernando came and sat down next me. "Here sister, will this help?"

I smiled at him. "You always knew what would help huh?"

We laughed and talked and smoked then soon I heard the car pull up.

"Is that Keith and them?" I asked.

Fernando got up to look. "Yep, better get the burgers on."

I got up and went towards the car. "Keith, hi brother, i'm glad you came. I wanted to be able to see you before I left."

He came up and hugged me so long, my tears were falling so I had to hide them.

"What's wrong sis, everythings fine." He said.

"That's not what I heard."

"Well, since when did I teach you to listen to what other people were sayin?" He said laughing and wiping my eyes.

"You know what I mean, you're legal?" He looked at me with that sideways smile and laughed a bit.

"You be careful, the last thing I need is to see my brothers on Americas Most Wanted at home in Durham watchin tv with my family there."

That made him smile and helping Brenda changed the subject. Getting out of the car with him was my sister and the kids, I couldn't believe how grown up everyone was, it's been to long.

I tried to get pictures and video, I got a little video but only for a minute. He figured his finger would suffice lol what a brat! I'm so thankful I have this little bit of time, it's better than no time at all.

"Hey Brenda, how are you doing, where's Cal?" She was corralling the kids in the yard,

"He didn't want to deal with all the people." She said.

"Never thought we'd hear something like that out of that man huh?" I said.

ANSWERED PRAYERS AND LESSONS LEARNED

That got us all laughing and we settled back into the yard. "I better go see if they need any help getting the food ready now."

I got up and looked around, Lucy and the kids, Fernando and Martha's and their kids, Marta and her grand-kids … if I kept going the list would just keep getting longer. It was still so different for me to be here with everyone I think about and miss on a norm every day when I'm home. I can't believe how grown up everyone is now.

The rest of the afternoon went by with lots of love and stories of memories, smiles and pictures. The hardest thing was having to say goodbye. Sharing hugs and tears, Miss Betty and I got into my perty little red P.T. Cruiser and headed out of the big city of Anchorage.

"Think we can find our way back to the highway?" I asked.

Betty laughed and gave me a kiss on my cheek. "Of course, and everything's going to be fine. We love you, never forget that."

"I love you to. I hate leaving my home in Chico and then I hate leaving this home to go back, what am I going to do?"

"That's easy. You're going to go home, take care of your family, write your heart out and finish our book. Then before you know it you'll be up here where the other half of your heart is." She said.

"I didn't know I would ever be able to make it this far in my life. To fall in love again and to be able to walk around Anchorage and the Valley and even Chico without fear of anything."

"I knew you would, your place in the world has always been to be with God. He had you go through the crazy things so that you could share your stories and help other women like me and you."

"Do you really think it's going to make a difference?"

She reached over and hugged me. "Oh honey, it won't only make a difference, your stories may help save a life, never underestimate yourself. I love you."

"I love you to."

I took Betty home and we said our goodbyes then I went to spend the evening with my girls, grandkids and John for dinner before I had to go to the airport. We had a great evening but leaving was never an easy thing to do.

⚘

I made it to the airport, returned my car and called Rick and the kids while I waited for my flight. Rick told me that Jasmine was graduating in the morning, I had scheduled my trip a day off, Oh My God this isn't good, how could I do something so stupid? He tried so hard to calm me down lol but that isn't very easy with him so many miles away and my baby girl graduating without her mom there, I was so disappointed in myself and couldn't stop crying.

Finally I mellowed out enough to get on my plane and when I got to Seattle I found my train. I missed the kids and my new granddaughter and Rick and the puppies and Charles and everyone so much! I'm so glad our family is so big, they were all there for her when she walked to get her diploma even though I wasn't. Our daughter Tina took care of Kelsey while Rick videotaped for the missing mama and the whole time I was on the phone with them listening to the graduation and getting to hear voices. Oh my, now I was crying and so homesick, what a mess I was I'm sure!

I'm so proud of our kids and our whole family, over the years we grew so strong for each other in so many ways!

I found out that the woman I had been working with online from New York hadn't been doing half of what I thought she had been and there were some other issues also. I was so frustrated and told her I had to let her go. After that I looked for someone local to work with me, I found a woman that I thought was going to work out great. After 1 ½ years I realized that she was sick more often than I was and I had to let her go also, we had gotten pretty close so it wasn't easy to do and I'm sure I didn't handle it the way I should have.

Every time I tried to work with someone to get my stories together it wasn't what I needed it to be. I have no idea what to do or how to keep up to God's expectations of the book He told me to write …

Love and Loss, Lives and Family

Coming home I knew it was Gods will I had gone on this trip and I don't believe in coincidence, what happened during my trip happened cause it was God's plan. I went up there ready to work, ready to go from house to house and brother to sister not caring what I had to see and deal with. I wanted my book to have the memories of the ones that lived with me through all the craziness, I figured it was worth getting to spend time with them and listen to the stories so it was worth my fears of what I was going to walk into, even though I knew there could be drugs or violence and no telling what kind of drama, but He didn't let it happen. He's always there to protect me, even when I don't know I need it.

Not to long after I got home I got a phone call from John telling me that Martha had been killed in a car accident. I wondered how many were going to die while I was gone and I'd never get to see them or tell them that I love them again! Aaww how sad, and having to tell the kids was never fun, there was no way I could make it up for the services.

I called Fernando to tell him I was sorry.

"Are you and the girls alright?" I felt so numb, had no idea what to do or say.

"Yea, they'll be fine, their remodeling the bedrooms right now, gonna open their space some. John's comin to stay with me for a bit and helping me out."

"Right on, I'm glad he's there for all of you, I love you brother and I'm so sorry."

"I love you to sister, don't worry about us, we'll be fine."

It was so strange to think that I had just seen her, I had just hugged her and talked to her. My heart broke for those kids and for my brother.

HER PLACE WAS WITH GOD

Home in Durham, our summer turned into fall and then into winter when I got an email telling me that my brother Steve, Emma's husband, had been killed in a car crash also. Oh my goodness, he was such an awesome man of God! My heart hurt for my sister, her and the kids were heart broke and here again, I couldn't believe it, we had just spend some real good time together, he's such a believer in the Lord and teacher of the bible.

And again I was 3000 miles away when I was needed …

Emma and I spent a little bit of time on the phone together every day for a while, I couldn't go without hearing her voice and knowing she was still walking and talking. Now her is getting better. I don't know how you get better from losing your life partner, she was doing the best she could, they had been married for 35 years. God is calling up the strongest and the truest, I had to fight between being angry and being sad and wondering why God does what he does and not understanding. Sometimes just plain not wanting to understand because my sister is on the other end of the phone crying so hard. I didn't know if she could ever stop and I couldn't hold her.

Still living in Durham it was Christmas 2007 and our friend Skip got real sick. They found lung cancer that had spread all over his body, then he had a stroke. Loosing him caught us all by surprise.

The guys got the shop cleaned up a bit and we were able to have his memorial there, it was a sad day.

Rick and I were on a trip with our puppies to Oklahoma, we had been there for two days and got two different phone calls. My sister Karen's boy, my nephew, had passed away. He was hit by a hit a run driver and killed on the side of the road. I was going to jump on a plane and come to her but then I wouldn't have any transportation so I decided I would drive up to Oregon as soon as we got home, her heart was so broke and we were all so sad. I honestly can't imagine the loss of a child, what do you say, what do you do? I would just go love her.

Then I got a call from my Jasmine and we found out her dad had passed away, oh my goodness, I was so far from home and from my daughter and couldn't be there for her. I was getting really frustrated with so much going on so far away so we didn't stay long and headed home soon as we could.

LOVE AND LOSS, LIVES AND FAMILY

When I got there Jasmine and I drove up and spent a few days in Oregon with Karen and went to her son's grave, it was sad but needed to happen. I so didn't understand all the loss and heart ache that was happening.

We lost sisters and brothers and children … how many more?

My Place Was With God and He Knew the Whole Time

God blessed me with an amazing family and the most loving and gentle man with his own past in the drug world, but in Jesus' name miracles happen and hearts change. He has spent these last 14 years loving me and our kids in the truest means of unconditional love, I have ever seen next to Gods. He allowed for my past to be a part of who I am, not as baggage I was carrying around with me like a burden, this was all Gods doing. He knew I would have to find some peace before I would be able to carry out the plans He has for me.

Our familys last Christmas in Durham was December 2009. The house was huge and after all the kids had moved out Rick and I decided to move out on our own, there's a first time for everything!

I was sad to not be living with our brother and kids after all these years, but I was excited for our new lives. The next month we moved up into the canyon between Chico and Paradise. Other than maybe up in the Matanuska Valley North of Anchorage, Mendocino and Switzerland lol, it's one of the most beautiful and serine places I had ever seen (when I was a little girl my mom and her friends and I would go tubing on Chico Creek here on Honey Run, I always thought of how amazing it would be to live here someday).

For years I have prayed to have women in my life that love Jesus like I do and for a Church I could call home. So many years had gone by and I had walked into and left so many of them. I even ran from one, I just didnt see it happening for me but I wasn't going to stop praying.

I was sitting at home on Facebook lol and as usual playing my favorite game potfarm. I was way up in the game spending every bit of extra time I had on it and planned my day around it. I was even spending a dollar here and two dollars there on

MY PLACE WAS WITH GOD AND HE KNEW THE WHOLE TIME

little things I wanted for the game.

I started noticing my niece Felisha posting about God, it made my heart so happy to see her thinking about Him, how awesome! Soon there were more and more posts about her life and God, then she started talking about Remedy Life Church.

This went on for about two months and then her mama, my sister Leah, invited me to Church there with her. I had no idea she was going also, how exciting! She was supposed to meet me in the parking lot so I got there early and parked way in the back to wait for her. I waited and waited then text her, she said she was running late and for me to go on in. lol not, that wasnt going to happen.

I sat there waiting and soon I heard a voice, 'Go on in Jenny', lol no Ill stay right here and wait. 'Jenny, go in you'll be fine', I heard again.

Oh My Goodness, the next thing I knew I was looking in the mirror at myself to make sure I looked alright then I was opening the door, getting out of the car and closing it behind me. I couldn't believe I was walking up through the parking lot and the whole time I'm thinking that I could stop and go back to my car and leave, but I wasnt doing it!

When I got to the door I opened it and the first person I saw with the most beautiful smile was a friend of our kids from when they were all in school in Durham. How awesome, she hugged me and showed me into the church. I went inside the doors where worship had already started and stood up against the wall trying not to be noticed or to dance, thankfully Leah was there soon and we went up closer. The music was mesmerizing and I could feel the smile that was stuck on my face, the love was everywhere.

After worshiping we all settled in our seats, I hadn't talked to anyone in the church and no one knew anything about me but every word Pastor Scott spoke was as if Jesus were calling me by my name and directing his every word into my heart. My life truly did have a purpose and I really was His child and I really did belong, at that moment I knew my heart was where it was supposed to be.

I felt as if I were in a tunnel, I knew others were around me but the Pastor had my undivided attention and the only part of the chair I sat on was the very edge. I was in awe and couldn't help but to share my amazement in looks of love, understanding and tears of joy with my sister Leah while we sat there and listened. I honestly am not sure why I couldnt stop crying other than being able to feel something I'd been waiting for, for so long was suddenly all around me, the Holy Spirit was stronger than I could ever imagine. I was where I belonged and God led me to this family as if they had been waiting for me to walk through the doors.

After the service Leah brought me to one of the Pastors for prayer, still feeling like there was no way I could do this, no way I could belong or be excepted in such an amazing place and live life in my world. I couldnt hardly keep from crying but it didn't keep anyone from being amazing and praying over me and introducing themselves to me, it was awesome. I even got prayer for my book, one of the women told me that maybe I had a new ending, a new last chapter ... I had been stuck and all of a sudden I had thoughts of wonder, how exciting!

I knew that after that day, January 7, 2012, things would be different, in my writing, my relationship with God and my family, everything in my life.

The next Sunday I was getting ready to go to church and decided to delete my potfarm Facebook game soon as I got home. Instead, before I left I got on line, went to my game and click, deleted it all, then went to church. No more game to take my time from God, my writing and my family.

Since Rick and I brought our families together in December of 1998, my every day has been more than amazing. Not everything was or is perfect and neither am I. Im not a perfect Christian, wife, mom or friend or a perfect daughter, sister, auntie or cousin. The difference between now and then is that I feel more secure and believe in who I am. I never knew there was a purpose to the madness we lived but now I know there was and that every day is special. It's another day I can strive to love with such a heart like Jesus has, I want to be a blessing so that I can bless others. I get to live, love and dream with and for Jesus.

It has been 1 ½ years now since I walked into the doors of Remedy Life Church and after 12 years of putting this book of my life together its finally here, which is of course obvious because ya'll are reading it lol. My secrets, most of them, are laid out here in these pages like dirty decorations on a table but now that I know I get to use my life to Glorify Him and for what He had planned the whole time, it doesnt feel as dirty anymore.

Im still living in my process, everyday im listening to and learning from God. I have dreams, ambitions and thoughts. Some that I have always had, some that have changed and some now that are new. God has amazing plans for me and my family and for you to!

My family had been raised as weed (marijuana) smokers so it has always been a norm in every aspect of our lives. Before I started at Remedy my smoking had been my medicine for my Anxiety and to sooth side effects from all my other medicines. Before

MY PLACE WAS WITH GOD AND HE KNEW THE WHOLE TIME

I would leave my house to go anywhere I would take bong hit after bong hit, one after another. Then I would go warm my car up and come take some more before I would go to town to do anything or see anyone. After a handful of months I realized I wasn't smoking at all for three to four hours before I went to church or to see my leader, go to a group or to do anything having to do with the church. As time went by and I heard Pastors word speaking to me and I heard God telling me that my medicine had become a habit, he was taking away my anxiety and I was getting stronger and healthier every day.

During my first year at Remedy I tried so hard to quit twice and even though I continued to give it to God all I would do is get emotional and feel like I was an addict or something. Also it was hurting my family because they didn't understand why I was doing something that made me feel so bad when I had taught them throughout our lives that smoking weed was what we did and that it's good for us and a part of who we are. It's legal and my medicine and that's just the way it had always been.

I went to my third Encounter at Remedy, Freedom Weekend. It's a three day retreat where the church comes together for a dedicated time of teaching, worship and prayer. We get to give up things from our past to the Lord, ask for forgiveness for what we had done to others and to forgive others for what they had done to us throughout our lives and so much more. The healing is amazing!

This one was different for me than the other two. I knew that me being dicipled, I may have a place in our church possibly as a leader one day like Angie is for me and other women. I couldn't imagine a woman in need texting me or calling me telling me she needed to meet with me and me not being able to because I was stoned, wow, something had to change and it had to change now. I went knowing that God has good things planned for my life and I truly only want to love like He loves. If I didn't take a stand now I would be hindering the blessings I may have for others, myself and for my family.

I went in total agreement to give my smoking to God and that was in early June of 2013, since then my new journey with Him has begun. Im not perfect of course and totally human so I can't say what will happen or when but even though it is around me and in my life I am free of 'needing' to get stoned. Wow, I wouldn't have ever thought that could happen. I have a sense of freedom now, something I never had in my past over my addictions and habbits, so exilerating!

I got to go see my kids and some of our family in Alaska this last June 2013, I had an amazing time with my girls, grandbabys and family!

I know that not everyone is doing 'great', but my heart feels so alive. I need them to know how much they mean to me no matter where their walk in life has brought them. The love and tears that we shared with each other have made us who we are today and now I am Gods child and it was awesome to get to share the new 'me' with them. I got asked questions about my new found faith in the Lord and not smoking weed lol that was awesome. It was obvious to them I was growing and changing and that my God was in control now, not me. My time with my kids was short but it was perfect and I look forward to every summer in the future and then some. Getting to hug them and live part of my life with them where the other half of my heart is.

Were all different and unique but perfect for Jesus! Rick Warren writes in The Purpose Driven Life, You are not an accident, long before you were conceived by your parents, you were conceived in the mind of God. He thought of you first. It is not fate, nor chance, nor luck, nor coincidence that you are breathing at this very moment. You are alive because God wanted to create you! The Bible says, 'The Lord will fulfill his purpose for me', and that includes you.

Today I know that by me giving my heart to God, my past becomes a part of the whole me that was already planned and expected. My Pastor said, when I live a life driven by purpose I stop being defined by my past and start living for my future.

Having such a blessed Pastor, my leader and church family I can see my life as a process now, specific as our fingerprints for each one of us. I have learned that the things I lived through, the things I did to others and that others did to me can be forgiven and learned from and then we get to help others know that they arent alone in their struggles. There are compassionate hearts that have been where you have been and have found a life of love and happiness on up the other end of the road where the Lord has been waiting for you the whole time.

Dreams become answered prayers and loving like Jesus loves is how I want to live, Ill strive for that every day for the rest of my life. I can't wait to see what amazing things happen in our lives next, I pray the same for you every day and love all of you with my whole heart!

MY PLACE WAS WITH GOD AND HE KNEW THE WHOLE TIME

COLLAGE PICTURE OF ALL TEN OF MY KIDS

Turn Around Valley

Standing on top of the mountain looking down, Gods world, my world, our world.

God knew my heart and blessed me with a home called, Turn Around Valley. Mountains strong and spirited surrounded the land like a protected blanket. Roads from here to there, connecting our single homes and land together so we could always get to each other when needed. God named this place Turn Around Valley because as we grew and changed and turned our lives around, we were allowed to move in. Each home was built to our wishes and dreams with waterfalls and green hills rolling everywhere. Creeks that were blessed with the sweetest tasting water, certain creeks were marked for fishing only, others for swimming. Trees lined each street giving homes a soft cool shade. Paths waved through town with parks and skating areas for our children. Super Markets, Shopping centers, Schools, and other businesses were ran by those who had been there the longest. Im sure that the best part of this world was that the people I love from both of my worlds, Alaska and California, were entwined together. Bringing sisters and brothers and families to a spot where they can spend their lives with each other as our dreams came true. I climbed back up to the top of the highest mountain and looked down with such happiness and pleasure.

Gods' world, my world, our world, together we can do anything! True hearts, knowing what is right and wrong and making choices that God smiled on pulled us so strongly together, in a world, one world for everyone I love!

Resources for Help

PLEASE look in the town you live for local help or call these numbers or go to the websites to get help!!

National Domestic Violence Hotline
thehotline.org
1800799SAFE (7233)

Catalyst Domestic Violence Services
catalystdvservices.org
18008958476

Safe horizon
Safe Horizon Moves Victims of Violence from Crisis to Confidence
safehorizon.org
1800621HOPE (4673)

Narcotics Anonymous
na.org
18187739999

Alcoholics Anonymous
aa.org

Salvation Army
salvationarmyusa.org
The Salvation Army has Rehabilitation Centers all over the United States and will be able to connect you to help where you are.

Acknowledgments

To the amazing one that gave this book to me, our God. My story is written for the Lord, he told me one day it was time to write my book and he told me the name. I, little ol' me, heard our Fathers words as if he were sitting over my left shoulder ... if I can hear God talking to me after everything I did, His wonders can happen for you to!

I'd like to say thank you so much to David Norum for donating funds to help me pay for my publishing fees. He is finishing his own book about a particularly hideous Domestic Violence case. He is a retired Sheriff's Detective and District Attorney Investigator from Monterey County (CA) who investigated and assisted in prosecuting hundreds of domestic violence felony cases in his career. He is currently the Executive Director of Sol Treasures, a small non-profit center for arts and culture in King City, California and I can't wait to read his book!

Thank you so very much to all of my family and friends that helped me with the costs and to all those that helped out and came to my fundraiser we had which earned the bulk of the monies needed and for all of the prayers and amazing words of encouragement I have received, what a blessing all of you are!

To our Kids - Michelle, Joshua, Jeanette, Jonathon, Tina, Jasmine, Mary, Melissa, Charlsie, and James (and to all our amazing kids with hearts of gold that have become ours through love). All of them have had to live the life of drugs, violence, and anger that we of lost moms and dads gave them. They will all come through on top but it takes a lot of falling and real scary roller coaster rides to get there. Through all of it though, my children have become courageous, strong, dependable, and genuine down to their hearts and souls, each and every one of them! They are compassionate and care

ACKNOWLEDGMENTS

about people and our world, somewhere through the years they must have been taught that God loves them because each of them shine with the Lord's glow and with His love in their hearts.

All of our kids hold a huge part of my heart and I will love you for an eternity.

To the fathers of my children. Without you and God I wouldn't have them, what more of a gift could anyone have ever given me? Thank you so much!

To my biological father ... I have never known you or my brothers and the rest of my family. It broke my heart for so many years, but now today with the Lord as my Father I am so thankful for you. Without you and my mom I wouldn't be me, thank you from my whole heart for my life that our God already had planned.

To my family, the families that raised me. They are the ones who gave me the solid understanding of what family means. Our mommy Joanne, our dad Vernon (rip, I pray he knows how much my sister and I love him and miss him) and my sister Dru. My Grandma and Grandpa Hoon and all my aunts and uncles and cousins and my niece and nephew. The memories we all share of growing up on Gramma and Grampa's farm are a part of our hearts that will never go away, im so thankful for that!

My dad's side of the family is like no other. The love of an Okie can truly warm the coldest heart. Both my sister and I have always been their very spoiled baby girls. My Granny Ruth's home, (along with my Gramma Hoons home), were two of the safest places in the world to be. W & L Auto Parts at the Dos Palos Y. We treasure our memories and will never forget the love our family gave us. Our Granny Ruth and Grandpa Earl, our aunts and uncles and cousins and Chocolate Gravy w/Biscuits n' all!

HER PLACE WAS WITH GOD

∽∞

I could not be whole without my family that has stood by my side and has helped nurse me through the hardest times of my being sick (side by side with all of my kids), and the most wonderful times at our Easter Day egg hunts and barbeques and birthday parties! Thanks to my sisters and brothers, I learned the sweetest love of a niece and nephew for their aunt and an aunt's love for her nieces and nephews. Having those special relationships in my life that mean so much to me, I thank God every day for my family here in Chico, I love you the world!

∽∞

To my family in Alaska, what a boring life I would have had and what a loss of love I would have had to live without you. You showed me how to feel a freedom only so few get lucky enough to be a part of, a life crazy enough to make a book out of (That was a funny haha lol)!

I think of every one of you always and there are so many of us that have passed away for one reason or another. I miss all of you and love you with all my heart. Without a one of you, I wouldn't be who I am today. You gave me a life time of memories with more to look forward to. There isn't a day that can pass by when you're not on my mind or in my heart and prayers!

∽∞

To my partner, my husband, my love, and best friend Rick. You have taken me from someone who was broken and totally devastated with life and gave me the means of being a better mom, partner and wife, friend, daughter, sister, cousin and Aunt. My health problems probably would have been a lot worse off if it hadn't been for your total love and acceptance. You allow me to be at peace with myself so much that I have actually been able to write my book to share with the world. I'm sure we were planned because God knew that without you there wouldn't have been this amazing love or a book at all. You are my love and my life, thank you Lord for leading me to find my matching rocking chairs!

∽∞

ACKNOWLEDGMENTS

To the man that shared some of the most amazing years of my life. My ex-husband and friend, John (Big John) who by the time reads this book, will hopefully finally see our lives as they truly were and allow God to heal him and comfort him. The reality that I lived, the pain our children and you and I have had to endure for so many years even after we were apart. If we had looked to God instead of the drugs, so many amazing things could have come to us, we were strong and we were loved by many and looked up to. I am so sorry for what we both have had to live with and without. Just know that our love was and is real and there will always be a special place in my heart that belongs only to you.

I hope and pray that you find your 'someone special' to grow old with in matching rocking chairs also …!

To all the men, women, children and families in the world who get caught up in the most fearful types of life styles. Living the life of a drug addict and/or in a violent relationship, takes you on a path so crazy and full of the unknown. The drugs, the violence, the danger, the humility, and the uncertainty of life on a day to day basis. I pray for you to open your eyes and your hearts and let God in because if by chance you can't, if you are in too deep and you just can't see through the cracks, there's no telling what can happen when the path goes off track. God and others are ready, step up and out, ask for help to find your way back, wherever you can, to anyone you can. There are people who love you that would die inside without you, I promise!

My Writing and Publishing Process

I had no idea what it would take to not only write a book, but to follow an instruction from the Lord. I'll never forget the day I heard Him speak to me clear as day over my left shoulder telling me it was time to write my book, His book. I had to continue on when I wanted to stop and persevere through it all.

He told me, "Jenny, it's time to write your book. The name is 'Her Place Was With God' and it will be your financial freedom."

At that point in my life I had taken an online creative writing class and wrote a handful of poems through the class, little did I know they were meant for my book. I began writing out stories of my life and throughout doing that it got harder and harder as some of the stores were scary, some were sad, and some were heart breaking.

I looked for and found someone to help me put my stories into readable form so that it read like a 'book' does but that didn't last long. I found three or so different people during my journey but nothing seemed to work. Soon I realized that I was supposed to put it together myself … I couldn't believe it, as I worked the chapters came together as did the book as a whole.

For many years after He told me what I was to do, I felt a heavy heart and blame for our family's and everyone's financial struggles in my life. I would think to myself, 'I know that Gods promises are real and if only I could finish this book our financial problems would all be fixed.' It didn't come to light until I found Remedy Life Church and my amazing spiritual leader Angie before I realized that I needed to grow in Him before I could comprehend what was to come. I know now that my life process and whatever does happen will all be for His glory and there will be others that will be saved by our God through my life and my story. One day I will be able to be blessed to be a blessing and to continue to learn how to love like Jesus loves.

The publishing part of writing this story has given me so much insight also, it has not been anywhere close to as easy as I thought it would be. There are specifics that

MY WRITING AND PUBLISHING PROCESS

have to be done, formatting, name changes, specific legality's and so much more. The finances to pay for self-publishing and picking the photos have been a challenge in their selves. My kids helped me plan a spaghetti feed fundraiser and so many amazing people volunteered, it was awesome. Family and friends shared their money, time, and prayer, their hearts are amazing! Through it all I am now on my way to finalizing all the details and getting the fee's paid. I have no idea what will come next in my Life but I do know that with God in control, everything will be just as He planned, perfect!

Hearing Gods words that He spoke to me were in the early 2000's, today we are almost to the new year of 2014 ... Thank you Jesus for taking me through this amazing journey and the next!

www.ingramcontent.com/pod-product-compliance
Lightning Source LLC
Chambersburg PA
CBHW082144230426
43672CB00015B/2843